Melanchthon on Christian Doctrine

Melanchthon on Christian Doctrine

Loci communes 1555

Translated and edited by
Clyde L. Manschreck

Introduction by Hans Engelland

BAKER BOOK HOUSE
Grand Rapids, Michigan 49506

ISBN: 0-8010-6143-1

PHOTOLITHOPRINTED BY CUSHING - MALLOY, INC.
ANN ARBOR, MICHIGAN, UNITED STATES OF AMERICA

A Library of Protestant Thought

A LIBRARY OF PROTESTANT THOUGHT is a collection of writings intended to illumine and interpret the history of the Christian faith in its Protestant expression. It is as variegated in its literary forms and theological positions as is the movement it mirrors. Tracts, letters, sermons, monographs, and other types of literature comprising the heritage of Protestant thought find a place in this series. Works that were originally composed in English, whether in Great Britain or in the New World, and works that were originally written in other languages, many of them not previously translated into English, are included. But it is neither necessary nor desirable that every segment of Protestant theology, piety, and ethics receive equal space. The trite theology, the conventional piety, and the platitudinous ethics always bulk larger in any tradition, also in the Protestantism of the past four centuries, than does the creative output of the religious spirit. The latter is our primary interest in this Library. While we have not felt obligated to grant them equal attention, we have included works that are typical of the more commonplace literature of the Protestant tradition. On the other hand, some works which logically belong in this series have not been included because they are readily available elsewhere.

In keeping with the fundamental purpose of this Library, the voices of Protestantism are allowed to speak for themselves, with only as much introduction, commentary, and exposition as will in fact allow them to do so. Wherever feasible, documents are reproduced in their entirety. A few representative selections have been preferred to more numerous but shorter passages, for the Library tries to depict the structure of thought rather than the genetic development of a man or a movement. Nevertheless, the variety of Protestant forms precludes a uniform treatment throughout. Our aim has been to be representative rather than exhaustive and to employ the best available tools of critical historical scholarship. Despite its ambitious scope, A Library of Protestant Thought is not an encyclopedia of Protestantism. It is a series of volumes from which not only clergymen and theologians, but students of philosophy, history, literature,

v

political science and other disciplines can gain a more balanced view of how the Protestant mind has thought and spoken since the Reformation.

The Board is grateful to the Hazen Foundation for an initial grant enabling it to begin its work; to the Sealantic Fund, Inc., for a grant making possible Board meetings, consultations, and editorial assistance in the preparation of specific volumes; and to the Oxford University Press for undertaking the publication of the Library.

THE EDITORIAL BOARD

Preface

Philip Melanchthon (1497–1560) presents an enigma that has puzzled researchers for more than four hundred years. On the one hand he is praised as the first systematic theologian of the Protestant Reformation, as the builder of the first public school system since the days of ancient Rome, as the preceptor of Germany through his promotion of education in Roman Catholic as well as Protestant universities. He was hailed by Martin Luther as the greatest theologian that ever lived, and the *Loci*, said Luther, should be esteemed next to the Bible. He wrote Protestantism's basic creed, the Augsburg Confession, and defended it in his theologically acute *Apology of the Augsburg Confession*, both of which have come to symbolize Lutheranism. He was Luther's staunch companion and colleague for twenty-eight years, and in an effort to compose differences and establish fruitful ecumenical relationships, he participated in almost every major colloquy of religion in his day.

On the other hand, the very same efforts for which he is praised bring him denunciations as a humanist, a rationalist, a synergist, and a traitor. Through his reorganizing efforts, his promotion of classical arts, his textbooks, and the hundreds of teachers trained under his tutelage, he allegedly introduced into the evangelical school system principles of reason that conflicted with the religious principle of justification by faith alone. He is accused of weakening the evangelical stand at Augsburg in 1530 by his compromising negotiations with the Roman Catholic contingent; and he appeared to be theologically subversive by changing successive editions of the Augsburg Confession. Differences between the early and the late *Loci* caused some contemporaries and later researchers to say that Melanchthon drifted away from the evangelical foundations established by Luther. When he sought to explain that the human will is not a stone and at least has to accept whatever is wrought by the word and the Spirit in conversion, he was labeled a synergist. When Melanchthon, despite misgivings, accepted the Leipzig Interim, which preserved justification by faith but allowed many Roman Catholic rituals as adiaphora, or nonessentials, he was vilified as a collaborator.

The enigma is not easily resolved, for neither the praises nor the denunciations are without foundation. Melanchthon was the acknowledged "preceptor of Germany" in his own lifetime,[1] and his work as a theologian, Biblical commentator, and active promoter of the evangelical cause is justly hailed;[2] but the denunciations also have a historical basis, and have persisted from the sixteenth century to the twentieth. These incongruous estimations are rooted in (1) Melanchthon's lifelong humanistic interests; (2) the fact that he did alter his thought on several controversial points of theology and seemed to veer away from Luther; and (3) the military defeat of Protestantism and the reaction of evangelical leaders to it.

Before Melanchthon arrived at Wittenberg in 1518, he was recognized as one of the most promising humanistic scholars of the day. He had written several pieces in the tradition of the humanists[3] and had received an accolade from Erasmus.[4] His great-uncle, Johann Reuchlin, had recognized his gifts quite early, and had initiated the changing of his name from Schwartzerd (black earth) to its Greek equivalent, Melanchthon, in keeping with the custom of humanists of the day.[5] And it was Reuchlin, one of Germany's leading humanistic scholars, whose recommendation won for Melanchthon the post of Professor of Greek at Wittenberg University.[6] There is no denying Melanchthon's strong humanistic orientation, for it was grounded in his formal education. John Unger[7] from Pforzheim tutored him in Latin grammar, and then George

1. Cf. Karl Hartfelder, *Philipp Melanchthon als Praeceptor Germaniae* (Berlin, 1899); Friedrich Paulsen, *The German Universities*, E. D. Perry, tr. (New York, 1895). The *Unterricht der Visitatoren* of 1528 became the model for scores of German public schools, and Melanchthon helped found or reorganize twelve of Germany's best universities: Cf. *CR* 26:7-28, 49-96; and Clyde L. Manschreck, *Melanchthon: The Quiet Reformer* (New York, 1958), chaps. 10-11.

2. For his works see *Corpus Reformatorum;* for a list of Melanchthon's works by years, see K. Hartfelder, *Melanchthon*, 579-620.

3. Cf. *CR* 1:1, 9, 14, 15, 18, 24, 46; 11:1; 17:1123, 1145; 18:124; 19:655; 20:3.

4. *CR* 1:cxlvi; Carl Schmidt, *Philipp Melanchthon* (Elberfeld, 1861), 29.

5. Cf. *CR* 10:469; 20:765; 1:cxxxi, 9; 2:520, 542, 558; 3:210 f.; G. Töpke, *Die Matrikel der Universität Heidelberg* (Heidelberg, 1844), I, 472.

6. Cf. *CR* 1:27-34.

7. Cf. *CR* 4:715; 25:448 f.; 28: *Annales Vitae*, 2; S. Bierordt, *D. John Unger, Melanchthonis praeceptore* (Karlsruhe, 1844); Schmidt, *Melanchthon*, 3; J. W. Richard, *Philip Melanchthon* (New York, 1898), 7.

Simler [8] at the Pforzheim Latin School promoted a deeper study of Latin and private lessons in Greek. When Melanchthon entered Heidelberg University in 1509, he had acquired a love of the old masters,[9] an affection which he subsequently extended there, especially with the inclusion of the writings of Rudolph Agricola (1445–1485),[10] who deeply influenced him in the field of rhetoric. He received the B.A. degree, June 11, 1511, after only two years of study at Heidelberg, but his application to take an M.A. was denied shortly thereafter because of his youthful appearance.[11] Understandably piqued, in 1512 he entered the University of Tübingen and immersed himself in the "new learning," studying Aristotle, William of Ockham, Johann Wessel, Virgil, Cicero, Terence, Livy, Hesiod, and even the Bible.[12] On January 25, 1514, the coveted M.A. degree was bestowed, and as a *Privatdocent* he began to lecture on the classics and to publish translations of Terence, Plutarch, Pythagoras, and Lycidas, along with *Rudiments of the Greek Language* in 1518.[13]

Melanchthon's successful teaching and publishing aroused professional rivalry at Tübingen, and also brought him to the attention of other universities and humanist leaders like Erasmus and Willibald Pirkheimer of Nürnberg.[14] The universities at Ingolstadt and Leipzig both sought to add him to their faculties,[15] but with Reuchlin's blessing he accepted the post at the recently established University of Wittenberg, where Martin Luther had in the previous year nailed his Ninety-five Theses to the door of the Castle Church. On August 29, 1518, just four days after his arrival in Wittenberg, Melanchthon delivered his inaugural speech, *De corrigendis adolescentiae studiis*, on the improvement of the studies of

8. *CR* 4:715; 10:259; 11:1001; cf. L. Geiger, *Johann Reuchlin* (Leipzig, 1891), 79; J. G. F. Pflüger, *Geschichte der Stadt Pforzheim* (Pforzheim, 1862), 292.

9. K. Hartfelder, *Melanchthon*, 23; cf. *CR* 4:715.

10. Cf. *CR* 4:716, 720; 11:280, 396, 439–42; Leonard Cox, *The arte or Crafte of Rhetoryke*, F. I. Carpenter, ed. (Chicago, 1899); *ZKG*, IV, 327, n. 7.

11. *CR* 1:cxlvi; 10:260.

12. *CR* 1:15, 87 f., 321, 1083; 4:718, 720 f.; 10:192, 259 f.; 11:332; 19:271 f.; 24:309; Joachim Camerarii, *De Vita Melanchthonis Narratio*, G. T. Strobel, ed. (Halle, 1777), 15 f.; Preface to *Farrago rerum, theolog., Wesselo autore* (Wittenberg, 1521).

13. Cf. *CR* 1:cxlvii, 9 ff., 13 f., 15, 24; 10:260, 297; 11:1, 14; 17:1123, 1137; 18:124; 19:655; 20:3; K. Steiff, *Der Erste Buchdruck in Tübingen* (Tübingen, 1881), for a long list of humanistic publications from Anshelm's presses, where Melanchthon was proofreader; and Richard, *Melanchthon*, 22.

14. See footnote 4, above; also *CR* 1:cxlvi, 22 f., 27 f., 34 n.; and C. F. Ledderhose, *Philip Melanchthon* (Philadelphia, 1855), 26 n.

15. *CR* 1:cxlviii, 42; 10:260 f.; Camerarius, *De Vita Melanchthonis*, 26.

youth,[16] in which he lamented the decline of the ancient classics, the languages of Hebrew, Greek, and Latin, and called for a recovery of the wellsprings of classical literature and Christianity and a return to Christian piety. He announced lectures on Homer and the Letter to Titus, for he expected to reform morality through a study of ancient philosophy and the Bible.

Luther enthusiastically welcomed a kindred spirit who was not afraid to venture,[17] and under the spell of Luther, fourteen years his senior, Melanchthon's interest in theology flamed. He helped Luther with the study of Greek, took an active role in the Leipzig Disputation, June 27–July 8, 1519, and soon found himself in the forefront of the evangelical struggle which Luther had initiated.[18] His interest in theology prompted him to study for the B.D. degree, which he received at Wittenberg in 1519;[19] in the theses prepared for this occasion he rejected transubstantiation and defended justification by faith and the authority of Scripture.[20] In 1521, when Melanchthon wrote the first *Loci*,[21] his stance was the same as Luther's, reflected especially in his view of man, whom he pictured as mired in a cesspool of self-love, too sinful to be capable of anything but hypocrisy. Unless overcome by Christ, he declared, this self-love blocks free will in man so far as justification is concerned.

But even at this time, according to some scholars, Melanchthon's humanistic outlook was merely submerged.[22] During the unrest at Wittenberg in 1521–22, when Luther was confined to the Wartburg and the radicals at Wittenberg were resorting to iconoclastic violence to destroy the old religious forms, many researchers hold, Melanchthon saw the necessity to seek in law and natural reason certain ethical requirements which would be binding on all men. These he found inherent in the

16. *CR* 11:15–25.

17. *CR* 10:302; Hartfelder, *Melanchthon*, 63; *Dr. Martin Luthers Briefwechsel*, E. L. Enders and G. Kawerau, eds. (Stuttgart and Leipzig, 1884 ff.), 1:220 ff., 226 f.; 2:280 ff.; *Martin Luthers Briefe*, Wilhelm Martin Leberecht de Wette, ed. (Berlin, 1825–28), 1:143, 196, 380.

18. *Cf.* Manschreck, *Melanchthon*, chap. 3.

19. *Cf. Martin Luthers Briefe*, 1:341, 380; *Martin Luthers Briefwechsel*, 280 ff.; *CR* 1:cxlix; Richard, *Melanchthon*, 59.

20. *Ibid.; CR* 1:137–46.

21. *CR* 21 and 22; *Loci communes von 1521*, Hans Engelland, ed. (Gütersloh, 1952), II, 1, *Melanchthons Werke*, Robert Stupperich, ed.; *Loci Communes*, C. L. Hill, tr. (Boston, 1944).

22. *Cf.* Adolf Sperl, *Melanchthon zwischen Humanismus und Reformation* (München, 1959); W. H. Neuser, *Der Ansatz der Theologie Philipp Melanchthon* (Neukircken Kr. Moers, 1957).

natural light of man's reason,[23] thus making a place for a philosophic ethic and the laws of men quite apart from scriptural justification by faith in Christ. However, Melanchthon never suggested that the keeping of such ethical laws could justify man with God, for he repeated emphatically that justification comes only through faith, for Christ's sake, without any dependence on any human merit; he simply felt that the rationality of man and communal living demanded such an external discipline.[24] If this was a subtle subversion of Luther's thought, Luther himself never protested.

In *The Freedom of the Christian Man* Luther declared that the Christian, that is, the man justified by faith alone, does good works as an expression of joy and gratitude for what God in Christ has done for him. Such a redeemed or justified man needs no law; his heart is so filled with the Holy Spirit that he spontaneously acts in accordance with love.[25] Paul called this faith acting through love (Gal. 5:6). Luther was speaking about such works in connection with the justified or redeemed man; Melanchthon could wholly agree; but he was also concerned about external discipline for the unredeemed man. His interest in education and morality led him to use the tools of humanism, not to destroy the insights of the evangelical reforms, but to establish a basis for discipline among even the unconverted. For Melanchthon the natural light as a basis for external, disciplined behavior for the unredeemed man had no bearing on the internal forgiveness and faith of the Christian. He was not using a humanistic principle to subvert justification by faith.[26] Significantly, Melanchthon broke his friendships with both Erasmus and with Reuchlin,[27] Europe's two leading humanists, and stood by Luther for twenty-eight years. Recognizing this fact, Luther did not object when Melanchthon broadened the curriculum to enhance the liberal arts. His

23. Cf. Engelland (ed.), *Loci 1521*, footnote 21 above.

24. *Ibid.; cf.* Lauri Haikola, "Melanchthons und Luthers Lehre von der Rechtfertigung," in *Luther and Melanchthon*, Vilmos Vajta, ed. (Philadelphia, 1961); Hill (tr.), *Loci*, 50–65, 71–76, 81–120, 154 ff., 166 ff., 170–77, 202–07.

25. *Works of Martin Luther*, II, W. A. Lambert, tr. (Philadelphia, 1943).

26. See footnote 24 above.

27. Melanchthon parted with Erasmus as a result of the controversy on free will between Luther and Erasmus in 1524–25. Reuchlin parted from Melanchthon in 1519 by joining the faculty at the University of Ingolstadt, where John Eck, Luther's opponent at Leipzig, was prominent. He implored his nephew to join him, but Melanchthon refused, and Reuchlin stopped corresponding in 1521 lest he be linked with a heretic. Reuchlin's valuable library was given to the monks at Pforzheim even though Reuchlin had sworn before witnesses to leave it to Melanchthon. Cf. *CR* 1:149 f., 362, 646.

continuance in the two faculties of theology and the humanities was an expression of his wide range of interests.[28]

In the 1555 *Loci* Melanchthon said the redeemed man would keep the Ten Commandments because they are an outward declaration of the will of God; such a man would wish to obey, to be in harmony with God's will, because of the indwelling Holy Spirit, not in order to merit justification, but because adherence to the Ten Commandments is God's expressed wish.[29] The unredeemed man should also abide by the Ten Commandments, at least externally, because they are a specific expression of God's divine natural law which, but for the Fall, would be clear to man's natural light. While the unredeemed man can neither inwardly nor outwardly keep the Ten Commandments in their fullness, especially the first commandment, the rationality of man, the natural light, tells him that external compliance is demanded by human social life.[30] The ancient philosophers clearly recognized this, said Melanchthon, and wrote noble treatises on the subject. Melanchthon's humanism was in the spirit of the Renaissance, but its epitome was the all-important *sola fides*, not the all-sufficient man.[31] Luther was so impressed by Melanchthon's work during this period that he stole Melanchthon's lectures on Corinthians and published them, then threatened to do the same with his annotations on Genesis, Matthew, and John — which he did![32]

Melanchthon was deeply influenced, even overwhelmed, by Luther in those early years at Wittenberg, but his thought was by no means set. The conflict over free will between Erasmus and Luther in 1524 and 1525 caused Melanchthon to re-examine the place of man's will in conversion. Melanchthon's doubts about the implications of predestination appeared in his *Commentary on Colossians* in 1527, which he called to Luther's attention.[33] In 1521, in the first *Loci*, he asserted that God controls everything through the mystery of divine predestination, but he sidestepped a discussion of it on the grounds that man should not be overly curious about God's mysteries. After 1527 and when he wrote the

---

28. Sheer overload, overwork, small salary, and a recognition of the desperate need of teaching the languages caused Melanchthon to hesitate about enlarging his theological endeavors. He married Katherine Krapp on November 25, 1520, and had the added expense of a growing family. *Cf.* Manschreck, *Melanchthon*, chap. 7.
29. *Cf.* Articles V–VIII, XIV.
30. *Ibid.*; see also "natural light" in index.
31. *Cf.* Hans Engelland's introduction, pp. xxv–xlii.
32. *Cf.* Richard, *Melanchthon*, 104 f.; *Martin Luthers Briefe*, 2:238; *CR* 14:1043.
33. *Cf.* F. Galle, *Versuch einer Charakteristik Melanchthons als Theologen, und einer Entwickelung seines Lehrbegriffs* (Halle, 1840), 274; *CR* 1:893; 2:457.

last editions of the *Loci,* he rejected the idea that "God snatches you by some violent rapture, so that you must believe, whether you will or not." [34] He did not include predestination in the Augsburg Confession lest any attempted explanation of it lead to more confusion.[35] Two things bothered Melanchthon. First, he could not accept "stoical fatalism," or determinism, for this meant that God was imprisoned by the causal laws of nature — a denial of miracles, prayer, and so forth. He could not find determinism in Scripture, nor could he tolerate the idea inherent in determinism that God is responsible for man's sin. Second, predetermined election seemed to undercut the Biblical message of salvation for all men. Also, a divinely forced justification would mean that man participated no more than a stone; he felt that man is responsible for accepting or rejecting the promises of God and that God does not force salvation upon a man as if he were inanimate.[36]

If the promises of God to have mercy are universal, that is, made to all men, then the reason some are saved and others damned must be that man is in some way responsible.[37] If man cannot comprehend this on account of the contradictions with *sola fides,* Melanchthon, in his *Cate-chesis Puerilis,* 1532, resolved to abide by the promises that God's word appertains to all.[38] In his *Commentary on Romans,* 1532, Melanchthon asserted that in justification "there is some cause in the recipient in that he does not reject the promise extended." Melanchthon was trying to assess the individuality and responsibility of man; he was not claiming that man is the author of justification.[39] The fact that man preaches the word and calls upon man to repent implies that the hearer does something. Melanchthon felt that predestination or election was contrary to religious experience and ignored the ethical personality of man. This led Melanchthon to his famous *causa concurrens:* the Holy Spirit and the word are first active in conversion, but the will of man is not wholly inactive; God draws, but draws him who is willing, for man is not a statue.[40] Man has a genuine freedom and responsibility which God does not abolish. Salvation is a gift, but it is not a gift if forced upon man. Melanchthon expressed this position in the 1535 *Loci,* and berated those people who refused to try to live morally on the grounds that, no matter what they did, they were either elected or not. He pointed to Saul and David, saying that

---

34. *CR* 24:43.   35. *CR* 2:546.   36. *Cf.* Articles IV, V, IX, XV.
37. *CR* 15:678 ff.   38. *CR* 23:179.
39. *Cf.* Galle, *Charakteristik Melanchthons als Theologen,* 291 f.
40. *CR* 21:271–74, 330; 1:637.

"the cause must be in man that Saul is cast away and David is accepted." [41]

Melanchthon could not accept a secret decree in God that inexorably meant some were saved and others damned, although he could not harmonize divine foreknowledge and human will.[42] He chose to rely on God's words of mercy.[43] In 1558 he declared that "Stoic necessity is a downright lie and a reproach to God," that "in external morality the will is not forced to commit adultery, theft, etc.," and that man is not a synergistic co-worker with God in conversion, nor does God force a man to accept grace.[44] The contrary would be "against God's word, injurious to all discipline, and blasphemous against God." [45]

Similar thought appeared in the 1544–45 Loci, which Luther knew about and to which he did not object.[46] And in De Anima, 1540, Melanchthon maintained that the will of man is not inactive in the moral struggle.[47] What others have since labeled synergism (man co-operating with God to bring about conversion) was far from meritorious work righteousness. It was Melanchthon's resolution of Biblical demands and evangelical experience. The 1555 Loci further explores these points of view.

Both humanism and an attempt to draw closer to Calvinism have also been blamed for Melanchthon's altered views on the Lord's Supper.[48] This was particularly noticeable in the 1540 changes which Melanchthon introduced into the Augsburg Confession. Such changed editions of the Confession came to be known as the Variata; the official Latin copy, presented to Emperor Charles V at Augsburg, was eventually destroyed by Philip of Spain, and the German copy disappeared from the imperial chancery. Melanchthon published the first edition, called the Invariata, from notes and copies which he had retained. Although the Augsburg Confession was a public document, he felt free to clarify and improve its expression from time to time. Article X of the Augsburg Confession, 1530, read, "Of

41. CR 21; Lutheran Church Review, XXVIII (1909), 325 f.
42. CR 5:109, letter to Calvin (1554).
43. CR 22:417; 24:478; 25:438.
44. Lutheran Quarterly, XXV (1905), 303–45; CR 9:766 ff.
45. CR 9:766.
46. CR 3:380; Lutheran Quarterly, XLVI (April, 1916), 184–88; J. W. Richard, Confessional History of the Lutheran Church (Philadelphia, 1909), 467 f.
47. CR 12:481; Lutheran Quarterly, XXXV (April, 1905), 303 f.
48. Cf. Peter Fraenkel, "Ten Questions Concerning Melanchthon, the Fathers, and the Eucharist," in Luther and Melanchthon, Vajta (ed.); S. S. Schmucker, American Lutheranism Vindicated (Baltimore, 1856); M. Reu, Augsburg Confession (Chicago, 1930).

the Supper of the Lord, they teach that the Body and Blood of Christ are truly present and are distributed to those who eat in the Supper of the Lord; and they disapprove of those who teach otherwise." In the *Variata* of 1540 Article X read: "Of the Supper of the Lord, they teach that with the bread and the wine the Body and Blood of Christ are truly tendered to those who eat in the Lord's Supper." "Tendered" replaced "distributed," and the note on disapproval was omitted.[49] At this time the German evangelicals were making overtures to John Calvin, and this change reflects a desire to allow a Calvinistic interpretation of the Lord's Supper, for Melanchthon himself had come to believe in a real, spiritual presence, which was a drift from the physical "distributable," "this-is-my-body" presence held by Luther. As early as 1519 Melanchthon had completely rejected transubstantiation, and by 1544 had eliminated the elevation of the host in Wittenberg.[50] Rationalistic humanism figured in the change: he had been searching the documents of early Christianity. In 1544 Melanchthon was ready to depart from Wittenberg if necessary; he had struggled with the problem for more than ten years.[51] Nevertheless, the tension did not result in a break.[52]

At the Marburg Colloquy in 1529 Melanchthon was paired with Zwingli and Luther with Oecolampadius in a discussion of the Lord's Supper, on which the participants agreed to disagree.[53] Afterward, Melanchthon's thoughts on the Eucharist gradually changed, due largely to a dialogue by Oecolampadius in 1530; it shook his confidence in the physical presence,[54] for Oecolampadius demonstrated that the early Church subscribed to both mystic and symbolic views of the Eucharist four centuries before the physical theories became the vogue. After the death of Zwingli and Oecolampadius in 1531 Bucer made overtures for union of the Zwinglians and Lutherans; though they were premature,[55] Melanchthon nurtured strong doubts about the physical presence in which he thought Luther believed.[56] To Melanchthon the presence had become a mystery, analogous to faith.[57] In 1533 Bucer sent Melanchthon a booklet, *In Preparation for Union*, that held some ecumenical promise,

49. Cf. H. Heppe, *Die Bekenntnisschriften der altprotestantischen Kirche Deutschlands* (Cassel, 1855), 340 ff.; H. E. Jacobs, ed., *The Book of Concord* (Philadelphia, 1882–93).
50. ZKG, XXXII, 292 f.; CR 7:877–89.   51. CR 3:537.
52. CR 5:474; *Dr. Martin Luthers sämmtliche Werke* (Erlangen, 1826 ff.), 32:29 f.
53. CR 1:1048, 1065, 1098; 23:727.   54. CR 2:217, 822, 824.
55. CR 2:470, 498, 787.   56. Cf. Schmidt, *Melanchthon*, 318 f.
57. CR 2:620, letter to Rothmann at Münster, Dec. 24, 1532.

but Melanchthon was not optimistic [58] because he felt bound to present to Bucer (at Cassel in 1534) Luther's view that "the body of Christ is really eaten in the Supper, that the body is actually torn with the teeth and eaten." [59] Nevertheless, Bucer and Melanchthon agreed that the body of Christ is given and received at the same time as the elements, that they are sacramentally joined without any natural mixing of their substances.[60] Luther agreed for the sake of peace, but Melanchthon had become convinced that his original views were contrary to those of the early Church fathers.[61] In the 1535 *Loci* he expressed an inward, spiritual communion with Christ as the essential aspect of the Eucharist.[62] This led to the Wittenberg Concord of 1536, in which the Swiss and the Germans agreed that "the true body and true blood of Christ are given and received, and not alone bread and wine," [63] that a sacramental union takes place and that "when the bread is held out, the body of Christ is at the same time present and truly tendered." [64] Melanchthon doubted that the agreement on words would last; rumors circulated that he was a Sacramentarian.[65]

In 1538 Melanchthon insisted that the sacramental presence was in the use, that Christ was truly present and effective then, the sacramental union being like the union of fire and iron.[66] By 1543 Melanchthon held that the sacramental union lasts only until the Communion is finished; then the elements are again simply bread and wine and may be treated as such.[67] When Luther wrote *A Short Confession on the Holy Sacrament, Against the Fanatics* in the tense year of 1544, Melanchthon expected to be attacked.[68] Instead Luther said, "I have absolutely no suspicion in regard to Philip," [69] but the Elector nevertheless took the precaution of forbidding Luther to attack Melanchthon.[70] Despite the tension in 1544, Luther's commendation of the *Loci* of 1544–45, which embodied Melanchthon's views on the Supper, were unstinted.[71] After

58. *CR* 2:675, 776; Schmidt, *Melanchthon*, 318 f.

59. Richard, *Melanchthon*, 251; Schmidt, *Melanchthon*, 319; *Martin Luthers Briefe*, 4:569.

60. *CR* 2:807 f.   61. *CR* 2:824.   62. Cf. Schmidt, *Melanchthon*, 371.

63. Cf. H. Eells, *Martin Bucer* (New Haven, 1931), 201; J. Köstlin and G. Kawerau, *Martin Luther* (Leipzig, 1903), 349.

64. Jacobs (ed.), *Book of Concord*, II, 284 ff.; *CR* 3:75 ff.

65. *CR* 2:837; 3:81, 180; Camerarius, *De Vita Melanchthonis*, 163.

66. *CR* 3:514.   67. *ZKG*, XXXII (1911), 292 f.; *CR* 7:877–88.

68. *CR* 5:474; *Luthers Werke*, 32:39 f.   69. *Martin Luthers Briefe*, 5:645, 697.

70. *CR* 5:746.

71. *Lutheran Quarterly*, XXXVI (April, 1916), 68.

Luther's death, February 18, 1546, Melanchthon branded the physical view of the Supper as bread idolatry.[72]

At Mühlberg, April 24, 1547, the Protestant military forces, betrayed by Duke Maurice of Saxony, were defeated by the imperial arms of Charles V. The Elector of Saxony and the Landgrave of Hesse were both imprisoned. Melanchthon and his family fled to Zerbst, and he greatly feared the uprooting of Protestantism by the forceful establishment of Catholicism.[73] At Maurice's insistence that he wanted to keep Wittenberg going,[74] Melanchthon returned, feeling that he should preserve what he could.[75] Other Lutheran professors went to Jena to set up a new university. When Charles V tried to impose Catholicism on Saxony in the Augsburg Interim of May 15, 1548, Melanchthon refused acceptance because it demanded episcopal rule, seven sacraments, papal interpretation of Scripture, transubstantiation, works of supererogation, invocation of saints, and other matters as nonessentials.[76] After extended negotiations, Melanchthon became convinced that an unfavorable interim adopted by the princes at Celle would be forced on Saxony.[77] Desperately Melanchthon rewrote certain sections of this document so as to preserve justification by faith, to omit the idea of meritorious sacrifice from the Mass, and to keep Scripture in the Church, "as she shall and cannot command anything contrary to the Holy Scriptures." Episcopal rule was accepted; confirmation, extreme unction, repentance, confession, and absolution were kept, but without auricular enumeration; the clergy were left free to marry; and much adiaphora, or nonessentials, such as bell-ringing, distinctive dress, and so on was retained.[78] Melanchthon was not pleased, but believed that it was the best that could be done under the circumstances.[79] This Leipzig Interim of December 1548 was in effect until the second betrayal of Maurice forced Charles V to negotiate the Peace of Passau, 1552, which led to the Peace of Augsburg, 1555, a settlement that made the religion of a territory the same as that of the prince. During the Leipzig Interim Melanchthon was sharply criticized.[80]

---

72. For views in the 1555 *Loci*, see Articles XIX, XXII, XXIII.

73. *CR* 6:198 ff., 230 f., 238 f., 381–90, 409, 520–33, 559 f., 599.

74. *CR* 6:563, 578–80.

75. *CR* 6:x–xvi, 26, 605, 610 f., 640; *Annales Vitae*, 1548.

76. *CR* 6:839 ff.; cf. B. J. Kidd, *Documents Illustrative of the Continental Reformation* (New York, 1911), no. 148.

77. *CR* 6:839 ff., 846, 853–85; 7:12–45, 92, 97, 113 ff., 215–21, 246–49, 255–59.

78. *CR* 7:260 ff.   79. *CR* 7:275.   80. *CR* 7:292–301, 332, 364–80.

Melanchthon's most persistent opponent was Matthias Flacius Illyricus (1520–1575) who had studied and taught at Wittenberg. During the dispersal of the university in 1547 he fled to Brunswick and then to Magdeburg, where he became the leader of a group of strict Lutherans — Amsdorf, Gallus, Faber, Wigand, Schnepf, Stolz, and others. Along with the faculty at Jena, which Flacius later joined, these men bitterly attacked Melanchthon, saying he had sold out to the Baalites, belly-servers, Samaritans, and papists. Melanchthon declined to answer their venomous charges, for the attackers seemed to make no distinction between the two interims.[81] Flacius called on all Christians to avoid the leprous adiaphora and to wield the sword of truth which the interimists would bury in concessions.[82] In *True and False Adiaphora*, 1549, Flacius argued that as preaching, baptism, the Eucharist, and absolution have been commanded by God, suitable ceremonies have also been commanded, *in genere*, for *cultus* reflects doctrine.[83] Melanchthon rejected this as a new type of "violent popery." [84] He insisted that his views on adiaphora were the same as those he and Luther had held earlier, and he lamented the "rage of the theologians." [85] Even after the Peace of Augsburg, Flacius and his cohorts tried to make Melanchthon publicly confess past errors, as at Coswig in 1557, but he would not admit either total or willful wrong.[86] The Formula of Concord, 1580, framed after much acrimonious controversy, called for bold confession in time of persecution with regard to adiaphora.[87] Flacius' extremist views cost him his post at the University of Jena in 1562, and he was further estranged on account of his treatise on original sin, in which he argued that the nature of man is essentially and totally corrupt, that original sin is the very substance of human nature, not something secondary.[88] The suspicion cast on Melanchthon was one of the major results of this controversy.[89]

The position that Melanchthon took on the Ten Commandments in the 1555 *Loci* was due in part to the opposition to law of Johannes Agricola (1494–1566).[90] In 1528 and 1537 he became embroiled with

81. *CR* 8:171 f., 455; Flacius, *Wider Das Interim* (Magdeburg, 1549).
82. *CR* 6:649 ff.; Flacius, *Omnia latina scripta contra adiaphoricas fraudes* (Magdeburg, 1550).
83. Flacius, *De Veris et Falsis Adiaphora* (Magdeburg, 1549).
84. *CR* 7:366 ff., 456–57, letter to Moller, 1549.
85. *CR* 7:477–78, 506 ff.; 9:1098.   86. *CR* 9:41–72; 8:840 f.
87. Jacobs (ed.), *Book of Concord;* Richard, *Confessional History.*
88. Flacius, *De peccati originalis* (Basel, 1562).
89. Richard, *Confessional History*, especially chaps. xix–xxvii.
90. *Loci*, 1555, Articles V, VII, VIII.

Luther and Melanchthon over whether a Christian should observe the law. Agricola maintained that Christians are free from the law, an antinomian position on the basis that justification by faith obviates observing any moral law, even the Ten Commandments. He went so far as to say Moses should be hanged. The controversy became so bitter that Luther requested the Elector to proceed against Agricola as a heretic, but Agricola hurriedly left Wittenberg for Berlin. There he published a letter addressed to the Elector of Saxony that appeared to be a recantation.[91] Luther did not accept it as such. He claimed that the Mosaic and moral law had the negative value of making a sinner aware of sin and thus preparing him for grace, and that it could help a Christian with his discipline and fight against sin. Melanchthon's emphasis on the Ten Commandments was virtually the same.[92]

Related to this controversy with Agricola was the one with Andreas Osiander (1498–1552), who in his disputations *De Justificatione* and *De Lege et Evangelio*, 1550, asserted that righteousness is not merely imputed to a Christian but is actually possessed by the believer as "essential" righteousness, for Christ is *in* the justified man; through this Christ we have God's grace, mercy, righteousness, truth, wisdom, and power.[93] Franz Hildebrandt states that this part of the Lutheran tradition was transmitted to John Wesley and the Methodists through Osiander, but that Melanchthon and Osiander both believed in the Holy Spirit's activity in man, and that Osiander was not Roman Catholic in this nor Melanchthon simply forensic.[94] Unfortunately, these and other controversies wracked Lutheranism before and after the death of Melanchthon.

Humanism, altered views, military defeat, and acrimonious controversies nourished the developing enigma of Melanchthon. Although much of Melanchthon is embodied in the official symbols of the Lutheran Church and in the Heidelberg Catechism of the Reformed Church, Melanchthon's contributions to the Protestant tradition were cast under a cloud. His name was stricken from the library books in France,[95] and

91. G. Kawerau, *Johann Agricola von Eisleben* (Berlin, 1881), 231 f., 486.

92. *Loci*, 1555, Articles V, VII, VIII.

93. *CR* 7:726; E. Hirsch, *Die Theologie des Andreas Osiander und ihre geschichtlichen Voraussetzungen* (Göttingen, 1919).

94. Franz Hildebrandt, *Melanchthon: Alien or Ally?* (Cambridge, 1946), 44–55. Cf. *CR* 8:557 ff., 783, 892 ff.; 9:403; 23:517; *Works of the Rev. John Wesley, M.A.*, Thomas Jackson, ed. (London, 1829–31), V, 236 ff.

95. "Melanchthon," in *Biographie Universelle*, XXVII, 546.

Melanchthonianism became a derogatory term, connoting humanistic deviation from Luther. Not until the middle of the nineteenth century did the study of Melanchthon receive its great impetus in the publication of Melanchthon's works by Bretschneider and Bindsell and of Carl Schmidt's biography.

But the mark of Melanchthon passed into the Reformed tradition through the Heidelberg Catechism in the *Palatinate Church Order* of 1563,[96] especially through Zacharius Ursinus, one of his students.[97] While it is almost impossible specifically to trace ideas in history, Melanchthon's genius in the Augsburg Confession passed over into the Thirty-nine Articles of the Church of England, and thence into the Twenty-five Articles of Methodism, as well as influencing the Synod of Dort, 1618, and the Westminster Confession, 1648.[98] Melanchthon's *Loci* was required reading at Cambridge, and Queen Elizabeth I memorized large portions of it in order to converse learnedly about theology.[99] In the Royal Injunctions of 1535 for Cambridge King Henry VIII commanded instruction in "Aristotle, Rodolphus Agricola, Philip Melancthon, Trapezuntius, &c. and not the frivolous questions and obscure glosses of Scotus, Burleus, Anthony Trombet, Bricot, Bruliferius, &c." [100]

In 1535 when Henry VIII sought to curry the favor of the Continental Protestants, Melanchthon dedicated his 1535 *Loci* to the king, and also wrote the Thirteen Articles that were agreed upon by Henry's commissioners and the Wittenberg theologians.[101] The articles bear a close connection with the Thirty-nine Articles of the Church of England and the Forty-two Articles of 1553. The Ten Articles of June 1536 repeated much of Melanchthon's phraseology. Through Thomas Cranmer Melanchthon's thought became current in England, for Cranmer not only circulated and used his works, but also repeatedly invited Melanchthon to come to England.[102] Cranmer used *The Consultation of Hermann*

96. *Bekenntnisschriften und Kirchenordnungen der . . . Reformierten Kirche,* Wilhelm Niesel, ed. (Zurich, 1938), 136–218.

97. *Cf.* Bard Thompson, "The Palatinate Church Order of 1563," in *Church History,* XXIII (December, 1954), 339–54; and J. W. Nevin, "Zacharius Ursinus," in *Mercersburg Review,* III (September, 1851), 490–512.

98. *Lutheran Quarterly Review,* NS XXVII (1897), 12 ff.

99. T. W. Baldwin, *William Shakspere's Small Latine and Lesse Greeke* (Urbana, Ill., 1944), I, 259.

100. *Ibid.,* II, 34; *Annals of Cambridge,* I, 375.

101. *CR* 2:921–30, for dedication; *cf.* Reu, *Augsburg Confession,* II, 454 ff. for discussion of articles; also, *CR* 2:1032–36; 3:1396 f., 1409.

102. *Cf. CR* 2:92–95; 6:715, 790–91, 801, 894, 918; 7:573; 8:119; 14:415; James Bass Mullinger, *The University of Cambridge* (Cambridge, 1884), II, 103 ff.

of Cologne, drawn up by Bucer and Melanchthon in 1543 for the reformation of the Cologne diocese, as the basis for his *Order of the Communion* of 1548.[103] Melanchthon was not exactly happy with the *Consultation*, but it was an extension of the evangelical reform, and Cranmer's writings, especially the Homilies, became one of the channels through which Melanchthon influenced John Wesley's Methodists on justification, good works, and assurance.[104] The reformers were even invited to England to compile the English Prayer Book! Although Melanchthon did not accept the invitations, his disciple Francisco Dryander was recommended and became Greek Reader to Cambridge.[105] A year later, in 1549, Bucer also began teaching at Cambridge. In 1559, after Cranmer's death, Queen Elizabeth directed scholars to read Melanchthon "to induce them to all godliness." [106]

Melanchthon's views on rhetoric spurred an improved dialectic and good Latin in Germany, and for two centuries his rhetoric was widely used in England. In the grammar schools of England about 1530 *In Rhetorica Philippi Melancthonis* was one of the five key works for the whole of the upper curriculum.[107] Leonard Cox, who knew and corresponded with Melanchthon, made the rhetoric widely available.[108] The rhetoric proved to be a link with William Shakespeare, for while Erasmus in 1511 used Terence to illustrate the structure of a play, it was Melanchthon who in 1524 "worked out the great pedagogical edition of the century showing how this application was to be made." [109] Terence was widely studied in the lower schools in England, where Shakespeare came to know the five-act play structure used by the boys as a guide in studying the plays of Terence.[110] Even the philosopher Peter Ramus Martyr, whose rhetoric and simplified logic became so popular in England, followed Melanchthon's recommendations.[111] This was an extension of the

---

103. The *Consultation* appeared in England in German, 1543, in Latin, 1545, and in English in 1547 and 1548. Cf. C. H. Smyth, *Cranmer and the Reformation under Edward VI* (Cambridge, 1926).

104. Cf. Manschreck, *Melanchthon*, chap. 18; CR 5:112, 142 f., 461, 464, 474, 708; Albert C. Outler, ed., *John Wesley* (New York, 1964), 122–23, 306.

105. Cf. Smyth, *Cranmer and the Reformation*, 144.

106. Baldwin, *Shakspere's Latine and Greeke*, I, 276.

107. *Ibid.*, 161.

108. Leonard Cox, *The arte or crafte of Rhetoryke*, F. I. Carpenter, ed. (Chicago, 1899).

109. Baldwin, *Shakspere's Latine and Greeke*, I, 641.

110. *Ibid.*; cf. II, 109 ff.

111. *Ibid.*; cf. II, 4–9, 20 f.; CR 1:1079 f.; 2:542–44; 13:413–16; 16:807 f.

humanistic side of Melanchthon, for his rhetoric and dialectic depended
heavily on classical authors — Cicero, Quintillian, Aristotle, Livy, Plautus,
Tacitus, etc. After 1573 Melanchthon's *De Oratore* and *Orator* were
widely used by scholars seeking perfection in rhetoric.[112] Three of Melanchthon's writings were studied by King James VI of Scotland, who
became James I of England: *Chronicon Melancthonis, Syntaxis Melancthonis*, and *Erotemata Dialectices*.[113] In this and similar ways too
numerous to document Melanchthon became part of the Anglican tradition.

Protestant research is deeply indebted to Melanchthon for the new
direction he gave to historiography. Luther preceded Melanchthon in
ascribing equal value to secular and spiritual factors in history, but the
latter established pedagogical arrangement and "scientific" approach. The
Renaissance humanists largely ignored church history, but the Reformation leaders could not. Melanchthon introduced didactic history with
an emphasis on divine direction, not only in his chronicles but especially
in his *Life of Martin Luther*.[114]

The irenic spirit of Melanchthon displayed in his many colloquies
looms large in the heritage of ecumenicity. The motto with which Peter
Meiderlin closed his *Paraenesis votiva pro pace ecclesiae*, 1626, did not
originate with Melanchthon but is expressive of his spirit: "In things
necessary, unity; in things not necessary, liberty; in both, charity." Significantly, the tract was addressed to the theologians of the Augsburg
Confession. It became a popular motto in England and was used by
Richard Baxter in his *True and Only Way to Concord*, 1679.[115] Hugo
Grotius (1583–1645), in his day the outstanding advocate of complete
unification of the churches, desired that men speak not of Luther and
Calvin but of Erasmus and Melanchthon when they discussed unifica-
tion.[116] In George Calixtus (1586–1656), the most outstanding of the
German Lutheran ecumenists, the Melanchthon tradition of peaceful
concord and unity lived on.[117] His father had been a pupil and admirer of
Melanchthon. And the irenic spirit of Melanchthon continued in Count

112. Baldwin, *Shakspere's Latine and Greeke*, II, 19 f.; cf. *CR* 16:685 ff.

113. Baldwin, *Shakspere's Latine and Greeke*, I, 235, 245 f., 248 f.

114. For a discussion of his contribution to historiography, see Emil Menke-
Glueckert, *Die Geschichtsschreibung der Reformation und Gegenreformation* (Leip-
zig, 1912); and L. W. Spitz, "History as a Weapon in Controversy," in *Concordia
Theological Monthly*, XVIII (1947), 747 ff.

115. Cf. John T. McNeill, *Unitive Protestantism* (Richmond, Va., 1964); Ruth
Rouse and Stephen C. Neill, *A History of the Ecumenical Movement* (London, 1954).

116. *Ibid.*, 95.   117. McNeill, *Unitive Protestantism*, 271.

Ludwig von Zinzendorf (1700–1760), organizer of the Moravian Church. Nevertheless, the seventeenth and eighteenth centuries, involved in violent strife and civil discord, "largely lost the ambitious vision of ecumenicity" of men like Melanchthon, even though the unitive principle survived.[118] In the nineteenth-century revival of Melanchthonianism in America, Melanchthon was hailed as "a champion of a progressive spirit . . . ready to adjust his opinions for the sake of overcoming the disunion of Protestant churches." [119] The Melanchthon Synod regarded him as "the leading early Lutheran exponent of conciliation, progress, development, and adaptation." [120] Yet the enigma remains, for he is blamed and credited for many different things.[121] Hopefully, this translation of the 1555 *Loci* will help clarify Melanchthon's significant part in our heritage.

Notes and Acknowledgments

Melanchthon's *Loci* of 1555 has not heretofore been translated into English, yet it represents a late influential phase of Melanchthon's thought. The original *Loci*, published in 1521, was the first systematic presentation of evangelical Protestant theology; over the years Melanchthon made a number of changes to reflect the development of his thought.

Melanchthon initially published the *Loci* because some of his students printed a premature, unsatisfactory version of his lecture notes on Paul's letter to the Romans, on which the *Loci* was based. Two editions of the popular *Loci* appeared in the first year, one printed in Wittenberg and the other in Basel. During the first period of the *Loci*, 1521–25, eighteen Latin editions and a number of German translations by Georg Spalatin were printed. In the second period of the *Loci*, according to Theodor Strobel,[1] 1525–35, Melanchthon enlarged, edited, and altered much of the content of his book. However, the greatest changes came in the third period, variously dated from 1535, or from the 1540's, to the end of

118. *Ibid.; cf.* Mullinger, *University of Cambridge*, II, 106.
119. Theodore G. Tappert, "Melanchthon in America," in *Luther and Melanchthon*, Vajta (ed.), 189 f.
120. *Ibid.*, 194.
121. *Cf.* R. R. Caemmerer, "The Melanchthonian Blight," in *Concordia Theological Monthly*, XVIII (1947), 321–38; Hildebrandt, *Melanchthon: Alien or Ally?;* Jaroslav Pelikan, *From Luther to Kierkegaard* (St. Louis, 1950), 24–48; Adolph Spaeth, "Melanchthon in American Lutheran Theology," in *The Lutheran Church Review*, XVI (1897).
1. *Versuch einer Litterär Geschichte von Philipp Melanchthons Loci Theologicis als dem ersten Evangelischen Lehrbuche* (Altendorf und Nürnberg, 1776).

Melanchthon's life, although only minor changes appeared after 1555. In the third period the *Loci* was not only enlarged to almost four times its original size, but was basically altered. In the second period Justus Jonas was the chief German translator, and in the third, Melanchthon attempted to give the *Loci* a wider audience by doing the German himself. This English translation is based on two German editions of the 1555 *Loci*, one edition published in 1555, now in the Melanchthon Museum in Bretten, and the other published in 1558, now in the Library of the University of Heidelberg. The translator is grateful to the John Simon Guggenheim Memorial Foundation and to the Committee on International Exchange of Persons, Conference Board of Associated Research Councils for Grants under the Fulbright and Smith-Mundt Acts, for making possible the study of these editions.

Numerous problems were involved in translating the *Loci*, and the translator only hopes that they have been resolved satisfactorily. Biblical references were quoted in the Revised Standard Version of the Bible whenever this could be done without altering the meaning of Melanchthon's German or when he was not trying to make a point through a particular rendering of a scriptural passage. Melanchthon sometimes apparently quoted from memory, so that his quotations are not always the same as in the RSV. These differences are retained wherever they have a bearing on the text. Footnotes have occasionally been added to explain certain references, but they have been kept to a minimum in order not to increase the size of the book. Most of the passages which Melanchthon wrote in the second person have been translated in the first or third person in order to avoid awkward inconsistency in person in the English.

Special thanks are due to Theo Clyde Manschreck for making the basic translation of Hans Engelland's introduction; to Mrs. Edward Meyer for consultation on various technical points; to Mrs. Diane Amussen for her editing of the manuscript; and to many scholars without whose previous work such a translation would not be possible. Thanks should also go to consulting editors Jaroslav Pelikan, Robert Stupperich, and Hans Engelland, and to John Dillenberger for their advice and encouragement.

CLYDE L. MANSCHRECK

Methodist Theological School in Ohio
Delaware, Ohio
Summer 1964

Introduction

On the twenty-ninth of August, 1518, Philip Melanchthon, a small, slender, unpretentious, almost timid figure, entered the Wittenberg Castle Church, which served as the great hall of Wittenberg University, and walked to the rostrum to give his inaugural speech on the reform of university education, *De corrigendis adolescentiae studiis*. It inaugurated a career that was to influence not only higher education but theology and the Church as well, for Melanchthon's influence brought about a spiritual outlook in Germany's evangelical universities that lasted for one hundred and fifty years, until the time of Wolffianism. Through the universities and the secondary institutions of learning which he created, his influence extended throughout the spiritual life of Germany.

Melanchthon, the son of an armorer, George Schwartzerd, was born on February 16, 1497, at Bretten in the Palatinate. He was the great-nephew of the famous humanist Johann Reuchlin, on whose recommendation he had been called to Wittenberg to the faculty of arts, and therefore to philosophy, to teach the Greek language and literature. However, he turned toward Luther and, in doing so, to theology. Early in the first year he stepped out of his specialized field by undertaking to interpret the Letter of the Apostle Paul to Titus, in addition to teaching Homer, whom he especially loved. In the following year, on September 19, 1519, after he was granted the degree of Bachelor of Theology, he began lecturing more in theology than in his own field; he offered lecture courses on Genesis and the Psalms, the Gospels of Matthew and John, Colossians, First and Second Corinthians, and, above all, Romans, a course which between 1519 and 1521 he offered three times. These theological lectures were well attended, the hall often being overcrowded, but he could draw only a few people to his philological courses, which the students often found hard to endure to the end of the semester. Yet in 1524, when Luther begged him to drop classical philology and to give full time to the theological faculty, of which he became a member in 1519, he refused to sever his dual faculty status, a sign from the beginning that he objected to faculty barriers.

Melanchthon enlarged his range of interests to include all the sciences, many of which he treated in his lectures. Like the later Leibnitz, he was a historian of many parts [*ein Polyhistor*]: he wrote many Latin speeches [*Declamationes*], which had historical content and revealed political understanding, as, for example, when he spoke on the election of Charles V; he revised the Chronicle of Carion, a world as well as a church history; and he edited the historical works of writers of antiquity, like Tacitus' *Germania*, which he valued highly. As a philologist he edited many Latin and Greek authors, often translating the Greek into Latin and interpreting it [*Ennarationes*], as he did some of the speeches of Demosthenes, passages from Homer, and the ethical and political writings of Aristotle. He dealt with juridical and medical themes and wrote on psychology, which he based on contemporary knowledge of anatomy. In the sphere of the natural arts, he delved into astronomy, geography, geometry, arithmetic, anatomy, and botany; he even wrote a book on physics, the focal point of which was astronomy. He did not acquire his medical knowledge in the lecture hall on anatomy or at the sickbed, for he studied Galen's works and other writings in accordance with the customary humanistic veneration of antiquity; nevertheless, he did not obtain all his knowledge from books. He knew the importance of personal observation, whether in the hall of anatomy or in the observatory. His lectures were enriched not only by the literary works which gave them a continuity with the past, but also by a vast exchange of letters with foreign scholars, princes, and kings. Thus Melanchthon personified the whole university in his time. In his person he became a symbol of the *universitas litterarum*. After his death this was even more evident, for his lectures on exegesis, ethics, philology, and history had to be divided among four men.

The Approach to Theology in the Older Melanchthon

The Theological Task of All the Sciences

Melanchthon's interest in all the sciences was ultimately motivated, not by an interest simply in man, but by his belief that the sciences all have a common theological task. In their common obligation they encounter one another; each is obligated to lead mankind to the knowledge of God.

According to Melanchthon's *Physics* (1549), the exploration of nature allows us to discover guides for spiritual living, especially in medical science, where we find arguments for refuting not only the Epicurean denial of God and his providence but also stoical determinism.[1] Even in his textbooks on physics he treats the question of the existence and providence of God, beginning his proofs for God with a causal conclusion a posteriori from ascertainable effects in nature produced by God.[2] In his *Dialectics* (1547) Melanchthon holds that the main task of the art of correct, orderly, clear teaching is to instruct mankind in the knowledge of God, the virtuous life, and the contemplation of nature.[3] Arithmetic should point to the unity of God and so guard against polytheism. We should "discern numbers in such a way that, when we hear of the unity of the Holy Father and of our Lord Jesus Christ, we do not conclude there are innumerable gods."[4] In the same manner geometry, which is so closely connected with arithmetic, should not exhaust itself in its practical applications, but should lift our eyes from earth to heaven and indicate to us the wonderful work and management of the world.[5] To be complete, astronomy must go beyond a consideration of the heavens to a contemplation of creation and the providence of God, and from this to virtue: "The laws of motion bear witness to the fact that the world did not originate through accident but was created by an eternal Spirit, and human nature stems from the heart of this Creator."[6] In the same manner Melanchthon turned toward astrology not only for its utility in the curing of diseases and the guiding of states but also for its religious lessons, for he saw in the "heavenly signs" an oracle of God which should not be despised.[7] The study of geography is "necessary in order to know God's ordering of kingdoms, where and when he manifested himself, left his imprint and made known his testimony, so that we may recognize the truth of his teaching and appropriate it."[8] Historical science, to be sure, has "worldly utility" in view, but over and above this, in an ethical, pedagogical sense, the task of historical science is finally religious; we learn from historical science about the beginning and course of religion, and about such things as the Church's doctrinal controversies and how they were decided; and without historical science we can hardly comprehend the prophets and the Holy Scriptures.[9] The task of philology also extends beyond the communication of the spoken word, for the Latin and Greek languages are not only receptacles of earthly things, but also of "heavenly doctrines." Greek makes possible a talk with the

---

1. *CR* 13:190.   2. *CR* 13:200.   3. *CR* 12:513.
4. *CR* 13:657.   5. *CR* 3:108.   6. *CR* 11:297.
7. *CR* 11:265.   8. *CR* 9:481.   9. *CR* 3:481, 877 f., 882.

Son of God, with the evangelists and apostles, "without an interpreter"; it alone opens the way to the history of the Christian Church and to doctrine in the first centuries; and the knowledge of Hebrew is requisite for the Old Testament.[10] And finally, philosophical ethics should not only lead to an external ordering of human life but also to the knowledge of God, to which it should conduct us by its distinctions between good and evil and questions about the goals of men.[11]

The sciences in their totality are somewhat like a huge mountain which from all sides aspires to and is complete in a single peak — the knowledge of God. The individual sciences have their specific places on the circle of knowledge, but all are turned to a common center — the knowledge of God. Thus they have a common spiritual orientation in which we can perceive their final unity, even though they approach it [the knowledge of God] from different directions. In the praise of God they unite to form one choir, the *integer artium chorus*.[12]

The Foundation of the Knowledge of All the Sciences

The synopsis of the sciences just given rests upon a common fundamental assumption, upon a certain theory of knowledge, derived from a Ciceronian concept, for Melanchthon developed his idea of knowledge on the basis of the "natural light" in man, *naturalis lux in intellectu*, or *lux humani ingenii*, or *lumen divinitus insitum mentibus*.[13] This "natural light" is the basis for certitude in all the sciences. It coincides with the general experience of man, the *experientia universalis*, which is perceived by the senses, and it is common to all men of sound mind in a similar manner. For example, fire is hot. Second, he developed his idea of knowledge on the basis of innate, ultimate presuppositions of knowledge, the *notitiae nobiscum nascentes*, the source of the individual sciences, through which they are known and made clear, and in which we concur without further confirmation.[14] Melanchthon divided the *notitiae nobiscum nascentes* into ultimate presuppositions of thought, the *principia speculabilia* of physics and mathematics (for example, the whole is greater than any of its parts); and the ultimate presuppositions of action, the *principia practica* of ethics, which direct the moral life and above all require distinctions between good and evil.[15] Third, the "natural light" renders possible syllogistic thought, through which we are able to bring together

10. CR 11:859, 709.   11. CR 16:166 ff., 171 f.   12. CR 11:414.
13. CR 13:150, 647; 21:712. 14. CR 13:647 f.   15. CR 13:649; 21:711.

those things which belong together and to separate those which do not agree.[16]

From this spiritual predisposition the innate *notitiae* lead to a consciousness of God; for this reason Melanchthon considers the atheist a deliberate liar.[17] With the help of the "natural light" he attempts to establish proof of God, and actually sets forth nine arguments. By virtue of the *principia speculabilia* it is possible to reason a posteriori from perceptible effects to God as the cause, and by virtue of the *principia practica*, to take for granted an immediate consciousness of God, which consists in the natural faculty to distinguish between good and evil and in a consciousness that we should obey God and be punished for disobedience. This immediate consciousness of God should actually be as clear and certain in us as the principles of thought which remain immutable, but man's defection from God created a barrier between man's heart and mind, and the heart is now moved by impulses contrary to the innate judgments about good and evil; consequently, men hesitate to approve the innate judgments. However, as this "divine light in the soul" cannot be extinguished, it should be "strongly aroused and the sense of it fortified so that we recognize, assert and confirm that the practical principles are just as sure and certain as the principles of thought, or even the immutable judgments of God." [18]

Melanchthon perceives this ethical-religious predisposition in the idea of the image of God, which though distorted after the Fall, nevertheless found expression, especially in the idea of law. Melanchthon then distinguishes divine, natural, and human law. The divine law is the law that God has imprinted on the human spirit as an "external and immutable precept of the divine spirit, a judgment against sin," [19] often proclaimed in God's word. The law of nature, which is given in the *principia practica* and which Melanchthon defines as a "natural knowledge of God and our guide in morality or judgment about good and evil, which is implanted by God in mankind like the knowledge of numbers," is the order in nature which corresponds with the moral part of God's law, summarized in the Decalogue. Thus Melanchthon can describe the law of nature as a "knowledge of divine law implanted in human nature." [20]

For his first proof for God Melanchthon turns to nature, where he beholds an order which, he says, could not have been brought about by an accident nor a development of matter, but only by an orderly Spirit.

16. CR 13:648.   17. CR 15:565.   18. CR 21:641 ff., 711 f.
19. CR 21:712, 686, 687.   20. CR 13:649 f.; 21:687 f., 712.

His second proof is derived from the rational nature of man, which he says can take its origin only from that which is rational. The third follows a posteriori from the natural power to distinguish between good and evil, order and number; a Spirit must be the architect of such power. Fourth, the existence of God follows (a posteriori) from the natural belief of all men in God, a *notitia naturalis*. Fifth, the conclusion (a posteriori) from the transgressor's qualms of conscience is that a Spirit has ordained this judgment. Sixth, the conclusion (a posteriori) from political society is that an "eternal Spirit has given man an orderly understanding for the sake of maintaining political community." Seventh, Melanchthon speculates on the sequence of cause and effect, and concludes that the causal series cannot infinitely regress because there would then be no necessary connection of causes; there must be a single first cause. Eighth, purposeful reasoning toward a goal implies the existence of concluding *causae finales*, with God as the originator. Ninth, prophetic announcements of future events indicate that a Spirit announces and points out the changes before they happen.

Reason and Revelation, Philosophy and Theology

From this naturalistic approach of Melanchthon's theology it follows that the revelation of God as attested in the Holy Scriptures can have only supplementary significance. Revelation only adds something to that which man himself can and ought to say about God. This fusion of reason and revelation becomes plain in the discussion about the providence of God. The proofs of God should both convince us about the existence of God and indicate certain characteristics in his being, for example, his providential care.[21] However, because the actualities of life do not always appear to reflect God's providence,[22] accepting it is more difficult than accepting God's existence. Therefore, the Biblical word is necessary to awaken and strengthen faith in his providence.[23] Thus, to the knowledge of God's existence revelation adds the certainty of his providential care.

The same complementary relationship between reason and revelation meets us in the idea of God in the doctrine of atonement. Melanchthon starts from the Platonic idea of God, that God is an eternal Spirit and the source of all good in nature, and then explains that "another, clearer, and more conclusive definition of the idea of God must be sought," because he [Plato] still "does not describe God as he has revealed himself."

21. *CR* 21:643.   22. *CR* 13:203.   23. *CR* 21:641.

It is necessary to add how God has revealed himself in the Trinitarian manner. In view of the atonement, man knows by virtue of the law of nature that God is just and kind to those who fulfill his will and that he is angry with those who do not. Through the gospel we first come to know that God for Christ's sake wants to be kind even to those who have not deserved it, for he justifies the sinner. This was hidden from Xenophon, Plato, Cicero, and Pompanius Atticus.[24]

Melanchthon co-ordinates revelation and the "natural light" in accordance with this complementary relationship. He says that in the Church, in addition to general experience, principles, and syllogisms, we have "still a fourth standard of certainty, namely, divine revelation, which occurs with clear and indubitable evidence in the prophetic and apostolic books." [25] Melanchthon here places reason and revelation in a coexistence, somewhat like two countries with a common border, living peacefully beside one another. Reason tolerates pretentions to something that is beyond its control and more than logic, something contrary to its knowledge, God; it tolerates a way of knowledge that is independent of general experience and logical axioms; for its part, revelation foregoes exclusive jurisdiction in questions about God and concerns itself with the function of completeness. Neither is limited, threatened, or repressed by the other.

Reason does not feel itself threatened by the fact that in its assertions revelation claims mathematical certainty. Just as every man of sound will should be certain that two times four equals eight, "so should the articles of faith, the divine warnings and promises, be for us certain and unshakable; and the one who does wrong should be just as certain that sins are forgiven for the sake of the Son of God, for whose sake he is heard and is an heir of eternal life. However, the grounds for the certainty are different. Reason grasps statements about numbers according to its own judgment. However the articles of faith are certain on account of the revelation which God has confirmed through sure and clear evidence, such as resurrection of the dead and many other wonders." [26]

This complementary relationship between reason and revelation consequently determines the relation of theology to philosophy as well as to all the sciences.[27] Theology, based in Biblical revelation, enlarges the natural knowledge of God in philosophy, and in this way *Heilsgeschichte* determines the construction of dogmatics.[28] But this revealed knowledge

24. CR 21:610, 733, 291.   25. CR 13:150 f.   26. CR 21:604 f.   27. CR 12:689.
28. CR 21:605 f.

of God in history is removed from philosophy's method of proof, which always starts from experience and principles.[29] Therefore, theology and philosophy are to be differentiated; they may not be mixed together like broth in the kitchen.[30]

However, though one cannot demonstrate revelation, one need not renounce methodical thought; it gives theology its scientific character, and without it theology would become an *inerudita theologia,* "in which important things will not be developed in an orderly manner, in which things that should be separated will be mixed, and things that according to their natures should be combined will be separated, and in which conflicting things will often be said, the immediate seen as truth, and peculiarities affected. . . . Nothing will hang together in it. One will perceive neither the point of departure nor the steps of progress nor the conclusion." [31] For this reason, in its conceptualizing theology must be able to define, limit, compare, and deduce.[32] It requires primarily dialectics in order to obtain a *methodus et forma orationis,*[33] a method and style of speaking, but it also needs the other sciences, especially physics and philosophical ethics, both to form concepts and acquire the contents of their knowledge, for example, their views of the soul or the will. Philosophy thus becomes the helpmate of theology,[34] its sciences, the *adminicula in doctrina coelesti,*[35] props for divine doctrine.

It is a fascinating spiritual structure which Melanchthon instituted and in which many generations of young people grew up. He projected it on one single goal of thought — knowledge of God. It served the schools and universities, and in it they saw their particular mission. And this structure was based on a single assumption, that "natural light" is capable of knowledge of God. With this doctrine of "natural light" Melanchthon gave the university a firm spiritual foundation and united all its sciences as fully as possible with the Christian faith. He first became *Praeceptor Germaniae* through this system of science.

The question concerning the rightness or wrongness of this naturalistic approach in his theology is posed by Melanchthon himself through an original and different approach in his *Loci Communes* of 1521, the first systematic theology of the evangelical Church.

29. *CR* 21:603 f.   30. *CR* 11:282.   31. *CR* 11:280.
32. *CR* 7:577.   33. *CR* 11:654, 280.   34. *CR* 11:282.
35. *CR* 13:657.

The Approach to Theology in the Young Melanchthon

In the young Melanchthon we encounter a completely different approach, manifested, of course, in the chapter on sin in his *Loci Communes* of 1521, in the reaction of God to the Fall of man. The question is whether man's departure from God only weakened and wounded the religious capacities of man, or whether it destroyed the spiritual bond with God so that man in a natural sense has completely lost God as the Creator and Sustainer.

Melanchthon sees the reaction of God in the departure of God's Spirit. "When God created man without sin, he was with him through his Spirit in order to move him to the right actions. This Spirit would have guided all the descendants of Adam if Adam had not fallen. But after Adam fell, God immediately turned aside from man, and would not be his guide." [36] This departure of the Spirit put an end to the spiritual union between God and man and had the following consequences:

1. *For the knowledge of men.* Melanchthon speaks of the consequences of this departure for knowledge in the chapter on "justification and faith." The theological position of his assertions is very significant, for he indicates that the capacity for knowledge with regard to the departure of God's Spirit is also related to the capacity for will and action. Single-handedly among the reformers, the young Melanchthon destroys the strict equilibrium between all the natural sciences. He sees in the question about the activity of God, in contrast to his later viewpoint, a genuine, yes, a cardinal question, which he expresses in his explanation of Genesis in 1523: "Is there a God? Was this world created by a divine power? Is it regulated by a divine being?" [37]

Melanchthon's answer actually undercuts the two ways to a natural knowledge of God which were known to him in the philosophical and theological tradition, the way from nature and the way from men.

First, the knowing of God from nature: Man "cannot comprehend the creation and the guidance of the world, and he supposes that things happen, originate, perish, and recur accidentally. Thus thinks the flesh in all." Or man thinks that "the ordered and regulated movements" are "but the course of nature which we see. What does God have to do with small and limited creatures? Each thing maintains itself by its own strength." [38] "Though you constantly read and reread, and even wallow in sacred books and doctrines, nevertheless reason [*Verstand*] will never

36. *CR* 21:97.   37. *CR* 13:761.   38. *CR* 13:761, 767.

thus believe that God exists, that he is merciful and just. You may hear the words and you may hypocritically imitate the words of Spirit, but in actuality you will not understand, and you will but uphold God's existence as poetic fiction. Human blindness is a deep abyss." After this Melanchthon comes to his basic declaration: "God's existence, God's anger, God's compassion are spiritual things, and therefore they cannot be known by the flesh." [39] For this reason, "the belief that everything is ruled through divine providence and that nothing happens accidentally undercuts our reason, which denies the existence of God and his care for us." To the being of God belongs not only "spiritual things" but also his existence. This means positively, "only as God affects our hearts and indicates with regard to creation that from him and in him and through him everything is can the heart receive trust in God." [40]

In the second place Melanchthon takes the possibility of the knowledge of God out of the natural conscience and thus denies that conscience is able by itself to know God and his will. Here emerges the problem of natural law. Melanchthon distinguishes three laws, the law requiring the honoring of God, the law prohibiting the harming of anyone, and the law enjoining the using of all things commonly. He draws the second and third law from the communal life of man, and the first, from Scripture, from Romans 1:20. Although he is convinced that Paul himself dealt with God's existence under the laws of nature, he considers it curiosity rather than piety to argue that God's existence can be concluded from a rational proposition. The meaning is still clearer in the altered second edition of the Loci Communes in 1522: "Human reason easily infers the last two laws, but how it could infer the first law, I cannot see, since reason was so darkened after the fall of Adam. . . . How the first law is to be included among the laws of nature, let others judge. Hebrews 11 says that creation is known through faith." [41] Melanchthon very plainly denies knowledge of God through natural law in the section on the gospel, in which he even takes away the aspects of natural law in the second law; indeed, he dispenses with the notion of natural law: "In addition to the natural law with which God impressed the spirit of man, God also, I believe, gave laws to Adam forbidding the taking of the fruit from the tree of knowledge and to Cain forbidding anger with or sin against his brother lest he murder him. In this manner the Spirit of God renews the knowledge of natural law that became obscured in nature because the spirit of man became blind through sin. Therefore, I would

39. CR 21:94, 160.   40. CR 13:762.   41. CR 21:117 f.

almost prefer to call the law of nature not a judgment which is innate
or implanted or impressed on the spirit of man by nature, but commandments which we receive from our ancestors and then pass on, as it were
from hand to hand, to our descendants. As Adam instructed his descendants with respect to the creation of the world and the honoring of God,
so he admonished Cain not to kill his brother." [42] Adam did not simply
awaken some remembrance of something that was in Cain from the
beginning, something lying dormant in his nature. He did not revive a
law of nature which had faded like an old writing; instead, he said
something unknown and new. For certainty concerning God's activity
Melanchthon looks back both to the certainty and the mystery of God,
which need proclamation through the word.

Melanchthon goes a step further. He makes a sharp religious judgment
on the value of all attempts of man to confirm the existence and will of
God by means of the two ways of natural knowledge. They not only
do not lead to the desired goal, but actually are an expression of revolt
against God. "What is known about the nature of God without the
Spirit of God, which renews and illuminates our hearts, is no more than
cold thought, certainly not faith, and for this reason nothing but sham
and hypocrisy, ignorance concerning God, and contempt, even though
the eyes of flesh do not see this hypocrisy. The Spirit sets everything in
order." [43] Proofs of God are but disdain and disbelief concerning the
majesty of God. Neither belief nor disbelief can be substantiated or re-
futed by proofs.

2. *For the will and action of man.* In turning from God man turned to
himself, and is now ruled by the basic emotion of self-love. This *amor
sui* "is the first and strongest basic motive ruling the nature of man (*primus
affectus et summus naturae hominis*); it overpowers him, and for its sake
he seeks and desires only that which seems to his nature good, pleasant,
sweet, and glorious; he hates and fears whatever appears hostile to him;
he avoids whatever opposes or whatever dictates to him; he does not pursue and seek what is not pleasing to him." [44] Because man does not have
this basic emotion under control, he cannot freely choose to hate and to
love; his love ends when one whom he may have loved up to that moment injures him.[45]

From this necessarily followed an antithesis to the scholastic theology
which at that time confronted the reformers, especially in William of
Ockham and Gabriel Biel. Men thought that the nature of man was not

42. *CR* 21:140.   43. *CR* 21:160.   44. *CR* 21:98.   45. *CR* 21:90.

injured through the departure of God, which meant that, as in the beginning, man still had the freedom in himself to call forth good acts, *actus bonos elicere*,[46] even the freedom to love God above all else.[47] This view said that man had to take the first steps on the way to justification and to dispose himself thereby for justification, as proclaimed in the classical sentence, "Do that which is given to you to do, and then God will give you his grace." [48] Melanchthon answers that man's self-love engenders additional hatred of God, for God is like a consuming fire to man. Only the compassion of God is able to overcome this hate, a compassion which produces a new affection of love for God so that man cannot but love God and return his love (*redamare deum*). No one can hate sin and repent except through the Holy Spirit.[49]

Thus Melanchthon establishes the impotence of man apart from God both in his knowledge of God and in his ability to will and act in accordance with God's command. For this reason, only God, through his Spirit, can again restore man. The approach of Melanchthon is thus not to define ever more closely what is human so as to have an analogy of God, but to return to the Spirit of God, for only the Spirit of God as it speaks to man in the word is able to direct his knowledge and will and action back to God.

Looking in retrospect on the approach through the "natural light," we must confirm that Melanchthon in his later theology de-emphasized the activity of the Spirit of God in man. The contours of tradition, which at first faded and were obscured by the brilliant light of the new knowledge, later came forward again. The consequences of the Fall from God are no longer universally understood, instead the "natural light" in man is a kind of sphere attributed to the Holy Spirit, as we saw in the question about the knowledge of God. This shaking change clearly appears for the first time in Melanchthon's commentary on Romans in 1532. Here for the first time we meet the proofs of God presented above, but, as in the *Loci* of 1535, only the first six; in the revision of the *Loci* of 1543–44 the proofs are enlarged to nine. Melanchthon never explicitly expressed the reason for this turnabout. Perhaps it was a defense against the enthusiasts, with their doctrine of the Spirit apart from the word, or an ethical-pedagogical interest over against their hostility to education, or

---

46. *CR* 21:91.

47. *Melanchthons Werke*, II, 1, *Loci communes von 1521*, Hans Engelland, ed. (Gütersloh, 1952), 31, n. 19.

48. *Ibid.*, 33, n. 27.   49. *CR* 21:98, 154.

perhaps a demand for a starting point for the proclamation of the gospel or for the study of the ancient philosophers, or perhaps all these motives combined.

Controversial Questions in the Interpretation of Melanchthon

The Relation of the Acts of God and the Acts of Men

The return to an approach to theology through man, with which Melanchthon returned to tradition, poses first of all the question as to whether this affected the central article of the Reformation concerning justification, and whether, with regard to the fulfillment of the law and the appropriation of salvation, a synergism penetrated Melanchthon's thinking.

With regard to the Decalogue, which now is understood as a short explanation and interpretation of the law of nature, man in his natural strength can fulfill only the second table, and that only in an external sense as *iustitia civilis* or *disciplina externa*. But Melanchthon had many reservations about the practical realization of this, because he saw it threatened by the weakness of original sin and by the power of Satan,[50] so that man even in this *disciplina externa* might easily fall if God were not preserving him.[51] Man is not able fully, in an inward sense, to fulfill the will of God, not even able to begin to do so.[52] "Without the Holy Spirit he cannot bring about the spiritual affections, which God demands, namely true fear of God, true trust in the compassion of God, true love of God, and patience and bravery in affliction and death." [53]

From this it is not to be expected that Melanchthon would be able to concede to assimilating grace in the natural will. He made several statements which, though misunderstood, in any case occasioned the suspicion of synergism, especially in his assertion of the three causes concurrently working together — the word of God, the Holy Spirit, and the will of man, which agrees with and does not resist the word of God. Yes, he could take over the formula of the "old"; the will is free in its ability to conform to grace (*facultas applicandi se ad gratiam*), "that is, it hears the promise and tries to agree and to end its deliberate sinning against conscience." [54] However, Melanchthon is speaking in the first assertion about the three causes which concurrently work together, not of a natural will but of a will that agrees, and he is thinking in the second of one who

50. CR 21:392, 401, 655.   51. CR 25:328.   52. CR 15:950.
53. CR 21:656.   54. CR 21:658 f.

is already reborn, as a conversation recorded by Jacob Runge shows.[55]
Many similar remarks corroborate this. "Trust and joy in the heart are
the immediate works of the Holy Spirit." [56] The will is active in conversion "in so far as God has healed it" (*quatenus sanari divinitus
coepit*).[57] Any nonresistance of the will results from the inducement of
the Holy Spirit.[58] Yes, God works during and after the conversion, and so
the will is not active; it remains purely passive. "It is very useful to know
this rule about the Holy Spirit, for it is true that God effects much wonderful enlightenment and activity in conversion and throughout the
lives of saints, which the human will only accepts, in which it is not a
co-worker but holds its own passively. Nevertheless, we must be taught
in all our anxious temptations to consider the word of God; we must
plead for his help and ask him to strengthen us with his word," and
"in this struggle the will is not inactive" (*in hoc certamine voluntas non
est otiosa*).[59]

These and similar assertions make it appear questionable that Melanchthon really advocates a form of synergism when he speaks of the activity
of the will. The assertions in which he speaks unqualifiedly and mis-
takenly are to be understood in accordance with the context in which
he stood. He himself names as adversaries the enthusiasts and the Manicheans who make the *ministerium evangelicum* useless, and he energetically
rejects the misunderstanding that the Holy Spirit deals with man as with
a statue, a piece of wood, or a stone.[60] God works in man not only in time
of crisis but at all times, which means that God works in ways that cannot be described in logical thought patterns but only paradoxically, with
the result that faith in one dimension appears to be the decision of the
Holy Spirit, and in the other dimension, the decision of man.[61] But in
Melanchthon's speeches about the activity of man still another motive
appears. Many assertions have a pastoral character; he intends them to
help in time of despondency and resignation, to assist in a resolution unto
faith. "I cannot, you say. On the contrary, you can, in a certain manner.
When the voice of the gospel rises in you, then ask God for help and
comfort yourself that the Holy Spirit is active in this, that in this way
God wants to convert. In view of his promises we should make an effort,

55. Cf. A. Herrlinger, *Die Theologie Melanchthons in ihrer geschichtlichen Entwicklung* (Gotha, 1879), 92; Fr. H. R. Frank, *Die Theologie der Konkordienformel*
(Erlangen, 1858), 198.

56. CR 15:97.   57. CR 24:316.   58. CR 15:680.
59. CR 9:468; 21:658.   60. CR 21:659, 663; 15:329.
61. See "*gleichwohl*" in the quotation in CR 9:468.

call on him, and struggle against our mistrust and other destructive emotions." [62]

The Relation of Justification and Sanctification

A second question is whether Melanchthon later gave up the unity of justification and sanctification,[63] which he originally taught when he joined Luther, thereby separating *regeneratio* from *iustificatio* and treating it as a second act of God, and understanding *iustificatio* itself as a mere *imputatio* of the *aliena iustitia Christi*, as mere forgiveness of sins. Melanchthon often speaks of justification as mere forgiveness or imputation of the righteousness of Christ or acceptance by God or a declaration of righteousness — without even mentioning sanctification. However, he does not intend to exclude sanctification but to console the terrified conscience under the judgment of God (*conscientia perterre-facta*) and to avert any Roman Catholic misunderstanding.

That basically he did not separate sanctification from justification is plain from the manner in which he speaks of Christ's mission. In the editions of the *Loci* after 1543–44 he says Christ came "in order to forgive us our sins and to begin in us new righteousness and eternal life through the Holy Spirit." [64] "Christ is our righteousness, that is, we are not righteous because the Son of the Eternal is righteous, but because his merit is credited to us for the forgiveness of sins and for reconciliation, and because he works a renewal in us, which some day in the eternal life will be complete righteousness." [65] He is "our righteousness, sanctification, and redemption, namely through his merit, his presence, and his strong activity in us." [66]

Because Melanchthon maintains this unity of forgiveness and sanctification in the mission of Christ, it recurs also in many of his teachings about justification. The new obedience must begin "because we are justified and our sins are annulled, and with that the new and eternal life actually begins in us, which is a new light and obedience toward God." [67] However, sanctification is not only the goal of justification but also its content. "Justification itself always brings new life and obedience with it,"

---

62. CR 21:659.

63. See especially Karl Holl, *Die rechtfertigungslehre im Licht der Geschichte des Protestantismus* (Tübingen, 1923). Cf. Karl Holl, *The Cultural Significance of the Reformation*, tr. by Karl and Barbara Hertz and J. H. Lichtblau (New York, 1959).

64. CR 21:854.   65. CR 12:410, thesis 34.   66. CR 8:612.   67. CR 13:1342.

and "the beginning of renewal always happens at the same time as justification." [68] Those who believe in the gospel "are justified, that is, through the Son and for the sake of the Son are received in faith and through him by virtue of the Holy Spirit are sanctified to eternal life." We are justified by faith "by virtue of the justice which God imputed for the sake of his Son and through the beginning of a new, pure life." [69] Righteousness is "reconciliation or imputation of righteousness through the God who declares us justified for the sake of his Son, and the gift and the activity of that righteousness and that life in us will be eternal." Thus Melanchthon includes sanctification in justification when he speaks with the Holy Scriptures of righteousness in the complete meaning of the word, *de toto beneficio*.[70] However, even if he had spoken only about forgiveness in the case of justification, sanctification would have been decided for him, for forgiveness means not only that God does not impute the sins, but also that it includes "at the same time the gift of the Holy Spirit, eternal life, and all the promises of the gospel that God grants to us as acceptors, assisting us and sheltering us. In short, all the benefits of the gospel (*omnia beneficia Evangelii*) are included in the idea of the forgiveness of sins." [71] Forgiveness and sanctification are like the light and warmth of the sun: "the world grows bright and warm in the sun; nevertheless, light and warmth are in themselves different." [72] Thus Melanchthon reproved Osiander only for his Catholic manner of speaking, not for his inclusion of sanctification in justification. In this way he protected the unity of justification and sanctification.

Predestination

A third question is whether Melanchthon later gave up predestination; originally he had joined with Luther in decisively advocating it.

Note first that he refers to the universality of the promises of salvation and blames man's debt on a miscarriage of the human will only, because God is not *causa peccati*, and in him is no *contradictoriae voluntates*. On the other hand, there seem to be assertions which do not fit within these limits. In the commentary on Romans in 1556 he answers the question, Why are so many men lost and so few saved, and why must the Church suffer in so many ways? "Not all the plans of God can be understood

---

68. *CR* 21:442; 28:401.   69. *CR* 14:1185, 579.   70. *CR* 12:410, thesis 39; 7:678 f.
71. *CR* 15:429.   72. *CR* 24:815; 14:86.

by human thought, but we must sustain ourselves in the revealed word of God. . . . Someday in the eternal school we will learn the reason for the divine plan." [73] In this connection he often speaks of a hidden decree of God (*arcanum dei decretum, consilium arcanum*), or of the hidden majesty (*arcana maiestas*). In view of God's decision with respect to Esau and Jacob, he declares that the same measure for measure is to be given only in the case of an obligation. "In the case of a gift or of compassion, it is not necessary to grant in the same measure." [74] "The sentence which says that there is an eternal election is true, and nevertheless it also remains true that we are not to investigate election without the word of God or beyond the word of God." [75] "We should agree to the word, even if we are not able to see all the connections in what is presented contradictorily" (*quae se in contrarium offerunt*).[76] "You must know that you should not judge a priori about your election, but a posteriori, that is, you are not to search in the hidden counsel of God to discover whether you are elected, you are to search in the revealed word." [77]

These statements indicate that Melanchthon does not reject predestination in principle — even in the sense of reprobation, but admonishes practically and pastorally about it. This would mean that a responsible decision of man and a sovereign decision of God take place simultaneously in the acceptance or rejection of salvation. In this assertion of dual activity Melanchthon is speaking in a paradoxical way, as he does in the question about the relation of the acts of God and of man in the formation of faith.

Melanchthon, therefore, stands theologically nearer to Luther than the traditional view indicates. The important theological deficiencies of the time following Melanchthon are more the responsibility of students who fragmented what he had fused.

In the teaching of the Lord's Supper Melanchthon may be distinguished from Luther in the fact that he established the real presence of Christ as possible in several places [*Multivolipräsenz*]. In his teachings on the Church, he vigorously clarified the Church's jurisdiction, so that afterward within orthodoxy the so-called pastoral churches could develop. And through raising the state to the guardianship of both tables of the Decalogue, he introduced a development that later expressed itself in the tenet "*Cuius regio eius religio*" and in the state church [*Staatskirchentum*].

73. CR 15:997 f.   74. CR 15:683, 981.   75. CR 25:681.
76. CR 24:921.   77. CR 24:478.

And finally, the enlightenment of the school of Christian Wolff, with its proofs of God and its combination of reason and revelation, can be traced directly back to Melanchthon.

HANS ENGELLAND

Dedication by Philip Melanchthon

Dedicated to Anna, the honorable and virtuous wife of our esteemed Joachim Camerarius, to whom I, Philip Melanchthon, wish God's grace, through his only-begotten Son, Jesus Christ, our Savior and true Helper!

Greetings to one both honorable and virtuous! That reverence, faith, trust, invocation, and gratitude may be awakened and strengthened through God's word and knowledge, all Christians should spend some time each day inwardly contemplating the gracious divine revelation and teaching in the writings of the prophets and apostles and in the creeds, for these are, and forever will remain, the source, the wellspring, and ground of our faith. Many books have been written, however, in which an alien meaning has been given to the divine word and the words of the prophets and apostles, and this has occasioned all sorts of quarrels. Rightly oriented teachers are needed, therefore, to clarify and preserve the proper meaning of the words of the prophets and apostles. And such true teachers do not invent new or peculiar doctrines about God; instead, they stay close to the unadulterated [*einigen*] meaning, which God himself has revealed through the words which are found in the writings of the prophets and apostles and in the creeds. The entire office of preaching, which God has ordained for public assemblies, is to present to the people these and no other writings, except the writings of the prophets and apostles, and the creeds, and thus unfold, as in a grammar, the true meaning of the words, what God is called, what created things are, and what such terms as body, spirit, person, law, sin, gospel, promise, faith, grace, justification [*Gerechtwerden*], and worship mean. To learn the true meaning of these terms and writings is to recognize sublime wisdom and divine light. This should be the purpose of a catechism.

After the almighty Son of God, Jesus Christ, graciously allowed his doctrine to shine again through The Reverend Dr. Martin Luther, and after he rebuked the error and idolatry of the Popes and the monks, and after I as a poor scholar drew up the Visitation and Confession,[1] I

---

1. *Unterricht der Visitatoren* (The Visitation Articles), 1528, drawn up by Melanchthon for the guidance of commissions inspecting the schools and churches of

xliii

was forced to dispute about many things with many people. In just this way I was moved to prepare this introduction, the *Locos Theologicos*, which I have written with a singular purpose. My intention was—then and now—to relate only that doctrine contained in the confession of the churches of Saxony, which was delivered at Augsburg in 1530.[2] With this in mind, as in a catechism when one tries to explain basic terms, I have drawn up this introduction for young people. Whether this be easy or difficult to do, those with understanding may judge.

But since I have found how difficult this is for me, I ask the Christian reader not to be an unfriendly judge, and I resign myself and all my writings to the judgment of the churches and universities which adhere to the aforementioned Augsburg Confession. And although many have written against this doctrine and against me — Cochlaus, Alfonsus, Perionius, Osiander, and others — I console myself still in the judgment of the true Church. Controversies occur constantly, and one has consolation enough against his foes if he himself before God knows that he teaches correctly and serves faithfully in his calling and witnesses to the true Church. I am sending you this work because, to a Christian who lives in true knowledge of God and in prayer and to one who attempts to rear her children in the same, this book in German may prove useful. May the Almighty God, Father of our Savior, Jesus Christ, for the sake of his Son Jesus Christ, graciously keep and guide your beloved husband Joachim Camerarius, you, and all your children.

Dated, Wittenberg, on the day of Matthew the Apostle, in the year 1553.

Saxony. The first part was a statement of faith, and the second part, a detailed school plan. Cf. *Corpus Reformatorum, Melanchthon Opera*, Carl G. Bretschneider and H. E. Bindsell, eds. (Halis Saxonium, 1834–60), 26:51–96.

2. In Luther's absence Melanchthon was the chief author of the Augsburg Confession, delivered to the Emperor Charles V by the evangelical authorities of Germany at the Diet of Augsburg, 1530. Cf. *The Book of Concord*, Henry E. Jacobs, ed. (Philadelphia, 1883), I; *ibid.*, Theodore G. Tappert, ed. (Philadelphia, 1959).

Foreword by Philip Melanchthon

God is a spiritual being [*Wesen*] who is wise, eternal, omnipotent, different from all creatures, true, good, beneficient, righteous, pure, and incorruptible, and independent [*freiwillig*]; he knows all hearts, judges and punishes all sins, and yet is merciful. God is the eternal Father, who from eternity begot the Son, his Image; God is the Son, who is the eternal Image of the eternal Father; and God is the Holy Spirit, who proceeds from the Father and Son. As the divine Majesty has himself graciously revealed through his doctrine and reliable testimony, the eternal Father together with his Son and Holy Spirit created out of nothing and preserves heaven and earth and all other creatures, and in accordance with the gospel is gathering to himself an eternal Church among mankind, for the sake of his Son Jesus Christ. He will give eternal blessedness to the holy and cast the godless into eternal punishment.

The Father is the first eternal person in the Godhead. He was not begotten and he does not proceed from any other person. But the Son was begotten by him from eternity, and the Holy Spirit proceeds from the Father and the Son. And the Father, together with the Son and Holy Spirit, out of nothing created heaven and earth and all other creatures, and preserves their being.

The eternal Son is the second eternal person in the Godhead, an essential [*wesentlich*] Image of the Father, whom the Father brought forth from his own being, in whom the Father contemplates himself. This Son has revealed to us that he is the person through whom the Father expresses the entire design [*Beschluss*] and order of creation and the restoration of man. He was sent that he might reveal to us the gospel, announce the gracious will of the Father, and take on himself human nature, that he might become the Reconciler, our Savior, and the Preserver of the Church.

The Holy Spirit is the third eternal person in the Godhead, who proceeds from the Father and Son, and is essentially the love and joy of the Father toward the Son, and of the Son toward the Father. He is revealed as the one who is sent into the hearts of the faithful to kindle in us the motion, love, and joy which he himself is, and to sanctify us to eternal life.

Whoever wishes profitably to teach himself or intelligently to instruct others must first comprehend from beginning to end the principal pieces in a thing, and carefully note how each piece follows the one preceding — just as a builder, when he wishes to build a house, must first construct the entire building in his thoughts and himself project a picture.

Thus, it is very necessary, in every art and teaching, to note all the principal pieces — beginning, middle, and end — and carefully to consider how each and every piece fits with the others, which pieces are necessary, which are false additions, and which are contrary to the right foundation; and the teacher and the hearer must accustom themselves to comprehend this in a very orderly totality. For if one is careless about doctrine and omits a few necessary pieces, delusion and error follow in other parts; and if one does not keep the end in view, it is the same as if one undertook a journey and gave no thought to the city to which one desired to go.

The order in which the pieces fit is what one should know if one would teach others. Cause precedes any finished work, so let us first speak of God; then of the creation of heaven and earth and of men; then of the fall of man; then of redemption. And such order is not difficult to bear in mind if we will merely reflect on what should precede or follow.

God himself has given us the most fitting order in the writings of the prophets and apostles. He puts his doctrine in the form of a story, for Genesis says that God created heaven and earth and then men. Next comes the story of how the first two people, Adam and Eve, fell into sin and death, and of how they were again graciously received. Then is given the twofold doctrine of the law and the promise of the future Savior who takes away sin and death.

And with this promise God once more established a Church, his own people, who are to have eternal salvation. For God was not willing that mankind's creation be wholly in vain and for eternal damnation. For the sake of his Son Jesus Christ he wants always to have among men a small company [*Häuflein*] to know and invoke him, and later to live with him in eternal blessedness, wisdom, righteousness, and joy. This Church of God is thus reconstructed when Adam and Eve are consoled with the promise of God's Son: "the seed of the woman will tread on the head of the serpent" [*cf.* Gen. 3:15]!

With this promise a Church is once again instituted, and Adam and Eve know that on account of the promised Savior they have been received, out of grace, and once more are justified and regarded as children of God. They know that by them knowledge of this Savior is to be preserved, that they are to invoke God in the knowledge of this Savior, to believe that God will certainly be gracious to them for the sake of this Savior, and that without knowledge of this Savior there can be no right invocation of God and no true Church.

Afterward, God repeatedly declared where his Church and people were; when Cain and others fell from the Church, God again recovered and declared his gracious promise, for he called Abraham. At the same time he gave his Church a particular [gewisses] land, for God wants his Church always to be known, and not to be thrust into a dark corner where none can either see or hear it; he wants it always to be high on a mountain, like a beautiful castle that can be seen from afar. God wants mankind to know him and the Savior, and to learn and believe his doctrine, law and promise, justice and grace.

Again and again there are stories in the books of the prophets about how God has preserved and guided this his Church; how the doctrine of law and promise is declared; how God punishes sin and nevertheless keeps a small company that invokes and becomes converted to him, as occurred in the Flood and then in Egypt. There are stories also about how mankind always has two parts; on the one hand, God's people; and on the other, a larger company of those who despise God. The latter follow their own wisdom, and want neither to hear nor accept God's word, but on the contrary, to persecute it; they are driven by evil, damned spirits who are God's enemies, the devils.

However, the Son of God throughout all time abides in the true Church of God; he watches over the small company in which his word shines, and he disperses the devils and does not allow tyrants completely to devour his Church.

All this is foretold in an orderly fashion in the books of the prophets; even the time of the year is given, and the different countries and the peoples are named, so that we may know, when, where, and how God with marvelous signs has revealed himself and given testimony of himself and of his Son and word. For he does not want to be unknown, and has always openly set before the eyes of many men of the world his testimonies, as he did in Egypt, and later as he did before Joshua, Gideon, Samson, Samuel, David, Hezekiah, and Daniel in Babylon.

Finally, the writings of the apostles declare that the promised Savior was born in the land of Judah to the Virgin Mary; that he preached; that he gave testimony to his doctrine through resurrections of the dead and other miracles; that he was put to death, gloriously arose from the dead, and that many men saw him after his Resurrection, visibly spoke many times with him, and also heard him preach. They also declare that he then visibly ascended into heaven, and afterward repeatedly gave testimony that he would be our Savior eternally, would visibly send the Holy Spirit, work great miracles through the apostles — such as resurrection of the dead and other miraculous works — and forever gather to himself a Church until the last judgment, when he would give everlasting blessedness to his Church and would cast the godless, with the devils, into eternal punishment.

Thus the books of the prophets and apostles, arranged as they are, constitute a complete and beautiful story, and a story is a good means of teaching. Just as a doctor in an orderly manner learns the parts of the human body and the malady of each, and in accordance with this prescribes medicine, so this story repeatedly sets forth all the articles of the doctrine of God's being; of human weakness; of law; of sin and punishment; of promise; of the Redeemer, the Son of God, and his suffering, Resurrection, and reign; of grace and righteousness; of the gathering of the Church; of eternal blessedness and eternal punishment.

Let the reader carefully note both the stories and the doctrine, and keep in mind the distinctions in the various articles of doctrine, and especially note carefully the difference between the law and the gospel, the latter being the benevolent promise of the Savior and of redemption, which we have through the Son of God by faith, not by our merit. The difference between law and gospel, or promise, will be explained later in this book.[1] And it is very essential to note this distinction, for the gospel, that is, the promise of grace and redemption through the Son of God, distinguishes God's people and secular godless companies. The heathen, being rational men, know how to solve problems according to their natural light, and they also know something about law, that is, about virtuous works — that parents should love their children, that one should not without cause injure any man in his person or property, that men should live together in harmony, in wedlock, and in mutual helpfulness.

However, the heathen know absolutely nothing about the gospel and grace, for this comes through a special divine counsel [Rath], above and

1. See below, Articles IX–XII.

beyond the natural reason of all angels and men. Out of his unmeasurable mercy God himself revealed that he would redeem wretched man through his Son, Jesus Christ, again receive him in grace, and bless him.

This doctrine must enlighten God's people, for as St. Paul says, "No other foundation can any one lay than this which is laid, which is Jesus Christ, the Savior" [1 Cor. 3:11]. And this foundation was often thoroughly obscured in the people who bore the name of the Church, as in the case of the Pharisees, and afterward the papists, as will be shown more fully later. This is mentioned here at the beginning so that the reader may more diligently note in all the writings of the prophets and apostles where the law is preached, and where the promise of God's Son, and of forgiveness of sins, of grace and blessedness is given, recovered [erholet], and explained.

Moreover, it is also necessary throughout this matter to consider that Christian doctrine is not dubious. We are on the contrary obliged to believe firmly, as the divine voice from heaven commanded: "This is my Son, in whom I have delight and joy; to him you must listen" [cf. Mt. 3:17]! And again in John 3:36: "He who does not believe in the Son will not see life, but instead the wrath of God will fall on him!"

We are carefully to consider these and similar statements, so that we may receive the pure Christian doctrine with true faith and not waver in our thoughts, nor invent devilish debates against it, as many evil men in all times have done and still do, like Celsus,[2] Porphyry,[3] Julian,[4] Mohammed, and others who ridicule Christian doctrine. We should carefully guard ourselves with faith and prayer against the deadly stings which the devils like to plunge into our hearts.

And then the Church in the time of the apostles set forth the chief articles of Christian doctrine in the Apostles' Creed, and afterward, in the Nicene and Athanasian Creed, a true explanation of the previous creed is given. At this point I want sincerely to give my eternal confession: All the articles in these creeds I truly hold, believe, and accept as divine

2. Celsus was a pagan philosopher of the second century, one of Christianity's first major critics. His bitter criticism, *True Discourse*, c. 178, is known through Origen's reply, *Against Celsus*, 248.

3. Porphyry (c. 232–303) was a Syrian-Greek Neoplatonist philosopher who questioned all religion and especially criticized popular superstition, the alleged inconsistencies in the Scriptures, and the lack of patriotism among Christian leaders.

4. Julian the Apostate (331–363), Flavius Claudius Julianus, Roman Emperor (361–363), sought to revive paganism and to cripple the Church. Wrote *Adversus Christianos*, recoverable through Cyril of Alexandria's refutation.

truth, and with God's grace I will always keep them, and I might add that all angels and men are obliged to accept these same creeds with true faith.

I will also arrange the principal parts in this book according to the order of the articles in these creeds, and explain them in this sequence insofar as God gives me grace. I will not invent any peculiar opinions or fancies, but will in all articles faithfully relate the doctrine as it is commonly preached, understood, and explained by the learned and God-fearing preachers who are in accord with the confession which was delivered through our Church at Augsburg in the year 1530. And I pray that God will keep this Church united in this his true doctrine throughout eternity! Amen.

The Most Important Articles of Christian Doctrine

Of God.
Of the one unified (einig) *divine Being, in whom are three distinct Persons*
  — the eternal Father, eternal Son, and eternal Holy Spirit.
Of the creation of all creatures.
Of the beginning of sin.
Of free will and human strength.
Of sin and the punishment of sin.
Of law.
Of the meaning of command or counsel in divine Scripture.
Of divine promises.
Of the gospel, and the abundant grace obtained through the Son of God.
Of the distinction between law and gospel.
Of how we are justified before God.
Of grace and eternal blessedness.
Of faith.
Of good works.
Of the distinction between deadly sin and other sins.
Of eternal predestination.
Of the difference between the Old and New Testament.
Of the spirit and the letter.
Of the sacraments.
Of baptism.
Of infant baptism.
Of the Lord's Supper.
Of sacrifice.
Of penance or repentance.
Of sin against the Holy Spirit.
Of confession.
Of compensation or satisfaction.
Of the keys and the power of the Church.
Of the Church.
Of human institutions.

Of Christian freedom.
Of offense [Scandal].
Of the kingdom of Christ, which is not a worldly kingdom ruled by the sword but a kingdom of eternal life, wisdom, and righteousness.
Of resurrection of the dead.
Of trouble and affliction.
Of prayer.
Of worldly authority.

These are the titles of the principal parts which follow in this book, and I have enumerated them in the beginning so that the reader can observe and consider these titles in sequence and better understand the order and totality of the Christian doctrine.[5]

5. These are numbered I–XXXVI in the following material, but Melanchthon's topics do not correspond exactly to his list. See the Table of Contents.

Abbreviations

CR   Philip Melanchthon, *Corpus Reformatorum, Philippi Melanchthonis opera, quae supersunt omnia*, C. G. Bretschneider and H. E. Bindsell, eds. (Halis Saxonium, 1834–60), I–XXVIII.

ZKG   *Zeitschrift für Kirchengeschichte*, Th. Brieger *et al*, eds. (Gotha, 1877 ff.), IV.

Table of Contents

❖

Loci Communes 1555

❖

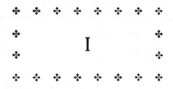

OF GOD

In earnest invocation of God it is necessary to consider what one wants to address, what God is, how he is known, where and how he has revealed himself, and both if and why he hears our pleas and cries. And our thoughts must not waver as the thoughts of the heathen who know a great deal — that God is an omnipotent, wise, and just Lord who created everything — but not where he may be found, nor if he will hear our cries. They cry to God only out of custom; they know nothing of his revelations, the Redeemer, and the promises. Concerning this blind invocation, Christ the Lord says, in the fourth chapter [v. 22] of John: "You worship what you do not know."

For this reason Christians are to shun the invocation of the heathen and Turks, and are to instruct themselves so that they may not fall into the error of addressing as God things which are not God. The first commandment in God's law is: "You shall have no other gods before me." This is to say, "You shall worship the Lord your God, and him only shall you serve"; that is, you shall invoke only this true God who revealed himself to his people with sure testimonies, and you shall not let your thoughts waver and wonder after other gods.

Remembering this is highly necessary, and it will often be repeated, particularly when prayer is considered. We state this in the beginning so that our thoughts will not rove at random, as do the thoughts of the heathen, the Turks, the unbelieving Jews, and all the godless; but instead, in great humility and earnest prayer, that we may consider the nature of God, how he may be known, how he may be found, and how we are to address and invoke him.

These considerations worried the apostles, for one of them says, John 14:8, "Lord, show us the Father, and we shall be satisfied." This was not a trifling request, for all sensible men would like to see God with their own eyes, and all are seeking where and how they may find him. The Son of

God, Jesus Christ, replies to this question consolingly and with a useful doctrine, for he says, "He who has seen me has seen the Father. Do you not believe that I am in the Father and the Father in me" [v. 9, 10]?

Ah, what a great comfort this is! Our thoughts should not rove about in error, for God has set before us his Son, Jesus Christ, who was crucified and raised up from death, and he has given his word, and with it, sure testimonies, even resurrection of the dead. This God who has thus revealed himself in and through Christ is the God to whom our hearts should look and speak, and we should firmly embrace this God, whose nature and will have been proclaimed to us through the Son. In this way our hearts speak to the true God, and do not address something that is not God. And let us diligently consider this word of the Lord, Jesus Christ, "No man comes to the Father, except through me. Whoever sees me, sees the Father" [Jn. 14:6, 9]! Since we are to seek God in Jesus Christ, his Son, and since our hearts and thoughts are to be bound to him, we may certainly conclude that we find and address the true God when we regard the true God as the one who has revealed himself in his Son. And as God has revealed himself, so should we regard him.

In beginning our invocation, it is very fitting for us [in our invocation] to reflect on the baptism of Christ. There the three persons are distinctly revealed. The Father declares, "This is my beloved Son" [Mt. 3:17]! The Son stands there in the Jordan in full sight and is baptized. The Holy Spirit overshadows him. Therefore, we must contemplate God's word and revelations for an understanding of his being [*Wesen*] and will, and because of this, recognize and believe that we are heard for the sake of the Son, as will be further explained later.

Having made this clear in the beginning, we will further consider other matters. At this point we might ask, If God is thus known through Christ, how did men long ago, like Adam, Abel, Abraham, and Moses, know God?

The answer to this is clear and certain. Just as John the Baptist, or Peter and Paul, knew and spoke to God, so also the saints of old knew and spoke to him. At the very time that he readmitted Adam and Eve to his grace, God revealed his gracious promise of the Savior. He gave them an obvious testimony that they had been rescued from the death which they felt in their hearts; and they later saw their sacrifices ignited by a fire from heaven. This true God who gave to them this promise, they knew as God, and they invoked him, relying on the Redeemer, the one who was announced to them, who visibly spoke with them, who later became incarnate. For this reason Jesus could speak these significant words: "Your father Abraham rejoiced that he was to see my day; he saw it and was glad" [Jn. 8:56].

Afterward this one and only true God erects a large, blazing sign in the first commandment, in which he says, "I am the Lord, your God, who led you out of Egypt" [Ex. 20:2]. With this large blazing sign he drew a distinction between himself and all the other gods who are imaginary. And we should know that all such revelations occurred in confirmation of the promise of the Savior Christ, as the prophets so well understood and declared.

From all that has been said, we should understand that at all times among God's people, from the days of Adam to the present, the knowledge of the true God has thus been maintained, and has included the promised Redeemer. As soon as Cain and other godless men scorned the promise and then forgot it, they no longer invoked the true God, for that which they addressed as god was a projection of their own false thoughts. And while men without God's word became ever more blind and wicked, they still wanted to worship and with holy works to propitiate God and obtain health, victory, fruits of the earth, and other blessings. In this blindness they erected new sacrifices and graven images, such as Jupiter, Mars, Venus, Juno, and Bacchus, and the devils drove the blinded people into false illusions so that they defied and insulted the true God.

These frightful examples should be considered, so that we may all the better learn where and how God is to be acknowledged and invoked, in the knowledge of his Son and the gospel, as St. Paul says, 1 Corinthians 1:21, "For since, in the wisdom of God, the world did not know God through wisdom, it pleased God through the folly of what we preach to save those who believe."

In protest, some ask, Is not man's rational knowledge of God the same as his knowledge of mathematics? By nature all men know that there is an eternal omnipotent being [Wesen], full of wisdom, goodness, and righteousness, that created and preserves all creatures, and also, by natural understanding [Verstand], that this same omnipotent, wise, good, and just Lord is called God. Many wise people, therefore, such as Socrates, Xenophon, Plato, Aristotle, and Cicero, have said that there is such an almighty, wise, good, just God, and that we must serve this one Lord in obedience to the light that he has built into our nature concerning the distinction between virtue and vice.

God implanted the knowledge of virtue in men precisely that we might know and be aware that God is, that he is a wise being, the fullness of virtues, and that he loves us and desires that we be like him, namely that we be obedient to him according to the light that he fashioned in us. Is this understanding of God not enough? Answer: This legal understanding [*Gesetzverstand*] of God is not enough, and furthermore, men do not find peace in this natural understanding, as one can see, for all wise people have grave doubts about whether God wants to help men, and in all times many gods are invented.

In the first place, it is clear that natural understanding is not enough because natural understanding speaks only of law and punishment; it does not say that God for the sake of his Son, out of grace, wishes to forgive us our sins and give us righteousness and eternal blessedness. About this, Socrates, Xenophon, Plato, Aristotle, Cicero, and Cato [1] know nothing at all! More about this later, in the distinction of law and gospel.[2]

Moreover, these same wise men find no peace in natural understanding; instead, they fall into doubt because they see how unjust it is for obvious despisers of God and tyrants, who mistreat countless men, nevertheless to have riches and a joyful life, while virtuous people live in misery and grief and are ingenuously killed by the tyrants. For this reason Cato [3] and Pompey said that they did not know whether God ruled or not so long as they, while doing what they thought was good, met with misfortune. Thus the natural light in wise people may become completely infatuated, and they suppose that God is neither a judge nor a helper. They then seek another fantasy, and become either Epicureans or Stoics. The Epicureans said, "God is nothing." The Stoics allowed God to be something, but they bound him hand and foot, and said, "All that happens, be it good or evil, happens necessarily according to a natural unchangeable order."

Thus has the devil disseminated much blasphemy in the world, through false deities in temples and through the insolent Epicureans and Stoics. One can easily see from this that the heathen did not find peace in the natural light [of man].

After Cain time and again only a few people heeded God's word and promise, and this is still the case in the world; but on the other hand, many people, not wishing to be like the Epicureans, retain a great fear of God. They would propitiate him with their own works, and they devise

---

1. Cato the Censor (234-149 B.C.).
2. See below, Article X.
3. Cato the Younger (95-46 B.C.), Roman patriot and Stoic philosopher.

ever more sacrifices and works. From this has followed the invention of as many new idols as there were false gods previously. One man made an image of the weather — Jupiter with his flashes of lightning; another made an image of war — Mars with his helmet and spears; and men invented special sacrifices for each image! Men practice such gross, frightful, devilish outrages, and fabricate new forms of worship, false idols, and false deities, when they lack true understanding of the gospel and when their hearts are not sustained through the Holy Spirit in right knowledge and invocation of God.

Having reiterated that we are to seek knowledge of God in his revelations and his clearly expressed words, and in humility receive the same with a firm faith, and having said that human understanding without God's word leads to gross blindness and doubt, let us now note what is the nature of God, what one is supposed to call the only divine Being, and what one is to call Truth.

We should diligently remind young people to differentiate God from all other things, that from the start they may realize that God is an omnipotent eternal being, the fullness of wisdom, righteousness, goodness, truth, and purity, and that all other things — heaven, earth, sun, moon, stars, and men — are created things, are not omnipotent and are not to be invoked. We shall say more about this in connection with the first commandment.[4] And this explanation and this definition will be drawn from divine Scripture.

God is not a physical being, as heaven and earth and other elements are; on the contrary, he is a spiritual being, omnipotent and eternal, unmeasurable in wisdom, goodness, and righteousness, one who is true, pure, independent, and merciful. This is God, the eternal Father, and the Son, the Father's image, and the Holy Spirit, which three persons created heaven and earth, and all other creatures. And God graciously revealed himself through the proclamation of the law and gospel, and with definitive miracles. Thus God has attested who is the true God, how he wishes to be acknowledged and honored, and that according to the gospel he will gather to himself among men an eternal Church, and bless it according to his promises.

This explanation is drawn from many clear divine statements:

That God is a spiritual being is plain from the statement in John 4:24, "God is a Spirit." And here *being* [*Wesen*] is rightly understood as the

4. See below, Article VI.

Greek word *ousia,* which is used often in the Church; it means something that definitely exists in and of itself, and is not dependent on some other foundation, as a contingent thing [*zufällig Ding*] is.

This also should be realized: that in God, power, wisdom, righteousness, and other virtues are not contingent things, but are one with the Being; divine Being is divine power, wisdom, and righteousness, and these virtues [*Tugenden*] are not to be separated from the Being, as the Valentinians [5] and others have so rashly claimed.

Omnipotence, eternity, wisdom, and goodness are proclaimed in the creation of all things in the first chapter in Genesis. Because God *created* all things, he is *not created;* he is eternal and omnipotent. And inasmuch as the text in the same chapter repeatedly says that God spoke, it is clear that God is not a being without understanding and wisdom [*Verstand und Weisheit*], for "to speak" means to consider and to articulate.

And besides, there are many testimonies in divine Scripture which clearly proclaim that God is omnipotent and eternal, the fullness of wisdom, righteousness, and goodness, pure and independent. In Exodus 6:2: "I am the Lord, who appeared to Abraham, Isaac, and Jacob; I am the almighty God." Note that God directs us to his revelation. This one only is God, the one who gave his promise to Abraham.

Psalm 33:13–15: "God looks down from heaven on all men, and perceives the hearts of all men and their works." To know, judge, and punish the heart is also a quality of omnipotence.

John 7:28: "He who sent me is true."

Psalm 5:4: "Thou art a God who hates sin."

Psalm 58:11: And men will say, "Truly God is judge in all the earth!"

Psalm 62:12: "Thou dost requite a man according to his works."

Psalm 115:3: "Our God does whatever he pleases," *i.e.* he is independ-

---

5. Valentinius was an important second-century Gnostic. His large following postulated an elaborate succession of pairs of aeons in the world of ideas or pleroma. When disturbed by the fall of Sophia, one of the lowest aeons, the pleroma produced Demiurge on the outside of its fullness. Demiurge created the visible world and became the God of the Old Testament. The aeon Christ was then sent to earth and united with the man Jesus at the baptism to reveal to men the gnosis for escape from this world of evil, material existence; but only the pneumatics or Valentinians could receive the gnosis and enter pleroma. Psychics, Christians who depended on faith and good works, could get only to the realm of the Demiurge, and the hylics, the rest of mankind, were damned. Melanchthon felt that aspects of Valentinianism persisted in the Christian tradition, creating pride, devaluing the Old Testament, slurring the creative power of God and his concern with the world, and questioning the reality of the Incarnation.

ent, self-subsistent, and unconstrained; he is not bound to creatures. He can draw back and hold up the sun, can make water stand still like a mountain, and he can raise the dead. It is necessary to note all this, and it is comforting to know that God will and can help us in that moment when we are abandoned by creatures.

The explanation of what God is comes from such statements. Now I want to cite statements which are testimonies that there is a unified [einiges] divine Being. And note that when we speak of God but not about that which is directly connected with his being, as when we speak of what God produces among creatures, we still are referring to the one God, for the three persons are at the same time a unified divine Being, and conjointly create. However, when we speak of how and what God is in and of himself, we must differentiate the three persons, of which more will be said later.[6]

In Deuteronomy 6:4, "Hear, O Israel: The Lord our God is one Lord"; and in Deuteronomy 4:35, "that you might know that the Lord is God; there is no other besides him"; and 32:39, "See now that I, even I, am he, and there is no god beside me." Isaiah 44:6: "Thus says the Lord, the King of Israel and his Redeemer, the Lord of hosts, 'I am the first and I am the last; besides me there is no god.' " Isaiah 45:18, 22: "For thus says the Lord, who created the heavens (he is God), who formed the earth and made it, 'I am the Lord, and there is no other. . . . Turn to me and be saved, all the ends of the earth! For I am God, and there is no other.' " Hosea 13:4: "I, even I who led you out of Egypt, am the Lord, your God, and you shall acknowledge no other as God. There is no other Savior except me!" Likewise, 1 Corinthians 8:4–6: "Hence, as to the eating of food offered to idols, we know that an 'idol has no real existence,' and that 'there is no God but one.' For although there may be so-called gods in heaven or on earth — as indeed there are many 'gods' and many 'lords' — yet for us there is one God, the Father, from whom are all things and for whom we exist, and one Lord, Jesus Christ, through whom are all things and through whom we exist." Also, Ephesians 4:6: "There is one God and Father of us all, who is above all and through all and in all"; in other words, "who is everywhere." And to say that God is everywhere also explains omnipotence.

Obviously the heathen invented many idols and false gods. And later they also invoked and honored dead men as God. Such blasphemies stand

6. See below, Article II.

in total opposition to the first article of faith, which teaches that there is one unified divine Being, and no more.

Many diabolical heretics, Valentinians and Manicheans, have spread throughout the world frightful lies and poisons against this first article. But these same lies can be countered and repudiated with the clear statements which I have just cited. When human reason beholds the great disorder and misery in human nature, it goes astray and thinks that if there were a wise and just God who could rule everything, he would not suffer such disorder. For this reason the Manicheans invented two gods, or a beginning of two kinds, both eternal, and diametrically opposed: one who creates all that is good, and the other who creates and sets in motion all that is bad and evil.

We should carefully avoid these and other lies and thoroughly learn the right doctrine and receive it with firm faith, in order that invocation of God may remain true and firm. We will say later how the Manicheans may be answered on the origin of sin. God is not the origin of sin; on the contrary, created spirits and men with their own free wills swerved away from God, and in this way sin and all evil began. Of this more later.

II

OF THE THREE PERSONS,

ETERNAL FATHER, ETERNAL SON, AND ETERNAL HOLY SPIRIT,

WHO ARE ONE UNIFIED DIVINE BEING

God built into our human nature an understanding of number and order and other distinctions, so that we might learn something about him, so that we might distinguish the only eternal Being from all the many created things, such as heaven, earth, water, air, fire, stone, wood, animals, and men. When we think about God, we must consider distinctions and number.

Now the first article of faith is that there is one unified eternal omnipotent Being, and nevertheless that there are three divine eternal omnipotent persons, eternal Father, eternal Son, and eternal Holy Spirit. And in the divine Being there are neither more nor fewer persons.

This is far beyond the wisdom of all creatures, angels, and men. But God has truly [*gewisslich*] thus revealed himself, and all angels and men must thus acknowledge and praise him, for we must believe God's revelation of his being and will. I will later give evidence and statements respecting this.[1]

First, however, I wish briefly to explain to the reader the word "person." *Person* is something which is not imagined; it is not a dead thought; and also it is not a contingent or changeable thing that depends on or adheres to any other being. *Person* is not a part or a detachable thing, but is instead an essence, a living thing in itself, not the sum of many parts, but a unified and rational thing, which is not sustained and supported by any other being as if it were but an addition to it. You are a person, but your body alone is not a person, for it is sustained by a nobler nature, namely by the soul; and if the soul separates from the body, the body disintegrates and decays.

1. See below, pp. 18–38.

The ancient Church used *hypostasis* for the term "person," and this is to be understood in the way in which I have just explained. Thus, one says that the Son of God is a person; that is, he is not simply an imagined thought but is truly a unified, distinct, rational entity [*Ding*], and is begotten by the Father.

This reminder, of the nature of a person is necessary because everyone must know this article in order not to fall into the Jewish blasphemy of imagining that there is only a human nature in the Messiah, as Ebion,[2] Cerinthus,[3] Samosatenus [Paul of Samosata], Photinus,[4] and in our time Servetus (who was burned in Geneva in 1553)[5] have contended.

For this reason we must know that in the divine Being there are three persons, no more, no less; for God has thus revealed himself, as the testimonies, which I will later set forth and clearly differentiate, prove.[6]

The first person in the divine Being is called the eternal omnipotent Father, the fullness of wisdom, righteousness, and goodness, neither begotten of another person nor proceeding from another; however, from eternity he has begotten the Son, his essential and full Image, and from him and the Son the Holy Spirit proceeds. This eternal omnipotent Father, with his eternal Son and eternal Holy Spirit, of his own free will [*freiwillig*] created out of nothing and sustains all creatures, heaven and earth, angels and men.

The second person in the divine Being is called the eternal omnipotent Son, the fullness of wisdom, righteousness, and goodness, begotten from eternity in the essential and whole Image of the eternal Father. He shows himself and is revealed to us as the eternal Father's Word, through which he pronounced the order of creation and the salvation of men, and as one who is sent primarily to proclaim the promise of grace. Through this second person the eternal Father preserves the office of preaching,

2. The Ebionites were an ascetic Jewish sect that believed poverty necessary for salvation, said the Holy Spirit invaded Jesus at the time of his baptism, and rejected Paul's letters. The Ebionites were active in the latter part of the first century and in the second century.

3. Cerinthus (*c.* 100), a Gnostic connected with the Ebionites, held that this world was created by a Demiurge and that Jesus was a mere man on whom the Christ descended at baptism, only to leave him at the Crucifixion.

4. Photinus, a fourth-century heretic whose views detracted from the divinity of Jesus Christ, was condemned at the Council of Constantinople, 381. He denied the pre-existence of Christ, while maintaining the Virgin Birth and Christ's superhuman endowments.

5. M. Servetus, *De trinitatis erroribus* (Hagenau, 1531), Bk. vii.

6. See below, pp. 13-18; also pp. 18-38.

through which this person effectively works. This person, born of the Virgin Mary, took upon himself human nature, and became our Mediator, Redeemer, and Savior, and forever is our King and High Priest. He upholds his Church and the office of preaching, effectively works through the gospel, and continually intercedes for us. He is Immanuel, that is, God with us; he protects and blesses us, raises up the dead, and finally brings us to the eternal Father, that we may clearly behold him. And he also gives eternal blessedness.

The third person in the divine Being is called the Holy Spirit, the fullness of wisdom, righteousness, and goodness, who proceeds from the Father and the Son, and essentially is the love and joy, like a flame, in the Father for the Son and in the Son for the Father. And he is revealed to us as the person who is sent into the hearts of the faithful to sanctify them, to kindle joy and love of God [*Freude an Gott und Liebe zu Gott*], and to work in us those impulses which constitute the Holy Spirit. As St. Paul says, 2 Timothy 1:7, "God did not give us a spirit of timidity but a spirit of power and love and self-control."

Explanation of the Distinctions

God created man as he did because he wishes to reveal himself to man; he wishes to give even himself to man, his goodness, light, wisdom, righteousness, joy, and eternal blessedness, and in return God wants man to acknowledge him, and offer thanks and praises to him. For this reason man is a rational creature, and fashioned in him are some clearer signs of God than in irrational creatures.

Because man has reason and can know his thoughts, can direct, control, and observe how one thing follows from another; because man knows there is a distinction between virtue and vice, and has the power freely to command the external members of the body to do good or bad deeds, we must certainly conclude that God is a wise, true, just, beneficent, pure, and independent [*freiwillig*] Being, one who punishes vice. From this we should further know that in the being of man there is first the being of the soul, then thought, and then will or choice, love and joy or grief. Thought is an image of all the things which one contemplates, and our words express the thought. When one remembers one's father, one has an image of him, and in words one says, "Thus is my father," after which love and joy or grief follow. All this is an indication of the Godhead:

the Father contemplates himself, and knows his thoughts, and in this contemplation his essential Image is begotten.

Our thoughts are perishable rather than essential images [*wesentliche Ebenbilder*]. However, when the eternal Father contemplates himself, an essential, imperishable Image is begotten; and this person in the creation and salvation of man is the essential Word, the Son of God. This Son of God announced the hidden wonderful news of Incarnation, redemption, grace, and salvation for man first to Adam and Eve. And the Son determined that through him the gospel should forever be upheld. He himself spoke with the fathers, and without a mediator raised up true servants of the gospel, and through the gospel he now enlightens the faithful. Therefore, he is called the Word of the eternal Father, for through him, without a mediator, the promise of grace is proclaimed, and he himself, without a mediator, forever upholds the gospel, and through him the eternal Church [*Kirche*] is gathered, and he himself works through the external word, and snatches the faithful out of hell by speaking comfort to their hearts; through him the Holy Spirit is given. And here it is useful to contemplate the first revelation, for the Son of God announced the promise of grace to Adam and Eve; he himself was the external voice. However, he was just as powerful in the hearts of Adam and Eve, and he snatched them away from death, and gave them life again, and as long as they kept the external word in their hearts, he himself dwelt in them and continued to give to them his Holy Spirit. Truly, all such things occur through the Godhead, the eternal Father, Son, and Holy Spirit. But it occurs in this sequence; the eternal Father sends the Word, his Son, through whom, without a mediator, the promise is proclaimed, and the Holy Spirit is given by the Father and the Son.

The Son himself says, John 8:25, "I am even as I told you from the beginning." Also, John 14:23: "If a man loves me, he will keep my word, and my Father will love him, and we will come to him and make our home with him." And John 15:5: "I am the vine, you are the branches. He who abides in me, and I in him, he it is that bears much fruit." Again, in Hebrews 4:12, 13: "For the word of God is living and sharp, piercing to the division of soul and spirit, and discerning the thoughts and intentions of the heart. And before him no creature is hidden, but all are open and laid bare to the eyes of him with whom we have to do." This passage teaches that the Son of God works through external preaching, which is for this reason called the living word. So, he himself also says, John 14:23, "If a man loves me, he will keep my word, and my Father will love him, and we will come to him and make our home with him." The Son himself is in the external word, and speaks comfort to the heart; he points to the gracious will of the Father, and through the Son the Holy Spirit is instilled in the heart. John 15:5, 7: "I am the vine, you are the branches. He who abides in me, and I in him, he it is that bears much fruit, for apart from me you can do nothing; so abide in me, and let my words abide in you." As the living Word of God, the very Son of God comes with the external word into the heart, so the heart through faith feels comfort. In Proverbs 8:29-31, wisdom, that is, the Son of God, speaks: "When he marked out the foundations of the earth, then I was beside him, like a master workman; and I was daily his delight, rejoicing before him always, rejoicing in his inhabited world and delighting in the sons of men."

Note in this text, for it is an excellent testimony, that the Son of God himself is in and works through the external word, for this wisdom, which preaches to the people, as written later in Solomon, has from the beginning of the world been the master workman, who has delight and joy in being with men, who proclaims the promise, upholds the office of preaching, and is effective therein. How can this divine wisdom speak more intimately and lovingly with us poor men than when it says that its joy and delight is to be with men? Ah, Lord Jesus Christ, enlighten us that we may know this!

From the foregoing passages we should learn that the Son of God is called the Word of the eternal Father, not only because he is begotten of the Father in his own self-contemplation, but also because he is the person through whom the creation of all creatures is pronounced and accomplished. And he is the one who is graciously sent to announce to men the hidden news of redemption and salvation, who repeatedly speaks with the fathers, upholds preaching, and gathers an eternal Church, who is himself powerful in the faithful. He is Immanuel, who speaks comfort to the hearts of the faithful, saying, "I will give you eternal life." Through him the Holy Spirit is given. All this you should carefully and humbly contemplate in order rightly to understand the Son of God and to learn why he is called the eternal Word of the Father.

If the term "image" means likeness, and we therefore say that the Son of God is the Image of the eternal Father, then note that the Father is for this reason wise, true, independent, good, just, pure, active against evil, and merciful, as he is proclaimed through the Word. Those with understanding are to ponder this term, for it is necessary to instruct the Church carefully about this in order to give the Son of God his honor.

Speaking further of the third person, the Holy Spirit, let everyone know that the term "spirit" here means something essential and eternal, not created, a movement; it means the love and joy in the Father and the Son. In other contexts the term "spirit" is often used to signify something ethereal among created beings, such as angels and souls, which are like flames, and not like the denser things such as earth, stone, wood, meat, and wine.

Distinction of the Persons

We noted in the introduction that there is a twofold distinction of the persons. The first distinction concerns the essential nature of the persons when compared with one another. The Father is the procreator; the Son is begotten of the Father and out of the Father's being, and throughout eternity the Son is the essential and full Image of the Father. The Holy Spirit proceeds from the Father and Son and is the love and joy in the Father and Son.

The second distinction concerns their activities and functions toward us; but here this old rule should be remembered, that every activity, be it creation or anything else, is an activity of all three divine persons. Nevertheless, in accordance with the order of the persons, each person has his own distinctive [ohne Mittel] work. As Augustine says, "The Son acts by himself, but not of himself."

The Son is the person through whom the eternal Father pronounces creation; the Son is the distinctive proclaimer of the promise and the perpetual upholder of the office of preaching. It was not the Father nor the Holy Spirit, but the Son who took upon himself human nature. Consequently, the Son is the Mediator, Redeemer, and Savior, not only because after the Incarnation he became a sacrifice for us, but also because he himself works in us, upholds the office of preaching, and speaks comfort to us through the external word. As Augustine says, "Wisdom is daily sent into the hearts of believers."

The Son is the living Word, and the Holy Spirit is given through him, as written in John 15:26, "I shall send to you from the Father the Spirit of truth"; and also in 1 John 4:13, "By this we know that we abide in him and he in us, because he has given us of his own Spirit." And since the Son gives the Holy Spirit in the contemplation of the gospel, the particular work of the Holy Spirit is to strengthen us in heartfelt joy and love toward God, and invocation of God, as St. Paul says in Romans 8:15, "You have received the Holy Spirit, whereby you cry, Abba, Father!" And as written in Zechariah 12:10, "I will pour out on the house of David a spirit of grace and supplication." Through the Holy Spirit we feel joy, know that we live in grace, and are brought to sincere invocation.

The believing heart, therefore, is a temple of God, in which God truly dwells and effects blessedness, and the three persons are there together. Through the outward word the Son of God is there and manifests the mercy of the Father, and the Father through the Son gives the Holy Spirit, as St. Paul says to the Galatians [4:6], "God has sent the Spirit of his Son into our hearts." Through the word comes knowledge; through the Holy Spirit, joy and love to God, and new obedience. Christians should diligently ponder all this.

In view of the particular nature of each person, it is proper when praying to observe a form which the prophets and apostles and later many holy learned Christian men used, and it is right that we differentiate our invocation from that of the heathen and consider to whom we speak, where and how God revealed himself, and why he will listen to us. For God has so revealed himself that our thoughts should not waver, as do those of the heathen, for we know that we address the one who is the true God and that this true God will hear us for the sake of his beloved Son. In John 4:22 the Lord Christ reproves the heathen, saying, "You worship what you do not know; we worship what we know." Also, "You shall have no other gods . . ."

We must remember this.

PRAYER

O omnipotent, wise, true, just, and merciful God, eternal and only Father of our Savior, Jesus Christ, out of thy great goodness thou hast revealed thyself, and hast said that we should listen to thy Son, Jesus Christ: Thou who hast with thy only begotten Son, Jesus Christ, and thy Holy Spirit, created heaven and earth, angels and men and all creatures: Thou who hast said, "As I live, I have no pleasure in the death of the wicked but that the wicked turn from his way and live" [Ezek. 33:11]! — I heartily beseech thee, have mercy on me and forgive me all my sins. Be always gracious unto me and make me righteous through thy Son Jesus Christ, whom thou in thy unutterable goodness and wisdom didst ordain to be a Mediator and Redeemer. Enlighten my soul and heart, make me holy, and guide me with thy Holy Spirit. Uphold thy true Church and good government for thy people. And may we in true thankfulness eternally praise thy great mercy. Amen.

In the passages that follow in which many useful doctrines are set forth, we should note carefully where *being* is indicated and where the distinction of the persons is intended. *Being* belongs in common to the Father, Son, and Holy Spirit, for the Son is of the Father's being, and the Holy Spirit is of the being of the Father and Son. For this reason the Church says that the Father, Son and Holy Spirit are *homousii, i.e.* in them is the same common [*gemein*] being. However, *person* pertains not to what is common but to what is distinctive; the Father is distinct from the Son, the Son is distinct from the Father, and it is quite necessary to note this so that faith may firmly hold that the Son, not the Father, took to himself human nature.

Testimonies about the Three Persons

With regard to God's being and will we should firmly believe what he himself has revealed, for it is written in John 1:18, "No one has ever seen God; [*aber*] the only Son, who is in the bosom of the Father, he has made him known." And in reference to the Son, God says, "Listen to him." Therefore, nothing is to be maintained about God save that alone to which God in his revelations gives testimony.

Resurrection from the dead and other miracles show that the Lord God is the one who repeatedly revealed himself in the Church from the time of Adam and Noah.

For this reason we want to present passages in an orderly fashion concerning each person.

Of the Eternal Father

First, that the person who is called the eternal Father by Jesus Christ is God is clear from these passages. Acts 3:13: "The God of Abraham and of Isaac and of Jacob, the God of our fathers, glorified his servant Jesus, whom you delivered up and denied in the presence of Pilate." Here it is clear that Peter is not speaking like a heathen about God, for, on the contrary, he knows by the revelation given to the fathers that the same one who sent Jesus Christ is the true God. John 3:16: "For God so loved the world that he gave his only begotten Son . . ." and so on. Many times the Lord Christ thus acknowledges and testifies that his Father is the true God. John 5:21: "For as the Father raises the dead and gives them life, so also the Son gives life to whom he will." Here Christ attests that his Father is the true God who gives life to the dead. With these and similar passages should be placed the promises in the prophets where God says that he will send his Son: "The Lord Jehovah (that is, the true God) said to me, 'You are my son . . .'" [Ps. 2:7]. Each person should himself carefully note similar passages, for listing them all here would take too long.

Of the Eternal Son

The very first passage in John shows that the Lord Jesus Christ, God's Son, is also truly God. After this person, Jesus Christ, took on himself human nature through Mary, there are two natures, one divine and one human; we will speak first of the eternal divine nature. The passage in John 1:14 shows both that the true God is the one who is the Father of the Lord Jesus Christ, and that this Son also truly is God.

Scholars say that John wrote his book that the Church might have a clear testimony against Jewish blasphemies, for at that time Ebion and Cerinthus were spreading the notion far and wide that in the Messiah there must be only a human nature. When Cerinthus was in the baths, at Ephesus, he gathered his followers, and together they argued furiously that there must be only a human nature in the Messiah; suddenly the house caved in and killed the slanderer and all those with him.

John 1:1 says, "In the beginning was the Word." He calls the Son the *Word*. This is somewhat easier to understand if we bear in mind that the Son is the person through whom the promise is made known and is also the one who afterward speaks directly with the patriarchs, as indicated in John 1:18: "No one has ever seen God; [aber] the only Son, who is in the bosom of the Father, he has made him known." This speaker is called the *Word*, as John later so designates him [1 Jn. 1:1]: "The Word of life appeared, that which was from the beginning, which we have heard, which we have seen with our own eyes, which we have looked upon and touched with our hands." And he is called the Word of life because through him the gospel is manifested [ausspricht] and life is given again to the faithful. Creation with the whole beautiful, wonderful order of all creatures if given [ausgesprochen] through this person, and for this reason John wrote, "In the beginning was the Word," namely this person who is the Image of the eternal Father, through whom the eternal Father revealed himself. Inasmuch as this *Word*, which is the *Son*, was before all creatures, it is clear that he is not a creature, and that he is omnipotent. Young people should be reminded that the term "creature" means a thing that was created out of nothing or that was made, begotten, or grown out of things already created. All angels, men, animals, heaven, and earth are such creatures. They are not omnipotent; on the contrary, they have their set limits; they have not existed from eternity; and their being is not upheld by their own power. They are upheld by God, who created them. John adds, "And the Word was with God." Here the distinction of persons is expressed. The Son was with the Father, and here the Father is expressly called God. Therefore, two different persons are indicated. Afterward John speaks of being, and says that this Word and Image, which is with the Father throughout eternity and is a distinct person, nevertheless has divine being and omnipotence; the text accordingly reads, "And God was the Word." Here one should note the grammatical arrangement of this sentence. The article in the Greek indicates that the sentence should read, "The Word was God." This being the case, we know that the text says that the Son is God.

Young people in school know the difference between subject and predicate. *Logos* in this sentence is the subject, and *Deus* is the predicate, which expresses what the being of *Subjecti* is. Accordingly, the Son is expressly called God, just as the Father. And although in Scripture the term "god" is used sometimes, but not often, to refer to men who, as God's representatives, bear divine offices, as the Psalm which speaks of kings, princes, and judges, "I have said that you shall be gods" (that is, divine officeholders); nevertheless, the term "God" in the Johannine text does not stand for an administrator; it refers instead to *being* [*Wesen*]. In this instance the entire sentence pertains not to administrators but to divine Being.

John immediately sets forth an attribute, namely omnipotence, which belongs only to divine Being, "All things were made through this Son." This and many other passages clearly show that he is omnipotent. John 5:19, 21: "For whatever the Father does, that the Son does likewise. . . . for the Father raises the dead and gives them life, so also the Son gives life to whom he will." Here belong all the passages which speak of the eternity and omnipotence of the Son. All show that the Son is *truly God*. John 8:58: "Before Abraham was, I am." John 17:5: "Father, glorify thou me in thy own presence with the glory which I had with thee before the world was made." John 5:17: "My Father is working still, and I am working." John 10:28: "I give them eternal life, and no one shall snatch them out of my hand." John 6:44: "And I will raise him up at the last day." Colossians 1:16, 17: "All things were created through him and for him, and in him all things hold together." Hebrews 1:2, 3: "Whom he appointed the heir of all things, through whom also he created the world. He reflects the glory of God and bears the very stamp of his nature, upholding the universe by his word of power." John 14:14: "If you ask anything in my name, I will do it."

These passages are quite clear, and incontestably show that the Son of God is omnipotent and existed before all creatures, yet he took upon himself human nature. The Christian reader should carefully note for himself other similar passages; I am presenting here only a few, so that one can daily strengthen himself when he is plagued with evil thoughts on this article.

Our Savior Jesus Christ also calls himself the only begotten Son. In saying this, he distinguishes between himself as the begotten Son and others who are received as children of God. This statement is at the same time a testimony to the divine Being that is in him, for whatever is begotten has the being of the begetter.

Inasmuch as the Son of God calls himself the *only begotten* Son, clearly he has his being out of the being of the Father, and this indicates a further distinction between the Son and other children of God. Adam, Eve, and Abel were not begotten out of God's being; they were created out of the earth or born of parents, and previously earth and heaven were created out of nothing. For that reason the [Nicene] Creed significantly says *begotten*, and not *created*. And this explanation is well stated in the Creed: "God of God, Light of Light," so that we may know that the Son is of the Father's being.

And this article has been preached not only since the birth of Christ, but from the beginning, for God's people must have known this Redeemer, and although there was a great lack of understanding in the people, the fathers and the prophets rightly acknowledged this Savior. He appeared visibly to many and spoke with them, with Abraham, Jacob, Moses, Joshua, and Daniel, who acknowledged him to be the omnipotent Son of God who would later take unto himself human nature.

Jacob speaks thus of him, Genesis 48:16, "May God and the angel, who redeemed me from all evil, bless these lads." This is in accord with the prayer given above. Jacob first names God and then the Mediator for whose sake God is gracious, and then he says that the same angel has delivered him from all evil, *i.e.* from sin and death. He also says that the same angel is to bless these lads. These are works only of divine omnipotent majesty, not of created angels or creatures.

Isaiah 7:14: "He shall be called Immanuel," which means, God with us; and then again, "His name will be God, and Everlasting Father" [*cf.* Is. 9:6]. Only omnipotent nature can bestow eternal life. And this statement corresponds with the statement of Christ, John 10:28, "I give them eternal life." In 1 Corinthians 10:4 *Paul* clearly says that the Lord, the Son of God, was with the people in the wilderness. In Psalm 72:17 the prophet speaks of the King who will be eternally worshiped, and says he was begotten before the sun came into being, and that all peoples are to be blessed through him, for they will be redeemed from sin and death. Micah 5:2 indicates that before the days of the world, he was, for the Messiah was begotten before creatures were brought forth. Thus the fathers and the prophets knew and called upon their Savior; they had the revelation that he is the eternal Son of God.

And note the following three testimonials which recur throughout the Old Testament.

First: The prophets very often say we are at all times to invoke the Messiah and to rely on him. Invocation rightly belongs *only to God*, because invocation acknowledges that the person that we invoke is omnipotent, one who sees beyond the physical and visible, one who searches the hearts of all men and knows and hears our inward sighs. If we are to invoke the Messiah and rely on him, which is certainly the case, then he is without doubt *omnipotent*.

Devilish invocation of the dead masked this beautiful testimony, and the worthy Dr. Martin Luther deplored this inexpressible loss.

The second testimony in the Old Testament is obviously that throughout its pages are promises which speak of the Messiah who will bless us, *i.e.* save us from sin and death, and again bestow upon us eternal life and blessedness. Such is often expressly reiterated, as in Jeremiah 23:6, "His name will be God, for he makes us righteous." Such action belongs only to divine omnipotent Majesty.

The third testimony: The Psalmist says, "I have today begotten you" [Ps. 2:7]. Only the Messiah is called God's Son, an only begotten Son, and this indicates that divine Being is in him.

A God-fearing man can clearly perceive that this article is true, necessary, and well grounded; the Messiah is God's Son, omnipotent and truly a divine person.

However, godless men argue and say that God is immortal, whereas this Messiah died. St. *Peter* answers this by saying that this Messiah suffered in his human nature. This has already been beautifully explained by Irenaeus, who was a righteous teacher and a disciple of Polycarp, and Polycarp was a disciple of the Apostle John. Irenaeus says that Christ was crucified and died, and still retained the divine nature in him, although the human nature was allowed to suffer and die; *i.e.* the divine nature did not use its power this time, but was obedient to the eternal Father in this amazing sacrifice.

In sincere humility we should consider this great thing, giving thanks to God that he so deeply humbled himself to help us, and beseeching him for understanding and grace. We will say more about suffering later when we speak of human nature, for first I wish to set forth the testimonies concerning the three persons.

Testimonies about the Holy Spirit

That the eternal Father and Son are two distinct persons is clear from the testimonies which I have given. It is also certain that *only* the Son, and not the Father, took upon himself human nature. From this it is clearly to be understood that the eternal Father and the eternal Son are two distinct persons. That the Holy Spirit also is a distinct *person* is clear from his appearance at the baptism of Christ in the Jordan, and again from his appearance on the Day of Pentecost. And because these have served all Christendom, both for doctrine and for witness, we should with heart and mind diligently contemplate them.

If the Holy Spirit were not a particular [*besondere*] person, but were instead only a created activity [*Wirkung*] in angels and men, he could not appear in a separate form. But the Holy Spirit is distinctly differentiated at the baptism of Christ because he obviously came in the form of a dove, and the Father draws a distinction between himself, the Son, and the Holy Spirit when he speaks first of the Son, "This is my beloved Son"[*cf.* Mt. 3:17], and then of the Holy Spirit, "on whom you will see the Holy Spirit . . ." [*cf.* Jn. 1:33].

The words which we use in baptism also show that the Holy Spirit is a distinct person. If he were not equal [*gleiche*], this command could not have been given: "Baptize in the name of the *Father*, *Son*, and *Holy*

Spirit." Here we are instructed to honor the third person just as we do the other two, about which we will say more below. In John 14:16, the Son says, "I will pray the Father, and he will give you another Counselor." Inasmuch as he says *another,* he speaks definitely of a distinct person. And the following testimonies show that this distinct person who is called the Holy Spirit is also God and that he is divine in being and omnipotence.

John 15:26, "When the Counselor is come, whom I shall send to you from the Father, even the Spirit of Truth, who proceeds from the Father, he will bear witness to me." *Counselor* is used for the term "paraclete," meaning an assistant, an advocate, one who gives advice to a person in a court of justice. Yet the Holy Spirit is not merely an assistant, like a friend who stands by one's side, as Cicero stands by Milo or as the angels hover about to protect us, like true friends traveling together on the road; no, the Holy Spirit dwells in our hearts. When we receive God's word, he produces joy and love to God and to our Lord Jesus Christ, and obedience, purity, strength, and patience in suffering, and other virtues. Thus should the term "Counselor" be understood. For this reason the Lord Christ also calls him "the Spirit of Truth," *i.e.* the one who produces and kindles in us true light and life.

Such statements abound. Galatians 4:6: "God has sent the Spirit of his Son into our hearts, crying, 'Abba! Father!' " Second Corinthians 3:6: "The Spirit gives life." First Corinthians 12:6: "The same Spirit produces all gifts." Second Corinthians 3:17: "Now the Lord is the Spirit, and where the Spirit of the Lord is, there is freedom," that is, the heart is freed from the devil's power, from despair, and from death, and is full of righteous joy and life. And also, "We are being changed by the Spirit of the Lord into his purity . . ." [*cf.* 2 Cor. 3:18]. For this reason the Nicene Creed says, "I believe in the Holy Spirit, the Lord and Giver of Life."

Now I have given testimonies to the effect that the Holy Spirit is a distinct person, and that this person produces in us joy and love toward God. With this we can be certain that the Holy Spirit is an omnipotent divine person, for this evidence is true and sound! Although the devil has devised and still does devise sophistry to the contrary, God-fearing men are able to perceive the truth. And this testimony which speaks of the work of the Holy Spirit should be carefully contemplated for three reasons:

First, to grasp the doctrine and to strengthen our faith that the Holy

Spirit is a divine omnipotent distinct person. Second, to contemplate the great goodness of God, who sent us his own Spirit, his own being. Indeed, God cannot bestow any greater gift than to give himself! Third, to lay hold on the comfort in the rich promises that God truly desires to give us this great gift and that he is more disposed to give than to receive. He wishes us in faith to desire this gift, and to beseech him for it; and he will truly give it to us if we but ask him, as the Lord *Christ* says, Luke 11:10–13, "All who ask will receive. . . . How much more will the heavenly Father give the Holy Spirit to those who ask him?" And we should sincerely thank him for this.

Again, we should note especially the words at the baptism of Jesus, and also previous testimonies in which this is expressly stated, "The Father will send you another Counselor," for it is a passage in which the persons are distinguished, just as in the statement at the baptism, where three persons are expressly named. Each bestows blessings; each is to be invoked; all are to be honored equally. This clearly indicates that there are three equal omnipotent divine persons.

And Christians should diligently contemplate their own baptism, in which God gave his gracious promises and in which a summary of his Church's doctrine is included. "I baptize you," means, "I bear witness with this baptism that you are now cleansed of sin, and that you are accepted into grace and everlasting blessedness by the true God who is the eternal Father of Jesus Christ, and by the Son, Jesus Christ, and by the Holy Spirit." We are thus received into this sublime grace, snatched from sin and hell, and established in eternal life by God, because of the merit of the Son Jesus Christ; and the Holy Spirit is sent unto us to work in us new light and eternal life.

Accordingly, we are baptized "in the Name," that is, in the power and invocation of the eternal Father, Son, and Holy Spirit. Now if the Holy Spirit works with the eternal Father and Son, if he is to be worshiped with them, then clearly he is an omnipotent divine person.

St. Paul says, 2 Corinthians 3:17, "The Spirit is the Lord," *i.e.* the Holy Spirit, which is given to us, is *God*. This is the proper understanding in Paul's own words.

And that this Holy Spirit existed even before the Son took upon himself human nature is clear from the statement of *Peter*, 1 Peter 1:11, "The Spirit of Christ in the prophets foretold that the Christ would suffer." Many passages in the prophets are in harmony with Peter's view; they bear witness that in all times the Holy Spirit visits saints and heirs of eternal blessedness, and that they are guided not simply by human power. To indicate this, let us point to a few prophetic statements. Isaiah 59:21: "This is my covenant with them, says the Lord: my spirit which is upon you, and my words which I have put in your mouth, shall not depart out of your mouth, or out of the mouth of your children's children, says the Lord, from this time forth and for evermore."

This cherished passage is filled with useful doctrine. First, the promise is made that there always has been and will be a Church of God. Bear in mind this consolation, for it reassures us that God will maintain his small company and will give them shelter and churches, even though the great empires, kingdoms, and principalities crumble.

This passage also teaches what the true Church is, and who God's people are, and how they are ruled, namely through the *Word of God* and through the *Holy Spirit*. Therefore, we should also learn from this that the true Church exists where the true doctrine of the gospel is preached. These words of Isaiah also show that the Holy Spirit was sent unto and known by the saints in the Old Testament. This passage further teaches that the Holy Spirit is a divine person who is sent into the hearts of believers, for the passage says, "My spirit, which is upon you." Here the person who addresses the prophet is distinguished from the person in him, namely the Holy Spirit. Zechariah 7:12 speaks of "The words which the Lord of hosts had sent by his Spirit through the former prophets." This also proclaims that the Holy Spirit is sent to the prophets and that God, together with his Word, gives the Holy Spirit. Also, the persons are distinguished; there is the Sender, and the Holy Spirit who is sent into the heart. Joel 2:28: "And it shall come to pass afterward, that I will pour out my spirit on all flesh. . . ." Note that God says "my spirit" in this passage, indicating that the being of the Holy Spirit is of the being of the Father and the Son, and nevertheless is a person who proceeds from both of them.

Now add the creeds to these testimonies. When we daily speak the Apostles' Creed we say, "I believe in the Holy Spirit." And in the Nicene Creed this article is further clarified: "I believe in the Holy Spirit, the *Lord* and Giver of Life." And so we say, "I believe in God, in the Son, and in the Holy Spirit"; and these words refer to persons. It is as if one said, "I acknowledge that this God exists, I believe his doctrine, and I trust in him." The Nicene Creed significantly calls the Holy Spirit *"the Lord and Giver of Life,"* openly acknowledging a person, one who is omnipotent. And the creeds should not be taken lightly, for they show what in their time was generally acknowledged and believed to be the true doctrine spoken by the apostles.

I will also present a few testimonies from some of the saints of old, men who were so close to the times of the apostles that they received doctrine from the teachers who lived with the apostles and were their loyal disciples.

Gregory of Neo-Caesarea

A man called Samosatenus [Paul of Samosata], a bishop at Antioch who was very proud and pompous, advocated the Jewish error that in Christ there must have been only a human nature. When his neighbors heard of it, many of the God-fearing men among them decided to hold a synod to repudiate this error. Involved in this was the bishop of Neo-Caesarea, Gregory, a man of many wonders. Eusebius wrote down Gregory's confession:

THE CONFESSION OF GREGORY OF NEO-CAESAREA

"There is one God, the Father of the living Word, his essential Image, the perfect begetter of the only begotten Son, who also is perfect; and there is one Lord, the one of the one, the Father's Image, the Word, through which everything was created, the true eternal Son of the true eternal Father. And there is one Holy Spirit, who has his being from God, who is manifested through the Son, who sanctifies believers that God and the Son may be known." [7]

This is a very clear testimony which men should bear in mind. It is especially pleasing in that the Holy Spirit is given the task of enabling us rightly to acknowledge and invoke God, which happens when our hearts are enlightened and guided by God's Word and Holy Spirit, as written in the prophet Zechariah, "I will pour out on the House of David the spirit of grace and supplication."

Irenaeus

At Smyrna was a bishop, Polycarp, who lived for several years with the Apostle John, and diligently devoted himself to learning from him.

---

7. Cf. *Ante-Nicene Fathers*, A. Roberts and J. Donaldson, eds. (New York, 1890), VI, *Gregory Thaumaturgus, A Declaration of Faith.*

Irenaeus was in turn a disciple of Polycarp, and he put into his writings the testimony of Polycarp. Irenaeus, an exceptional teacher, was eventually killed in Hungary because of his Christian faith. This same Irenaeus speaks of the Son in the second chapter of his third book,[8] saying:

"The Son was in the beginning with the Father, and everything was created through him. He has always been with those who are God's people, and in recent times, as determined in the counsel of the Father, he took to himself human nature, to suffer and to die for all mankind."

Eusebius of Palestine

Basil quotes the following passage from Eusebius as a testimony of the three persons: "We invoke the Holy Spirit, who together with our Savior Jesus Christ created all things."[9]

Tertullian

In the book against Praxeus, this very important doctrine is specifically explained: In Jesus Christ, who was born of the Virgin Mary, there is not only a *human* nature but also a *divine* nature, and the divine nature, the Image of the eternal Father, is an eternally distinct person.[10]

Epiphanius

After the Council of Nicaea, God-fearing men such as Basil, Nazianzus, and Epiphanius adequately explained this in lengthy writings. Here, however, I will only refer to the statement of Epiphanius. He, too, gives testimony that the Holy Spirit proceeds from the Father and the Son, *i.e.* that the Holy Spirit is of the being of the Father and the Son. Later this caused war and strife among the Greeks. These are the words of Epiphanius: "There are three distinct persons, the eternal Father, the eternal Son, and the eternal Holy Spirit; and the Holy Spirit is one of the being [*Wesen*] of the Father and the Son. *Spiritus sanctus est Homousius Patri et Filio.*"[11]

8. Cf. *ibid.*, I, *Irenaeus Against Heresies*, III, 18.
9. Cf. *Nicene and Post-Nicene Fathers*, H. Wace and P. Schaff, eds. (Oxford and New York, 1895), VIII, *St. Basil: Letters and Select Works, On the Spirit*, chap. 29.
10. Cf. *Ante-Nicene Fathers*, III, *Latin Christianity: Its Founder, Tertullian, Against Praxeas*, chap. II.
11. Cf. *Die griechischen Schriftsteller der ersten drei Jahrhunderte*, K. Höll, ed. (Leipzig, 1915-33), 25, *Epiphanius, Heresies*, 33, 66–68, 77; *Ancoratus*, 7, 7 f.

It is quite true that belief should and must be grounded in the word of God, and when we pray our hearts should dwell on God's word and be strengthened by it. Yet God himself, for the sake of his Son, wants always to have a Church. He wants a Church in which true confession shines for the strengthening and teaching of others. The Lord Christ says to Peter, "When you have turned again, you should strengthen others" [Lk. 22:32]. For this reason it is useful to see what was the expressed confession of the ancient true teachers, especially with regard to the important things about which there was severe war and strife. If we find that our faith is based on the word of God and is likewise in agreement with the true Church, then our hearts will be that much more content and our invocation and faith that much more strong and joyous.

Finally, we should also know that there are no more and no less than three divine persons, as the words of baptism and likewise the creeds show. He alone is God to whom omnipotence is ascribed, and only he is to have divine honor and to be invoked. This is said only of these three persons.

In order that our invocation may be further distinguished from that of the heathen, we must frequently remind ourselves that Christians are to let their hearts dwell often upon, and in prayer bear in mind, two very important distinctions pertaining to God's being and his will; that is, we must recall where and how God has revealed himself, that our addresses and appeals may be directed, not toward things, but only to the one who is the true God. The heathen run after the sun or the moon, and the papists run after the dead, St. Ann or St. Jacob. We must also know that God is willing to receive and hear us for the sake of his Son, *Jesus Christ*.

This doctrine is beautifully illustrated in the baptism of Christ, a glorious revelation that came to pass and was recorded, not only to strengthen John, but for the benefit of us all. I also do not doubt that Mary and her sister were there, and that many others beside the disciple John saw and heard this revelation.

And as often as we pray, let us imagine that we, too, are standing on the Jordan, and speaking to the true God who revealed himself there as Father, Son, and Holy Spirit, three distinctly different persons. The Father says, "This is my beloved Son"; the Son stands in the water and is baptized; and the Holy Spirit descends on him in the form of a dove. And for the sake of the Son, this unified divine Majesty will receive us and will send the Holy Spirit into our hearts. We should remember the baptism of Christ, and thereby further separate our invocation from that of the heathen, the Mohammedans and others, for they openly blaspheme the Son and the Holy Spirit. In doing so they also blaspheme the Father, because it is written, "Who honors not the Son, honors not the Father," and similarly, "No one comes to the Father, except through the Son" [Jn. 5:23, 14:6].

Let us remember that there are no more and no less than these three divine persons, even as stated in the much-loved passage in 1 John 5:7, "There are three who bear testimony in heaven, the Father, the Word, and the Holy Spirit; and these three persons are one unified being." This statement about the three divine persons is true and clear, and will, I hope, console, and help the Christian to remember and to accustom himself to such a form in prayer, as set forth above.

Let us also remember that with reference to the Son we say, "He was *begotten* by the eternal Father"; with reference to the Holy Spirit, "He *proceeds* from the Father and the Son." Although we will learn only in eternity the high wisdom of this birth and procession, nevertheless, now, as God's children, we are to learn the language, and without changing these words, contemplate: Birth is of the knowing power (*nasci est a potentia intelligente*); but the procession and the flame of love is of the will (*procedere, amor, agitatio est a voluntate*). The differentiation can be made more explicit if we note the distinction of powers in ourselves. Thoughts in the knowing power are images; but love and motivation burn in the will and heart. God thus created angels and men in his image, that we might perceive in them something of him; but our thoughts and love are not in essence persons; they are but dying shadows.

That the Eternal Son of God Took upon Himself Human Nature

Now follows the article about the eternal Son of God taking on himself human nature. Although this great miracle is also far beyond the understanding of all men and angels, certainly and obviously this article is given by God, is substantiated by the resurrection of the dead and by many miracles, and God's immutable will is that we learn and confess this article and seek comfort in it. For with this miracle redemption and blessedness are presented to men, as we will later discuss.

And for the sake of clear instruction, take the Gospel of John; it teaches in an orderly fashion about the two natures. The Son who is the living and eternal Image of the eternal Father is from eternity with the Father, before all creatures. This Son has been our intercessor since the miserable fall of Adam and Eve. He resolved that he should take upon himself human nature and bear the punishment for our sins and reconcile God's anger. After Adam, therefore, this is repeatedly prophesied, that this Son will take to himself human nature and redeem us. At the appointed time this happened. The eternal Lord took upon himself human nature in the womb of the Virgin Mary, and received her blood, which God purified. An inseparable union of both natures, human and divine, occurred in the person of this *Jesus Christ* in the womb of the Virgin Mary. Therefore, the Lord, born of the Virgin Mary, is a unified, whole person, and yet two natures are in his person, the eternal second person of the Godhead and this human nature.

And although we cannot give an exact example of the union, this might serve as a guide: Two natures can be in one unified person even as soul and body can be in one unified person. This is not wholly parallel, but it may be instructive.

But we should know that the divine nature took upon itself not the body alone but the body and soul. This divine nature and the soul and body of Christ are inseparably united; the divine nature does not separate from the soul and body of Christ after he is born of the Virgin Mary. The human nature, soul and body, is supported [*getragen*] by the divine, in such a way that there is a unified person, as one's body is supported by his soul in such a way that he is a unified person. Origen uses this analogy: The divine nature glows in the human nature throughout the soul and body, as ore glows in red-hot iron.[12] Again, this analogy is not quite parallel, for iron and fire are not living persons and they are separable, but it is a rough guide.

We should also know that in taking human nature Christ took all the natural characteristics, including mortality, but without sin. The properties of each nature remain; the human nature needs food and drink and sleep; it has hunger, grows, and is mortal. Although the properties of each nature are different, as they are in a person (for your soul can count, but your body cannot), this *Jesus Christ*, God and man, nevertheless is a unified person. And this *entire* Jesus Christ is our Redeemer; in his human nature he died for us, and although he still possessed his divine nature, he did not use its might, but manifested his humility to the Father, as Ire-

---

12. Cf. *Ante-Nicene Fathers*, A. Roberts and J. Donaldson, eds. (Grand Rapids, Mich., 1956), IV, Origen, *De Principiis*, II, chap. 6, par. 6. Also *Ante-Nicene Christian Library*, A. Roberts and J. Donaldson, eds. (Edinburgh, 1869), X, *The Writings of Origen, De Principiis*, II, chap. 6, par. 6 (the 1956 edition of *Ante-Nicene Fathers* is an American reprint of this 1869 publication).

naeus says. Thus it is written in 1 Peter 4:1, "Christ suffered in the flesh," *i.e.* in his human nature, and the submission in his divine nature is of such deep humility that no creaturely wisdom can fathom it. We will, however, learn such secrets in the life eternal. In this life we should contemplate with humble gratitude the marvelous wisdom of God that humanity should be rescued in this manner! that the eternal Son of God should be our Intercessor! that he should take upon himself human nature, and become a sacrifice for us, that he should be cruelly slain and conquer death! All pious people should diligently learn the story, as written by the evangelists, and think about it often.

But we must also remember that the evil spirits know the story very well; nevertheless, they remain in eternal punishment. We must learn, therefore, that this Son of God, with his sufferings and his triumph, brings us to blessedness.

For this reason we should know why and to what end the Son of God is sent. This is expressed in the creed: He is a blessing unto *men*, and for our salvation he descended from heaven, as written in John 1 and Romans 3 and 4. Similarly, it is written in 1 Timothy 2:5, "There is one mediator between God and men." This does not say, "between God and the devils."

We should know that this Mediator merited for us forgiveness of sins, righteousness, and eternal salvation. But we should know something more, namely that we obtain these his benefits through faith, and not through our own merits. We should acknowledge that we are sinful and tremble before God's wrath, but we should also seek comfort in the Son of God and firmly believe and conclude that our sins are truly forgiven for the sake of this Mediator, without merit from us, *freely*, and that this Savior's righteousness is imputed to us through *faith*. If we thus believe in him, we truly have forgiveness of sins, imputation of righteousness; and the Son of God is working in us a new obedience and righteousness, and giving to us the Holy Spirit and an inheritance of eternal blessedness. More will be said about this and the Mediator's benefits in the article about forgiveness of sins and righteousness. This is set forth here that we may contemplate why this truly marvelous event happened — why the eternal Son of God took upon himself human nature.

Here our hearts say, "Could redemption not have happened in some other way?" In the next life we will know the divine wisdom pertaining to this question. Nevertheless, we can begin to think about it now. And although we cannot fathom such [wisdom], from it we are to learn, that divine righteousness has a great and terrible wrath against sin, and in eternity will not forgive the devils their sin. When God accosted and rebuked him, Adam could only have thought that he was eternally damned — until he heard the promise, "The seed of the woman will tread on the head of the serpent" [cf. Gen. 3:15], and was consoled anew and rescued from hell.

God's great and justified wrath against the sin of man was not allayed without an equal and even greater payment, lest the righteousness of God be effaced. And so both mercy and righteousness are present in this deed. Out of a great love and mercy for mankind the Son prays, and out of a great mercy the divine Majesty receives man. Nevertheless, so that righteousness may be upheld, the punishment, or an equally great payment, is laid upon the Son. This is the wondrous counsel which determined that the union with human nature should be made, that the Son should humble and take upon himself human nature, and that this Son of God and man should become a sacrifice!

Contemplate now how high and great are God's righteousness, God's wrath against sin, and the punishment which is laid on the Son. And then contemplate how great is the love in the Son, and the mercy of the three divine persons toward us.

First, note that inasmuch as mankind fell into sin, the one to be punished and to pay the penalty had to be a man, but one without sin.

Secondly, in order for the payment to be equal and even better, the one who pays is not simply a man or an angel, but is a divine person.

Thirdly, no angel and no man could have borne the great burden of divine wrath against our sin. For that reason, the Son of God, who is omnipotent, out of immeasurable love and mercy toward men, laid upon himself this great wrath.

Fourthly, no angel and no man is able to walk in the mysterious counsel of the divine Majesty. The Mediator prays for all men and especially for every petitioner, and the divine Majesty hears their desires, and then acts accordingly. All this pertains to an omnipotent person. In the Letter to the Hebrews, when only the High Priest enters into the *Sanctum sanctorum* (Holy of Holies), when only the High Priest, and no one else, is allowed to go into the secret altar in the temple, it means that only the Redeemer is to be in the secret counsel of divine Majesty, and wholly see and know the heart of the Father.

Fifthly, no angel and no man might have conquered death and taken life again, for this belongs only to an omnipotent person.

Sixthly, the Redeemer is to be a power [*kräftig*] within us; he bears and sustains our weak nature, beholds the hearts of all men, hears all sighs, prays for us all, is and lives in the faithful, and creates in them new obedience, righteousness, and eternal life. All this pertains only to an omnipotent person; this is Immanuel, *i.e.* God *with* us and *in* us.

In our daily prayer we should consider the source of these things, and acknowledge, praise, and give thanks to the Son of God that the two natures, divine and human, are united in him.

With this in mind, note the statements that are used in the Christian Church by those who are God-fearing and prudent. We should avoid strange statements which only bring about discord and error, even as St. Paul says, "Let your speech always be gracious" [Col. 4:5].

There is a great difference between saying, "The body lives," and, "The body is life." *In concreto* it is true and right to say, "The body lives." However, *in abstracto* it is incorrect and false to say, "The body is life." This difference is also found in the Christian Church. *In concreto*, the following statements about Christ are correct and proper, "Born of Mary," "God is man," "God was born of the Virgin Mary," "God suffered," "God died and arose again." Likewise: *"Christ is God; Christ is a man; Christ* died and arose again."

For in these statements the entire single person is understood, although only the human nature died. This is as if I said, "This man counts and calculates his money." Such is rightly spoken, although only the soul (mind) can count and calculate. However, a person is soul and body.

And the prudent should learn what the Christian Church calls *Communicatio Idiomatum, i.e.* the property of one nature may be attributed to the entire person, as when we say, "God is dead." Here the property of one nature is stated of the entire person, for the *whole Christ* is Redeemer, Mediator, and Savior, and the heart should at all times invoke the *whole* Lord Christ, just as, in thinking of a friend, we think of the *whole* man, body and soul.

However, such statements as the following are not correct and not proper: "The divine nature is human," or, "The divine nature died," for this form speaks not of the whole person but in particular of the divine nature *in abstracto*, and does not maintain the distinction of natures.

"Christ is a creature," must also be repudiated. The Arians sought to deceive when they spoke thus, for they mingled with their error the contention that Christ was not really God, but a person, created out of nothing, like the angels. We must earnestly repudiate and counteract this frightful error.

Now let us answer several related arguments.

First, if God is immortal, how can Christ be God, since he died? Answer: Christ died in accordance with his *human* nature, just as he ate, drank, and slept in accordance with his human nature. Nevertheless, the divine nature, which is not mortal and needs neither food nor sleep, remains in him. The merchant calculates only with his soul, but his body is always there, for the soul and body constitute one unified person.

Second, in the Gospel of John, Christ says, "The Father is greater than I," and also, "Father, glorify thou me" [Jn. 14:28, 17:1, 5]! Now how can Christ be God and omnipotent if he is not equal to the Father in power and glory? The Arians particularly used this argument, so a clear, well-grounded answer should be given.

Let us very diligently note the distinction between statements that refer to being and those that refer to the office of preaching or to an actual service. The statements about being always refer to equal power and glory, as in the first chapter of John [v. 1, 3], "The Word was God; all things were made through him," and in the fifth chapter [v. 19], "Whatever the Father does, that the Son does likewise."

However, many other statements refer to the office of preaching, and to the time of the actual service which he was obliged to undergo, as when he says, "My God, my God, why hast thou forsaken me" [Mt. 27:46; Mk. 15:34]? This statement and others like it do not refer to being, but to the then present performance in which he humbled himself, is pierced for our benefit, and in which he became a priest and sacrifice for us. To this extent he is as one sent, a servant, and in this capacity is subject to the divine Majesty, who sent him and who poured out on him his great wrath against our sin. In the distress of the moment he is small and weak — not that his being is not otherwise, only that his power is not in this moment manifested. So God ordained for our sake, out of his marvelous wisdom and great compassion for us.

Thus God-fearing man can understand that passages about being must be differentiated from the passages which pertain to the service and the deep humility in a particular time when Christ in his compassion blessed us. And note carefully the passage in Irenaeus which we mentioned above. "Christ was crucified and died." *Quiescente verbo;* the divine nature in him remained silent, that he might suffer and die, *i.e.* the divine nature by a wonderful counsel was subject and obedient to the Father.

And it remained in check; his divine power was neither manifested nor used.

This beautiful passage from Irenaeus is in accord with the one in St. Paul, "He humbled himself and became obedient unto death . . ." [Phil. 2:8].

One might also ask: How could Christ have anxiety and fright if he continually contemplated his Father and was blessed? This and many similar questions are raised by certain people who have not considered the wonderful counsel of God that caused his anger to be poured out upon the Son. The same answer as before holds true: Make a distinction with regard to the time, the humiliation, and the exaltation. Although the Lord was at all times blessed, he was nevertheless ordained to be a sacrifice and at a certain time to bear the wrath. For that reason, the light of divine joy did not always shine with the same intensity in him, and as his body could feel the wounds and the pain, so also his soul felt fright and anxiety more deeply than any other man or angel can imagine. His great anxiety drew drops of blood and the deep lament, "My God, my God, why hast thou forsaken me?"

Therefore, the text in Hebrews 4:15 says, "For we have not a high priest who is unable to sympathize with our weaknesses, but one who in every respect has been tempted as we are, yet without sinning. Let us then with confidence draw near to the throne of grace, that we may receive mercy and find grace to help in time of need."

This text reminds us not to pose impertinent questions, but to contemplate the truly wondrous sufferings of the Lord, so that we really become aware of God's wrath against our sins, and tremble, and afterward contemplate his great grace in that God is thus reconciled; he truly desires to forgive us our sin, to receive us, and he wants this his Son to be active in us, and to give us salvation. Thus, in the midst of fright we should receive consolation.

For those who fear God, this reminder should be enough. We are to consider this truly wondrous mystery with humble hearts and pray that God himself will teach and enlighten us. We are not to waste time with impertinent questions, as, unfortunately, we have done too often.

We are to consider all these articles in earnest prayer, for in prayer it is necessary for us to think about whom we address, where God revealed himself, how he desires to be acknowledged, and why he wishes to favor us. Previously we gave a form of Christian prayer, which we will here repeat with a conclusion.

PRAYER

"O almighty God who art the only living, true God, eternal Father of our Savior, Jesus Christ, in unity with thy only begotten Son Jesus Christ and Holy Spirit, creator of heaven and earth, men, and all creatures; thou who art wise, just, good, true, and pure, a judge and yet merciful, for thou hast said, 'As I live, I have no pleasure in the death of the wicked, but that the wicked turn from his way and live,' I call on thee, and beseech thee to be merciful unto me, and forgive me all my sins. Be gracious unto me and make me righteous for the sake of thy beloved Son, Jesus Christ, through him whom thou didst out of thy wondrous goodness and wisdom ordain to be our Mediator, Reconciler, and Redeemer unto righteousness. Make my soul and heart pure and holy with thy Holy Spirit; teach me, guide me, and give me eternal bliss. Gather and forever uphold in our midst an eternally true Church. Give us good Christian government, and protection, and daily bread. Drive the grim devils from our paths, so that they may not lead us into sin, blasphemy, and ruin. Sustain thou us that we may rightly invoke thee, praise and give thee thanks in eternity. Amen.

"I believe that thou wilt favor me, for the sake of thy Son Jesus Christ, and that this prayer for his sake will be efficacious. Thy beloved Son, Jesus Christ, is our High Priest. He prays for us, and brings before thee our troubled desires. And wouldst thou through thy Holy Spirit graciously strengthen my weak faith and weak invocation."

And so that we ourselves may more strongly recall the Mediator and our High Priest, the Son of God, Jesus Christ, we should address him with names, such as he uses in calling us to himself. "Come unto me all you who labor [in Angst seid] . . ." [Mt. 11:28].

"O almighty Lord Jesus Christ, eternal Son of God and Image of the eternal Father, thou who for us was crucified and arose again from the dead and liveth and reigneth eternally in divine power, thou who was ordained to be our Mediator, to reconcile us, and to make us righteous and blessed: I beseech thee with heartfelt cries, have compassion upon me, forgive me my sin, and pray the eternal Father on my behalf. Be thou in me, and through thy Holy Spirit bring to pass in me a new light, purity, and blessedness. Forever and ever gather in our midst thy eternal

Church, and give us good government, that we may throughout eternity
with joyful hearts give thanks and praise to thee. . . ."

THIS FORM IS ALSO CORRECT

"O almighty God, Holy Spirit, thou who didst reveal thyself visibly
unto the apostles, thou whom the Son of God didst promise unto us:
Have compassion upon us, and for the sake of the Savior Jesus Christ,
kindle in us true knowledge and invocation of the divine Majesty — of
the eternal Father and of the Son Jesus Christ in unity with thee. Let us
not be seduced and fall into error. Make pure and holy our hearts.
Awaken in us a fear of God, true consolation, faith, hope, and love
toward thee. Forever uphold God's Church and govern her with right
doctrine, wisdom, and unity. In worldly government give us good counsel, peace, and welfare. So may we throughout eternity offer unto thy
divine majesty, in unity with the eternal Father and Son Jesus Christ, our
heartfelt thanks and praise. Amen."

In our invocation we should contemplate and practice sound doctrine,
and at the same time learn what true invocation is, and know that we are to
invoke nothing except the omnipotent divine persons. Invocation is to be as
God himself has taught us. To invoke the dead, be it Anna, Mary, Jacob,
or George, is unmitigated, execrable idolatry; later this will be explained
further.

When we pray to anyone whom we neither see nor hear, our invocation implies in that person the omnipotence of knowing the hearts and
desires of all men. This honor belongs only to the omnipotent divine
Majesty.

All Christian teachers should know that they are obliged to give honor to
God by keeping the first commandment: "You shall have no other gods
[before me]." They should earnestly flee and repudiate all errors which
the devil has invented by working through the blasphemous Jews, heathen, Mohammedans, Samosatenus, Arius, Manicheans, and others called
by other names. The learned should inform others and with God's word
strengthen them against all error.

III

OF THE ARTICLE THAT GOD CREATED
ALL OTHER THINGS

Of Creation

In the foregoing article we spoke about eternal omnipotent being, the fullness of wisdom, goodness, and righteousness; about that which is true, holy, and pure; about that which is called God. Now we will go a step further and speak about things which are created through this divine Majesty. As the divine Majesty, in his boundless goodness, wanted to reveal himself, he created beautiful works — heaven and earth, air and water, angels and men. That he might be known, he imparted his wisdom and goodness to angels and men. We should earnestly contemplate this origin and purpose of creation.

This article about the creation of heaven and earth, and men, and so forth, is expressed first in Genesis and often afterward in the writings of the prophets and apostles; and it is reiterated in the creeds, so that faith should easily apprehend this article.

Created things are all the things other than God, like heaven, earth, air, water, angels; that is, rational spirits, trees, plants, irrational animals, and men. The divine Majesty — the eternal Father, together with the eternal Son, the eternal Image of the Father, and the Holy Spirit — freely and voluntarily created all these out of nothing, and to all living things he gave life, as written in the beginning of Genesis.

The divine wisdom in this wondrous work may not be fathomed; nevertheless, men should often contemplate that God desires this beautiful work to be a testimony of him. He created everything that he might reveal himself, as I just said.

If the beautiful order in this wondrous edifice which God made should be a testimony of him, and truly is an open testimony, then rational people should behold and contemplate this order, especially the singular wisdom with which heaven, air, water, etc., were formed, and the fact that man has reason, the ability to calculate and differentiate, to distinguish between virtue and vice; that there is joy in the good conscience if one has followed right reason, and, on the other hand, chilling fright if one has acted against the implanted reason, as in unjust manslaughter or incest.

We should note further that a wise architect ordered heaven and earth, for we behold the convenient ordering of time into day and night, summer and winter; we see that at a certain time the earth receives seed and produces, that at a certain time fruits become ripe. We should note that all the herbs on earth have their special powers, and are wisely apportioned so that one serves the liver, another the lungs, etc.

Although young people think less about this order than the old, we should accustom ourselves to such contemplation, and note that these evidences of an orderly design are set before us as reminders that none of this happened by itself, but was ordained and made by a wise, omnipotent Architect.

Six things are to be remembered in connection with this article about creation:

First, the three divine persons, the eternal Father, the eternal Son, the Father's Image, and the Holy Spirit, created all things. This is indicated in Genesis 1:26: "Let us make man in our image." This refers to three persons, not to one only.

In John 1:3 it is written about the Son: "All things were made through him, and without him was not anything made that was made." This statement is important, and clearly it is written about the Son. Genesis 1:2 is written about the Holy Spirit: "The Spirit of the Lord was moving over the water," *i.e.* he was upholding and preserving all created things.

Second, that all things outside of God were created out of nothing is shown by this statement in John 1:3: "All that was made, was made through him." If it is true that God created everything, it follows that there was never anything outside of God out of which other things were made, as the philosophers imagine, and so forth.

Third, everything that God created and that which he effects in all times is of his own free will, *undetermined* and *unforced,* and he is able to set in motion or to check the processes [*Gang und Wirkung*] of created nature, just as he made the sun stand still in Joshua's battle, and as he made a way through the Red Sea for the Israelites. For this reason Psalm 115:3 says, "He does whatever he pleases"; and Psalm 135:6: "Whatever the Lord pleases he does in heaven and on earth."

Fourth, human blindness thinks that God is like a carpenter who, having built a ship, departs and abandons it to water and weather, and has nothing further to do with it. Men imagine that after creating this earth and mankind, God departed, and now has nothing to do with this realm of created things. We must root these false thoughts out of our hearts with God's word, and we must learn the solace of true doctrine and believe that God is truly present in all places, that he sustains the being of all things, and that everything that has being or life [*Wesen oder Leben*], so long as it remains in being or life, is sustained by God. So the heavens, sun, and moon remain in being and have their ordered courses; the earth annually yields fruit; angels, men, and animals live; and all this happens through the concurring activity [*Mitwirkung*] of God.

This concurrence is to be understood as freely done on the part of God, for God is not bound to created things. He can stop, alleviate, soften, and harden as he pleases, just as he often alleviates illnesses and many other cruel effects of nature for those who call upon him.

Concerning this present and concurring activity of God, note these passages:

Acts 17:28: "In him we live and move and have our being," *i.e.* through him our being, life, and strength are given and upheld.

Hebrews 1:3: "God upholds the universe by his word of power."

Colossians 1:17: "All things are held together in him."

Acts 17:25: "God gives life to all that has life."

John 5:17: "My Father is working still, and I am working with him."

Therefore, we should know that the article of belief on creation also includes the *upholding* of being and life. And if we say the creed, "I believe in one God, the Father, omnipotent Creator of heaven and earth," we should likewise in our hearts acknowledge and give thanks to him through whom the being and life of all things is also continually sustained. This sustaining is called the general activity of God, *actio Dei generalis*.

Fifth, when human reason hears about the concurring activity of God in created things, it asks if God is bound to created nature and if God must act as the rule of nature dictates. It also asks if God's concurring activity is present in sinful works, as the horribly lewd blasphemies of the Stoics, and afterward the Manicheans, suggested; they said that God is bound by natural necessity, *ad causas secundas, etc.*

If God could not act except as natural necessity dictated, then invocation and pleas for help would be useless. The Turks are stronger than we, and if God acts in accordance with strength, then it is useless to invoke God for help and victory.

To this and to many more questions of blind reason, and mad Stoicism, there is an eternally true and sure answer: God acts voluntarily [*freiwilliglich*]; he is not imprisoned in nor bound to created nature; on the contrary, he can and often does will to give counsel, volition, movement, and strength to angels and to men, which they of themselves, in their own natural ability, cannot have. This is quite apparent. He gave such counsel, volition, boldness, and strength to Jonathan so that, with a single servant, he attacked the enemy and slew them in flight. And there are many such examples among the heathen. God gave the youthful Alexander the Great this counsel, volition, boldness, and strength so that he attacked the powerful kingdom of Persia, and God protected him in the great battles.

Think how many times God checked Saul so that he was unable to seize David!

Such gifts, help, or hindrances occur in the hearts and minds of men, but for all that, God does not change the order of nature in heaven and on earth with regard to water and air. It is one activity to affect the mind and will in man and to alter human strength, and another to effect a change in the natural order of heaven, earth, and water. Nevertheless, God is not bound to the natural order of heaven and earth and water, for when he wishes to punish, he may make this natural order harsher, as when he withheld rain from Israel for three years. He often punishes with violent storms, famine, pestilence, and illness; and on the other hand, he often mitigates the natural order, for he rescued Hezekiah from a fatal illness, and made a way through the sea for the Israelites. To the suffering Hagar, when she was cast out with her son, he gave a well of water just when she thought she was doomed to die of thirst.

And be sure to remember this truth: The order of the righteousness of God is vastly higher and firmer than all the created orders of natural things of the sun, moon, earth, and water. God is so benevolent that for the sake of the Mediator he mitigates and stays his just and rigorous wrath, forgives sin, and does not punish as severely as we have deserved. Indeed, it is much easier for God to stay the course of the heavens or the order governing water than to mitigate the high order of his stringent righteousness. This should be considered carefully.

As we said with regard to invocation, we should know the passages which teach us that God truly is present in created things, and that he cares for us and hears us and can and will help us when no help is possible from the natural order or our natural powers. God acts freely, and is not bound to the natural order and to necessity, as the Stoics have bound him.

Deuteronomy 8:3: "Man does not live by bread alone, but by every word that proceeds out of the mouth of the Lord."

Psalm 72:12: "He delivers the poor and him that has no helper."

Psalm 27:10: "My father and my mother have forsaken me, but God has delivered me."

Psalm 23:4: "Even though I walk through the valley of the shadow of death, I will fear no evil; for thou art with me."

Psalm 10:13: "Why does the wicked renounce God, and say in his heart, 'Thou wilt not call to account'? Thou dost see; yea, thou dost note trouble and vexation, that thou mayst take it into thy hands. The poor commit themselves unto thee; thou art the helper of the orphans."

Isaiah 57:15: "God dwells with the afflicted and the distressed."

Job 13:15: "Even though God slay me, yet will I trust him."

Even though God does not help me in this mortal life, I will not turn away from him; I will trust in him, for I know that he will help me in eternity. This mortal life in which there is so much misery, even if it has some peace, must still come to an end, and man in death is left without the help of creatures, but the faithful are not forsaken by the Lord Christ.

John 10:28: "No one shall snatch my sheep out of my hand."

Matthew 21:22, 21: "Whatever you ask in prayer, you will receive, if you have faith. If you say to this mountain, 'Throw yourself into the sea,' it will be done."

Romans 4:3: "Abraham believed and had hope, when there was no hope in natural power."

Ephesians 3:20: "God be praised, for he is able to do far more abundantly than all that we ask or think."

The example and prayer of the prophet Jonah is clear proof that God can and will help, even though we be forsaken by all creatures.

Adam and Eve, after their first sin, were forsaken by all creatures. This example we should consider often.

Matthew 10:29: "No sparrow will fall to the ground without your Father's will. Even the hairs of your head are all numbered." . . .

[Melanchthon further cites Ps. 104:27; 100:3; 33:13 f.; 147:8 f.; 36:6; 55:22.]

This article — that God is present in all created things, cares for us, will help us in concurrence with or outside the natural order, and will protect us against the fuming devil — we should remember daily when we pray, "Give us this day our daily bread," and also when we say, "Lead us not into temptation," *i.e.* drive the devil from us, and strengthen us against all temptation; and also when we pray, "Deliver us from evil," *i.e.* save us in time of trouble, etc.

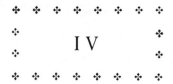

IV

OF THE ORIGIN OF SIN,

That Man Was Not and Furthermore Is Not Forced to Sin,

and of "Contingentia"

A sixth thing,[1] of which we must also speak, and about which great strife has often arisen in the world, is this: Whenever someone says that God upholds all created things, someone else immediately asks about the origin of sin.

What sin is, we want to explain more fully later;[2] right now we want simply to take up the short statement in 1 John 3:4: "Sin is everything that is contrary to God's command." In these few words John, like a true master of dialectic, has very significantly pointed out what sin is. This is as if one answered the question, "What is darkness?" by saying that darkness is a lack of light. Here God's wisdom and will is the eternal immutable rule and measure of righteousness. And this rule he proclaimed in his law, which is his eternal wisdom precisely duplicated in words. Whatever diverges from this rule and breaks this divine order is *wrong;* it is called sin, and is condemned by God's judgment and wrath.

It is very necesary to recognize that sin is not caused by God. God has no pleasure in it, does not will it, and does nothing to effect it; he neither compels nor drives anyone to sin. On the contrary, he is an earnest enemy and punisher of sin. Man's will and the devil's will are the sources of sin! First the devils and then men themselves, of their *own free wills, unforced by God*, departed from God and fell into sin.

1. Melanchthon considers the sixth item in his previous listing (*cf.* p. 40) significant enough to make it a separate major article.
2. See below, Article VI, p, 70.

Verification and Definite Testimonies about This Article

Genesis 1:31: "God saw everything that he had made, and behold, it was very good."

Psalm 5:4: "For thou art not a God who delights in wickedness."

Zechariah 8:16 f.: "Render in your gates judgments that are true and make for peace, do not devise evil in your hearts against one another, and love no false oath, for all these things I hate, says the Lord."

John 8:44: "When the devil lies, he speaks according to his own nature, for he is a liar and the father of lies." Here is a distinction between creation that is from God and the sinful corruption that is not from God but from the devil. For this reason the text says a lie is the devil's particular work.

Romans 5:12: "Sin came into the world through one man."

First John 2:16: "The lust of the eyes is not of the Father but is of the world."

First John 3:8: "He who commits sin is of the devil; for the devil has sinned from the beginning."

By these clear, definite testimonies we are to stand steadfast; we are confidently to repudiate the devilish lies of the Stoics and the blasphemies of the Manicheans, and to realize that sin is not something caused by God. Sin is a corruption, a breach, a disorder in the rational, very beautiful, good, and noble order of created things, spirits and men, and this disorder came first through the free will of the devils, and afterward through Adam and Eve, *who themselves freely* turned away from God, as will be discussed later.

The following two ideas are not contrary to one another: The being of the spirits and the body and soul of men were created by God, and also are upheld by God; nevertheless, the disorder and the rent, or breach, in creation is not of God, but is of the free will of devils and the first men. And even after the rent occurred, God upheld broken nature, as is the case now.

Speaking further about actual sin after Adam's fall: Although men were corrupted after Adam's fall, so that original sin is inborn in us, and we in our own strength are not able to heal this great injury or to set it aside, nevertheless, the wound in Adam and Eve first came, unforced, of free will.

We must also admit, even as Scripture certifies, that after Adam's fall this freedom remains, so far as rational external activity is concerned. We are able to restrain external members, such as the hands and feet, the tongue and eyes, to keep discipline, and to refrain from doing external works of shame.

Although Cain burned with jealousy, hate, and anger, nevertheless, speaking of the powers in him, he might still have held back his hand and not murdered his brother. And although the devil drove him, and the evil bent was itself strong in him, even so he still had this power and freedom, so that he was not forced to use his external members to commit evil, as I wish soon clearly to demonstrate in the article on free will.

Holy Scripture openly proclaims that there is an external uprightness which man can of his own power effect. To this extent a free will remains; man can control and rule his external members, even as Achilles did. Although he was provoked to anger, and drew his sword, and could have pierced Agamemnon, he restrained himself. Of this, more later.[3]

Because God does not will and has no pleasure in sin, and because sin first originated not of God's will but of the free will of the devils and of Adam and Eve, and because man retains a freedom in external works, it follows that we should not keep saying that our wills were first forced into sin,/or that we are still forced to commit external acts of evil, or that David had to take the wife of his faithful, upright servant, and so on.

It also follows that we should not insist that everything that happens must happen just so (as the Stoics have said of their fate), and that God and the wills of men are bound. If all that happens *must happen as it does*, then Nero necessarily practiced his horrible vices. Such horrible, filthy lies should not be brought into the Church before the ears of God and the angels. I pray that all God-fearing people will guard themselves against this.

To counteract this, people cite the passage about Pharaoh: "I will harden the heart of Pharaoh" [Ex. 4:21; 7:3]. Here the words read as if the hardening is a deed that God himself wills and effects in the heart of Pharaoh. To this the true, established, and right answer is that there is a great distinction between doing something oneself and allowing or not preventing another to do it. What God himself does and creates is good. Moreover, when the devils or men act against God, that is not God acting, even though God allows such to happen and does not actually prevent it, except in his own time.

Now the Hebrew reads thus: "I will harden him," that is, I will in the

3. See below, Article V, p. 51.

course of time let him become even harder, more arrogant, furious, and delirious. In the Hebrew this is a very general way to speak; the words are used as in the Lord's Prayer, "Lead us not into temptation," that is, do not let us fall into temptation, etc.

It would be superficial to compile such examples in great number, but they should especially be noted where punishment in particular is mentioned, as in Psalm 89:39, "Thou hast renounced the covenant with thy servant; thou hast defiled his crown in the dust." These are words, so to speak, that have a veil. God himself does not make genuine worship unclean, but he does veil the punishment of those who murder the saints, as do the Mohammedans, Turks, and papists.

This raises very complicated arguments about necessity and contingency, *de necessitate et contigentia,* that is, whether everything — the good and the evil, the holy and the sinful — must happen as it does, whether David *had* to commit adultery, and so on. I do not wish to speak at length about this now, but I beg all the pious to be forewarned, and for the sake of God's honor to maintain with firmness that God does not desire sin, that he effects nothing pertaining to sin, and that sinful deeds *do not of necessity* happen. Brooding over this matter is either shameful curiosity or malicious obstinacy. However, for the sake of instruction, we will set forth a few things to remember.

This very consoling and beloved passage in Matthew 10:30, "Even the hairs of your head are all numbered," is cited to show that *everything* must proceed in a set order, and cannot proceed otherwise.

The answer to this and to many similar statements is that there are divine consoling promises which proclaim that God indeed beholds our misery, cares for the faithful, graciously preserves us from falling into temptation, hears our cries and appeals, and helps us; as written in the Psalm 34:15, "The eyes of the Lord are toward the righteous," to protect, guide, sustain, and at last to bring them to eternal blessedness.

From such words of comfort and promises *only* this follows, that God cares for the faithful, preserves them, and wishes to aid them against their enemies, the devils and tyrants. It does not follow that devils and tyrants must of necessity undertake their blasphemy, unchastity, and murder.

Many people also use this argument: God knows everything, and he has decided what he will do and what he will veil, and everything happens just as he knows it. Some will conclude from this that everything must happen thus and so.

To answer this it is necessary to know that "to be necessary," or "must be," has several marked distinctions and degrees of meaning.

The first degree is this: Some things are immediate and necessary in and of themselves, and *must* thus be throughout eternity, namely God is; he is eternal, omnipotent, living, wise, good, and righteous. This is *necessary;* it must be thus, and it cannot be otherwise. This is called *necessitas absoluta*, "absolute necessity."

The second degree: Some things are necessarily in accordance with the order in which they are created. The course of the sun necessitates the order of day and night; it is the nature of fire to give heat, of water to give dampness, etc. God can alter such things, as when the sun stood still in Joshua's battle. For this reason they are not completely necessary, but rather are in accordance with the natural order. When God does not alter nature, then it performs exactly as it is created.

The third degree concerns the good works in which God's will is effective, but which nevertheless are not in and of themselves necessary, and, of course, God is completely unforced, but they [these good works] do follow as *necessitate consequentiae*. Although they are decided by God, and are proclaimed so that they assuredly will happen — as, for example, all men will be raised from the dead, Israel will be led out of Egypt to Canaan, and the Jews will return from Babylon to Jerusalem — these and similar works do not happen in and of themselves. They invariably happen, however, since they are decided and announced. And as long as they are good deeds, God's will and work are therein. The Son Jesus Christ is sent, the dead are raised, and Israel is delivered out of Egypt.

The fourth degree concerns evil works, which God does not will. Although he both knows and sees them, for nothing is hidden from his eyes, they are not his will and work. He veils the punishment ordained for them. He himself speaks of Sennacherib, saying that he will put a rein in his mouth and lead him back again.

Thus God draws a curtain over Pharaoh and Saul, and sets them a limit so that their boldness and bluster come to an end. While the punishment is decided, the end of Pharaoh comes from foregoing causes and is not in and of itself necessary. It is necessary only because it follows, *necessitate consequentiae*. Pharaoh, Saul, and the like were not forced to practice their spite and wantonness, and if they had desisted, the punishment would not have followed, as in the case of Nineveh, which was spared.

These degrees are to be carefully noted, so that everything is not lumped together and made equally necessary, without considering the particular causes. The madness in Cain, Pharaoh, Saul, and Judas is from their own free wills, even though the devil drives them with it, as the text says, "Satan entered the heart of Judas" [Lk. 22:3]. However, they were not forced, and this is not God's activity and doing.

And note the answer to the argument which declares that because God foreknows all things, as is written, and because God is not deceived, so then everything *must* happen as it does. The truth is that God's knowing does not force the human will to commit sin, and God has no desire to perform his will through sin. Sin is not necessary.

Although many perplexing questions are raised in this matter, nevertheless a God-fearing man should be bound and ruled by God's word, which significantly and frequently says, "*God is not the cause of sin; on the contrary he is definitely the enemy of sin.*" And the dispute is also to have a limit, for we cannot fathom everything, and the pious who want more information and better understanding might talk about this with people who love truth and do not seek unnecessary wrangling.

The following article on free will explains further.

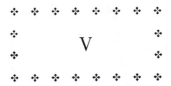

OF HUMAN STRENGTH [1] AND FREE WILL

To speak about *free will* is simply to speak about man's strength or weakness, which everyone, as much as possible, should contemplate in his own nature. However, some people introduce extraneous questions: Do all the natural effects in the air, in the water, and on the earth, all the good deeds and all the evil, happen of necessity? Does God's knowing in advance force the human will to act in a certain way? As was said previously, we should not be sidetracked by these questions. The Stoics should not be judges and masters in the Christian Church. When we speak of free will, we are simply talking about the deterioration of human strength through sin, man's inability to free himself from sin and death, and about the works that man is able to do in such a state of weakness.

And first to be considered is how man was created and what his greatest strengths are. Of the latter there are five: First, he is able to digest food and drink and thus sustain his physical life. About this we need say nothing more.

Second, he has five external senses: sight, hearing, taste, smell, and touch, and three inner senses in his brain so that he can draw distinctions, find similarities, and remember.

Third, in his soul he has understanding and knowledge and can command some of his external members.

Fourth, he can have true desires in his heart and will without hypocrisy.

Fifth, he can stir and move his external members from one place to another; he can keep his hands, feet, tongue, and eyes still or move them here and there.

Originally man was thus created, to be God's image; that is, his understanding [*Verstand*] was endowed with a great light. He knew about number, he had knowledge of God and the divine laws, and he could

1. *Kraften,* also translated as "power."

distinguish virtue and vice. With this light his heart, his heart's desire, and his will were without hypocrisy. His heart was created full of the love of God, free of all evil desires. His will was free, so that he could choose to keep God's law, and his heart and external members could be fully obedient without any hindrance. It was also possible for his understanding and will to choose something else, as happened later.

Accordingly, when free will is mentioned, we mean understanding and will, heart and will; and they belong together, without hypocrisy.

Man was created wise and upright, and before the Fall he had a free, unimpeded will.

However, as Adam and Eve fell into sin and incurred God's wrath, God withdrew from them and man's natural powers became very weak. The light in his understanding became very dim, although some remained, for man can still use numbers and make distinctions between good and evil works and the teachings of the law. God wants all men to recognize sin; he wants to punish us by means of our own conscience; and he wants all men to maintain external discipline. For that reason knowledge remains in this corrupted nature, although it is dim and full of doubt and uncertainty about God, not knowing whether God wants to be man's judge or helper, or whether God wants to receive and listen to men — of which more will be said under law and gospel.

Further, all good virtues toward God in the heart and will were also lost — love of God, trust in God, and true fear of God. God is not received where the Holy Spirit has not first enlightened and kindled the understanding, will, and heart. Without the Holy Spirit man cannot of his own powers perform virtuous works, such as true faith, love of God, and true fear of God. And therefore the miserable human heart stands like a desolate, deserted, old and decaying house, God no longer dwelling within and winds blowing through. That is, all sorts of conflicting tendencies and lusts drive the heart to the manifold sins of uncontrolled love, hate, envy, and pride. The devils also spread their poisons.

When we speak about this great ruin of human powers, we are talking about free will, for man's will and heart are wretchedly imprisoned, impaired, and ruined, so that inwardly man's heart and will are unlike the divine law, offensive and hostile to it, and man cannot by his own inward natural powers be obedient. This is said about true inner obedience, without hypocrisy.

Now to speak of the movement and motion of external members of the body. Although the heart and the inner will, as we ourselves are aware, neither hear nor inwardly obey the law without hypocrisy, nevertheless God has left the understanding free to govern in that it can move and control the external members of the body. The understanding may say to one who is sick with a fever and very thirsty that he should hold his hand and not drink, and he restrains his hand from seizing the mug. Even in this corrupted nature God has allowed such freedom with regard to external motions of the body. He wants all men to have external morality [*Zucht*], and thereby learn the distinction between powers that are free and powers that are bound; thus we can think in some degree that God acts freely and is not a prisoner or a bound Lord, as the Stoics have pictured him with regard to his created nature.

Whoever looks at himself and systematically considers the nature of the soul, the understanding [*Verstand*], will, and heart, and the motion of external members of the body, can in large measure inform himself and others about free will; and it is very useful for virtue to learn as much as possible about how all the parts of the body operate and what such words as the following mean: *understanding*, the true will which is like the heart, and the *rationalizing* [*gedichteter*] will which is not like the heart, but concerns itself with thinking and commanding the external members of the body to follow understanding, as in the case of the thirsty man with a fever whose hand is restrained from seizing a mug. The hypocrite has such a rationalizing will. Esau considered himself to be his brother's good friend.

In divine Scripture, the heart is often mentioned as the highest power in the soul. For this reason, if the heart is not in agreement with the will, then there is no true will, just thoughts and a rationalizing will which controls only the external forms.

Although with this much as a basis it is not difficult to answer questions about free will, I want nevertheless to mention a few additional items.

The First Answer

Let this be the first answer to the question about free will in this corrupted nature. Even though they are still not reborn and are not sanctified through the Holy Spirit, men have the power to move or to restrain external members of the body through thought and will. As far as external works are concerned, there remains in man a free will, as previously said about the thirsty man who restrains his hand. So also with Achilles; although his heart burned with rage so that he drew his sword, he checked himself, sheathed the sword, and departed from Agamemnon.

Honorable morality is to move or restrain the external members of the body in accordance with right reason [rechter Vernunft] and God's law. Passages in St. Paul show that this freedom remains in man, for St. Paul often speaks of external righteousness [Gerechtigkeit], and calls it justitiam carnis, a righteousness of the physical nature which has not yet been reborn. To have such righteousness, man must also have the possibility of moving and using his external members — such as the tongue, hands, and feet — in the performance of commanded works and duties. Otherwise, no one could have such external righteousness. And if this freedom were not in men, then all worldly law and all education of children would be in vain. However, it is certainly true that through worldly law and the education of children God wants to force men into honorable customs, and such pain and work are not totally in vain.

For this reason St. Paul says to Timothy "that the law was given to the unrighteous that they might have curbs and prisons to keep them from becoming worse and doing other shameful deeds" [cf. 1 Tim. 1:8–11].

When young people hear that works do not merit remission of sins, they often become even wilder in their daily intemperance and immorality, and do even less praying, reading, and contemplating of Christian matters. In this way they open the door still wider for the devil. Contrary to such shameful indulgence, we should know that God earnestly desires all men to curb themselves with true morality, and the reasons for this are four in number.

The first is, on account of the divine commandments, for all angels and men are obliged to obey God.

The second is, to escape punishment in this and in the next life, for God truly punishes obvious external sins, like manslaughter, adultery, incest, robbery, fraud, perjury, Epicurean blasphemy, idolatry, and magic. He punishes these sins not only in the next life but in this present one, just as the text about manslaughter says, "Who takes the sword will by the sword perish." This clearly refers to physical punishment; and the same is said about stealing and fraud. "Woe to the robber, for he will be robbed"; and of immorality, Hebrews 13:4, "God will punish whores and adulterers"; and of contempt for parents, Deuteronomy 27:16, "Cursed be he who does not honor his father and mother." The Scriptures are full of such testimonies, and in our daily experience we can see the same right before our eyes, for manslaughter is not concealed and it does not go unpunished.

It is a foolish senselessness and delusion of the devil that, despite their consciences, men proceed in evil acts, immorality, robbery, and murder, in the hope that physical punishment will not follow, although it happens unfortunately that distress comes to the innocent as well as to the wanton and tumultuous people. The devils take great pleasure in this delusion, and when physical punishment comes, many such deluded people fall into eternal blasphemy, fear, and despair. Even though we have a short reprieve, we should not think anything except that physical punishment will most certainly come soon. In the Scriptures are many earnest warnings, and we should often read them and take them to heart. The Lord speaks to Abraham, saying that he will punish Sodom because he wants his anger against sin to be proclaimed far and wide.

Solomon says that the people become fearless when punishment does not immediately follow. But this is a lamentable blindness, for the impious will be punished and the pious will at last be blessed.

From the book of wisdom [cf. Sirach 8:10] we should know that "with that with which we sin, with that will we also be punished." And Christ says, "As you judge so shall you be judged" [Mt. 7:2]. David committed adultery, and with the same he is later punished. His own sons practiced murder and immorality on his descendants and on his wives. In every land we see how the wicked have been disinherited and how governments have been torn apart. In Jeremiah 5, the prophet says, "They have abandoned me, although I gave them blessings and nourishment; they have multiplied adultery and murder. Shall I not punish them for such evil" [v. 5; cf. v. 24–29]?

The third reason is that God requires moral living so that other people may have peace. We were not created to use the world wantonly; our living should honor God and serve other men, for this is why we were created and redeemed. As God says, "You shall love God with your whole heart, and your neighbor as yourself" [Lk. 10:27].

The fourth reason is, as St. Paul says, "The law is a schoolmaster to lead us to Christ" [Gal. 3:24]. That is, external morality is necessary, for in a life filled with dissolute, immoral, persistent adultery, gluttony, robbery, and murder there can be neither instruction in the gospel nor acquaintance with it. And in such foolish, mad people who continually and wantonly persist in sin against their own conscience there can be no effective work of the Holy Spirit. For this reason we are to preach about God's wrath and the punishment that he inflicts, as seen in the earth's great misery and wretchedness, war, evil government, tyranny, sickness, poverty, discord, shame, and all kinds of plagues. He wants worldly authorities to serve with genuine sincerity to further the maintenance of honorable morality.

All punishment through the authorities and others should remind us of God's wrath against our sin, and should warn us to amend our lives. We should carefully think about all this, so that those who are not yet reborn may learn that they are required to obey God and live in honorable morality. Those who have been reborn also need to know about this, for St. Paul warns, "Change with great care, not as fools do . . ." [cf. Eph. 5:3-20; Gal. 3:3].

In addition this should be noted. Although this capacity, or freedom, remains in man's corrupted nature, so that we can move or restrain our external members, the expression of this freedom has two obstacles — our own weakness and the devil's activity. Few people can resist evil tendencies. When we burn with love or anger, we often do a thing that we know is injurious to ourselves. We say, therefore, that one's own weakness conquers his freedom. But men, incited by the devil, fall even more dreadfully, for the devil drives men to murder, insurrection, adultery, and blasphemy, and in doing so the devil becomes ever more influential [stärker], so that he is like an invited guest, for men develop a lust and love of evil things and do not want to turn away from the source. Concerning this, the ancients say that if one does not want to fall into sin, he must turn away from the source. (Vitare peccata est vitare occasiones peccatorum.)

All this is related to assist us in contemplating our great weakness and miseries, for we are deeply mired in sin and death, and in our external works are easily overcome by our own weakness and by the devil's inflaming activity. And we should lament that we are so hardened and intractable that our wretchedness and danger do not touch our hearts. Not for a single moment of our lives are we without doubt; we err and often fall; we merit punishment and God's wrath; the devil hunts us unceasingly; and there is no man on earth who associates with people who does not encounter all kinds of persecution and incitement. What great punishment many people behold in their own children! All fortune is unstable. How many great kings and princes are dislodged, exiled, confined, and imprisoned to die! This proverb is still true. "In an instant the mighty fall and are no more."

We should contemplate all this as a reminder to fear punishment and to live morally. On the other hand, we should also know how God, because of his great mercy and for the sake of his Son and through his Son, wants graciously to hear and assist his Church, those who rightly call upon him; and we should know what are the graces and gifts which the Son of God has obtained for us. About this we will speak later.[2]

This also should be noted. Although it is certainly true that all men are obliged to live in external morality and that God earnestly punishes external depravity in this life, and in the next life will punish all those who do not become converted, we must also know that external morality *cannot merit* forgiveness of sins and eternal life. *It is not* a fulfillment of the law, and *neither is it the righteousness by which a man is justified and received before God.* Only the Son of God has merited forgiveness of sins for us, and for his sake we are received, *out of grace* and *mercy, by faith, without our deserving it.* Of this more will be said later.[3]

The Second Answer to the Question About Free Will

This is quite obvious: No man by his natural power can take away death and the inborn evil tendency of this nature. Only the Son of God can do this, the Son who says, "O death, I will be your death." Man has no power to accomplish this. Further, it is also certainly true that no man can *merit* forgiveness of sins, as is clearly indicated in Titus 3:5, "Not because of deeds done by us in righteousness, but in virtue of his own mercy, he saved us."

And place before your eyes Adam and Eve after the Fall, when they stood before God in judgment, trembling with fear. Then they knew that there was no help or counsel to be had from any creature. They had merited God's wrath and eternal death, and they would have sunk into eternal death if God in his great mercy had not revealed the promise that the seed would trample on the head of the serpent, and if the Son of God had not thus wrought in them comfort and life.

There Adam and Eve discovered that they were rescued from sin and death, but not through their own powers and free will. From this example we learn how such rescue may also happen in us.

Further, it is also true that we still do not have enough power to keep God's law; we cannot begin inward obedience in our hearts without divine help and without the Holy Spirit. We cannot continue to produce obedience without the Holy Spirit, for we cannot in and of ourselves

2. See Articles X–XII.
3. See Articles IX–XIII.

ignite in our hearts a firm belief in God, a truly burning love for God, trust in God, patience in suffering, and joy in God. God is neither known nor loved if the Son of God through the Holy Spirit does not first enlighten our soul and heart, creating therein light, comfort, and ardor. The following passages show this:

Romans 8: "It is impossible for the law to make us righteous" [cf. v. 3].

First Corinthians 2:11: "The natural man knows not the Spirit of God," that is, if God is not present in our natural powers, in our heart and soul, then we are full of doubt and have no firm belief in God. In this condition we pay no attention to God's wrath, are secure and hard, and proportionately feel punishment if we are not comforted through the gospel and Holy Spirit; if only natural power is active in us, we face empty despair and eternal death, as seen often in frightening cases like those of Saul, Ahithophel, and Judas.

Let it be further known that for this reason God accordingly gathers to himself an eternal Church and is active in the saints. As soon as Adam and Eve heard the words, "The woman's seed shall tread on the head of the serpent," the Son of God kindled faith in them through the Holy Spirit, and they felt comfort, and were drawn out of death, out of the throat of hell, and afterward dwelt with God as the text says, John 14:23, "Whoever loves me will keep my word, and my Father will love him, and we will come to him and dwell in him!" And, therefore, through God's activity in Adam and Eve, a firm belief in God began, based on the promise, as well as trust and love and other virtues. The obedience which the divine law teaches was born [angefangen] in their hearts.

Thus the Son of God, through his gospel and the Holy Spirit, is continually active in his saints in his Church; he will be with them and dwell in them. We should acknowledge this gracious presence of God in us, and heartily thank God that he receives this miserable, weak nature so graciously, for the Mediator's sake; that he dwells in us, kindling faith, light, and true obedience in our souls and hearts, healing our weakness, taking away sin and death, bringing about eternal life, and shielding us so that the devil does not overthrow and assassinate us.

We should be warned and with great earnestness repudiate the lies and blasphemy of Pelagius, who taught that man in his own natural strength can fulfill the law, merit forgiveness of sins, be righteous before God, and merit eternal life. The Pharisees were stuck in this blindness, and they did not know the meaning of law, sin, or righteousness. And through this error the knowledge of the Lord Jesus Christ and his grace and the true teaching about faith are utterly obliterated.

Therefore, we should know that God has given his gospel and established preaching so that he may effectively punish sin and produce in our hearts genuine and dreadful fright, so that we know and feel that God is a true judge and is angry on account of sin. King Hezekiah speaks of this fright: "Like a lion he has crushed all my bones" [Is. 38:13]. And in the midst of such fright God wants also to effect comfort and life through the gospel, and for the sake of his Son he announces forgiveness of sins and grace through the Son of God. Whoever then does not fall into this fright and in his anxiety does not despair, but takes refuge in the Son of God and comforts himself with the promise, as we will explain later, in this the Son of God, through the Holy Spirit, is certainly working and kindling in the heart right belief and trust in him, the Son of God, and hope, comfort, and joy in God, love to God, true fear of God, patience, true invocation, chastity, and other virtues. And with this the obedience which the law teaches, not just external obedience, is begun in the heart.

In this conversion, in fright and in comfort, we learn what law and sin are and also the nature of faith, comfort, Christ's grace, righteousness, and true prayer. This occurs through the Holy Spirit when we contemplate the gospel, for St. Paul says, "The gospel is the power of God for salvation to all who believe" [Rom. 1:16].

Second Corinthians 3: "The gospel is an office of the Holy spirit" [cf. v. 3, 6, 8, 18], that is, the Holy Spirit works through it, and so forth. Without this activity of the Holy Spirit in our hearts, there is no true faith and comfort and love to God, as the following passages show.

Romans 8: "Whoever has not the Spirit of Christ, he is not of the Lord Christ . . . Those who are led by the Spirit of God are the children of God" [cf. v. 9, 16].

John 15:5: "I am the vine, ye are the branches. He that abideth in me and I in him will bring forth much fruit, for without me you can do nothing."

Galatians 4:6: "Because you are sons of God, God has sent the Spirit of his Son into your hearts, who produces the true cry, 'Abba, Father.' "

And there are many more such testimonies, for God wants us to know that the Son of God dwells in his saints in his Church and is active in them through the Holy Spirit, and that there is this distinction between the saints and the godless. These promises of divine activity in us were not written so that we might live wildly and savagely, even though some imagine that if they cannot come to God, they will then be drawn to him through the Holy Spirit, and so they are pleased to wait until they are pulled by the hair to God. And in the meantime they pursue their lust.

To these thoughts much should be given in reply, but for now let this reminder be enough: The passages about divine activity were spoken to us for comfort. We should not think that a man is a piece of wood or a stone, but as we hear the word of God, in which punishment and comfort are put forth, we should neither despise nor resist it. We should immediately rouse our hearts to earnest prayer, for the Lord Christ says, "How much more will your heavenly Father give his Holy Spirit to you if you ask him!" He is not speaking to the scorners who continue in their sins against their conscience, who resist punishment and comfort. It is very necessary to remember this.

Chrysostom says that God draws man. However, he draws the one who is willing, not the one who resists. (*Trahit Deus, sed volentem trahit.*) [4] And Basil says that God comes first toward us, but nevertheless that we should also will that he come to us. And take the wonderful parable in which the son who had squandered and wasted his inheritance in riotous living comes home. As soon as the father sees him from afar, he pities him, runs to him, falls on his neck, and kisses him. Here the son does not run back, does not scorn his father, but instead goes also toward him, acknowledges his sin, and begs for grace. From this illustration we should learn how this teaching is to be used and how this passage in Basil is to be taken. *Tantum velis, et Deus praeoccurrit.* We need only to will, and God has already come to us.

Revelation 3:20: "I stand before the door and knock. Whoever hears my voice and opens to me, I will come in to him. . . ."

By remembering this, we can learn that the passages about divine activity are very comforting. The Son of God will be with us, come to us, and will give us aid, because he knows our misery. Only let us not push him away, but ask him for aid, as did the poor fellow whom hunger forced to return to his father. Whoever even faintly thinks that he would like to be in the grace of God again has made a beginning, and God will strengthen him, as this wonderful passage in St. Paul says, "God effects the will and the fulfillment of that which is pleasing to him" [*cf.* Heb. 13:21; Col. 1:9, 10].

---

4. *Cf.* Chrysostom, *Homilies on St. John,* 5 (St. John 1:3–5), 10 (St. John 1:11–13), 45 (St. John 6:28–40), 46 (St. John 6:41–53); *Homilies on First Corinthians,* 2 (1 Cor. 1:4–5).

This is a promise to comfort the weak who feel in their hearts a small spark and longing to be in the grace of God again; they should know that God both made the beginning in them and will further strengthen them, but they should at the same time exercise the faith they have and pray, as Christ says, "Ask, and so you will receive. . . . How much more will your heavenly Father give to you his Holy Spirit, if you ask him for it" [Lk. 11:9, 13]!

Many men alarm themselves with this doubt: "I do not know whether God pays any attention to my sighs and longings; I do not know if he wants to receive me." To combat this doubt, we should be well instructed in the doctrine of faith, for God's earnest will and command is that we should believe in the promise, and even though faith is weak, we should let heart and tongue speak, even as the troubled man in Mark 9:24 speaks, "Lord, I believe, but I beg you to help my weak belief." God will be with us, as the Scripture says, "*Spiritus adjuvat infirmitatem nostram;* the Holy Spirit helps us in our weakness" [Rom. 8:26]. This we learn in daily anxiety and true invocation.

Some people complain that speaking of our impotence in this way makes people lazy and leads them into despair. But this is not true, for at all times men can and should maintain external discipline; this becomes easier for the reborn than for others, because the reborn have the help of Christ and his protection against the devil. In those who have turned to God regeneration has begun, and after that heart and will are active. The Holy Spirit is not a lazy being; he kindles light and fire in the soul and heart in such a manner that the soul and heart also possess a better knowledge of God and an initial love and longing for him; as St. Paul says, "The image of God in us shall again be restored in true righteousness and holiness . . ." [*cf.* Eph. 4:24].

Of Passages Connected with This Question

Various passages are brought together in connection with the two parts of this question [of free will], and often are interpreted very badly. In considering these passages, the reader should carefully consider and understand each without sophistry.

As Solomon says in Proverbs 16:9, "Man's heart devises a way, but God directs his steps." From this and similar passages some conclude that man's will does nothing at all. Such an interpretation is much too coarse. Solomon himself says that man has a plan, and so he devises something.

However, accomplishment requires much more, namely God's will and gracious help.

And this is a very necessary doctrine which frequently is reiterated in divine Scripture, that we may learn to undertake only commanded and necessary works, and that, in doing so, we should invoke God, and therein work and endure with trust in him. Moses led the people out of Egypt, but not on his own; he asked God for help and worked and endured in trust in God. Thus was God with him, manifesting himself in the work commanded and directed by him, and giving victory and a happy end to it.

On the other hand, however, when we on our own begin something that is not commanded and is not necessary, it rests on human wisdom, power, and pleasure, and will result in endless unhappiness and wretchedness. When Pompey began the great war against Julius, which was not necessary, he trusted in his own power and party, and in the end there was great wretchedness. And there are many such examples in all times which come under the principle expressed in Psalm 127:1, "If God does not build the house, they labor in vain who build it." Also John 3:27: "A man can of himself do nothing, unless it is given to him from heaven." That is, if God does not assist, then our plans, labor, power, and everything are too weak.

Let everyone consider how necessary it is to know and to keep this rule in this life, and let no one purpose anything that is unnecessary, that is not what God has commanded; on God we should call for help, and trusting in him we should work and endure, as the Psalm teaches, "Be obedient unto God, and beseech him. . . . Commit your way unto the Lord, and he himself will lead you" [cf. Ps. 37:3-5].

This beautiful, necessary doctrine which teaches us fear of God and invocation of him, and also says what true comfort is, eclipses the foolish, childish explanation of these passages as meaning that man's will has no activity at all.

Having properly recovered these passages in their true meaning, we should note that *electio* and *eventus* are vastly different, that is, the choice or design which we have and the carrying out of the design are vastly different. For example, Pompey and Josiah freely chose war. This was a work in the individual effected by his own will. However, in the carrying out of one's choice, not only must one's will be present, but the will of many others who also help and give a hand, first among which is God's will and help, and then the help of a faithful, steady people.

Solomon speaks often of this: "The human heart has a design, but God directs his steps" [cf. Prov. 16:9]. He reminds us of reverence for God, humility, and invocation, as when he says, "Behold, dear friend, how many great things men devise which prove to be very evil" [cf. Ecclus. 29:25; Prov. 1:31–33; 6:14–15]. The pseudo-undertakings of such very wise people — Saul, Pericles, Demosthenes, Pompey, and thousands of others — proved to be evil. Therefore, we should not be arrogant and audacious; we should ponder not only what we should do but where God will bestow his grace and aid. Let us undertake commanded works, invoke him, and work and be patient in trust in him. Clearly, Solomon is not a Stoic, for he does not say that the human will does nothing; he talks instead of different choices and how we execute them.

Sometimes the choice is man's free will and has nothing to do with God, as when David decided on his own that he would claim Uriah's wife and gave the command that she be brought to him. But in Joseph, when he would not consent to adultery, there was a virtue that was certainly from God, who was ruling and strengthening him so that his will obediently followed, unforced, and ordered the eyes, mouth, hands, and feet to shun this passion. In such activity the will is not a block or a stone; God commands us diligently to bring all our members under control. Therefore, it is said, *praecedente gratia, comitante voluntate;* divine grace and help move men to good works, but nevertheless so that the will follows and does not resist. David fell of his own accord; he was not forced; and Joseph might also have fallen.

From Jeremiah

Jeremiah says in chapter 10:23, "I know, Lord, that the way of man is not his own!" Some people interpret this fine, comforting passage to mean that man's will does nothing, but Jeremiah is speaking here of himself and of all the great prophets, and of the deeds and professions of consecrated regents, who have been reborn, and who in their professions [*Stande*] and callings are not idle; and the word "way" means the entire calling or profession. Thus spoke King Hezekiah: O Lord, this kingly rule is much too difficult for me; it is your work. Thou givest good rule, and I beseech thee graciously to give to me thy good counsel, to rule my reason and heart, and to grant to my labor fortune and victory. Mercifully forgive my frailty and lack of wisdom in office [cf. 2 Kings 19:15–19].

Jeremiah's words are just such a lament and prayer, which all men

should contemplate in their respective professions, both to confess their
burden and to call on God for help. And there are also answers in this
passage. Jeremiah does not say that the human will does absolutely [*ganz*]
nothing, rather he speaks of understanding, choice, and execution, all of
which, however, are very weak without God's help. Josiah errs in judgment when he decides on war, and he fails later in the act. Israel is right in
opposing Benjamin, and does not err in judgment, but later good fortune
fails to come for other reasons. By such examples Jeremiah's words may
be easily understood.

It is deplorable that some explain these comforting passages to fit their
own understanding and employ childish fantasies, so that consciences
become confused and humility and invocation are not served.

Jeremiah reminds us to recognize our weakness in judgment and in
deed. Men can easily err, and many very exalted persons have erred
frightfully in judgment, as David did in taking a census of the people, and
as Josiah, Pericles, Demosthenes, Pompey, Brutus, and others have done.
Moreover, even if we do not err, we may still lack good fortune if God
does not help us.

For this reason, as previously stated, in all our undertakings we should
carefully consider these three things:

First, whether we are following God's command, and not undertaking
some unnecessary thing because of our own forwardness.

Second, whether we are obeying God's command in our calling, and
not neglecting the work of our calling, for Scripture says, "Each one is to
labor in his calling" [*cf.* 1 Cor. 7:20, 24].

Third, whether in our hearts we are crying to God for help, and
trusting in him, waiting for final deliverance, and asking that we not
depart from him in sorrow and misfortune. . . .

From Sirach [5]

These words are in chapter 15 of Sirach: "God first created man and
gave him power to choose good or evil . . ." [*cf.* v. 14, 18].

The Pelagians have extended this passage much too far. Even though
Adam and Eve before the Fall had the freedom to follow God's law
unhindered in their hearts and their works, after the Fall human nature
was so wretchedly corrupted, the human heart, so full of doubts about

5. Ecclesiasticus.

God, so inconstant, so empty of fear and love of God, that men could not fulfill God's law.

For this reason we should not extend this passage, as the Pelagians and monks do, to mean that men can fulfill God's law by their own natural powers, without divine activity within. The Pelagian meaning is contrary to the whole of divine teaching and the promises which God had from the very beginning given and revealed to his Church.

All men should know that after the Fall the freedom to move and control the external members of the body remained, so that we are able to maintain external morality. In this respect the statement of Sirach is still true even of this weak nature, for we do have such external freedom, and Sirach has scored against the devilish Stoics. We should not say that God has forced us to sin and that God has deceived us, for sin is an abomination to God. This should be enough about the passage in Sirach, for he is speaking of external morality.

However, Augustine and others have said much more. The passage in Sirach should be understood as including, not excluding, the grace of Christ, for all sayings about the obedience which is pleasing to God must include the grace of Christ. That is definite, as will be said more fully later. And it is necessary to explain what the word "grace" means. So when Sirach says, Stretch your hand out to good or to evil, this should be understood as meaning with the grace and help of the Savior Jesus Christ. In this much is included, but first of all there is the thought that we have forgiveness of sins for the sake of Christ, and that God is pleased even though our initial obedience is very weak and paltry.

The second thing that it means is that the Son of God will himself help us, guide us through his Holy Spirit, protect us against the devil, and always be a Mediator and Intercessor for us in the heavenly council of the divine Majesty.

For this reason, in our obedience, calling, and labor we should earnestly cry out daily to God and with firm faith ask him for the sake of his Son *Jesus Christ* to forgive us our sins, accept graciously our poor weak humanity, and to bestow upon us his Holy Spirit for guidance. We should ask for counsel and help in all our works, so that our labor may be useful to ourselves and to others for the maintaining of divine knowledge and good government, and we should ask for protection against all the cunning and temptation of the devil.

In this invocation and practice we may learn better to understand this and other passages, for it is certainly eternally and unchangeably true that we must include the grace of the Lord *Christ*, as the passage in St. Paul says, "Through faith we keep the law," that is, without faith we cannot begin to keep the law, for works without faith are only external shadows and do not please God [*cf.* Gal. 5:6, 14; Rom. 9:30–32].

Two Passages from Hieronymus [St. Jerome]

In Hieronymus we find two passages which are often quoted and which sound as if they contradict one another. They are old rules which were given in different councils. This first one is: "Cursed be all who teach that God's law can be kept without grace."[6] This is quite right, and was directed no doubt against Pelagius and similar Pharisaical teachers, such as the monks and papal teachers like Thomas, Scotus, and many others who have spoken in the same heathenish way, saying that we can entirely keep God's law in our hearts and in external works, without the aid of the Holy Spirit. In other words, they are saying that man can merit forgiveness of sins with such works. These lies and blasphemies should be known, condemned, and execrated. They blot out the true meaning and use of divine law; and they obscure the distinction between law and gospel, and the meaning of faith, grace, and righteousness, which we have through the Son of God, Jesus Christ.

On the other hand, this passage is put forth: "Cursed are all who teach that God's law could be kept without grace."[7] We should rightly understand this sentence. First, we should know that the word "grace" means more than just the help which the Holy Spirit effects in man; *grace* also means mercy and gracious reception for Christ's sake, even though our works are still weak and impure. It is not sufficient to explain this sentence by saying, "If the Holy Spirit helps, then man can keep the law"; for even though obedience has begun in those who are reborn, much weakness, impurity, and sin still remains in them in this life, and even the saints cannot fulfill the law in this life. Therefore, they must still trust that, notwithstanding, they are pleasing to God through grace, that is, through the mercy and gracious reception which is promised to them for the sake of the Mediator, Jesus Christ.

6. *Cf. Nicene and Post-Nicene Fathers*, H. Wace and P. Schaff, eds. (Oxford and New York, 1893), VI, *Principal Works of St. Jerome, Letter* cxxxiii: 5–9; *Against the Pelagians*, 1:23–24.
7. *Ibid.*

Further, it should also be known that this sentence does not speak of external morality, which even the heathen like Scipio,[8] Cato,[9] and Atticus [10] can maintain, but of faith, fear of God, love for God, trust in God, and joy in God in suffering. Therefore, this sentence should be understood as if it read, "Cursed are all who teach that the law of God can be kept in the heart without grace, that is, without the activity of the Holy Spirit." That is to say, this cannot be done without grace, which is mercy and gracious reception whereby the believer is pleasing to God for the sake of Christ as long as Christ is in him and covers his weakness, although this weak nature may still not be able to fulfill the law.

The second passage in Hieronymus reads, "Cursed are all who teach that it is impossible to keep God's command." [11] This sentence is directed against the Manicheans, and requires a careful explanation. The Manicheans espoused many poisonous errors, many derived from the Stoics, which are such frightful blasphemies that I do not want to relate them. Basically there was the error that one part of human nature was created for evil and must continually perform external evil deeds. For example, Cain had to kill his brother Abel, and could not have held back his hand.

Opposite this devilish blasphemy is the sentence which says, "God's command is possible to keep! " However, we should understand this as pertaining to external works and also to deeds of the heart with the help and activity of the Holy Spirit; good works become possible with the grace of *Christ* and the activity of the Holy Spirit in the heart, as we will explain in the following articles. The true voice of the gospel must re-

---

8. Scipio Aemilianus Africanus Numantenus, Publius Cornelius (185–129 B.C.), known as Scipio the Younger, was a Roman military tribune and statesman noted for his integrity, stern morality, and honesty in diplomacy. He promoted Greek literature and learning through the Scipionic circle, which included Terence, in whom Melanchthon was interested. Scipio leaned toward Stoicism in philosophy and was made the chief speaker in Cicero's *De Republica*.

9. Cato, Marcus Porcius (95–46 B.C.), known as Cato the Younger, was a Roman military leader and Stoic philosopher who was celebrated by many ancient authors, including Cicero, in panegyrics of his devotion to duty, opposition to bribery, and strict virtues. Marcus Porcius Cato, (Cato the Elder 234–149 B.C.), was known for his adherence to the old Roman moral customs and objections to the inroads of Hellenic culture in Roman society. He was among the first writers of Latin prose to achieve prominence, but Melanchthon is probably referring to Cato the Younger.

10. Atticus, Titus Pomponius (109–32 B.C.), a friend of Cicero and a patron of letters, was known for the tranquility and happiness of his private life. He wrote a Greek history of Cicero's consulship and some annals of Roman history, neither of which is extant, and edited a volume of letters from Cicero to him.

11. See note 6, p. 66.

main, the voice which says that without the Son of God, *Jesus Christ*, no man on earth can completely fulfill God's law; no man can be without sin in this life. The Psalmist says, "Before thee no man in this life is justified" [Ps. 143:2], that is, no one fulfills the law. In Romans 8, St. Paul says, "By the law it is impossible to make yourself righteous" [*cf.* v. 3, 7, 8; also 3:20, 28].

Let this be enough about free will as a human power. And I pray that Christians will not let themselves be involved in strange Stoical disputes about this; such disputes do not belong in the Christian Church, and cause people to err. What I have said is in keeping with the teaching of the true Church since the time of Adam, as may be seen clearly in the prophets and in the writings of the apostles. Ever since the time of the apostles there have been holy men who have known and preached this truth, some more clearly and purely, some more obscurely than others — Basil,[12] Ambrose,[13] Augustine, Prosper,[14] Maximus,[15] Hugo,[16] Bernard,[17] Tauler,[18] Wessel,[19] and Luther.

12. St. Basil (329–379) was the bishop of Caesarea, one of the most important fathers of the Greek Church, an opponent of Arianism, author of several Biblical commentaries, and the founder of monastic institutions.

13. St. Ambrose (*ca.* 340–397) was the bishop of Milan, and one of the greatest of the early Church fathers; he successfully opposed the Arianism of Empress Justina, defended orthodoxy in his many sermons and writings, forced Emperor Theodosius to do penance for premeditated massacre at Thessalonica, and greatly influenced Augustine.

14. Prosper Tiro, or Prosper of Aquitane (*ca.* 390–465), a disciple and friend of Augustine. Poet and rhetorician, and an opponent of Pelagianism, he defended Augustine against Vincent of Lérins and John Cassian, versified much of Augustine's theological thought, and compiled an *Epitoma Chronicon* of the French Church down to 455.

15. St. Maximus (*ca.* 580–662), a Byzantine theologian, secretary to Emperor Heraclius and afterward abbot of the monastery at Chrysopolis, vigorously defended orthodoxy and the primacy of Rome in the Monothelite controversy. He was imprisoned, banished to Thrace in 655, and seven years later brought back to Constantinople, where he suffered scourging, mutilation of his tongue and right hand, and exile for his beliefs.

16. Hugo, or Hugh of St. Victor (1096–1141), was the head of the abbey of St. Victor in Paris. He was a mystic philosopher, theologian, and author of many commentaries and treatises, including *De Sacramentis Christianae Fidei*, a synthesis and defense of dogma. He opposed Abelard and believed that God's existence could be proved from internal and external experience.

17. St. Bernard of Clairvaux (1090–1153), abbot of Clairvaux, was the reformer of French Cistercian monasticism and preacher of the Second Crusade in 1146. He arbitrated so many ecclesiastical and political impasses that he was known as the "conscience of Europe."

18. Johannes Tauler (*ca.* 1300–1361), a German mystic of Strasbourg, was a Domin-

We should also diligently note what should be reproved in papal and monkish teaching, as so much relates to what they write:

First, that man can of his own natural power, without the Holy Spirit, be obedient in his heart to God's law.

Second, that with such works forgiveness of sins and grace are merited.

Third, that after being reborn, man can in this life keep the law in its entirety.

Fourth, that with such works and fulfillment of the law eternal life is merited.

These are errors which we should reprove and repudiate. What they have attached with regard to perfection and other things I will mention later.

---

ican monk influenced by Master Eckhart. He became one of the "Friends of God," a brotherhood of lay and clerical mystical pietists who objected to mechanical sacerdo-talism in the Church, and sought to express his convictions in vigorous Christian living.

19. Wessel Gansfort (*ca.* 1420–1489) was an opponent of scholastic theology who emphasized Scripture as the source of faith and insisted that sin can be forgiven only by God. He directly influenced Melanchthon and Luther, and in 1522 the latter published and wrote a preface for his *Farrago Rerum Theologicarum.*

VI

OF ORIGINAL SIN

If we want to speak about original sin, we must first consider why and how man was created. This we will briefly discuss to give the young people an introduction to true contemplation of this. By multitudes on earth this doctrine about creation and the Fall of human nature is looked upon as a fable. However, against this human blindness in the Christian Church we should first strengthen ourselves with the divine revelation in which God has given testimony about himself and his teaching, as in the exodus of Israel out of Egypt and the resurrection of the dead.

Secondly, we should earnestly beseech God to enlighten our souls and hearts, and to inflame, increase, and strengthen in us our faith.

Thirdly, it is useful to consider here how God has fashioned evidence of himself in our nature. All this we should contemplate if we are to discuss creation and the Fall of man.

As to the first: Because of great miracles, the resurrection of the dead and other events, it is certain that the teachings of the Church were given by God, and we should believe the same and not go rushing about, seeking sources for death and human weakness in such things as the atoms of the Epicureans. As divine revelation teaches, in Moses and in St. Paul, "Sin came into the world through the first man, and by sin came death" [Rom. 5:12]. Although this is alien and strange to human reason and philosophy, and although there are always many people of an Epicurean stamp who ridicule the divine doctrine about original sin, we who know and invoke God should not deviate from divine Scripture.

As to the second: I heartily beseech thee, O Lord, omnipotent, true, living, and wise, eternal and only [*einiger*] Father of Jesus Christ, Creator of heaven and earth, together with thy only begotten Son, Jesus Christ, and the Holy Spirit, be merciful to me, for the sake of thy beloved Son, Jesus Christ, and enlighten and strengthen my soul and heart through thy Holy Spirit, that I may know thee with a firm faith, know that thou hast truly created and dost maintain this visible nature, and that thou dost gather to thyself an eternal Church among us, and will be with us to dwell in us. Give to me in my heart thy truth and light, that I may rightly call upon thee, and abide always in obedience unto thee.

As to the third: After contemplating divine revelation and after the prayer, let us look at ourselves. Man is a clear public testimony of God, and man was created that he might be a testimony of God. Man was created that God might be in us and reveal himself to us, and impart to us his wisdom and other blessings, and that we might acknowledge, praise, honor, and glorify, and give testimony of him. We behold in ourselves many fine gifts, namely wisdom in distinguishing between virtue and vice and in understanding about number and order. As often as we look on these gifts, our hearts should be convinced and we should recognize that a wise masterworker, even God, has performed his work with wise counsel, for the fine orderly works, the heavens, sun, moon, men, and so forth, did not just float together with neither master nor counsel.

Our nature tells us that this is so. Therefore, we should not be uncouth [*grob*] or indolent; we should note the evidences of God within ourselves. If our nature had not fallen into sin and darkness, we could see these evidences much better; but even so, we should still be aware of them as much as possible.

If we think of how man was before sin and the Fall, we can more fully apprehend our own great wounds and the shame which followed sin, and our misery of mind should lead us to seek the help of God's Son.

All men should know the passage in Moses about the creation of all creatures, and recall often that this article of belief is grounded therein. Note God's words, "Let us create man in our image, after our likeness" [Gen. 1:26]. And afterward the text says, "And God saw everything that he had made, and it was very good" [v. 31].

These sentences show that man was originally created to be an image of God, that in man himself there was evidence of God from which he should have learned that God truly exists; that God is a living, wise, good, righteous, true, pure, chaste, free and uncontrolled being; that God is irritated by all disorders which are contrary to his character [*Eigenschaften*], such as unrighteousness, falsehood, and impurity; and that he punishes and blots out such disorderly things which are contrary to him.

In speaking of God's image and likeness, these characteristics are first of all to be considered, for God is living, wise, good, righteous, true, pure, chaste, free; the one who punishes all disorders contrary to his character. St. Paul speaks thus of the image. Truly the eternal Son is the full, perfect, essential likeness of the eternal Father, and we are in the likeness of the Son. Likeness is foremost among these characteristics.

It follows from these words about likeness that through the Holy Spirit God kindled in Adam and Eve the wonderful light of wisdom, through which they knew God, number, order, virtue, and vice, and their hearts and members were pure and in true order, and obedient to the light in the understanding, and their hearts glowed with love and joy to God and other virtues. The will was free and unimpaired, and there was still no sickness and no death.

And this wonderful human creature was pleasing and righteous before God, and God would have had his dwelling in this nature and would have imparted continually his wisdom and virtue unto us, and had joy and delight in us, and we on the other hand would have known, praised, loved, and had joy in him.

Thus was man before sin. From this we should understand that original sin is a wretched destruction of this wonderful image of God.

However, we should pause and contemplate the great love in the divine Majesty toward human nature. First, inasmuch as God poured out upon us his noblest characteristics — life, wisdom, goodness, righteousness, truth, purity, and freedom — and wished to dwell with us and have joy in us, and because nothing higher can be given than himself and this likeness of his characteristics, it is very clear that his love toward us was not a cold, indolent [*fauler*] thought, as a Stoic might argue, but a genuine, earnest, burning love.

Consider further how, after the Fall, the Son of God manifested his love toward us. The anger of divine Majesty against sin is also not a cold, indolent thought, as one Stoic jeered, but is truly a consuming fire, as Moses says, as horrible punishments daily show, and as Adam and Eve experienced many times. Indeed, in this wrath the eternal Son of God laid himself before the eternal Father, asked that this creature not be blotted out in eternity, and to satisfy divine righteousness, he willed and took upon himself the punishment and made payment for us.

Consider in the third place this testimony of God's great love. After the acceptance of man, God again renews in us his image and likeness, and gives us his Holy Spirit, which dwells in us, which is the flame drawing our soul and heart again to the eternal Father and Son, so that we know the eternal Father, eternal Son, and the Holy Spirit. The likeness in us is again restored so that we have eternal joy and life in God. And where the Holy Spirit is and is active, there also is the entire Godhead.

In our contemplation we should acknowledge God's love, give thanks to him, and cry unto him to enlighten our hearts and to stir up in us his great love, and cast us not away.

We ought to know how Adam and Eve were deceived and driven by the devil and fell into sin. Moses described this, and note the order and wisdom in the account.

In the creation God placed a light in man, through which we might and should acknowledge him. With it we may still clearly know that he particularly loves us, and that we should be his eternal Church, that he desires particularly to be active in us in a way in which he is not active in irrational animals. For the natural light he also expressed his word, that therein we should know him; and this one who has given this word we should invoke as God, and be obedient to him, and practice obedience in the works which he has commanded in his word; and no one should believe, follow, or append anything contrary to this clear, commanded word, as he through his expressed word again builds his Church.

After Eve believed and followed the devil and veered from God's word, and Adam did likewise, then both Adam and Eve fell under God's wrath and eternal punishment; and they lost the Holy Spirit and the wonderful virtues which they enjoyed previously, both for themselves and for all mankind, who were to have a beginning in them, and were naturally to come from them. They stood in the place of future mankind. To them the gifts were given; the same would have devolved on their successors if they had remained steadfast in obedience. But when they fell, they lost the gifts for themselves and for all mankind who were naturally to be born of them.

This fall and shame is very well depicted in the parable in Luke 10 about the man who desired to go from Jerusalem to Jericho and was robbed and beaten by murderers, and then lay dying. A priest and Levite passed by the wounded man and did not help him. Then came a Samaritan, who showed mercy to the dying man, went to him, and poured wine and oil on his wounds, and bandaged them. Afterward he put him on his donkey, and took him to an inn to be cared for. The next day, as he desired to travel again, he gave the innkeeper two groschen and commanded him, saying, "Take care of him, and whatever you spend extra, I will repay you when I come again."

In this wonderful much-loved parable the Son of God has depicted this doctrine for the entire Church: The man represents Eve and Adam, who were going from Jerusalem, that is, out of a peaceful, divinely pleasing, righteous, and immortal condition, to Jericho, that is, toward their inconstant thoughts and lusts, for Jericho means the moon, which signifies inconstancy in these physical things. On the way Eve and Adam were unexpectedly attacked by murderers, that is, by the evil, furious, murderous enemy of God, the devil, and were robbed of righteousness, with which God had adorned man, so that after the Fall they were no longer pleasing to God, and God was not pleased to dwell in them, and the soul no longer had the wonderful light and knowledge of God as before. The will and the heart no longer burned with love for God, no longer had joy in God, were unable to kindle again the former joy and love, were now weak and in confusion, and all mankind had lost life and eternal blessedness.

In the Fall man's powers were all impaired. The understanding was greatly weakened, and became full of doubt about God and unable to know things as Adam knew them before the Fall, when he had from God, through the eternal Word, the Son, such clear magnificence of wisdom that he could reflect on God and the order of creation and much besides. Respecting this, John says, "The Word was the light of men" [cf. Jn. 1:4].

And just as the Holy Spirit before the Fall activated a burning love and joy toward God in the will and heart, and all man's inclinations and mores [Sitten] were in the right order, so after the Fall, when the Holy Spirit was removed, false flames and pernicious sores grew in the will and heart; inordinate love, wrath, fright, and anxiety lacerated the heart. All men feel this, particularly when they have no comfort in time of death and in other great troubles. Therefore Jeremiah says, "The human heart is perverted and full of affliction [Schmerzen]," [cf. 17:9], and Saul in his last extremity felt the most dreadful affliction.

And now we in our time are robbed and beaten, and have fallen into sin and eternal death, and the priest and Levite pass us by, that is to say, the sacrifices and the law and the doctrine of works cannot rescue us from sin and death, cannot again give us grace, life, and righteousness. But then comes the Good Samaritan, the Son of God, Jesus Christ, whom Jacob saw on the ladder at Samaria. He takes away sin and death; bestows grace, eternal life, wisdom, righteousness, and eternal blessedness [Seligkeit]; and pours wine and balm on our wounds, which is to say, with the office of preaching he reproves sin and through the holy gospel and the Holy Spirit gives comfort and dresses our wounds. That is, he covers the sin with forgiveness and the imputation of his righteousness. He lifts us up and puts us on his donkey, that is, he himself bears our sins with his sorrows. He leads us to his inn, that is, to the Church, where we should grow ever stronger.

In this wonderful parable both the impairment [Schade] and the healing are described. I have drawn on it here in the beginning, and I ask the reader to consider it often because it is a good introduction to an understanding of this article.

What Original Sin Is

To be in original sin is to be in God's disgrace and wrath, to be damned on account of the fall of Adam and Eve. On account of the wretched loss of the divine presence, light, and activity in us, on account of our blindness and doubt about God, and our perverted, evil tendencies which are opposed to God, we are sinful and damned.

Note the difference between this short explanation of the Christian truth about original sin and papal fantasies about it. The monks and the papists imagine that original sin is not a great impairment [Schade]. They shamelessly say that doubt about God and evil inclination are not sins, but something indifferent [Mittelding], like eating and drinking. They also say that a man can by his natural power keep the law of God, that man merits forgiveness of sins through his own fulfillment of the divine law, and that man is thus righteous before God through his own fulfillment of the law. These are vain, devilish lies, which blot out the gospel of grace and redemption which we have through the Son of God, Jesus Christ. Therefore, we should be careful to mark well the difference between false and true doctrine.

It is surely true that these impairments of human nature, namely this blindness, doubt about God, and evil inclinations in opposition to God, are sinful and damned, and that man for this reason is damned if he does not receive baptism and continual forgiveness through faith in the Lord Jesus Christ. Although by special divine counsel sufficient capacity has remained in our weak nature to enable us to perform external honorable works, such external discipline is not a fulfillment of the law, for the blindness, doubt, self-assurance [Sicherheit], and evil inclinations in the heart are great sins against God, as mentioned above and as further discussed later. Note well that although the law points out what God is like, such righteousness cannot be in anyone unless God himself dwells in him and gives him his light and glory. Thus the law is entirely fulfilled in us only in eternal life, in eternal righteousness, when we have eternal joy in God, and God has become All in All. Of this, more is said later.

Anselm's often quoted sentence agrees with our explantion: *Peccatum originale est defectus justitiae originalis;* original sin is a defect in the original holiness or righteousness which was imparted to us at the time of creation, when nature was without any evil tendencies, when Adam's heart was full of the divine spirit and light and joy in God. Then Adam knew and saw God and his inexpressible goodness and boundless mercy much more distinctly than we now see sin. Then he was joyfully and entirely obedient to God. Pure, true fear of God, heartfelt, ardent love for God, and gratitude for the wonderful unending gifts of God welled up and filled his heart without ceasing.

Through Adam's fall and sin we have lost all this, and man's powers in body and soul are so wretchedly corrupted that we cannot obey God's command; and for us who have lost the bright, beautiful light and knowledge of God there necessarily follows a horrible blindness, disdain of God, animosity and bitterness toward God, doubt and vacillation. We forget God entirely, fear human risk, build with complete trust on human help, solace, and advice, and fill our hearts with evil ideas, raging passions, and inordinate desires contrary to God and his will. Accordingly, when Anselm expounds his definition, he points out that he has included both *defectum* and *concupiscentiam.*

Bonaventure also speaks well and rightly about this, saying that there is no difference between the two; one may say, original sin is *concupiscentia,* evil inordinate desire, or one may say it is a defect. Speaking still more fully and more clearly, he says that one includes the other. For this reason several of the newest teachers, without any basis for doing so, have fought about so many words when they have contended that original sin is a defect and not *concupiscentia.*

In the schools our opponents use foreign words, *materiale peccati* and *formale,* which many of them do not themselves understand. We do not need such unfamiliar words. We can use familiar words to speak intelligently about what is true and right in itself.

This impairment, or sickness, remains in the saints, as it is born in us. However, it is forgiven and is not reckoned for condemnation against believers. As St. Paul says, "There is now no condemnation in those who are in Christ" [Rom. 8:1]. Psalm 32:1 also reads, "Blessed are those whose sins are forgiven!" The Psalmist calls the impairment sin, but it is forgiven.

I do not want to trouble the German reader with how the opposite is talked about in the schools. For many understanding people, even their associates, know that they erred when they said only the *materiale* pertains to evil desire. Evil desire, defect, and blindness pertain to both material and formal sins. However, *formale* should be called the oath to condemnation.

Where Did Original Sin Begin?

When Adam fell, he lost his noble gifts, holy knowledge, innate holiness, and righteousness; he felt God's wrath and frightful judgment; he was cast into death and the power of the devil, and robbed of his noble purity and holiness. What was born afterward of Adam was born of evil, corrupted, sinful nature; it came into being through sin. Accordingly, by nature sin has devolved on all the descendants of Adam, and all are born in sin and are under God's wrath.

Of the Punishment of Sin

The scholastics say that evil desire is a punishment for sin, but that evil desire in itself is not a sin. We say that evil desire is a punishment for sin and is also in itself sinful and damnable. Death is a punishment, laid on man on account of sin. The foremost, the highest, and most frightful punishment, however, is that we are thrown, because of sin, into the dreadful power of the devil. Moses speaks briefly of such frightful punishment when he says,[1] Genesis 3:15, "And you will bite him on the heel."

The devil, then, rages dreadfully against our poor, weak human nature, distressing it with all kinds of horrors, with temptation to all kinds of despair [*Herzeleid*], and with great danger. And finally, when the hour comes, he strangles us, for he is a liar and a murderer. In addition, he provokes man's poor human nature to all sorts of gruesome sins, errors, heresies, blasphemies, and often to murder, riot, and all sorts of adversity. From the beginning of the history of the world there have been many

1. Melanchthon, like most of the scholars in his day, assumed that Moses wrote the first five books of the Old Testament.

excellent people who have applied themselves to honesty and virtue with the greatest diligence, and nevertheless, on account of the weakness of nature and the cunning and power of the devil, have come upon great misery.

Passages from Scripture Showing that Original Sin Is, and What It Is

In Psalm 51:5 the prophet says, "Behold! I was brought forth in iniquity, and in sin did my mother conceive me."

He is not lamenting the sin of his mother, but his own inborn sin, as if he had said: I was conceived and shaped in the womb; in my flesh and entire being was great impurity and sin. The prophet acknowledges that the sin in men is that which they bring with them out of the womb.

St. Paul, Ephesians 2:3: "We were by nature children of wrath, like the rest of mankind." There Paul says clearly that both Jews and heathen are born in such misery that they are born in wrath, i.e. in God's disfavor. In Romans 5 this article is clearly expressed, and this passage should be known by all men, for in it is testimony against the condemned doctrines of the Pelagians, Anabaptists, and others with similar views. It would take too long to set forth the entire text, but the Christian reader should diligently contemplate the following sentence.

"As sin came into the world through one man, and death through sin, and so death spread to all men, then all are sinful" [Rom. 5:12]. Note the word "all" and the word "sinful," i.e. all are repugnant to God's will and law, and are therefore in disfavor and eternal, just punishment. As John says, "Sin is whatever is repugnant to divine law" [cf. 1 Jn. 3:4], that is, whatever is contrary to divine wisdom and will, for God has proclaimed his wisdom and will in the law.

And Romans 7 and 8 explain that inborn impurity is blindness and evil inclination contrary to God's law. All men must feel and acknowledge that they harbor doubts in their hearts about whether God will be our judge or whether he will grant us a favorable hearing and be gracious to us. All men feel inordinate love, hate, and other flames. Although certain people, so long as they live in easy peace, pay little attention to sin, God teaches us that it is this dreadful impurity which arouses his wrath, and for that reason all men remain condemned if they are not reborn through baptism and faith in the Lord Christ.

This doctrine has always been preached in the Church. As early as

Genesis 8:21 these words appear, "The imagination of man's heart is evil from his youth." Jeremiah speaks likewise, "The human heart is perverted and full of misery" [*cf.* 17:9]. "Perverted," *i.e.* turned from God, full of inordinate love, self-assurance, and pride. Accordingly, when God punishes, there is misery of heart, fright, anxiety, flight, and wrath against God. Although the prophets speak briefly, as is their custom, we should nevertheless diligently consider them in order to learn the very important things that they utter.

What is original sin? Answer: Some uncivil men judge that original sin is only the evil inclination in the body to such things as debauchery, inordinate love, and hate. However, we should know that it is blindness and disorder in the soul, in the heart, and in the other powers of man. As long as the soul is not God's temple, it is full of doubt about God, and for this reason the heart is also full of erroneous tendencies.

Pharisaic, Pelagian, Papal, and Anabaptist Errors in This Matter

In opposition to this article about original sin, one called Pelagius and many others have said that man brings no sin with him at birth, that only the evil deeds which a man does afterward are sins. And although the papists speak of original sin, they are fundamentally Pelagian, for they say that inborn doubt and evil tendency are not sins, but things indifferent, like eating and drinking.

They further say that a man can, with natural strength, entirely fulfill God's law, that man can merit forgiveness of sins through good works, that man thus becomes upright before God, and that God is pleased on account of the external good works.

From the time of Cain human reason in certain people has thus rationalized this matter. So the Pharisees taught, and until the end of the world such pharisaic, Pelagian errors will be voiced by many people. The true Church, knowing the divine judgment against sin, must combat this error, and must preach the voice of the gospel of the Son of God; as John says, "Behold, the Lamb of God, who takes away the sin of the world" [1:29]! He who imagines, as do the Pharisees, Pelagians, and papists, that our works merit forgiveness of sins robs the Lord Christ of his glory.

He who imagines that man in his weak nature can fulfill the law, *i.e.* that he can be and is consonant with the law, is blind and full of lies. In addition he destroys the gospel of the Savior Christ, for by faith, for the sake of the Lord Christ, we are justified and pleasing to God, not on account of the law.

Having this reminder, we should understand that it is very necessary to know the right doctrine about original sin, and on the other hand to combat all pharisaical, Pelagian, papal errors and lies. Here we should also note that although human nature is corrupted, God has allowed some knowledge to remain in man; he has the gifts of number and measure; he can build; he has great wisdom, and he knows natural law. These gifts are divine light and truth, although they are in a corrupted vessel, where God himself does not dwell and does not rule the heart. By nature men have some good tendencies and virtues, such as parental love, which is called στοργή, and respect, and mercy for the poor who are unjustly opposed, and zeal against vice, as in the case of Tola protecting the children of Hercules. Heroic valor in Achilles and in Alexander are particularly God's works. But such things are not a fulfillment of the law, for these virtues are not rightly directed in a corrupted heart in which God does not dwell and in which there shines no knowledge of God, faith, love, and joy in God. As long as these virtues are in a state of disorder and are inwardly polluted, they are also sinful. However, when man is converted and God dwells in the heart, and faith, love, and joy in God are kindled, then the same virtues in the reconciled person are better directed and please God, as in the case of Abraham's love toward his children.

Here I want briefly to append this reminder about the defects and evil tendencies in the saints. The blind papists shriek that *concupiscentia* is not sin after baptism, and they support this with many sophistries. However, St. Paul, in Romans 7:7–25, calls our innate defects and evil tendencies sins; his words are clear: "They strive against God's law" [*cf.* v. 20, 23]. Therefore, they certainly are sins. However, the converted and reconciled are forgiven. We will report more fully on sin in the saints later.

About Actual Sins

If one would speak about sins, he should always contemplate the excellent sentence in 1 John 3:4, "Sin is whatever is against God's law"; all defects and tendencies in all human powers, in the understanding and in the heart; all errors, evil plans, and unrighteous desires which are opposed to the divine law; all external works which counteract God's command. Although reason cannot set straight inner blindness and sin in the heart, it can decide external works when it has learned the divine law; therefore, no longer explanation is now needed. When one sees the divine commands, it is easier afterward to decide that actual sins mean all desires and works which knowingly or unknowingly occur, and all the evil designs which are contrary to divine commandments.

We should look at all the misery and the human lives in which we see so many open, gross, actual sins, for this is testimony that human nature is corrupted, and that our hearts do not live in God and are not ruled by God. Human weakness and one's own evil will are sources of gross sins, and the devils also drive many men into horrible depravity, as the passage about Judas says: "Satan entered into him" [Jn. 13:27]. The devils poison men against God and Christ. They rage against the poor human race, using all sorts of methods and stratagems; they drive them to idolatry, to false doctrine, to manslaughter, to war, to dreadful immorality, to destruction of orderly government, to devastation of the land, to murder of small children, to obstruction of good discipline and the cultivation of divine doctrine, and to actions displeasing to God and Christ. They prepare much blasphemy!

There is no doubt that physical punishments in this life follow from gross, actual sins, even as Scripture says, "Whoever takes the sword will perish by the sword" [Mt. 26:52], and, "Alas for the robber, for he will in turn be robbed" [cf. Is. 33:1]. This applies also to unchastity and incest. "Take care not to do these abominations, lest the land vomit you out, as it did the nations who were there before you" [cf. Lev. 18:26, 28]. This rule remains true: after gross, actual sins, physical punishments follow. God wants these punishments to remind us that he is wise and upright, and will punish sins, although it may not happen immediately. God places before our eyes the fierce punishments of death, sickness, poverty, hunger, war, gallows, the rack, and many plagues, that we may learn to consider his great wrath against sin.

One should not make light of this doctrine, for God earnestly demands external discipline from all men, both converted and unconverted. The Scriptures say, "The law is strong and firm against the unrighteous" [cf. 1 Tim. 1:8-11], which is like saying, God's terrible anger is earnest and severe against the unrighteous.

Although physical punishments are decreed by divine wisdom and righteousness for the destruction of sinful nature, the greatest requital is the eternal punishment, which assuredly comes to all sinners who are not converted to God by faith in the Savior Christ. As John says, in the third chapter, "Whoever does not believe on the Son will not see life, but the wrath of God rests on him" [v. 36].

And it is well to observe that as often as we speak of sin and explain it is that which is contrary to God's command, we should also speak of the wrath of God, eternal and corporeal punishment in this life, which is embraced in this word; for that which is contrary to God's command is also contrary to his wisdom and justice. When filled with wrath, the divine just Majesty destroys everything which is against him. Therefore, sin being everything which is contrary to the divine commands, [the sinner] is ordained by a just and divine wrath to eternal and temporal punishment and will be everlastingly rejected if he is not recommended for forgiveness of his sins through the Son, Jesus Christ. . . .

All men should often contemplate the wonders of reconciliation. God is righteous, and truly angered by sin, but he is also merciful. He again receives miserable fallen man, without relinquishing his righteousness and righteous anger. Our Intercessor, the Son, *Jesus Christ,* makes payment and feels the terrible wrath which no creature could have borne. In the eternal school we will learn about this wondrous decree of divine wisdom, and here we can begin to learn about it by remembering that sin is a terrible thing and that divine righteousness is seriously angered by it, as God's wrath in breaking our nature in death reveals. God's wrath is laid on the Son, to satisfy divine justice, but divine mercy is given, for the sake of the Son, to make man acceptable. Consider how great a love this is, that the Son would take on himself this inexpresssible wrath. Let this be a brief reminder for the God-fearing, who, I pray, will humbly contemplate this great wonder.

VII

OF DIVINE LAW

Let me first set forth the old and customary divisions. The law in Moses has three parts. The first part is called *lex moralis,* that is, laws about virtues; henceforth in this essay I will call this *eternal law,* or the law about the judgment of God against sin. The second part is *lex cerimonialis,* that is, laws about the Church, which are concerned with external works, like sacrifices, and prohibited eating of the flesh of swine, all of which were established for a certain time, as in ancient Judaism. The third part is *lex judicialis,* that is, laws about civil government, about justice, inheritance, and peace. There is a great difference between the first part, which pertains to the eternal, and the other two, which pertain to the temporal. All men should know that the laws about ceremonies in the books of Moses, and also the laws about the civil government of Israel, were intended only for Israel and were to remain only until the coming of the Messiah and the true expiatory sacrifice.

God established the government of Israel that there might be a certain people and land in which the Messiah would appear and preach and perform signs, suffer, and rise from the dead; and that there should be a certain school in which God would reveal himself and perform signs, and give, explain, and maintain his promises. God chose a suitable place almost in the middle of the known earth, between the great empires of the Chaldeans, Assyrians, and Egyptians. There he established, in the eyes of all, the successors of Abraham. Along with the promise of a Messiah, he also decreed a temporal government, which does not now bind us, for it ceased with Judaism. This can be gathered from Acts 15 and the entire Letter to the Galatians. This should be remembered in order to avoid falling into the fantastic contention of Thomas Münzer,[1] who says that a

---

1. Thomas Münzer (*ca.* 1489–1525) was an Anabaptist German reformer and theologian who studied with Luther and then attacked his evangelical teachings as too "honey sweet." He claimed direct communion with the Holy Spirit and his radical

Christian in court must render judgments according to the law of Moses; he would destroy the Roman law which is now used. He who does not distinguish between such temporal law and eternal law will suffer many errors. Eternal law is given the weak name *lex moralis*. We refer to the Ten Commandments as the eternal law because the principal parts of eternal law are included in the Decalogue. However, when we use the term "Ten Commandments," this should not be childishly understood as referring only to ten sentences but rather to the entire law, which is called *lex moralis;* but we will not here quarrel about words.

First, however, I want to give this definition: The divine law, which is called *lex moralis*, or law of virtues, or law of the judgment of God, or the Ten Commandments, is the eternal, unchangeable wisdom and principle of righteousness in God himself. A portion of this wisdom was imparted to man in the creation and later God's word was given that we might know the nature of God himself and his demand that we be like him in wisdom and righteousness. He did this that we might not vex him in mind, heart, or works, and that we might know his anger toward all who do not have perfect obedience, and his condemnation of them to eternal punishment.

Our childish thoughts about law are a great impediment, so that we pay little attention to the law's great wisdom. When we hear the words "divine law," let us think about God. He has described his Ten Commandments as divine law, and he has taught us that he is not an unreasoning, changeable thing, but that he exists, and is eternally wise, good, true, righteous, chaste, and kind. He makes the criteria for virtues and vices, and is an earnest judge and requiter of all vice. He terrifies our hearts so that we feel that we are repugnant to this divine wisdom and righteousness. But when our conscience is overcome by terror, we begin to understand.

Inasmuch as this eternal law is divine wisdom itself, first fashioned in us in creation, and explained in the divine word from the time of Adam to our own, it is clear that this law binds all rational creatures in all times.

---

preaching of rebellion caused disturbances against the established authorities at Zwickau, Prague, Allstedt, and Mühlhausen, from all of which he was expelled. Returning later to Mühlhausen, he gained control of the city and established a communism of goods. In the Peasants' War he mustered an army of peasants which was defeated at Frankenhausen, May, 15, 1525, by Philip of Hesse and other nobles. Shortly thereafter Münzer was tortured and beheaded.

This law did not originate with Moses, and did not pass away with Judaism; it is and always will be; it shows us God's nature, and tells us that he wants us to be like him, and that he abhors sin. This voice of the law is the judgment and fire with which he terrifies and slays our hearts. As St. Paul says, "Through the law comes knowledge of sin"; and, "The law brings wrath, terrors, and death" [cf. Rom. 3:20; 4:15]. In just this way the prophets, the Son of God, and the apostles preached law, and it must be preached in the Church of God. Now we will briefly recall to mind, one by one, the Ten Commandments, for these sentences contain the most important parts of what is termed *lex moralis*.

The First Command in the Ten Commandments

All men should know Exodus 20, for it describes the glorious story of how the divine voice from Mount Sinai delivered the Ten Commandments. Now we are not giving any new doctrine, but only a summary of the Commandments in a short and orderly fashion. And we are to remember, as I have often said, that no creature can fully comprehend God's high wisdom. Nevertheless, one must learn something about it.

Note that the first command speaks of the foremost, highest, and most necessary wisdom, namely the knowledge of the true God. Now the heathen, even in their darkened natural understanding, know that heaven and earth, men and other creatures, did not of themselves just come together, but that a wise omnipotent Being exists who originally created and still sustains all things. However, the heathen and other idolaters depart in many ways from the true God. For this reason a precept is established that directs us to the true God and teaches how rightly to acknowledge God. God has always placed before us *external* testimony by which he wishes to be known and differentiated from all whom other men invoke. Such testimony is given in the exodus from Egypt. "Him you shall keep for God, who led Israel out of Egypt, performed great miracles, promised the Messiah and gave the law" [cf. Ex. 20:2, 3; Deut. 10:20; 2 Kings 17:36; Gen. 3:15]. As the Israelites in their time differentiated this true God from all the false gods of the heathen and in accordance with this testimony invoked the one who led Israel out of Egypt, who previously gave the promise of the Messiah, through whom he would take away sin and death; so in our invocation we are to reflect on this testimony, together with that of the Savior *Christ*, who has now appeared, and who says: "No one comes to the Father except through the Son. He who does not honor the Son, does not honor the Father! He who sees me also sees the Father" [Jn. 5:23; 14:6, 9]!

Therefore, let reason and heart differentiate the true God, who revealed himself through the Lord Christ, who died on the Cross and arose again, from all the invented gods, and know that he alone is God who reveals himself through his promises and afterward through the Son, Jesus Christ.

This is the first doctrine in the first command concerning the right knowledge of God. Such a distinction between the true God and false gods is necessary, that one in all invocation may appeal to the true God, and not mingle heathen idolatries with Christian doctrine. . . .

If human nature had not fallen into sin and darkness, we would have had a much higher, clearer, and more certain knowledge of God. Instead, we speak weakly about it. Nevertheless, God is known to us in his revelations through his word and miracles, and especially through his *Son, Jesus Christ;* all miracles and promises came to pass to give us knowledge of the Lord *Christ,* and we should be guided by such.

Of the knowledge of God, I would like to say more; however, it is all so high that one cannot express it in words. But I covet for the God-fearing an introduction to this high wisdom of God, for in great tribulation God gives light in this matter to those who seek comfort in the Lord Christ through his word.

With right knowledge of God, faith should burn in man, so that one may firmly and without doubt believe God's word and also have fear, love, and trust in God. Man should be in accord with Deuteronomy 6:5, "You shall love the Lord your God, with all your heart, and with all your soul, and with all your might."

But we must all confess that, unfortunately, we are not as we should be. Human hearts pay little attention to God, cling to creatures contrary to God's will, and do not fear his judgment, much less love him. And these deep sins are pointed out in the passage in Paul, Romans 8:7, "The mind that is set on the flesh is hostile to God." Ah, how great a misery this is in human nature!

From this it is obvious that human nature does not keep this first command, and by natural powers is not able to begin to keep it, and the monks teach nothing but absurdities when they prevaricate, saying: Men are able to keep God's command, and to do it with their own natural powers, without the conversion which the Lord Christ effects through the gospel and his Holy Spirit. Also when they say that men can do still higher and better works than to follow the command: "You shall love the Lord your God with all your heart."

Here this question arises: Can no man be pleasing unto God? Can man make no beginning in keeping this command? Although more will be said later about how obedience begins and why it is pleasing to God, we must nevertheless say something about it now, and also indicate the good works in this command. For there must be a beginning, even though, unfortunately, in all men it is very weak.

This beginning occurs when the heart, truly terrified before God's wrath against our sin, hears the gospel through which God, for the sake of the Lord Christ and through him, gives forgiveness of sins and also gives the Holy Spirit. Then, through faith in the Son of God, the heart is snatched out of anxiety and hell. Thus the heart knows God's wrath and also his mercy. Next, along with this faith and solace, the Holy Spirit effects in the heart joy and love to God, and obedience to this command is thus begun in us through the Lord Christ. And although much impurity still remains in our corrupted sinful nature, we are justified, that is, pleasing to God, through righteousness imputed to us *for the sake of the Lord Christ*. Therefore, the Son of God is the fulfillment of the law, as Paul says: "For us he has borne the punishment and is the Reconciler, and for his sake we have forgiveness of sins" [*cf.* Rom. 5]. In addition, he produces in our hearts solace, joy, and eternal life. This solace and joy is the beginning of obedience in us.

When one relates the good works in this command, even the most worthy saints grow weak, but we may learn something from naming them.

The first is: To have *right knowledge of the true God*, to receive it in faith (that our hearts may know and invoke this true God as the God who has revealed himself through the Lord Christ, his word, and miracles) and to reject idolatry and contrary teaching.

The second work: *Truly to tremble before God's wrath and to fear him.*

The third work is *true faith*, in which there is *trust* in the *Son of God, Jesus Christ,* for whose sake, even in Adam's time, forgiveness of sins, grace, and blessedness were promised to man. Without trust in the Mediator no one can have solace and forgiveness of sins, and without this Mediator no one can know and invoke the true God and seek grace. David and all the saints understood the first command as pertaining to the

God who gave them the promise of the Messiah through whom they have forgiveness of sins and grace, and through whom they know and invoke the true God. God speaks of himself, Exodus 3:6, as "the God of Abraham, Isaac, and Jacob"; that is, as the God who revealed himself to Abraham and who gave him the promise which speaks about the seed through which we are all to have grace and blessedness.

The fourth work is *love to God* and *solace* and *joy in God*. As the heart receives forgiveness of sins and grace through faith, and is snatched out of hell, it feels solace and joy in the mercy of God through *Christ*. The heart then loves God, and humbles itself, yes, the Holy Spirit burns in it and makes it one with God. Thus the heart begins to have faith, and to rely on, to love, and to fear God, to be obedient to him in truth, in chastity, in praise, in gratitude, in humility, in helpfulness toward our neighbors.

Thus *love* of God is kindled *through faith*.

The fifth work is *hope*. It is a firm expectation of eternal blessedness through the Mediator. This hope follows out of faith and trust. Thus says Peter in 1 Peter 1:13, "Set your hope fully upon the grace that is coming to you at the revelation of Jesus Christ." This hope brings solace in all affliction, for to the degree that we hope for deliverance or alleviation by God, to that degree the heart exhibits good and becomes joyful and alive.

The sixth work is *patience, i.e.* obedience to God even in the sorrow which he has commanded us to carry, so that we do not depart from God, but find alleviation of sorrow in the contemplation of God's will, his presence, and his help. David is patient when he is hunted; he is obedient to God in his punishment and does not depart from him, as Saul did. He finds comfort in contemplating God's will, God's presence, and his help.

The seventh work is *humility*, which includes many virtues: knowledge of one's own weakness, fear of God, keeping of vocation, trust in God, and patience in sorrow. Jonathan is humble; he knows that he is too weak for the kingdom; he knows that blissful rule is God's work alone, and he has fear of God in the knowledge of his sins and unworthiness. He remains in his calling; he does not wish to make himself king; he does not wish to push David aside; he relies on God, who helps and gives him success in his station. Later he is obedient to God, even though God removes him entirely away.

This command contains such a lofty wisdom that no creature can thoroughly explore or sufficiently understand it, and angels and men will have to learn about it in eternity. Nevertheless, it is very necessary to point in this life to the frightful sins and depravity which oppose this first command, so that we may contemplate the dimensions of misery in the human race, and recognize and put away the grossest sins.

This first and highest command is the most necessary, for God created angels and men to have knowledge of the true God, to be like him, to acknowledge, invoke, praise, and love him, and to know that he truly gives us life, wisdom, righteousness, nourishment, and all good things. For this reason we should be thankful and obedient. Because men depart from this true God, especially by breaking his most important command, they are terribly condemned. We are to think carefully about this, that we may acknowledge God's righteous wrath, tremble before him, and seek grace through faith and reliance on the Mediator, *Jesus Christ*. And for instruction, we are to consider these uncouth depravities one by one.

SIN AGAINST THE FIRST COMMANDMENT

The first stage of sin against the first commandment is *to imagine* or *to say*, "There is no God," or that God is not a righteous judge, that he pays no attention to men, or that he is a being held captive in nature, unable to effect anything outside the physical laws in beasts and men. We should consider the hundreds of thousands of men in this first stage, who are constantly raging against God. In this multitude are many wise philosophers such as Epicurus, the Academicians, and the Stoics. It is indeed a wretched situation when men, who should be the image and mirror in which God chooses to reveal himself, fall so far from God that they imagine he does not exist. This absurdity is contrary to reason; the devil has inflamed Epicurus and his ilk and strengthened their fantasies.

The second stage, at the opposite extreme, is to invent *other* gods, and to give divine honor to creatures, as the heathen have done. Thus images are adored as if they were God, and dead men are invoked, as when the papists invoke saints. They run to the images of Mary, Anna, Jacob, etc., and imagine that God or Mary is the power behind some so-called miracle which is nothing but a dreadful deception set in motion by the devils.

The third stage is *sorcery* in its sundry forms: To resort to magic is to make an alliance with the devils, to seek help from the sworn enemies of God, and to put trust in them. The same may be said for gazing in a crystal ball, hexing sickness away, and other unnatural practices not ordained of God. *All* this is strictly forbidden in Leviticus 20:6: "If a person turns to mediums and wizards, playing the harlot after them, I will set my face against that person, and will cut him off from among his people."

The fourth stage is: All the *Jewish, Mohammedan, heretical,* and *philosophical* errors of those who invent their own God after their own thoughts and will not acknowledge and receive the God who revealed himself through his Son, the prophets, and the apostles. Opposed to the first commandment are all heretics, such as the Manicheans, who invent two gods, one good and the other evil, both eternal; and followers of Samosatenus, who imagine that in Christ there is no divine nature, but only a human nature. Mohammed and many other heretics had the same idea.

The fifth stage is *carnal self-assurance,* whether in hypocrisy or in open sins. In this stage men are without fear of God, without reliance on God through the Son, and God does not dwell in such a heart. Matthew 17:5 pertains to the first command, "This is my beloved Son, with whom I am well pleased; listen to him," and also Isaiah 66:2, "Where will God dwell? in the contrite heart which trembles before my words."

The sixth stage is *despair,* and note moreover that the other side of this great sin is self-assurance. Despite their self-assurance Saul and Judas sink in despair. To combat these dreadful sins we should fear God, and in our fear look to *Jesus Christ,* and rely on him, believing that forgiveness is truly presented to us for the sake of the Mediator. In this faith the heart should feel comfort and joy in God, as we will amplify later.[2] Romans 10:11 speaks of this faith: "No one who trusts in the Lord will be put to shame." It is a sin for terrified hearts to remain in doubt, even though the papists teach that one should always doubt whether he is in grace. This is the blasphemous error which the blind bishops and monks in the Council of Trent have authorized.

The seventh stage is to set up or admit the validity of peculiar *worship services,* sacrifices, satisfactions, and monastic works, or to glorify such works as if they merited forgiveness of sins, as the monks teach with regard to their orders, the Mass, and so forth. This robs *Christ* of the glory that belongs only to his obedience.

The eight stage is *arrogance,* a reliance on one's own holiness, power, and sagacity, an attempt to exceed one's calling, trusting only in one's own power, as when Sennacherib undertook of himself to destroy Jerusalem, and Pompey hoped to subdue Julius.

2. See Article IX–XII.

The ninth stage is *impatience*, in misfortune to depart from God and become enraged against him. Saul is angry, and impatience drives him to pursue David and to slay the priests. Such rage breaks the first commandment, for we are required to be obedient to God in misfortune, as Peter says [1 Pet. 5:6], "Humble yourselves under the mighty hand of God"; *i.e.* humbly pray for patience in time of punishment and acknowledge that God is righteous. First Corinthians 10:10 enjoins, "You shall not murmur against God"; and Psalm 37 bids us to be subject to God and to hope that he will help us.

These stages are mentioned so that one may learn to reflect a little on all that is contained in this commandment. For although no angel and no man can fathom the depth of this commandment, in this life we must at least begin to do so.

The Second Commandment

"*You shall not take the name of your God in vain.*" Note that the *first* commandment speaks about understanding and the heart, and the *second* speaks about the tongue and speech. For God wishes to be acknowledged, and external speech is the manner in which this is done. With peculiar wisdom the words establish the negative; they forbid all misuse. In such statements the affirmative, or correct use, is implied.

Now this commandment is also beyond our power to grasp fully, but we must nevertheless make a start toward learning it. And note henceforth that in all the commandments the first is always included. Although this reminder may seem trifling, it is very necessary to remember that no work is pleasing to God unless fear of God and faith have previously come to the heart. Although Scipio [3] acted laudably in not touching the virgin who was engaged to another, but instead sent her back to her parents undefiled, this was not a divine service, for he was living in idolatry and did not acknowledge the Son of God.

And now to relate several stages of good works in this commandment:

The first stage: In true fear and faith to invoke God, as he himself has ordained and has taught, with knowledge and faith in the Mediator, the Son of God, as will be said in the section on invocation. [4]

The second stage: In true fear and faith to thank God, confessing that spiritual and physical gifts come of him, and are neither attained nor

3. See note, p. 67.
4. See Article XXXIII.

maintained through blind fortune or through our wisdom and power. Therefore the Lord says, Psalm 50:15, "Call on me in the day of trouble; I will deliver you, and you shall glorify me," *i.e.* give thanks to me and confess that I have helped you. And Christ says in John 15:5, "Without me you can do nothing," that is, nothing that is good and pleasing to God. If one is rescued from sin and punishment, it occurs through Christ.

The third stage: In fear and true faith rightly and purely to preach law and gospel, which is frequently commanded, Galatians 1:9, "If anyone preaches any other gospel to you, let him be accursed."

The fourth stage: In fear and in true faith, to confess true doctrine every time confession is demanded. Christ says, Matthew 10:32, "Everyone who acknowledges me before man, I will also acknowledge before my Father who is in heaven."

OATHS

Customarily and rightly oaths are placed among the works of the second commandment, and it is very important that people be instructed well with regard to them, for an oath is an important, serious, potent thing. We should know first of all that an oath intrinsically is an invocation of God in which we do two things: We represent him as a witness who is truthful and cannot lie, as he himself has said we should represent him in the confirmation of the truth, and he approves the truth and damns and punishes falsehood. Accordingly, in an oath we ask God as the punisher of falsehood to punish us in earnest if we are lying.

And because of divine righteousness and the order of things punishment inevitably follows the false oath, just as it follows homicide. God loves truth and hates falsehood, and for this reason he punishes the liar. But he punishes a perjurer even more severely because the perjurer insults God, who is *truthful*, by placing a lie before him for confirmation; the perjurer mocks God by insincerely asking for punishment. Such insult and mockery are extremely grave sins, for which punishment will be more severe, for God, who remains true, will indeed punish us, even as we have asked him to do, if our words are false.

What cannot here be said about oaths, for lack of space, the reader may find in other books, but I want one general rule to be remembered: *Juramentum non sit vinculum iniquitatis.* It is wrong to promise or to swear to commit sin. And if one has thus sworn, it is not a [true] oath, and it should not be kept. For example, Herod should not have killed John under the pretense of an oath.

SIN AGAINST THIS COMMANDMENT

If we place right use and misuse over against one another, we will have a means whereby to understand this commandment a little better. Therefore, let us note several stages of misuse.

In the first stage in the misuse of the divine name are all the blasphemies which are uttered or written by the Epicureans, who say that there is no God, that God is nothing; that God judges no one, helps no one, punishes no one; that God is a being imprisoned in physical nature, and, as the Stoics have said, that he can do nothing contrary to the order of nature. Having considered stages in our hearts and thoughts in connection with the first commandment, so now in connection with this second commandment let us consider stages of slanderous speeches and blasphemies. For these two commandments, the first and the second, are closely bound; out of good hearts proceed good speeches; out of evil hearts, evil speeches.

The second stage: All the false invocations which the heathen have made, and still do make, to their many idols and human images, even as the papists invoke departed saints. Likewise: the neglect of true invocation.

The third stage: All sorts of sorcery, invocation of devils, and pacts with the devils.

The fourth stage: All sorts of false doctrine, heretical errors, similar to what is seen among the Jews and Mohammedans and heretics like the Manicheans, Ebionites, Arians, and many papists and Anabaptists; and all sorts of apostasy or falsehood in our confessions of doctrine.

The fifth stage: All false invocation, by all the heathen, Jews, papists, monks, and others who, without true fear of God and without trust in Christ, pray in hypocrisy. A large part of mankind is included in this stage.

The sixth stage: All sorts of false oaths and perjury, for in the first place, the lies in themselves are an insult to God, and in the second place, God is further insulted by being asked to confirm the lies.

The seventh stage: All the deranged curses in which we beseech God to destroy other people, all those curses in which we mention the sufferings and wounds that Christ endured to win grace and blessedness for us, those curses in which we ask that Christ's marvelous obedience be used to serve our unrighteous anger in the desecration and condemnation of others. Such curses harbor multiple sins, not only because unrighteous anger and vindictiveness are intrinsically opposed to God, but also because such absurd curses insult Christ's suffering and obedience, which are meant to bring us solace and healing and for which we should always be thankful; but thus we would change them into swords for the murder of others. If we considered this frightful inversion of the sufferings of Christ and remembered that shaming the sufferings of Christ provokes God to wrath, our hearts would tremble before such curses.

The eighth stage: Neglect of thanksgiving. This sin is so common on earth that even the saints punish themselves because they do not more heartily and frequently offer thanks to God.

The ninth stage: All forms of self-praise in which we extol our own wisdom and power, as Ajax did in boasting that he did not need God's help for victory, as we do in murmuring against God in impatience, and as the Israelites did in saying that God would not lead them out of Egypt and that Moses was a deceiver.

The tenth stage: All false show, by which one pretends to honor God, but actually seeks for himself power, glory, money, pleasure, and status, as the Pope and many others do under the pretense of the office of preaching. Their arrogance, tyranny, and insatiable avarice make the office of preaching a cover for ignominy. In 2 Corinthians 2:17 *Paul* calls this "peddling God's word." The world is so full of this sophistry that horrible wars have been launched under the pretense of celebrating God's glory, when actually men were but seeking their own personal status or vengeance.

The eleventh stage: The scandal [*Ärgerniss*] connected with all evil works and things. The devils and evil men celebrate their victory against God as soon as they have accomplished some scandal, for many men follow evil examples. When lords are adulterers, then adultery among their servants is also common. Evil examples cause many people to keep fewer precepts and to pay less attention to God's anger. Seeing the great lords and doctors living in open sin and mocking religion, many people become more wanton and learn thus to mock religion. There is no doubt that evil examples prompt many serious vices.

I have given this crude introduction to indicate some of the important things that this commandment embraces, even though we cannot plumb its depths.

Let us note also that positive punishments are appended to both the first and second commandments, for law without punishment is empty talk, even though truly the principal punishment of sin is the eternally terrible anxiety, the pain, which accompanies it. This remains with all who are not rescued by faith in the Son of God.

However, specific punishments in this life are also decreed by God, and God himself is the one who punishes, as the text in Hebrews 12:29 says, "Our God is a consuming fire!" Through external punishments God wants us to realize that he is wise and righteous, draws a distinction between virtue and vice, and destroys everything that is contrary to his wisdom and purity. Physical punishments in this life are the beginning of eternal punishments for all who are not converted to the Lord Christ.

To the extent that the law speaks of physical punishments in this life and to the extent that they are the beginning of eternal punishments, to that extent the law includes eternal punishments; but the law says nothing about forgiveness out of grace, for the law is only a frightful judgment of God against our sin.

All men should be instructed and firmly believe that God, even in this life, fiercely punishes external disobedience with plagues, illness, poverty, hunger, war, disastrous government, and even adversity for our children, for the first commandment says that God will punish unto the third and fourth generation.

In a matter of such gravity it is wanton impertinence to dispute, saying, Why does God punish the children when the parents have sinned? Concerning such a question, let this be said: the gospel offers forgiveness of sins and grace to all. Whoever is converted to the Lord *Christ* has forgiveness of sins, and is blessed, for he is delivered from the wrath which the law proclaims. Yes, even physical punishments are alleviated. Where there is no conversion, then law, God's wrath, and physical and eternal punishment remain. And all the wisdom in men and devils is not enough to comprehend the enormity of striving against and despising God's wisdom and will. We cannot set limits for God, saying how far his punishment should extend, nor are we to frame impertinent questions; but rather we are to contemplate his righteous anger and tremble before his wrath. For he desires to dwell in the hearts of those who fear his words and believe on Christ our Lord.

The Third Commandment

"You shall keep the seventh day holy," and so on. The first commandment speaks of the heart; the second, of the tongue; and the third, of ceremony, that is, about the keeping of the office publicly ordained by God for preaching and for administering the sacraments. God wants all mankind to know him and the Savior, *Jesus Christ*, since for that purpose we were particularly created. Therefore, he wants his Church to be in the light and to be known as the place where his word is preached, and he wants public, honorable gatherings with preaching, invocation, thanksgiving, and the sacraments. It was for this reason that in Israel he set aside the seventh day; from the time of Adam the first fathers kept it as a day on which they put aside the work of their hands and met publicly for preaching, prayer, thanksgiving, and sacrifice, as God had ordered. When we speak of the Sabbath, then, we should understand it as referring to the keeping of the entire public office of preaching.

Very important doctrines are included in the word "Sabbath," but this third commandment chiefly means keeping a public office for preaching and for administering the sacraments. This meaning should not be deemed insignificant and childish, for we should know that public, honorable gatherings for preaching and administering the sacraments are extremely important for planting and maintaining true knowledge and invocation of God, good discipline, and peaceful government.

Because we were created not to live alone but to live with one another, some must instruct and others rule, and all must help one another; and, as it cannot be otherwise, public, honorable gatherings are necessary so that there especially people may come to understand that God has bound them together and to himself and wants to be the leader [Haupt] and the true protector of this miserably weak company and to be acknowledged by them. All this should diligently be considered, for it is comforting to know that God wants to maintain a visible Church and the public office of preaching. Consequently, he will not allow the devils, the Turks, and other tyrants completely to destroy his true churches, schools, and the houses and cottages of his followers. But we are not to disdain this commandment; the Church is not to destroy itself with false doctrine and idolatry, or stir up trouble with unnecessary wrangling, or in any way to forego true preaching and the sacraments, as unfortunately now often occurs.

And for the instruction of young people, let me explain a childish contention: "We have already been told that Levitical ceremonies have been abolished, and, inasmuch as the law of the Sabbath is a Levitical *caerimonia*, and inasmuch as St. Paul explicitly says, Colossians 2:16, 'Therefore, let no one judge you for not keeping the Sabbath,' why do you make so much of this commandment?"

The answer. In this commandment there are two parts, one general, which is always necessary for the Church, and one specific, which refers to a special day that pertains only to the government of Israel. The *general* part pertains to the true public office of preaching and the divine ceremonies which God commanded for all times. This general commandment is binding on all men, for all rational creatures, in accordance with the rank and vocation of each, are obliged to praise God by helping to maintain the office of preaching and public worship. But the *specific* part about the seventh day is not binding on us; therefore, we have gatherings on the first day, namely on Sunday, and on other days according to opportunity. And scholars know how to develop this further, for *general* in this commandment pertains to that which is moral and natural and permanent, namely the keeping of the Church's worship; and the *specific*, which points to the seventh day, pertains to ceremony.

To do good works in this commandment one should assist according to his rank, in true fear and faith, in the keeping of the office of preaching and public Christian gatherings; preachers should teach the gospel in its purest form, and maintain a true usage of the sacraments, and not interpolate false doctrine or untrue worship. Hearers should listen carefully, and learn to enjoy coming to public Christian gatherings where they may invoke God, give thanks, and receive the sacraments. Hearers should not withdraw unto themselves and cause others to withdraw from Christian gatherings, for the Lord Christ specifically promised in Matthew 18:20, "Where two or three are gathered together in my name, there am I in the midst of them," and the Psalms often say, "In a great congregation I will praise thee."

In addition, the hearers, and especially the rulers, should appoint true servants for the proper maintenance of the office of preaching, and they should protect and help them so that our youth may be reared in Christian doctrine and useful trades and good discipline. Rulers are especially commanded to do this work, for Isaiah 49:23 says, "Kings shall be your foster fathers, and their queens your nursing mothers." And the rulers and men who faithfully do these things will receive specific assistance and gifts, as the Lord *Christ* says, "Whoever gives to one of these little ones even a cup of cold water because he is a disciple, truly, I say to you, he shall not lose his reward" [Mt. 10:42]. And I could point to other fine examples, such as the widow of Zarephath, Obadiah, and others [*cf.* 1 Kings 17:8–16; 18:3–16].

SINS AGAINST THE THIRD COMMANDMENT

Sins against this third commandment include all sorts of contempt and destruction of the true office of preaching and of Christian gatherings.

The devils, Turks, and tyrants try openly to exterminate Christian gatherings; but heretics, and all sorts of false teachers and idolaters, papists, and others, are also destroyers of the true Church.

So do those who do not, or who seldom, gather for preaching and the administering of the sacraments. So do those who influence others by their bad example.

So do the Donatists, who produce unnecessary cleavages by saying that the office of preaching and the administering of the sacraments are invalid if the priests, even though they teach correctly, do not have praiseworthy habits or are otherwise unpleasing to them.

The Church is also destroyed by crude, beastly persons who rail at ministers and will not give them that which is prescribed by authority in laudable and approved regulations. On account of such robbers of the Church, God himself proclaims, in Haggai 1, that he will let the fruit of the fields rot, and will punish the people with famine, so long as they will not help with the necessary building of his Church. In summary, an understanding of this delightful commandment about the Sabbath is very important to our understanding about the Church and the office of preaching, of which it is necessary to say more later.

Still, let the reader diligently contemplate the teaching about the Sabbath in Genesis 2. After God created man, Adam and Eve, he created no new creature; he wanted this human creature to be the end, to be the crowning creature in whom he would have his rest, habitation, joy, and delight, to whom he would impart his wisdom, righteousness, and joy, and by whom he would be praised. And this would occur by the Son of God, who is the Word of the eternal Father, first revealing God through his external word, and at the same time working in the hearts of believers, so that the eternal Father and the Holy Spirit would dwell in believers who would then be the temples of God, and God would have joy in them and be praised by them. This was the Sabbath before the Fall. But even after the Fall the Sabbath was re-established when the gracious promise was given that there would be a second peace of God, that the Son of God would die and would rest in death until the Resurrection. So now in us our Sabbath should be such a dying and resurrection with the Son of God, so that God may again have his place of habitation, peace and joy in us, so that he may impart to us his wisdom, righteousness, and joy, so that through us God may again be praised eternally. Let this meaning of the Sabbath be further pondered by God-fearing men.

Of the Fourth Commandment

In Moses it is written that God commanded him to make *two* stone tablets on which God then wrote the Ten Commandments. This is significant, for the two tablets indicate a distinction among the commandments. The first three commandments speak of the true knowledge of God, how he reveals himself to us through his word, how he imparts to us his wisdom and knowledge, and how we must accept him, first and before all others. These three commandments constitute the first table; the following seven commandments constitute the second. . . . [They pertain to the social order and reflect God's nature.]

But the first must be included in all the commandments, so that God may be obeyed and honored as he has decreed. True knowledge of God comes in faith, fear, and trust. We must first know *Jesus Christ*, the Son of God, and receive forgiveness of our sins through him, before we are pleasing to God and become his dwelling place.

After this, obedience in the second table is highly pleasing to God, a divine service, for Christ says in Matthew 22:39, "The second commandment is like the first, you shall love your neighbor as yourself!" Note that Christ deems this social obedience of the second table so highly that he says, "These commandments are equally as high as the first and highest commandment." No angel and no man would dare to speak so if the Son of God had not himself thus spoken; but note that Christ wants the knowledge of God and the virtues embraced in the first table to come first and to burn in every heart. The tables are similar in that as God himself is, so are these commandments, beneficent, true, and pure; for he maintains an unalterable distinction between virtue and vice; and he truly wants rational creatures to be like him. The obligation to both tables is equal, for the second table becomes a divine service when done in obedience to the first commandment.

This should be contrasted to the open, cruel lies which the devils themselves spit out, so that through the Anabaptists they may cause more and greater confusions of the divine order. Just as in times past, Marcion, Manichaeus, and Tatian caused terrible immorality and tumult by condemning marriage, worldly authority, judgment [*Gericht*], and property, so the Anabaptists have caused even greater confusion in the orders of creation.

And let this be a constant maxim: All who condemn marriage, worldly government, judgment, or property owning are truly filled by the devil, and we should flee far from them. We will see that God also is against them, and that he maintains his order by publicly treading them to the floor, as we have seen in the case of Münzer and Pfeiffer [5] at Mühlhausen in Thuringia, and in John of Leyden [6] at Münster in Westphalia. The passage of Paul, Romans 13:2, stands fast: "Whoever resists authority is resisting what God has established, and will be punished."

The commandments in the second table are also given that we may learn the specific distinction between many virtues and vices and bear in mind the nature of God himself. For example, the fifth commandment, "You shall not kill," points to the distinction between goodness and tyranny, and testifies that God is good and righteous and wants to condemn no one without true cause. However, the devils are murderers and tyrants, for they provoked and drove Cain, Pharaoh, Saul, and Nero to unrighteous bloodshed, and continue to do the same to others now. The sixth commandment, "You shall not commit adultery," points to the distinction between chastity and immorality, certifies that God is pure and moral [keusch], and loves purity and has a profound wrath against all kinds of intercourse outside of marriage. But devils drive men to unchastity, incest, adultery, and unnatural lust — not that their nature, which is not flesh and blood, may have delight in lust or the sexual act, but that they may disgust God, and arouse God's wrath against men. The eighth commandment, "You shall not bear false testimony," shows the difference between truth and falsehood, and certifies that God is true and loves truth, and vents his wrath against falsehood. However, devils delight in lies, sophistries, and all sorts of deceit, in order to promote blasphemy and to create misery for men. They well know that lies are not useful to themselves, but they are useful for making strife among men more terrible.

So throughout the Ten Commandments we should consider, not just

5. Heinrich Pfeiffer was a radical Anabaptist preacher who helped Münzer gain control of Mühlhausen (see note, p. 83).

6. John of Leyden, or Jan Brockelson, and Jan Matthys were Anabaptist leaders who gained control of Münster by force and attempted to establish a model communal government. Matthys declared he was God's prophet and ruled by daily revelations, one of which sanctioned polygamy. When Matthys was killed in a sortie against the besieging army of the bishop of Münster, Brockelson had himself crowned king. Fanatical excesses of lust and cruelty followed, and many were executed. The town finally fell on June 25, 1535. Brockelson and others were fiendishly tortured to death and their bodies exhibited in cages on St. Lambert's steeple.

what *we should do*, but what *God himself is*, for he has set before us this mirror, namely the Ten Commandments, that we may learn of his nature and strive to be like him.

This fourth commandment reminds us that we owe obedience to our parents, of whose bodies and blood we have received our body and blood. But all creatures owe much more obedience to God because they were created by him, and have their being and lives from him. And just as parents have an inexpressibly great natural love toward their children, which has a special name στοργή; so God has an inexpressibly great love toward his only begotten Son, *Jesus Christ*, and toward *us*, poor creatures, who have refuge in *Christ*.

In this fourth commandment we should be able to see that God earnestly wants order and government instead of the kind of freedom in which everyone may exercise all his wantonness, as a wolf in the forest that runs wild and plunders and eats whatever he can overtake.

Now the corrupted nature in men is such that it would like to live freely, without God, without law, without any fear. One sees godless, wanton people, tyrants, Cyclops, and Centaurs living thus, and they give to this desolate existence the honorable name of freedom. But there is no freedom when there is no order, for then no man is secure from others. A wanton and malicious man might by sheer force deprive his neighbor of life or seize his neighbor's wife, or daughter, or property, as Cain did in murdering his brother, and Tarquinius in shaming Lucretia, and as Ahab did in taking Naboth's inheritance. Such disorder and unbridled living is not human freedom, but wolfish license; to call it "freedom" is to misuse a noble term, for freedom means an orderly use of one's own body and goods, by choice, in accordance with divine law and other true statutes. Note the speech which Cicero received from Crasso: *Legum servi sumus, ut liberi esse possimus, etc.* ["We are servants of the law so that we can be free."] In all of life and in the use we make of all creatures, the Ten Commandments, that is, the divine law, should be our bridle, should bind our hearts, mouths, hands and all our members, as God frequently has commanded, in Deuteronomy 4, "You shall heed the ordinances that I have commanded, that you may live!"

I have mentioned these things about the second table, even though all this is but a trifling and childish introduction, for it is impossible for any creatures fully to comprehend the exalted wisdom in any commandment.

But now let us briefly speak about the principal works embraced in this commandment. God establishes the order between rulers and subjects, and the beginning of all rule, by which man is to be guided, is the rule of father and mother. Then follow the overlords, who bear the sword, and schoolmasters, who, along with parents, by divine order and by command of the parents, should work for the maintenance of good discipline, virtue, and God's glory.

First, no matter how briefly we speak about the office of rulers, about father, mother, overlords, kings, and princes, and even of mayors and schoolmasters, one thing is very clear and obvious: All authority is first of all ordained of God especially to give voice to the Ten Commandments. And that this voice may not be ineffectual, father and mother and overlords should be God's servants and tools in punishing the disobedient for external vices. If they are lazy and will not punish, then God himself is the righteous judge, punisher, and executioner.

There are four very important reasons for physical punishment in this life.

The first: God is a wise and righteous being, who out of his goodness created rational creatures to be like him. Therefore, if they strive against the One who is the order of righteousness, he blots them out. The first reason for punishment, therefore, is the order of righteousness in God.

The second: the need to curb some men. If murderers, adulterers, robbers, and thieves remained in our midst, nobody would be safe.

The third: example. If some are punished, others will be reminded to consider God's wrath and to fear his punishment. And thus the source of punishment will be lessened.

The fourth: the importance of divine judgment and eternal punishment, which men will not escape if they are not converted to God. God's punishment now shows that he upholds a standard of virtue. He is a righteous Judge, and thus reminds us that after this life all sinners who are not converted to God will be punished.

So the first and foremost command for all potentates, fathers, mothers, and guardians is that they uphold divine law in the presence of their subjects and punish external trespasses with gravity. Overlords have power to make special laws that are conducive to peace; yet they are not to govern contrary to divine law. In the article about worldly authority more will be said about this office.

As for those who are ruled, obedience is commanded in the strongest terms, in the respect [*Ehrerbietung*] that goes with: "You shall honor your father and mother." Respect is the spring and beginning of true obedience, and respect includes these five things: (1) Knowledge of divine order and virtues in superiors, (2) humility in the heart, (3) external submission, (4) forbearance in the physical infirmity of a reigning prince, and (5) thanksgiving to God and prayer that he will establish good government.

The first stage of respect is a knowledge that divine wisdom did not ordain that we have a wolfish freedom, but that first of all we be bound to God. Out of his goodness, and not out of tyrannical caprice, he wishes that we be subject to him; for if we cling to him, he can impart to us his wisdom and goodness.

To draw us to himself, and to keep us, he revealed his law and doctrine, and established an order of authority. He maintains this order without which there can be no peace and welfare, as the Psalm 127:1 says, "Unless the Lord watches over the city, our watching is in vain."

The foundation of respect is the knowledge that God himself out of his exalted wisdom made and sustains this order, and is himself present in government, that he gives good counsel to the best sovereigns, and guides their hearts and hands in their vocation. In this knowledge one also knows that law and judgment are not expressions of tyranny, but, instead, of divine wisdom and righteousness.

The second stage of humility proceeds from the first. As we behold God in the ruling order, and know that this rule is not an expression of tyranny nor of wanton offense, but is instead divine wisdom and order, our hearts can humble themselves and esteem God in his wisdom and righteousness. Our hearts can surrender themselves and love these great gifts and the Lord. And we can also love the tools, the men who are in the government, through whom God gives peaceful, disciplined existence and life. For example, when a God-fearing man in Israel beheld David, his heart could rejoice that God in the miracle of Goliath's death and in other ways gave testimony that he would maintain the government, and for this gift he could thank God and at the same time could have a sincerely good attitude toward David. This first stage of respect, then, is knowledge of divine wisdom and humility.

The third stage of respect is external submission, which even the heathen understand. But, about the first stage they know nothing, for it comes through the Church. And external submission means doing with one's body and possessions what parents or authorities command, if it is possible and not contrary to divine law.

The fourth stage is patience with regard to physical infirmities in parents and in rulers. The weakness of human nature and impediments, well placed by the devils, make it impossible for any government in this life to be entirely pure and wholly wise and virtuous. Respecting this, Solomon says: There is no one on earth so righteous, even though he does much good, who does not also commit sins and cause harm. For example, David was a very beneficial ruler, but he committed sins and caused harm with his adultery and murder, and with his impertinence when he counted the people. Cyrus was highly praised, even long before his birth, and did become a holy king; he conducted great wars, and he finally set the Jews free. But he committed a great piece of folly in an unnecessary march [*Zuge*], when he was captured and lost a great people.

Now we might ask, since all rulers are vulnerable and often act unjustly because of indolence, and so forth, how can any ruler have a good conscience? Are not they all tyrants? Here we need to recognize that a tyrant is a ruler whose evil will and design is wantonly to do injustice to his people, even though at times he does some good. Caligula and Nero were tyrants, for their will and design was wantonly and continually to do injustice to the people, and they acted unjustly more frequently than otherwise. God has condemned such rulers, and they will be judged by these commands: "You shall not kill; you shall not commit adultery; you shall not steal." Divine commandments are binding on all rational creatures, kings, princes, and subjects, just as Isaiah 3:14 and others often say, "The Lord enters into judgment with the elders and princes of his people." Ezekiel 34:10: "You shepherds, hear the word of the Lord: Thus says the Lord, I myself will punish the shepherds, and will require my sheep at their hands, and will make an end of them, so that they shall no longer be shepherds."

Also in this life this rule is frequently demonstrated: "All who take the sword will with the sword perish." To take the sword without the command of true law is to resort to one's own wantonness. We see from experience that slayers do not escape the sword. And tyrannical kings and princes are usually reduced, through wars or otherwise. Apryes,[7] the mighty king of Egypt, killed the prophet Jeremiah. But afterward this proud king was captured in a battle, and later hanged. Phokas killed the emperor Mauricium; but afterward Piscus and Heraklius captured him and had him run through. History is full of such examples. Now and then, punishment falls on the children. Herod drove away his own sons,

---

7. Pharaoh-hophra of Egypt (588–569 B.C.) sought to divert the Chaldeans, who were besieging Jerusalem, 588–586 B.C. (*cf.* Jer. 37:5–10; Ezek. 17:15; 2 Kings 25:1–7). According to tradition Jeremiah was killed by Jewish exiles who forced him to flee to Egypt.

and even killed some with his sword. David's punishment fell on his sons, and he himself was driven out; but God used him as an example to indicate that he would mitigate the punishment of those who turn and call upon him, for as the prophet says: "In anger God remembers mercy" [cf. Ps. 78:38; Is. 12:1, 48:9].

On the other hand, they are not tyrants but qualified rulers if they will and intend to do rightly, and in a majority of cases do it, although they may occasionally, because of human weakness, thoughtlessly, but not wantonly, neglect justice or fall into sin. This definition is grounded on two passages: St. Paul says, "God requires us to be true" [cf. Rom. 2:12–16]; that is, that we have both the will and the intention of rightly conducting our office, and of learning to do with industry whatever is necessary. Even though men like David, Hezekiah, and Josiah have a strong will to act rightly and to do useful work, they often make false steps and the devil adds many obstacles. "There is none on earth so righteous, even though he does much good, that he is not also sinful" [cf. Ps. 14:1-3; Rom. 3:10; 1 Pet. 4:17-18].

On account of previous sin, governments experience periods of unrest and, like the weather, are unstable. Hezekiah had no such victories as David, and even though God manifested his wonderful help, Hezekiah's enemies wrought great devastation in the land. But true rulers can with good conscience hold office. To the degree that they have true faith in God, and acknowledge and invoke the Lord Jesus Christ, they please God and are heirs of eternal salvation. Such were David, Jehosophat, Hezekiah, Josiah, Constantine, and Theodosius. For the good of the Church God occasionally gives such pious sovereigns, who are particularly gracious tools, through whom God again quickens the land, relieves it of the burdens of robbery and extortion, and again establishes discipline, justice, fear of punishments, virtue, the Church, and true doctrine.

The *patience* to bear the frailties of rulers is very necessary in the fourth stage of respect. To maintain peace and to alleviate whatever you can through your vocation is to recognize that God is the source of all government, that he will not suffer man to fall into complete ruin, and that for this reason he will give good government to some. But in doing so he also punishes our sins, for governments are not always equally orderly and smooth.

Compassionate patience in suffering is both wisdom and virtue. When Noah lay uncovered, his son Ham wantonly mocked him, and today young people often mock infirmities in true rulers, and by talking about them, they poison people against rulers and cause tumult. In our time this is very common. In Proverbs 16 Solomon speaks about such poison-bearing people, and says that slanderers create schisms among princes. The reviling of those in authority is expressly forbidden in Exodus 22:28, "You shall not curse a ruler of your people." This is spoken of tolerable rulers, not of the bloodhounds and tyrants, of which more is said later.

The fifth stage of respect is prayer, in which we should thank God for the laws through which he imparts to us his wisdom and establishes external discipline in governmental rule, and in which we should earnestly beseech him to be with us, to watch over us with his holy angels, to drive away the devils, and graciously to give peace, counsel, and strength to our rulers. It is comforting to know within our hearts that orderly governments are God's work and gifts, to thank him for them, to praise his wisdom and righteousness, and at the same time ask him graciously to impart to us these his gifts continually. Moses prays: "Ah, Lord God, if you yourself will not go before us, then lead us not away," and God says that he will travel along with him.

These five stages are included in the word "respect" [*Ehrerbietung*], but this is merely an introduction and a basis for reminiscence about a wisdom that far exceeds man's comprehension.

GOOD WORKS IN THE FOURTH COMMANDMENT

The following good works pertain to this commandment:

First, parents, schoolteachers, sovereign authorities, and all rulers, high or low, in true knowledge of God and of the Lord Jesus Christ, in fear of God and in faith, should love those subject to them, charge and rule them with this table of the Ten Commandments, and punish external disobedience, each one after his calling. They should protect the obedient, and help them to maintain body and life, reputation and profession—all to the end that they may know God, be in his true Church, and praise him in eternity. That they may call on God, let each one truly serve in his calling, and grasp not at a foreign vocation, nor make an obstacle for others and a confusion of order. In 1 Thessalonians 4:11, *St. Paul* charges the brethren "to aspire to live quietly, to mind your own affairs, and to work with your hands."

And children, students, and subjects, of high or low status, in true knowledge, reverence, and faith, should love and esteem their fathers and mothers, schoolteachers, and the persons who provide good government, law, and justice, as if all were by divine wisdom ordained. They should be obedient to them in externally commanded works, each in his order, after his calling and station. They should thank God for good government, and heartily beseech him to be the father of every house and to be present in all government.

Each one should understand his calling and his office, and truly serve therein, and should not grasp after a foreign calling, thereby causing dissensions, tumult, hate, homicide, and destructions.

In general, the gratitude of all is embraced in this commandment. One who helps another in distress acts as a father or mother. But what is gratitude, and why should one who has been helped give thanks?

These are extraordinary questions; for the virtue which one calls "gratitude" is itself extraordinary and not well known.

Gratitude [*Dankbarkeit*] is a virtue which comprises two other important virtues: truth and justice [*Gerechtigkeit*]. First, there is the truth that we confess with our hearts and mouths when we speak of whom we have received help, when we are not proud and do not boast that we have ourselves with our own wisdom or our own strength done so and so. Second, there is justice, for in gratitude we behold our special obligations to the benefactor and feel that we must return as we have received. By divine wisdom justice is an ordained equality of exchange. Buyers and sellers should maintain such equality, and others also, for men could not live with one another if one part only took and devoured and the other part only gave and suffered. Rational men know well that justice is of this nature. To preserve the equality of justice, God ordained that truth in rulers be matched with truth, and benefit with benefit. Solomon speaks of ingratitude, saying [*cf.* Prov. 17:13], "From the house of the ungrateful, misfortune will not depart." The curses in Deuteronomy 27, where the ingratitude of children to parents is mentioned, are also based on this sense of justice.

To be grateful is to practice truth and justice, and from this it is easy to understand why God taught and commanded gratitude.

First, with regard to truth, it is obvious that God is truthful, and exhibits great wrath against lies. Therefore, we are to confess of whom we have received benefit; God is angered if we boast that we have helped ourselves, for such boasting contains two vices which God cannot suffer — lying and arrogance, which occur when we elevate ourselves, and in false pride make ourselves great.

Further, God wishes us to practice this confession that we may also know him and be grateful to him; that we may through confession realize that we truly have and receive life, wisdom, nourishment, his word, help and protection, grace and eternal blessedness from him, and that we are not wonderful magnates and squires who do not need God. In summary, the practice of gratitude should point us to God, for in giving thanks we confess that he is our Helper and Savior.

Second, this may be noted about justice or equality of exchange: God himself rewards good with good, and sin with destruction. Thus he keeps equality. He hates sin, whether in David or in Saul. Yet he will forgive all who turn and seek refuge in the Lord Christ. He will graciously receive, hallow, and bless them, Manassah the same as Hezekiah, Paul the same as John the Baptist. God thus teaches us that justice is a stabilized equality, so that we may know that he himself is not tyrannical, but carefully equates gifts and punishments. Therefore he has ordained equality of exchange in buying and selling, in borrowing and repaying, in wrong-doing and punishing, that we may be reminded of what he is like. Men cannot live if orderly justice is not maintained, benefit given for benefit, punishment for vice, etc.

Gratitude includes justice: equality should prevail, and benefit with benefit be recompensed, even though external gifts of recompense cannot always be equal. Joseph's brothers could not give to Joseph the same goods which he gave to them. Nevertheless, in truth they acknowledged him from whom they received benefits, and in their hearts they felt love for Joseph and knew they should manifest external kindness.

Gratitude is seriously commanded by God. Thus we may learn through practice to manifest and confess to God that we have received many goods from him, some directly, some indirectly; that afterward our hearts may be bound to him in service.

SINS AGAINST THIS COMMANDMENT

First, the gross sins in all rulers, fathers, mothers, schoolteachers, authorities, and princes are relaxation of necessary works in one's vocation, as when parents do not provide small children with food and physical necessities, do not impart a knowledge of God, and do not punish for vices. Lack of diligence often prevails in schools, both in teaching and in discipline. Government authorities often fail to do what is necessary to maintain right teaching and good discipline and to insure justice and protection for the oppressed. On the other hand, they often introduce obvious tyranny, such as insufferable taxes and plundering of the land. As it is true that leaders are divinely established to protect their people and their lands, it is also true that divine command obliges subjects to give rents and interest to their overlord according to their means. Nevertheless, rulers should observe John's preaching: "Let each of you be satisfied in your wages, and do no one an injustice with lies or out of spite" [*cf.* Lk. 3:14]. Rulers should consider the story of God's judgment in the case of Naboth and know that God maintains a rule for great kings and princes: "Alas for the robber, for he will in turn be robbed" [*cf.* Is. 33:1].

Sins against this commandment include all the designs and disquietude of one who steps outside his calling to seize another office, and of those who cause disturbances, war, and destruction. Alcibiades could not rest: he practiced mean tricks against neighboring rulers for such a long time that Athens and he himself became nothing.

Second, for subjects the great sins against this commandment are: disobedience of children against parents or schoolteachers; any kind of misdeed which causes sorrow in the hearts of parents: disobedience against orderly government and tolerable authority: public tumult in which subjects, many or few, draw swords against the proper authorities, and defying true order, undertake to make themselves a new government and to blot out orderly authorities. Absalom marched against his father, and a few years ago Thomas Münzer, a preacher at Mülhausen in Thuringia, mustered poor people on the field of battle to expel or kill the princes, counts, and lords, and to make a new government. Later the Anabaptists at Münster perpetrated even more gruesome misdeeds; and Thomas Münzer and the self-styled king at Münster [8] were finally and justly punished. Later generations should note these and similar examples, and should bear in mind that God cannot suffer tumult; in times of great distress they should purify the Church.

Rebellious tongues only bring injury and create disdain of authority, from which disturbances in government arise.

All the unkindness married people practice against one another, or that brothers and sisters and other blood relations carry out against one another are usually included among the gross sins against this commandment. An example would be the hate of Esau for his brother Jacob. All the ingratitude which is manifested in so many men: one man helps another to escape the gallows, and his thanks is to be brought to the gallows himself! Examples abound. The high priest Jehoiada saved the life of young Joash and preserved his kingdom [*cf.* 2 Kings 11, 2 Chron. 23]; but afterward Joash killed Jehoiada's son, Zechariah [*cf.* 2 Chron.

8. John of Leyden, or Jan Brockelson (see note, p. 100).

24:20–22]. Simon Maccabaeus was overcome by his daughter's husband, Ptolemaus, to whom he had given land and goods [cf. 1 Mac. 13–16]. Dion was overcome by Kalippus, whom he had raised out of poverty to great authority, Kalippus later being killed by the same sword with which he murdered his lord Dion. Julius spared Cassius' life, and restored him as one of the great lords. But afterward Cassius was chief among those who plotted Julius' ruthless murder. However, Cassius received fitting payment for his ingratitude; he killed himself, using the same sword with which he had previously stabbed Julius.

Many ungrateful men are strangely punished in God's providential ways.

A rich promise is attached to this fourth commandment, for obedience brings reward, just as disobedience brings punishment and destruction. If punishment did not follow disobedience, the law would be empty. However, I will say more in general about rewards and punishments at the end of this discussion.[9]

The Fifth Commandment: You Shall Not Kill

We pointed out above that these divine laws are the eternal immutable wisdom and righteousness in God, and we said that men should conform to this divine wisdom and righteousness with mind and heart and all the powers of their being. Our Lord Christ explains that commandments pertain to the heart as well as to external works. An example is this commandment to Saul: "You shall love your faithful servant David; your heart shall not burn with hate and envy against him" [paraphrase, cf. 1 Sam. 17–31].

I will not append a long explanation here, but it is necessary to remember that this commandment, "You shall not kill," signifies that we shall not kill another person out of anger, hate, or envy. It does not forbid all killing. God himself established a definite order, wherein he maintains moral equality [Gleichheit]; he ordained authorities, tribunals, and penalties, and commanded the authorities to kill blasphemers, murderers, sorcerers, adulterers, and others defiled with incest. Through these punishments he wants us to know that there is a difference between virtue and vice, that he is righteous, and that he will destroy and blot out the unrighteous. Men could not live in community if murderers, robbers, and ruffians were not restrained.

9. See below, pp. 122–28.

God's wisdom and righteousness ordained the authorities and tribunals through which public wrongdoers, in the due process of law, may be subjected to death; and God maintains this order by powerfully sustaining and strengthening the authorities, tribunals, and penalties. And if the authorities are too weak, he punishes directly, as Sodom, Pharaoh, Saul, David, and many hundreds of thousands were directly punished, temporally and eternally, through divine wrath.

Therefore, we should make a distinction between the office of authority and this commandment: it means that those who are without divine command shall not kill anybody. Nevertheless, even though their office entitles the authorities to kill, this power is limited.

God says, "Vengeance is mine; I will repay!" God carries out punishment both directly, as in the case of Sodom and Pharaoh, and indirectly, or through the authorities, as when he punished Catilina,[10] through the council at Rome, or when he punished the filth of Antony and Cleopatra through Augustus. Let it be known, then, that divine vengeance and punishment pertain to the office of authority, but God says, "Vengeance is mine."

Here, moreover, we should note that the commandments are worded so as to forbid evil deeds, because *oratio negativa* or *prohibitiva*, a prohibition, extends further than *oratio adfirmativa*, a permissive statement. Whenever vice is forbidden, by contrast, virtue is commanded.

And there are virtues or good works in this commandment: righteousness, that is, a maintenance of equality with one's neighbor by not injuring his person, wife, children, rank, or profession. All this is included in, "You shall love your neighbor as yourself," for God created men for communal living, that together they might acknowledge and praise him. As numbers in a series are mutually dependent, so are men for the sake of the whole. And righteousness and mercy are commanded, particularly toward pious men who might need help.

To have mercy is to feel the pain of another's misery, especially the misery of pious or misled men, and in the spirit of that feeling [*aus ziemlichen Ursachen*] to mitigate the punishments by giving them aid. David and Julius were merciful when they showed consideration to citizens who had been compelled or misled into opposing them.

God is this way. He is righteous. If we were without sin, he would heartily love us all equally, and give to us all a happy life now, and in the

---

10. Lucius Sergius Catilina (108?–62 B.C.), a Roman patrician who perpetrated numerous crimes.

next world, eternal blessedness. But he is also merciful, for as long as we are deceived by the devil, our misery moves God to compassion, and he helps us through his Son. He restores to life all who accept the Son, and he daily mitigates many punishments.

On the other hand, there are gross sins and vices against this commandment, for example, the unrighteousness of injuring or craving to injure men. Such unrighteousness is manifested in homicide, physical violence, envy, unrighteous wrath, and hate, and also in mercilessness, as in the case of the man who wanted his servant killed simply because he had broken a beautiful glass.

Such unrighteousness is also seen in joy and mockery when pious men are in misery, as Shimei's mocking when David was driven from the town [2 Sam. 16].

The Sixth Commandment: You Shall Not Commit Adultery

Here adultery is forbidden; therefore, we must know what marriage is, for in forbidding all extramarital sexual intercourse this commandment sanctions marriage. Here we must remember the rule that virtue is commanded in the prohibition of vice.

Marriage is a natural, inseparable union of only two persons, one husband and one wife, for whom God has not forbidden coition, for he thus ordained reproduction to avert impurity.

God revealed his will in this order of creation. He created man and wife, and he wants mankind to procreate continually until the resurrection. But men are not to run about like beasts that know no difference between chastity and unchastity [*Keuschheit und Unkeuschheit*]. God is a pure, chaste, orderly being, and wants us to acknowledge him as such; and while we cannot see him physically and may not embrace him physically, he nevertheless wants us to keep him in our hearts as a pure, chaste, orderly being and to distinguish him from all irrational, unprincipled, impure natures, from beasts, from devils, and from men. This virtue, this chastity, constitutes a very clear, evident distinction between God and the devils. We should diligently consider all this, not only to recognize the virtue of "chastity," but also to discover how, when, and why God ordained it. And because he is a pure, chaste being who hates all lewdness in the devils and in men, so we in our prayers should consider and address God as a wise, omnipotent, true, good, just, chaste, pure, and independent being.

The distinction between chastity and unchastity is revealed in the very beginning in Paradise, when God says, "The two shall be one flesh" [1 Cor. 6:16], *i.e.* only a single man and a single woman should be joined together for reproduction, and they should be inseparable. In these words the institution of marriage is established, all extramarital intercourse is prohibited. If a single man and a single woman are to be inseparably joined, it follows obviously that they should not stray about, neither man nor wife. Adam and Eve clearly understood this serious divine word, and recognized therein God's wisdom, and afterward preached it to their children.

Plainly this understanding is germane to the commandment, "You shall not commit adultery." For although these words are brief, they are nevertheless to be understood as God himself has so often explained them. That marriage is pleasing to God is clear from sentences in Genesis 2 and from statements of our Lord in Matthew 18 and 1 Corinthians 7. That all extramarital intercourse is forbidden by God and is a deadly sin is clear from Leviticus 18, and from the words of St. Paul in 1 Corinthians 6 and Galatians 5: "Who acts thus will not inherit the kingdom of God." In these and similar words God has explained this sixth commandment, and he has indicated his earnest will in the terrible punishment visited on Sodom, Canaan, Benjamin, and David. These are set before us so that we may recognize that God's wrath, in the form of temporary and eternal punishment, shall fall on all who are lewd if they remain unreconciled to God.

God himself establishes this rule in Leviticus 18: "Do not practice the abominations of the Canaanites; for if you practice such iniquity, the land will vomit you out, as it vomited out the Canaanites" [*cf.* v. 24–30]. God keeps this rule. His punishments prove his anger against lewdness, as history and daily experience show, and there is no doubt but that great empires, kingdoms, and cities have been destroyed on account of idolatry, tyranny, and lewdness. For these reasons the Canaanites were blotted out; the empires of Egypt, Syria, and Macedonia, changed; the cities of Troy, Thebes, and Sparta, destroyed. These sins account for the devastation that the Turks have wrought, and still do, from Syria all the way to Germany.[11] We should look to our own lives for the sources of our

11. Early in the sixteenth century the Turks had expanded into Asia Minor, Persia, and Egypt. Suleiman the Magnificent besieged Vienna in 1529, took Hungary in 1541, and vied with Charles V of Spain for control of the Mediterranean. He dominated a huge crescent of territory from Algeria to Hungary. Melanchthon and other reformers regarded the advances of the Moslem Turks with great concern.

particular misfortune in our own generation and children, for God commonly maintains the rule which is written in the Book of Wisdom, "As one sins, so shall he be punished" [cf. Wisd. of Sol. 3:10, 11:16, 12:23]. Therefore, it follows that the unrighteous use of one's seed will be punished in the seed, that is, in one's children. *Peccata in semine puniuntur in semine*, as was the case with David, whose children committed murder and rebellion.

Worldly authorities are earnestly to punish adultery and incest; if they are lax, and allow it, God himself punishes, as he did at Sodom, at the same time removing both the evildoer and the authorities.

This pertains to temporal punishments which come from external sins, but we should know that sins include not only external lewd acts, but also inordinate lusts in the heart, as explained in connection with this commandment in Matthew 5. So let each of us look into his own heart, and see how beastly and inconstant the heart is, how it vacillates with love and flames of lust. We should recognize our weakness, and turning to *Jesus Christ* for grace, we should ask him to forgive us our weakness and uncleanness, and guide us with his Holy Spirit.

GOOD WORKS ACCORDING TO THIS COMMANDMENT

The foundation for all good works is a true knowledge of God and faith in Christ. When the heart is turned to God, when true reverence and faith enlighten the heart, when sin does not plague the conscience, then marriage and the bond of marriage are truly works pleasing to God. And the heart is not to follow inordinate passions into adultery, but is earnestly to resist them, and to lead a sober life.

Such matrimony is also chastity. For living in matrimony in accordance with God's commandment is chastity; or, to put it another way, chastity is shunning all extramarital relations and resisting inordinate passions. Thus Adam and Eve, Abraham and Sarah, Isaac and Rebecca, and Zechariah and Elizabeth were chaste married couples and pleasing to God, as many thousands of married couples have been.

The second stage of good works in this commandment is to live unspotted outside of matrimony, that is, to avoid all forbidden sexual intercourse and to resist inordinate passions. This is possible for children and youth who still do not feel strong lust, and also for elderly people; but not all men in the years between are able to live unspotted outside of matrimony, only those who have a special divine gift for it, like John the Baptist, or Mary, the mother of Jesus, or the widow Hannah.

To maintain this gift, one should avoid even the occasion for sins, and should live soberly, in prayer and in contemplation of divine doctrine.

SINS AGAINST THE SIXTH COMMANDMENT

All extramarital intercourse is a mortal sin against this commandment. So also are all inordinate passions and lusts; all unattractiveness through gorging and swilling, associations, lewd speech, gestures, grimaces, and so forth.

The Seventh Commandment: You Shall Not Steal

Note how beautifully God has regulated men and political society. Note also that God is as he makes himself known in his law: the fullness of wisdom, goodness, truth, righteousness, and purity.

In the first table he speaks of the highest wisdom, of true knowledge and invocation of God.

In the second table he first speaks of regents, father and mother, and their authorities.

And after that he gives us regulations as to how we should live with one another. First we are to be just, to kill no one, for it would not be possible to live together if we devoured one another at will.

And from this it follows that we should be chaste, that order should prevail in the estate of matrimony, for God himself is a pure being who loves purity.

Now in this life we must have food and drink, shelter and clothing, and the seventh commandment provides a basis for such physical needs; and note once more that a prohibition points to something already ordained. *Prohibitio significat, aliquid ordinatum antecedere.* Because stealing is forbidden, possession of property must be pleasing to God.

Therefore, let us learn from this commandment that God himself has established ownership of property and reasonable laws to regulate it. It is comforting to know that the laws by which we live and have property are pleasing to God, for then a believing man can work with a clear conscience to maintain himself in such an order, and can invoke God's blessings and aid. For it is truly a part of God's order for us to have food and drink and shelter in this life.

Note this in reference to the devilish Anabaptists. They argue that all goods must be held in common and boast that it is a mark of great holiness to break up property. Such contention attracts many evil men who, instead of working, intend only to live in debauchery and to exercise lewdness, as happened at Münster. Against such madness one should consider and uphold the beautiful wisdom contained in this commandment.

Because possession of property is right and pleasing to God, about which more will be said later,[12] God erects a strong wall around each householder for the sake of his shelter and goods, namely this his law, "You shall not steal." Our hearts and hands should not desire another's goods nor acquire them, except as God has ordained an exchange by agreement and equal payment. In this life we need various things, and God gives to one the fruits of the earth, to another, wool and cloth. Therefore, to facilitate exchange, God himself ordained contracts, buying, and selling. He desires us to use these means to preserve equality, for otherwise we would soon consume one another. Thus he would have us remember that justice is equality [*Gerechtigkeit Gleichheit ist*], and that God is just; he himself hates sin, yet he is merciful to all who take refuge in the Lord Christ. He wishes us to maintain equality [*Gleichheit*] among ourselves, according to his divine order; the strong should not trample the weak, nor encumber them only to boast, as Saul sought to crush David, who had served him faithfully.

And with this wall, namely this commandment, "You shall not steal," which is more than mere words, God ordained authority, the tribunal, and punishments. And although the authorities often do not punish, and themselves become thieves and robbers, God, who is a righteous Judge and Executioner, dispossesses them, and takes from thieves and robbers the goods they unjustly acquire. Accordingly, Isaiah says, "Woe to the robber, for he will also be robbed" [*cf.* 3:11, 33:1].

GOOD WORKS IN THIS COMMANDMENT

If knowledge of God, fear of God, and true faith are in the heart, and a good conscience prevails, then to have and to use property in an orderly fashion is work truly pleasing to God; and our hearts should thank God, and beseech his further blessings, that we might help those in need.

The second stage of good works in this commandment is to maintain equality in buying and selling, renting, and so forth, instead of seeking unjust gain by fraud, pressure, usury, theft, or robbery. To honor God we should willingly maintain equality in all buying and selling, remembering that God is just, and wishes us to be just toward one another.

12. See below, pp. 116-18.

The third stage is to let our hearts and hands, to the extent of our capacity, practice generosity toward the Church, and toward the poor, for God is good and generous, and wishes us to be likewise. And this generosity should be as Solomon says, "You are to let others come to your springs and rivulets, but you should remain master over them." [13] Let us give of the fruits of our possessions, but maintain our houses and fields. God's earnest divine commands and gracious promises have often touched on the generosity which we are to practice in obedience and faith; as in Luke 6:38, "Give, and it will be given you."

The fourth stage lies in not squandering our substance in carousing and idle display, but in maintaining and properly using it as God's gift. For Solomon thus speaks, "You must not give your substance to aliens nor to those who are unmerciful." [14] That is, evil companions help us to waste our possessions, and they mock us when we are reduced to poverty. Thus three virtues are given in this commandment, *justitia, beneficentia, et parsimonia:* justice, generosity, and economy.

SINS AGAINST THIS COMMANDMENT

The first stage: Willfully acquiring alien goods by robbery, fraud, undue pressure, or usury. It also pertains to an unequal exchange in buying, selling, loaning, and renting.

The second stage: Not giving suitable help in times of common necessity, to the Church, to friends in need, and to those who are poor.

The third stage: Wasting one's goods in useless pleasure and luxury, so that one's own children or countrymen are injured. This includes three vices, *injustitia, sordes, et prodigalitas;* injustice, stinginess, and wastefulness.

The fourth stage: Not thanking God for a reasonable amount of this world's goods, but avariciously coveting and continually scheming to seize more for oneself.

Divine commands such as, "You shall not kill," and, "You shall not commit adultery," are binding on all men. And this commandment is no exception; "You shall not steal" binds all men, kings, princes, lords, subjects, husbands, wives, young and old. "Cursed be everyone who does not abide by all things written in the law" [Gal. 3:10]; and Isaiah declares, in the third chapter, "God will enter into judgment with the great princes" [*cf.* v. 14], and in Ezekiel 34, the Lord says, "Alas for you

---

13. Source uncertain; *cf.* Prov. 3:27; 5:15–17; 21:13, 20; 22:9.
14. Source uncertain; *cf.* Prov. 1:10–16, 26, 27.

shepherds in Israel; because you yourselves rob and oppress my sheep, I will get rid of you" [*cf.* v. 1-10].

John says, "Be content with your wages" [Lk. 3:14.]. These and many other passages clearly indicate that subjects may also have property, and that subjects are not to seize their master's goods, nor are the lords to deprive the subjects of their property. An example that should be noted is the case of Ahab and the vineyard of Naboth.

The Eighth Commandment: You Shall Not Bear False Witness

To maintain life, safeguard marriage, and protect possessions, courts of justice and penalties are necessary. This commandment pertains to courts of justice, for in these short words, "You shall not bear false witness," everything is contained that is necessary to true judgment.

But again, two things should be stressed. The first is that a prohibition implies that the opposite is commanded; in this case, truth. If one is forbidden to lie, the implication is that truth is commended, and also, by contrast, that truth is right and pleasing to God.

The second thing to remember is that God himself ordains truth, which implies that God is true and steadfast, even as Christ our Lord says, "He who sent me is true" [Jn. 8:26]. And truth is the virtue of understanding a thing as it is, speaking of it as it is, giving it its intended meaning, and avoiding discrepancies in word, thought, and deed. This explanation is based on the words of our Lord in Matthew 5:37, "Let what you say be simply 'Yes' or 'No.' "

The virtue of truth is highly acceptable to God; for he understands everything just as it is, speaks thus of it, and varies not. God says, in Malachi 3:6, "I am the Lord, and I do not change." We are not to doubt his words. God's earnest wish is that truth prevail in angels and men. The evil angels fell from truth, however, and their distinctive mark is that they are deceitful; they have a passion for lying, first with regard to God, and then with regard to other things. Devils have filled the world with idolatry; they have impelled blind men to call God that which is not God, and to keep as right that which is not right, such as sundry kinds of lewdness, sacrifices to the dead, and the persecution of Christians who confess the true God.

Inasmuch as this commandment speaks of truth and falsehood, any rational person can easily discern that it includes a great part of human life: it embraces courts of justice, accusations, responses, testimonies, motives, and the promises one finds in convenants of buying, selling, lending, and renting. In governing this pertains to judging or not judging rightly and in education, to teaching rightly or not teaching rightly. In general speech this pertains to praising and blaming others truthfully, to inventing lies about them, and to twisting what they say. The scope of these matters is so wide that no man on earth can fully comprehend this commandment; nevertheless, one can think about it, and learn to recognize and shun the grosser transgressions of it.

As a full explanation of this commandment would be too long, I pray only that everyone will consider what this commandment says about truth, how great a virtue it is in God and men, and how necessary. For how can one man deal with another if there is no truth, if promises are not kept, if false reports are given within and without the court? Here one may clearly discern that God is earnestly opposed to lies and deceit, and will punish them.

In Deuteronomy 19:16 ff. God has commanded that anyone who gives untrue testimony that jeopardizes a man's life shall be put to death.

Proverbs 12:22 says, "Lying lips are an abomination to the Lord."

And a passage in Proverbs 19:9 declares that "A false witness will not go unpunished, and he who utters lies will perish."

Zechariah 8:16 f. says, "Speak the truth to one another . . . do not devise evil in your hearts against one another, and love no false oath, for all these things I hate, says the Lord."

GOOD WORKS IN THIS COMMANDMENT

If in your heart there is the right knowledge and fear of God and faith in our Lord, then the works enjoined in this commandment are good and pleasing to God. This would include observing truthfulness instead of deceit or sophistry in testimonies, judgments, accusations, responses, opinions, counsel, promises, reports, instruction in education, and in speaking of virtue or vice in other people. In this world there are many kinds of sophistry, underhanded machinations and practices. The Thracians agreed to a thirty-day truce, but by night they unexpectedly attacked the enemy, saying that the agreement pertained only to days. Such owlish trickery is very common in law courts and diplomacy.

The second level of good works here is to speak truthfully about the virtues or vices of others rather than willfully to repeat rumors and maliciously twist certain things. The Pharisees put a malicious interpretation on Christ's eating with the tax collector [cf. Mt. 9:9–13; Lk. 5:27–32;

15:1–2; 7:34]. Concerning such suspicious and unfounded interpretations the Lord says, "Judge not, that you be not judged" [Mt. 7:1; cf. Lk. 6:37–38].

SINS AGAINST THIS COMMANDMENT

On the first stage are the gross sins: Giving lies in our testimonies, judgments, accusations, responses, opinions, and counsel; deliberately speaking untruth in promises and reports; giving false instruction in the arts; and willfully spreading slanders and lies about other people, as Potiphar's evil wife did about Joseph, and Ziba about his master in 2 Kings [2 Sam. 16]. Ulysses falsely suspected Palamedes of conspiring with the enemy, and killed him.

On the second stage are the sins of coloring lies with sophistry, leaving a false appearance, and seeking to evade. Such would be the case with one who owes a debt but evades paying by saying, as often happens, that he was not able to get word to the proper place.

The great princes in Persia invented a sophistry in order to destroy Daniel by leaving the impression that Daniel had not kept the king's commandment. The world is full of sophistry, which some people think is wisdom. However, Sirach [Ecclus.] says, chapter 37, "Whoever practices sophistry (i.e. designs false appearances) is to be hated; there is no wisdom in him; and God gives to him no grace" [cf. v. 20–21]. Such is the case with monks. When they maintain and embellish their errors with sophistry, with invocation of the dead, and with masses for departed souls, then obviously they are outside of God's grace, are in blindness.

A third stage of sin with regard to the eighth commandment is the harboring of unfounded suspicion, and the interpreting of right things or things that do not matter as if they were evil. Saul suspected David of trying to take his kingdom and interpreted all David's good deeds as attempts to elevate David to the throne. Tiberius suspected Germanicus and had that good young prince killed. Much disorder arises from suspicion between persons of high and low degree. One sees examples of this in all countries; and such suspicions and interpretations are fundamentally opposed to the virtue called truth. Truth is well-founded knowledge, not precarious imagination nor poisonous perversion.

The fourth stage is to perpetrate a deceptive or taunting irony; i.e. to speak as a conspirer, to speak so that another is taunted, or led to act blindly, as when the devil says to poor Eve, "You will become like the gods" [cf. Gen. 3:5]. One often gets such devilish, ironic advice if one seeks counsel from such a conspirer, one who does not want to disclose himself and who has no *categoricam propositionem* in mind when he says, "Forward, forward; you are on the right track, you will be like the gods!" I will let this short reminiscence suffice, for all divine commandments are so deep that neither angel nor man can fathom them. Nevertheless, think for a little while about this commandment which concerns lies, false words, sophistry, misleading statements and false reports, and falsely obtained promises. How great a part of human activity is included in this one commandment!

The Ninth and Tenth Commandments

The two last commandments pertain to improper inclinations [*Neigungen*] or desires, and further explain the foregoing commandments, namely that not only external evil works but also their roots are against God, *i.e.* the miserable disorganization of human nature and blindness and doubt about God keep God from shining in the understanding and from reigning in the will and heart. Instead, man's will and heart are without fear of God, without love of God, without true invocation, without trust, and without dependence on God; man's will and heart are full of improper inclinations and passions. This entire disorganization is against God; it is sin; and for it God damns men if they are not born again through the Lord Christ and the Holy Spirit.

Paul speaks about this sinful disorganization and gives a lucid explanation of these two last commandments when he says in Romans 8:7, "That which the flesh (*i.e.* human nature without the Holy Spirit) devises, intends, wishes, and craves, is enmity against God; it does not submit to God's law; indeed, it cannot." Reflect on what a frightful statement this is, for he is speaking of enmity against God, not only in external evil works, but in all human intention, wisdom, and virtue which are without the Holy Spirit. For such wisdom and virtue do not establish a claim on God, as they do not produce what God would effect in our lives. This innate sin is more fully discussed in the article above on original sin.

The monks maintain that natural blindness, doubt about God, and evil inclinations are not sins if we do not sanction them, and so they interpret these two last commandments by sanction. This teaching of the monks is false. Romans 7 clearly shows that both evil inclinations and sanction, both the root and the fruit, are sins.

This doctrine is often expressed in divine preaching, and is included in this commandment; God in his special wisdom has proclaimed his law with great signs so that we might know him as he is, and how he created us, and that we might know that we became unlike him when we sinned, for which we encounter death and punishment. His righteousness is against sin; he has a great wrath and a consuming fire against it. This is revealed so that we may tremble before God's wrath and learn to acknowledge the Mediator, the Son of God, and take refuge in him, as is discussed below.[15]

About Punishments Appended to the Law

In external worldly government, a law without punishment has no more force than sound carried away by the wind. Divine law would be the same if terrible punishments were not appended. And so God in his righteousness has appended to the law the greatest punishment, namely eternal wrath, which thrusts all into eternal anguish and pain who are not acquitted through the Son.

These punishments have their beginning in this life in physical death, and in all sorts of anguish and difficulty. God wants us in this life to remember that he is wise and righteous, and that he punishes unrighteousness. Physical death and all sorts of plagues are decreed by God, and he maintains this order in his punishment. The great sins, like murder, adultery, sex contrary to nature, robbery, and perjury, he commonly visits in this life with physical punishments, as the passage [Rev. 13:10] says, "He that taketh the sword (*i.e.* other than under an established order) will also perish by the sword." And God uses physical punishments, as indicated, first, that we may learn that he is wise and righteous, and also that his righteousness blots out everything repugnant to it. And second, punishments are attached for mankind's sake, so that civil life with many people living together may be tolerable. If God himself did not protect civil life, and did not punish murderers and robbers, then there would be nothing but devastation on earth. But God wants to maintain civil life, for until the resurrection of the dead, he wants continually to gather to himself a Church among men. Third, he wants physical punishments to remind us that we are to turn from sin to him.

Of a Threefold Use of the Divine Law

Man does not have forgiveness of sins through the law, or by the merit of his own works; neither is he justified, that is, he does not please God,

15. See Articles IX, X.

even though he lives an externally moral life. No man can fulfill the law; that is, no man can really be conformed to God's will as he in the law has indicated that we should be. No one in this corrupted nature is without sin. So one may ask, For what, then, is the law useful? Answer: There are three principal uses of the law.

The first use is civil; law teaches and with fear and punishments forces one to keep his external members under discipline, according to all the commandments about external works. The tongue is not to speak outrageous words about God; the hands are not to kill and not to steal another's goods; the body is not to practice external immorality; and the tongue is not to speak lies. This civil use is binding on all men, although the works are not holy; and this external obedience is possible for all men on several levels, as previously indicated with regard to free will.[16] God's earnest pleasure is that all men observe external morality [*Zucht*]; he punishes external vice with public plagues, with the sword of the authorities, and with illness, poverty, war, dispersion, distress in children, and with various misfortunes [*Verderbung*]. And he who is not converted to God falls into eternal punishment. But remember that although this external morality does not merit forgiveness of sins, and although it does not justify a person before God, it is pleasing to God, even though it is a long way from a fulfillment of the law.

The second use of the law is more important; namely to preach the wrath of God. Through the preaching of the law God accuses the heart, causes it to be alarmed, and drives it to such anguish that, as Hezekiah notes, men say, "Like a lion he has smashed all my bones" [*cf*. Is. 38:13]. Men feel God's wrath against sin, and if they do not receive comfort through the Christ, they sink into eternal anguish and flight, as did Saul and Judas. Hundreds of thousands of men fall into eternal punishment, even for a small sin, when God glances at us angrily.

St. Paul often speaks of this use. In Romans 4:15, he says, "The law brings wrath," that is, fright, anguish, and flight in the presence of God's judgment [*Gericht*] against sin. Hundreds of thousands of men live in apparent security, but this judgment finally comes to all. Moreover, many men who feel this judgment are comforted, converted, and blessed again through the gospel, but some fall into despair and eternal anguish. Deuteronomy 4:24 says, "God is a devouring fire."

Psalm 58: "Surely there is a God who judges and punishes men" [*cf*. v. 11].

16. See above, Article V.

Psalm 62:12: "Thou dost requite a man according to his work."

Psalm 50: "Surely God will come, he will not keep silence; before him will go a devouring fire, and the heavens will declare that God is a judge" [cf. v. 3, 6].

Nahum 1:2: "The Lord is avenging and wrathful, and keeps wrath for his enemies."

Zephaniah 1: "God will come, and with his light will search out those people who take their ease and say: 'God will not do good, nor will he do ill' " [cf. v. 12]!

Job 9: "I know that thou dost punish the sinner" [cf. v. 2].

Solomon 8: "Sin does not remain unpunished" [cf. Eccles. 8:12, 13].

And in the last chapter, "All men shall fear God, and keep his commandments; for God will bring everything that happens, good and evil, even though it be secret, into judgment" [cf. Eccles. 12:13, 14].

To summarize: God is equally just [gerecht] toward all; therefore he punishes sin in all, although it may not happen at the same time. He created knowledge of his law in our nature, that we might know his righteousness [Gerechtigkeit]. He proclaimed great miracles, that we might know his nature, what he calls right, what sin and injustice are, and he has from the beginning of the world, especially in his Church, maintained knowledge of all the necessary commands. He uses his law to strike down our sinful hearts. As Paul says, in Romans 7: [cf. 13], "Sin works death through the law." Job 6:4 says the same: "The arrows of the Almighty are in me; the terrors of God are arrayed against me."

Whoever has felt divine judgment and this sorrow of heart well knows that it is the same as death if God does not again grant comfort through our Lord Jesus Christ.

Contemplate the fact that God will judge and that his judgment is very serious, for the law is God's wisdom. We cannot eradicate the light that God planted in men when he created them. And he openly proclaimed the Ten Commandments, to the accompaniment of miracles, so that the light would not be extinguished by the doubts of the human reason in our disorganized nature. God added eternal and temporal punishments to the law, for he wants physical punishments to remind us of his law when human reason disputes it.

God also ordained the office of preaching, that it might take his place in combatting sin through the word, and, for the sake of Christ the Mediator, proffer grace. Through preaching God produces terror and comfort. The Son of God himself originated the office of preaching in Paradise by saying that he will accept fallen men again, and will rescue them from death. At first he punishes the sin and says, "What have you done" [cf. Gen. 3:13]! It was no jest when Adam and Eve heard the divine Majesty himself speak, for then and there they felt death. But the Son of God himself voiced a wonderful absolution, and said to them, "The seed of the woman shall bruise the head of the serpent" [cf. Gen. 3:15]. From this they understood that they would not die; the woman would have a seed; and they understood that they would again be returned to grace, because the seed of the woman would again overthrow the power of the serpent, and would again give righteousness [Gerechtigkeit] and life. This comfort the Son of God wrought in the heart of Adam and Eve when he spoke the external word.

In the office of preaching in his Church God wants us to proclaim what he is and how he ennobled human nature in creating it in his own image. But against God's will, human nature fell away from God, and is no longer the image of God. Therefore human nature is under God's disfavor; no longer to be like God is to be in sin. In his law he indicates that we are to be as he is and as he wishes. He will maintain this very important doctrine in his Church.

One needs the preaching of law, as St. Paul says, for "Through the law comes knowledge of sin" [cf. Rom. 3:20]. Yes, the law is not only a witness to what sin is, but to what God is; one must learn what sin is if one is to know what God is and what is repugnant to his divine wisdom and order.

St. Paul says in Romans 1:18 that sin is to be punished through the word of God in the office of preaching: "The wrath of God is revealed from heaven against all ungodliness and wickedness of men." Christ speaks in the same way when he says that he has not come to destroy the law, but to fulfill it. The highest law, which we call *lex moralis*, is the eternal unchangeable wisdom and righteousness in God himself, which he nevertheless revealed to us. No one can obliterate this wisdom and righteousness in God himself; it is and remains eternal, and at all times it condemns that which is repugnant to it. Because of this wisdom and righteousness in God the awful wrath of God against our sin was poured on Christ the Lord; thus we are accepted for his sake, as will be described more fully later.[17]

Christ the Lord himself preaches and explains the Ten Commandments. He says, "The Holy Spirit will punish the world on account of the sin of

17. See below, Articles IX, X.

not believing in me" [cf. Jn. 16:8 f.]. Through the office of preaching, God punishes the world's frightful, terrible ignorance, in that men know not the Son of God, nor the promise of the Son of God and the forgiveness of sins and grace; and the heart that does not call on the Son of God in true faith and trust does not receive forgiveness of sins. The Holy Spirit punishes such sins as contempt of God, false security, doubt of God's word, and indolence in the maintaining of divine doctrine. The Holy Spirit also punishes sins against men, such as tumult, hate, envy, murder, adultery, robbery, and lies. Paul frequently says, "Whoever sins will not inherit the kingdom of God" [cf. Rom. 2:2–11; 1 Cor. 6:9–10; 15:50; Gal. 5:21; Eph. 5:5]. In these and similar words the apostles preach and explain the Ten Commandments, and command us to know and always to preach them in the Christian Church, that through such preaching hearts may be freed from blindness and false security, and earnestly consider and feel God's wrath.

Christ himself said, "Preach in my name repentance and forgiveness of sins" [cf. Lk. 24:47]! And since we are to feel repentance and terror in our hearts, we must know what sin is in its many forms.

This involves the second use of the divine law, and we should remember it well, so that we may earnestly and firmly maintain and preach the true meaning of the Ten Commandments. For several years the Anabaptists have been clamoring that one should not preach the Ten Commandments, on the grounds that whoever is born anew is led by the Spirit to do good works without the aid of the word, and that such good works supersede the commandments. Such statements of the Anabaptists display empty blindness and entail many errors and blasphemies. In contrast to this, consider that even Christ himself preaches and explains the Ten Commandments, and give thanks to God for his wisdom in revealing his nature and ours, and for the revelation that after the resurrection we shall again be like him.

Also consider that the light of natural law was planted in man when he was created, but in the heathen it has been obscured, and they have allowed terrible sins which are contrary to the natural light in men, that is, contrary to the natural law. They have invented many gods and have imagined all of them to be eternal; they have even invoked dead men. They have allowed adultery and exchange of wives. Such blindness has prevailed among the heathen, but in his Church God has maintained the true understanding of his law. It is a devilish blasphemy, therefore, to say that one is not to preach the divine law, for this is to assert that one is not to say what God is like, nor to point out the distinction between God, who is wise, true, good, just, and pure, and other things, which are not. The divine law is God's wisdom imparted to us. And the ingratitude of those who despise this gift of God is enormously great, whether in devils or men. One cannot speak too much of this wisdom of God.

The third use of the preaching of the law is concerned with those saints who now are believers, who have been born again through God's word and the Holy Spirit, of whom this word was said, "I will put my law in your heart" [cf. Jer. 31:33; 32:37–41; Heb. 8:8–12]. Although God now dwells in these and gives them light, and causes them to be conformed to him, nevertheless, all such happens through God's word, and the law in this life is necessary, that saints may know and have a testimony of the works which please God. Since all men in this mortal life carry in themselves much weakness and sin, daily penance before God ought to increase, and we ought even more to lament our false security and impurity. Such can come about through the divine word, through a consideration of the punishments on others, or through our own punishment.

All this is the preaching of law. The holy king Zechariah learned through the Ten Commandments, and through great suffering when he saw the destruction of Israel, and through his own wretchedness when Sennacherib came, that he should have lived in great fear of God and earnestly invoked him. In short, God has given his Church knowledge of his eternal and unchangeable law, which is called *lex moralis*, or the Ten Commandments, and he wants the Church to maintain it so that men may have a divine testimony of what is right and of what sin is; so that through the punishment of sin in all men, the unconverted may be converted, and the converted be strengthened in the fear of God.

The saints are free from law in that it does not condemn them. Although they carry within them in this mortal life weakness and sin, since they believe, for Christ's sake they are pleasing to God, and sin is not counted against them [*zuggerechnet*]. About this more will be said later. Yet this eternal unchangeable wisdom and order remain; all rational creatures are to be obedient and subject to the true God, their creator, about which a longer report follows.

This brief, simple introduction to the law is given in the hope that every God-fearing man will accustom himself to consider often and diligently the Ten Commandments; then he will continually acquire more understanding, and will love more fully this very beautiful wisdom of

God, and thank God for this light and revelation. Each one will also perceive more clearly his own uncleanness, and such contemplation will cause him to stand in fear of God's justice. And although those great asses, the monks, have taught that all men are naturally endowed with the capacity completely to abide by God's law, this teaching of the monks is but a frightful, devilish blindness. However, intelligent Christians have other information from the word of God, and know that our miserable human nature is condemned precisely because it does not conform to divine law. And they also know that there is such high wisdom in the divine law that no man can fully fathom it.

Of Natural Law

Many ask, what is natural law? The answer is that it is precisely the eternal unchangeable wisdom in God which he proclaimed in the Ten Commandments. However, we should understand this law, as God himself clarified it through Christ, the prophets, and the apostles. God planted the glory of this, his own unchangeable wisdom, in men in the first creation. As the numbers 1, 2, 3, 4, 5, 6, 7, 8, 9, and 10 are in us, so also is the light that God is an eternal omnipotent, wise, true, good, just [gerechtes], and pure being, who created all things, who wills that all rational creatures be like him in virtue and who will punish and remove the rational creatures who are repugnant to his wisdom and righteousness.

This is a legal understanding of the law, and it remains in man even after he sins. For God wants us to know his nature, and so in us the judgment against sin remains. External civil life is to be regulated according to this natural light, and note well that this natural light and the Ten Commandments, when truly understood, are one single wisdom, doctrine, and law.

Now, one might ask, since an understanding of the Ten Commandments is implanted in all men at their creation, why then did God proclaim the Ten Commandments with so many great miracles before so many hundreds of thousands of men? Answer: There are many important reasons for this open magistral proclamation, but two are especially important. In the wake of sin, the light in human reason was not as clear and bright as before. Men became ever more shameless and savage, and incurred more blindness. The heathen invented and invoked many eternal beings and repugnant gods. They permitted all sorts of frightful immorality, and did not record it as vice. Against such blindness God not only proclaimed his law on Mt. Sinai, but has sustained and upheld it since the time of Adam in his Church, and has given public testimony to this in the story of Cain and Abel, the punishment of Sodom, and so forth. However, the proclamation on Mt. Sinai is the most magnificent, and it has many strong testimonies, so that this doctrine may not be entirely obliterated in human reason.

The second reason is that it is not enough that man know that he is not to kill other innocent men, nor rob others of their wives and goods. One must first of all know God's nature and know that God earnestly wants us to be like him, and that he is enraged against all sin. Therefore he proclaims his commandments himself, that we may know that they are not only in our minds but that they are *God's law*, that God is the judge and executor against all sin, that our hearts may recognize God's wrath and tremble before it, and may know that in all sin we not only act against human welfare but also offend God. . . .

Also it is necessary that the saints clearly know from the word of God which works please God and are divine worship, that they may not invent works according to their own reason, one thus, another so. God also proclaims his law because human reason without God's word soon falls into error and doubt. If God himself had not graciously proclaimed his wisdom, men would fall still further into doubt about God's nature, right and wrong, order and disorder. So that we may know God's nature and have a positive distinction between God and devils, right and wrong, order and disorder, God himself has instructed and strengthened us in this proclamation.

VIII

OF THE DISTINCTION OF COMMANDMENT
AND COUNSEL

(COUNSELS)

The Anabaptists flit about and pretend great works of holiness, and in their hypocrisy say they have nothing of their own. They fake great patience and practice no vengeance and no resistance. Just so, a thousand years ago similar devilish hypocrites flitted about. Carpokrates and his companions desired not only to have their money in common, but also their wives. Although this is a frightful example to mention, it is necessary for us to remember that we must consider how terribly the devil fumes and rages when he has an opportunity; and that we must be forearmed, prepared, and strengthened with pure doctrine, and daily cry to the Lord Christ to enlighten and guide us with his gospel and his true Holy Spirit, and drive the lying devils far away. At present the monks have not raged as grossly as the Anabaptists and have not said that it is necessary to make inheritance and money common, but they have said such is a counsel of perfection. In these speeches of the monks there are many great lies; therefore, I will give a brief reminiscence.

A commandment is so called because it speaks of necessary obedience. Everything that is contrary to the commandments is sin, and this brings eternal punishment if man is not converted to God.

A counsel is a doctrine, not a commandment; it does not demand a work, even though it praises the work as blameless and useful.

Now the monks have selected three such works, namely, not to exercise vengeance or resistance; not to have property; and to live chastely without matrimony. The monks say that the gospel has counseled these three works, and they then devise lies, saying that these works merit forgiveness of sins, that they are perfection, and that they are higher than the works of divine commandments. In our times the Anabaptists particularly have written books which are full of frightful errors and lies. Although basic and lengthy instruction on these topics would be very useful, I will here speak briefly. Whoever has learned the other articles in order — what law is, the difference between law and gospel, how before God man is justified through faith, and that God has ordained worldly authority — can from this basis also determine what one is to do about resistance, property, and chastity.

First, it is obvious that our works cannot merit forgiveness of sins; so also are our works not perfection, for in this weak life we are still far from fulfillment of the law, and much sin, doubt and disorder remain in us, as Job, chapter 9, says, "No man is justified before God" [cf. v. 2; 25:4]. Therefore it is empty blindness when men extol their own works as perfection, as if such works were a complete fulfillment of the divine law, and as if such holiness were higher than commanded works.

Of Vengeance, Punishment, and Resistance

It is obvious that God has ordained both the offices of preaching and worldly authority, and we will now indicate the difference between them. For worldly authority God has commanded first of all these four offices:

The first, that it shall be a voice of the Ten Commandments in external morality.

The second, that with physical power and with the sword and gallows it shall punish all who have done external works against the divine commandments; shall protect the innocent; and, if possible, shall drive away murderers and robbers.

The third, that worldly authority shall make its own laws for morality and peace, but these are not to be opposed to divine commandments.

The fourth, that it shall physically punish those who disobey these commandments.

These are the foremost works of worldly authority, and God has earnestly commanded that the worldly authorities execute them, that is, protect the innocent and punish the disobedient, as Romans 13 has clearly expressed, "The authority is God's servant for good, and the one who executes his wrath on the wrongdoer" [cf. v. 4]. Here the worldly authorities are expressly commanded to exercise vengeance or punishment and resistance in God's stead. And thus this is a commandment which belongs to the authorities, and is not merely a counsel.

On the other hand, all subjects, ministers, and other men whose office does not require this public execution and resistance are commanded not to exercise their own vengeance; they are not themselves to punish the wrongdoer in accordance with the wrong, but may and should request in an orderly fashion that the authorities do so. Especially they are not to exercise power against the authorities, are not to instigate tumult, and are not to join the rabble [Haufen] to overthrow orderly authority. About individual vengeance our Lord Christ says, Matthew 5:39, "I say to you, Do not resist one who is evil." This is to be understood as outside the command of authority, for our Lord Christ speaks in the same sermon especially about each person's heart, and the same chapter contains nothing about authority. Concerning this, however, God clearly gives instruction in other speeches, as is hereafter more fully discussed. So one should now know that vengence is twofold: the office of vengeance, which God has ordained and commanded; and its opposite, individual vengeance, which outside of this office is earnestly forbidden, as our Lord Christ says to Peter, "All who take the sword (to be understood as out of defiance, outside of constituted authority) will by the sword perish" [Mt. 26:52; cf. Jn. 18:11].

From this explanation, obviously the admonition against [exercising] vengeance is not a counsel but a command and prohibition. The authorities are commanded to execute what God has ordained for protection and punishment. Subjects are expressly forbidden to seize authority, and note what disorder follows if one thinks that it is a counsel not to exercise vengeance or punishment. If the authorities did not exercise vengeance or punishment, government would no longer exist; on the other hand, if the subjects themselves were allowed to exercise vengeance or punishment, there would be nothing but tumult, and no government at all.

Observe that this fundamental true instruction is against the Anabaptists and the blindness and errors of the monks, who strive against God and against proper government. And hereafter consider further what great sins follow when one deviates from properly established order — when the authorities become corrupt or untrue, and tyrannical, when they do not protect the innocent, when they strengthen vice and fail to punish the wrongdoer. Consider the sins that follow when one resolves to seek his own vengeance in the fury of his own hate, seeks the suppression of the one who is his enemy, and creates the factions, partisans and plots that bring tumult. At Rome Catiline practiced trickery against Cicero, to take advantage of him and to strengthen his own party and Cassius against Julius [Caesar], and at Athens, Critias against Theramenes. And this poison is still more wicked when it happens in the Church, when Cain is infuriated with Abel; Saul, with David; Arius, with his bishop. In our own times we see many examples of the learned vengefully inveighing against one another. This fury does great harm, and to lessen and recognize these great sins, God's word repeats that we are to have patience toward one another, are not to seek our own vengeance, are not to rend the Church because of pride and the hate which follows from pride, of which I could give many examples. I know a person who hoped to mount high enough to make it possible for his dogs to urinate on Lutherans, but God severely restrained him. Therefore, I say that everyone should learn patience, and not vindictively destroy the poor Church, nor hinder the invocation of God.

Christ says, "Learn of me, for I am gentle and lowly in heart" [Mt. 11:29]. Bear in mind how noble this word is! Pride and vindictiveness are related, and commonly are the principal causes of the greatest wars and destructions. Marius and Sulla, Pompey and Julius, clashed with one another principally out of pride, and yet if each one had been moral, he could have maintained his position without war.

Against these devilish passions Christ sets two virtues, humility and gentleness, which we are to contemplate in him, and even in a small way to learn and practice; we are not to destroy the Church and orderly government out of pride and desire for vengeance, as Cain and Saul did.

We are to contemplate what pride and vindictiveness, humility and gentleness, really are. To be proud, haughty, and arrogant is to be secure from fear of God, to have great regard for one's own wisdom, strength, or might; to elevate oneself above others and to do unnecessary works outside one's calling, to increase oneself so as to overwhelm another. Antony, secure from the fear of God, thought that he was nobler and mightier than Octavius [Augustus], and for this reason wished to be the sole manager, and to take Octavius' position. The devil beheld his own wisdom and virtue and despised the Son of God, who was humble, and wanted to be higher than he.

Although the explanation is short, it is easy to understand from this that pride and arrogance [Hoffahrt] trespass against many of God's commandments. It is against the first commandment to be falsely secure and fearless, and to rely solely on one's own capabilities; and it is against the second table to step outside one's own calling and to hinder and overwhelm one's neighbor in his.

On the other hand, to be humble is to fear God and to acknowledge one's own weakness; not to esteem one's own wisdom, strength, or might as great; not to rely thereon, and not to step outside one's vocation, but to serve God in one's vocation, in the hope of divine help, untroubled about another's vocation, loving and honoring others as God's instruments, and knowing that all good government is God's work, and that God also can make use of others. And all this is to the glory of God. For example, Jonathan is humble; he fears God and knows that good government is not by human power, that one does not make himself king. He does not desire to raise himself above his calling and, since he knows that God has called David to kingly sovereignty, he does not wish to vex him; instead he loves and honors him as God's instrument, and rejoices that God himself has chosen a man who will be a useful servant, to whom he gives the testimony of great miracles. Jonathan does all this to the glory of God.

Humility is not present in many men, and so it is difficult to talk about and to recognize. The example of Jonathan provides an introduction, but that of our Lord Christ is much higher. He has divine wisdom and omnipotence and is nevertheless obedient to the Father; he takes our punishment to himself and does not use his power to avoid it. He draws us poor, miserable men to himself, and establishes in us a great glory, that God will again be gracious to us and that he will impart to us in eternity his wisdom, righteousness, and joy.

Vindictiveness is a great anger, stemming from pride, one's own wantonness to overwhelm or to blot out others without the orderly office of authority; such pride is often great, even though the perpetrator has no reason, as Cain, for imagining that God honors only the other and wishes to do nothing for him. This is very common, and all rational beings can understand that this vice is repugnant to many divine commandments. Pride, through which anger is kindled like a fire in the heart, is against the first commandment. Saul wishes to drive David out of the way in order that he alone may have authority. This unrighteous anger, this jealousy and hate and thirst for blood are against the commandment, "You shall not kill." It is also against the same command about rending the divine order of justice [Gerichten].

On the other hand, to be gentle is, with humility and patience, and for God's sake and glory, to keep anger, jealousy, and hate quiet, and not to allow them to begin burning. It is to exercise no vengeance, to instigate no tumult, partisanship, plotting nor war against proper order, nor hatefully and jealously to rend the churches with unrighteous controversy.

From all this it is clear that "not to exercise individual vengeance" is a commanded work, and is not simply a counsel, as the monks speak of it. But here one may ask, "Is it then wrong for me to protect myself against a murderer on the street?" Answer. It is right to protect oneself against murderers; God has so ordained in his system of rights [*Rechten*]. In such a case authority delegates the sword, and in this situation the sword pertains to the office of vengeance. Thus, one may protect himself with force against unjust force, since justice has ordained such. This applies to a murderer on the street, or to a mass of murderers who initiate unjust war. That God has commanded protection for the innocent is discussed more fully under "authority." [1]

Of Poverty

"Poverty makes woe." This is a true proverb, and it is necessary to understand it, for the monks say that it is a counsel to be poor. The first distinction to be made is between poverty and not having property, for one can be very poor even though he has property. How many hundreds of thousands of heads of households have for themselves and for their poor children their own cottages, beds, clothes, and food, and nevertheless have not all the necessities of life! These are called poor, and are truly poor, although they have property, and more is to be said later about bearing poverty in patience. [2] These, however, the Anabaptists attack, saying that Christian men should not own property, but should have all goods in common, and they make a command of this. The monks are subtler; they say poverty is a counsel, a special holy work.

These opinions of the Anabaptists and monks are erroneous and false. The seventh commandment, "You shall not steal," shows that it is right, and a divine order, to have property. These grave words of the seventh commandment confirm the right to property for every one, and they draw a wall about each one's house and trade [*Nahrung*].

And this should be noted very carefully: the orderly regulations of the human race in authority, courts, punishments, marriage, property, buying, and selling are so decreed and maintained through divine wisdom and power, that the devils which oppose such regulations may not completely destroy them.

And order in the human community is a clear testimony to God; for in the punishments of murderers and the like, one acknowledges that God

1. See below, Article XXXVI.
2. See below, p. 136 f.; also Article XXXIV.

exists, that he is a just Judge, and is present among men. Through his beautiful order God would be known, and through such means and bonds he wants us to be drawn together, and to serve one another, as do the Son of God and angels who are pleasing to God.

Works of such service are divine worship in the faithful, for men acknowledge God by being obedient to him in his ordained order; and men are not to be torn from God's ordered stations, but should be maintained and honored in them. The Lord speaks frequently in the prophets, as in Zechariah 7, "I have not commanded you to fast, but I have commanded you to render true judgments," etc. [cf. v. 4–10].

Knowing now that this [characteristic of the] physical order, ownership of property, is pleasing to God, one should further know that abandonment of property is of two kinds: that which is compelled and that which is hypocritically chosen.

Forced abandonment occurs when pious Christians, because of their confession, are exiled and compelled to leave their goods and children.[3] In this abandonment, having patience is to invoke God; it is to worship and to do a work pleasing to God, even as it is a good work to remain firm in one's confession, even though life is taken away. This patience and firmness in confession are commanded and necessary works, not simply counsels. The Lord Christ speaks of this abandonment when he says, Mark 10:29 f., "There is no one who has left house or brothers, or sister or mother or father or children or land, for my sake and for the gospel, who will not receive a hundredfold even in this life, despite persecutions, and in the age to come eternal life."

Poverty can also result from many other misfortunes, such as fire or war, in which house and castle are destroyed. In these and similar misfortunes, those persons who turn to God have patience and do good work and worship.

Hundreds of thousands of God-fearing householders are poor, although they possess property; that is, although they own something, they and their children do not have the proper necessities of life. This is called poverty. In this circumstance patience is a good work, pleasing to God, as the text says, "Blessed are the poor in spirit" [Mt. 5:3], that is, those who for God's sake are patient in their poverty, although they work and

3. This often happened in the sixteenth century. In the Peace of Augsburg, 1555, the Lutherans and Roman Catholics agreed that the official religion of a territory was to be the same as that of the ruler (cuius regio, eius religio), and that those of another persuasion were to be tolerated or allowed to leave without hindrance. This agreement, though shaky at times, prevailed until the outbreak of the Thirty Years' War in 1618.

maintain property, as much as God permits to them. For it is God's will that all be not equally strong nor equally rich. It is virtue and strength from the Holy Spirit, wisely and rightly to bear poverty, and not to design evil, dishonorable things to become rich, as Judas and many others did. Patience is to be further discussed later.[4]

However, the voluntary abandonment of one's own goods in the erroneous opinion that begging is a holy work of divine worship is not only not a counsel but a lie, a mistake. "Vainly they honor me with the commandments of men" [cf. Mt. 15:8–9; Is. 29:13]! Also, whoever obtains bread from another by begging, if he himself has property and has forsaken it without being persecuted, if he does not perform some honorable work such as teaching to obtain bread, if he is able and not prevented from working, he is a thief. The cloisters, therefore, have always been full of thieves, and this is still more sinful in that they have sold the Mass and dead pageantry.

This also should be noted. When God gives property and a tolerable trade, we should first of all know that having property is pleasing to God; and we should acknowledge it as a gift of God, thank him for it, and ask God to sustain and bless our poor children with the benefits of our trade. And we also should ask about the correct usage. With regard to this, everyone should look carefully at the lovely passage in Solomon, "Out of your spring let the little brooks flow; however, you alone are to remain master of it, so that it does not become alien to you" [cf. Prov. 15:15–17]. You should preserve the ground and the principal benefit for the virtuous rearing of your children, but as much as possible you should distribute the fruits to others, to the churches, to schools, and to the poor. This passage expressly confirms property, and gives instruction about its use, teaching both how to economize and how to limit liberality. From the spring let the brook flow out to others, but this does not mean that you are to repudiate your house and goods. And an understanding of this lovely passage, which God speaks through the wise king Solomon, discloses much useful doctrine, which should be well known in order to combat the hypocrisy and the lies of the Anabaptists and the monks.

Of Chastity

Chastity, strictly speaking, is the avoidance of all prohibited sexual relationships [*verbotene Vermischung und des Samens Missbrauch*]. It is also living by the rules of marriage, without any sexual promiscuity outside of

4. See below, Articles IX and XXXIV.

marriage, and this virtue should be in external members and in the heart; that is, the heart should not have improper passions for forbidden persons.

All these are commanded works: in marriage, to avoid all forbidden sexual relationships; and outside marriage, to live purely without any misuse of sex. If one has not the gift to live purely or chastely outside marriage, then he is commanded to get married.

If one, however, has the divine gift to live purely outside marriage, he may so remain, as did John the Baptist and the widow Hannah. Getting married is not commanded but shunning all prohibited sexual relationships is an eternally unchangeable commandment.

And all men should know which sexual relationships God has forbidden, and should consider the punishments which God has appended to his prohibitions and which he himself executes, first of all in this life. For God firmly maintains his rule truly to punish in this life external lewd immorality [*Unzucht*], adultery, and incest, even though worldly authorities pay no attention to and do not want to punish such vices. The Lord expressly says in Leviticus 18:29, "All men who do these abominations shall be cut off from among the people." Thus, on account of their immorality the Lord blotted out Sodom, Gomorrah, the Canaanites, and many other great cities. And there is no doubt that great destructions here on earth occur on account of idolatry, murder, and immorality. Everyone can recall cases in our time in which persons of high and low degree have fancied adultery and have been frightfully struck dead, or cases in which other great punishments following immorality have fallen on the children, for sin is punished in one's descendants.

The wrath of God is even more terrible when poured out in eternal punishment on those who are not reconciled to God before their end. St. Paul expressly says in 1 Corinthians 6, "Adulterers, fornicators, those who commit incest, and so forth, will not inherit the kingdom of God."

It is very necessary to know all this, and to consider it often, so that one may rightly understand what chastity is and be obedient to God in this virtue. For God's great wrath against immorality shows that this is a very grave matter with God. Consider why: God has placed his law in his rational creature, has given him the knowledge to distinguish between virtue and vice, so that we may know God's nature and differentiate him from evil, unordered things. Now chastity provides a very clear distinction between God and the impure spirits and men.

For this reason, when we speak of God, we should characterize him in our contemplation as wise, almighty, true, just, pure, chaste, and merciful. We cannot embrace God with physical arms, but we are to contemplate him with faith in our hearts, as he has revealed and distinguished himself from all creatures, and especially from wrongdoers. Because chastity makes this clear distinction, God wants this virtue to be well known to us. That this is a very grave matter to God is evident from the fact that devils furiously drive poor men to immorality. Because they know that God is especially displeased by such sins, they drive still more furiously, just to vex God. The devils also know that other great vices stem from immorality.

Consider this carefully and frequently, and exercise obedience to God by living purely and chastely in marriage, or outside of marriage. We should beseech God to strengthen us against our own weakness and against the devils, so that we may not fall into immorality. God wants us to seek this help of him; he wishes to be even more gracious because he knows the poisonous evil of the devil herein.

Also note very carefully that only in the true Church of God has the true understanding of the sixth commandment, about chastity, remained. The heathen and the heretics have openly approved of frightful immorality, about which much might be said; and the papists, with their prohibition of marriage, have caused frightful sin. But this is a wonderful comfort: only in the true Church of God has the doctrine about chastity and marriage always remained pure. One should know this mark of the true Church and should also note that because the heathen and the heretics, and now the papal persecutors, break the sixth commandment, this true doctrine about marriage, they are not the Church of God. This is quite obvious.

Whoever has a true understanding of the sixth commandment and wants to live purely and chastely, to the glory of God, must himself judge whether he shall live within marriage or whether he can live sinlessly outside of marriage. All men should frequently contemplate this unchangeable rule, 1 Corinthians 6:9 f., "Adulterers, fornicators, the immoral, etc., shall not inherit the kingdom of God." Accordingly, under this topic belongs the entire doctrine about marriage. All men should have information from divine Scripture, concerning it, *e.g.* Matthew 19, 1 Corinthians 7, Leviticus 18.

When St. Paul says, "It is better if one remains free and unmarried" [*cf.* 1 Cor.7:8, 32], he himself explains that he is speaking of persons who are qualified for the unmarried state. Previously he says, "It is better to get married than to burn" [1 Cor. 7:9], that is, than to live in immorality and impurity. And it is obvious that married people who have many children and children's children, who are in poverty, to whom come other anxieties such as illness, misfortune, and discord — it is obvious that these carry a great burden. Whoever does not think so is a grossly absurd man. Concerning this, Paul says, "It is better to remain unmarried and free," better for the one who is qualified for it, not on account of holiness, but on account of the physical hindrances. Unmarried, he would have fewer physical hindrances than if he were married and had children and were burdened with the accidents that befall children.

So far we have spoken about law, but now follows the important article about the gospel and the promise which, through Christ and for his sake, brings forgiveness of sins, grace, justification, the Holy Spirit, and eternal life. This promise is quite different from the law; and all men are carefully to learn the difference between law and gospel. The monks, and before them, some ancient scribes, greatly obscured the light. With offense to the Lord Christ and the corruption of many souls, they obliterated the necessary and happy comfort of forgiveness of sins *through faith, without merit*, and many other errors have followed. Remember this, so that the following may be more easily understood.

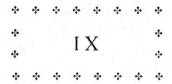

I X

OF THE GOSPEL [1]

The word "gospel" in the old Greek language means "joyful tidings," and God undoubtedly chose to make common this beloved word about the preaching of grace in order to remind us that this preaching about Christ is far different from law. The law proclaims to us the great wrath of God against our sin, and says nothing about the forgiveness of sin, out of grace, without our merit. But John knows the Son of God, and says, "Behold this is the Lamb of God who takes away the sin of the world" [Jn. 1:29]; and the gospel preaches about the same Son of God, and about forgiveness of sins, justification, the Holy Spirit, and eternal blessedness, which we by the same Mediator, the Son of God, *Jesus Christ, without our merit, through faith,* assuredly receive.

We should carefully note this distinction, and listen not only to Moses, who proclaims the curse, saying, "Cursed be everyone who does not abide by all things written in the law" [Gal. 3:10; *cf.* Deut. 27:26], but also listen to the preacher, who directs us to the *Son of God,* saying, "Behold, this is the Lamb of God who takes away the sin of the world."

At the very beginning of his book John has indicated this distinction between Moses and Christ, between the law and gospel, with these words: "The law was given through Moses; grace and truth came through Jesus Christ" [Jn. 1:17]. *Grace* really denominates the gracious forgiveness of sins and acceptance without our merit; and *truth* denominates eternal benefits [*Güter*], life, right knowledge of God, and the kind of justification [*Gerechtigkeit*] that is not just an external shadow, but is the divine light, splendor, and activity — yes, God's own presence in our hearts, as Paul says, "God will be all in those who are saved" [Phil. 2:13; *cf.* 1 Cor. 15:28]. John speaks of full salvation, and he says that Moses has not given this, for Moses only proclaimed the law; but the Son of God, Jesus Christ, has obtained and given us these benefits.

1. In this article Melanchthon includes Of Divine Promises and Of the Difference Between Law and Gospel, which he listed in the foreword.

For grace to be known, we must previously know our great misery and recognize that God is profoundly angry on account of our sin. He even commanded the Lord Christ to preach *poenitentiam et remissionen peccatorum* in his name, that is, repentance and remission of sins. He says, "The Holy Spirit will punish the world on account of its sin so that it may believe in me." [2] Through the preaching of the gospel, God actively produces terror and comfort. Therefore, for the sake of instruction, the following explains what the gospel is.

The gospel is the *divine* proclamation in which men, once they have heard of God's anger against sin and truly tremble before God's wrath, are presented with the most gracious promise that God, *for the sake of Christ*, graciously, *without merit on man's part*, wants to forgive them their sins and to justify them, and that the Son of God will bring comfort to those who believe and bestow on them the Holy Spirit and an inheritance of eternal life — all of which is to be received through faith.

This explanation should especially be noted because this is what distinguishes the true Church of God from other peoples. For example: When God for the first time re-established his Church after the Fall, when he punished miserably fallen man with the proclamation of death, they undoubtedly felt terrified; but at the same time God comforted them with the promise of a future Redeemer, and, when they heard the promise, at that moment the Son of God effected comfort and life in their hearts.

This promise was maintained in the Church of God as its main proclamation, and was clarified in divine revelation again and again. However, at the same time many people departed from the true Church, for although they upheld the law, they entirely obliterated knowledge of the Redeemer and the promise of grace; they are not God's Church. There have been and still are such groups which are simply Mohammedan; although they have the law, they still are not God's Church. For this remains eternally fixed, 1 Corinthians 3:11, "No other foundation can any one lay than that which is laid, which is Jesus Christ"; and John 14:6, "No one comes to the Father except through the Son"; and, also, John 5:23, "He who does not honor the Son does not honor the Father."

We must conclude from this and similar clear passages that the churches of God are only those gatherings in which the holy gospel of the Lord *Christ* is rightly preached. Only in those gatherings do the heirs

2. Source uncertain; cf. Is. 13:11; 24:21-23; 26:21; Amos 4:6-12; Joel 2:10-13; Ps. 9:8-10; 22:25-28; 96:10-13; 98:7-9; Jer. 44:29; Mt. 13:41-43; Rom. 10:18-21; Jn. 3:17-18; 16:8; Rev. 3:9-13.

of eternal blessedness exist, not among the heathen or Mohammedans, nor any other persecutors of the Lord Christ. Concerning this, more will be said in the article on the Church; this is said here so that we may draw a distinction between law and gospel.

Although wise men among the heathen, such as Hesiod, Phocylides, Plato, Xenophon, and Aristotle, say much that is true about law — for law is in many respects a natural light,[3] like number — these same wise people among the heathen say absolutely nothing about Christ and the forgiveness of sins. Knowledge of Christ and of forgiveness of sins is not a light that naturally shines in us; we are not born with it, as we are with a knowledge of number. But God in his mercy has made forgiveness known in revelations extending back to Adam, he has repeatedly confirmed it in miracles, and he gathers to himself an eternal Church, which first began in the revelation of the future Redeemer, when God said, "The seed of the woman will tread on the head of the serpent" [Gen. 3:15].

Note that the promises are twofold. The first, the highest and most necessary, is the promise of the Lord Christ himself, the promise of grace and eternal salvation. This promise must be the first and highest, for if we did not have forgiveness of sins, and remained bound by eternal death, the temporal promises would be of little comfort. . . . Therefore, we ought first to know and contemplate this chief promise about the Lord *Christ* and eternal blessedness. And this chief promise is, strictly speaking, the *gospel.* Although the promise is clearer in the writings of the prophets, it was revealed in the beginning and was included significantly in the first passage about the person of the Mediator and the eternal blessedness which he brings with him. Both the person and the grace and eternal blessedness which are given to us through the Son of God and the *seed of the woman,* and for his sake, must be known in the Church. The holy fathers, Adam, Seth, Enoch, Noah, and Shem undoubtedly saw the Son of God with their own eyes, for he became visible, as to Abraham; and they felt and recognized his activity in their hearts through the word. This is the reason the Lord Christ says, "Abraham has seen my day and rejoiced" [*cf.* Jn. 8:56].

3. "Natural light" refers to a given intelligence or endowment which Melanchthon believed to be common to all rational men, whereby they know the fundamentals of mathematics, morality, and order. Even though sin affects the full use of the natural light, it is still with man. Melanchthon considered the rudiments of law as part of this natural light (*cf.* Jer. 31:31–34 and Rom. 1:18–32). For specific references to natural light, see index.

Note the promises, from Adam's time to the present, and carefully consider the comfort in them, even though we cannot explain each one now. The first passage is, "The seed of the woman will tread on the head of the serpent"; that is, I will again give you a Savior, who will be born of a woman, without the seed of a man, and will destroy the power of the devil, will take away sin and death, and bring again eternal justification, eternal life, and eternal joy. Here the person and grace are included, and Adam and Eve through these words felt in their hearts that this reported person would be the Savior, and through faith they were rescued from their terrors and from death.

This promise is later reiterated and established for the heirs of Abraham: "In your seed shall all people be blessed" [Acts 3:25; cf. Gen. 12:1-3; Gal. 3:8]. In the preaching of this promise the true Church through faith, according to this promise, is to be gathered, and the true God, who gave this word, is to be distinguished from all imaginary gods. The saints invoked the God, who revealed himself in his promise and in his testimonies, and they felt comforted in their hearts through faith, according to this promise, and they prayed, hoped, waited for, and received help in their calling from the future Savior. As Jacob prays, "May the almighty God, and the Angel, who rescued me from all evil, bless you" [Gen. 48:15-16]. This Angel who rescued Jacob from sin and all evil is certainly the *Son of God.*

Afterward the promise is established in the stem of David, for the Savior is to be born out of David's line. This is explained through the prophets. One should know this revelation and explanation, and often consider it.

This promise of the Son of God and of grace is vastly different from law: basically, the law is a teaching which commands perfect obedience and does not freely impart forgiveness of sins without merit on our part. The law says no one is justified who is not as the divine law indicates one should be. But the gospel has the Reconciler *Christ* and this difference: *freely, without merit.* The entire obedience of the Lord Christ is our merit. This is very important, for in true anguish the heart struggles not particularly with whether God is merciful, but with whether God will be gracious to anyone who has sinned, whether he will be gracious to one who has no merits, whether he will receive us, even though [we may know] he has received others. Here the heart must know that for the sake of the Lord *Christ* the gospel truly and freely bestows, without merit on our part, forgiveness of sins and grace, and that we receive this great grace with faith. The second thing that the heart must know is that forgiveness and faith are for all men, are *universales*.

All men in their corrupted nature have sin, and God truly hates sin in *all men*. Therefore, the preaching of wrath indicts everyone, as *Paul* says, Romans 3:23, "All have sinned." On the other hand, the preaching of grace in the gospel is also *universalis*, and promises forgiveness, mercy, justification, the Holy Spirit, and eternal blessedness for *all* who accept this grace *with faith* and trust in the Lord *Christ*. There is absolutely no doubt that the commandment to receive the Son of God and to trust in him is a commandment for all men, as the eternal Father says, "This you shall hear." And in the second Psalm, "Kiss the Son!" And Matthew 11:28 says, "Come to me, all who labor and are heavy laden, and I will give you rest." In the number "all" everyone should include himself, and with faith in the Lord Christ should ask for help.

This promise of the Son of God and forgiveness of sins, grace, and eternal salvation is often confirmed with a divine oath, so that we may not remain mired in doubt and the despair therein. Thus says Psalm 110:4, "The Lord has sworn and will not change his mind, 'You are a priest for ever after the order of Melchizedek.'" Ezekiel 33:11: "As I live, says the Lord God, I have no pleasure in the death of the wicked, but that the wicked turn from his way and live." This oath one should often consider carefully in order to strengthen faith.

In addition, there are promises of temporal help in this mortal life, as in Matthew 6:33, "Seek first his kingdom and his righteousness, and all these things shall be yours as well." Matthew 10:30: "All the hairs of your head are numbered." And St. Paul says, 1 Timothy 4:8, "Godliness is of value to all, as it holds promise for the present life and also for the life to come." Why God also gave temporal promises is worth considering, and there are at least four reasons:

First: For the knowledge of God and of creation, that is, that we might think of God and remember that he creates and maintains everything, and also that the distribution of temporal goods happens with his counsel, not as Epicurus imagines, without God's counsel. Here one is to note the passages about creation and distribution, in Deuteronomy 30:20, "God is your life and the length of your days"; Psalms 127:1, "Unless the Lord builds the house, those who build it labor in vain"; and in Proverbs 10:22, "The blessing of the Lord makes rich." And from this one should learn this important wisdom and rule, that human counsel, work, cunning, and strength alone, without God's support and help, cannot be fruitful. Pompey thought he was so strong that he could always triumph, but nevertheless he did not triumph, because triumph is of God. Proverbs 21:31 says, "The horse is made ready for the day of battle, but the victory belongs to the Lord."

The second reason why temporal blessings are given and promises announced is this: Maintenance of the Church in this mortal life; for it is God's order and will that his eternal Church be gathered in this mortal life only through the office of preaching. If people are to preach and learn now, they must live, and this requires food, drink, health, and shelter, for as the Psalmist says, "The dead cannot praise God" [Ps. 115:17]. In order that a Church can be and live, God makes the earth fruitful, gives us, as his children, food and drink; gives government and shelter, and comforts us; and proclaims the promise of these temporal goods that we may know that he will sustain the Church and for this end will give life, health, nourishment, shelter, and government. The Lord *Christ* speaks about this in Matthew 6:32, "Your heavenly Father knows that you need them all."

The third reason is that God wants us to exercise faith, invocation, and thanksgiving through temporal aid, so that the light in our hearts concerning God's works, presence, and fatherly will may become ever stronger. Thus he speaks in Psalm 46, "Call on me in time of trouble, and I will rescue you, and you shall praise me." This commandment we are to note carefully and to exercise daily, and with it consider the purpose of this invocation and thanksgiving, namely that in our hearts God may so much more be known, honored, and loved.

The fourth reason is that the temporal promises are a reminder of the Lord Christ, and the eternal promise, and here two things obtain. First, all temporal goods are given and promised *for the sake of the Lord Christ;* the eternal Father himself gathers his Church out of love for his Son, but because the Church must have its beginning in this life, God gives us physical goods, which are necessary for us in this weak life. As *St. Paul* says, 2 Corinthians 1, all promises are proclaimed and given to us for the sake of the Son.

Moreover, in all invocation, even for temporal aid, the heart must think about the Son of God and the eternal promise and forgiveness of sins, for the heart cannot fruitfully call on God without a consideration of the Lord Christ. Conscience always flounders and wonders, since it has sinned and is still sinful, whether its cries to God will be heard. Here knowledge of the Lord *Christ* and *faith* that the forgiveness of sins is received must light the way and strengthen the prayer for temporal help.

Although there are many reasons why the Church of God is placed under the cross, of which we will speak hereafter, one reason is that God wishes through various temporal dangers and anguish to compel us, not only to seek temporal help, but much more, to know the Lord *Christ* and to seek eternal blessings. . . .

Note that the gospel proclaims that God wishes to sustain the Church and will give temporal help, and at the same time that the Church is laid under the cross and must suffer persecution. These two statements appear to be contradictory, but not really, for the Lord Christ himself includes both suffering and help, Mark 10:29 f., "There is no one who has left house, . . . lands . . . for the sake of the gospel, who will not receive a hundredfold now in this time, with persecutions, and in the age to come eternal life." And Isaiah 30:20 speaks of eternal goods, suffering, and maintenance of the Church, "Though the Lord give you the bread of adversity and the water of affliction, yet your Teacher will not hide himself any more, and you shall hear his word."

Although these words sound as if they are in opposition, they are merely parallel statements. It is true, the Church lies under the cross for many reasons, but God maintains it in this mortal life, so that his gathered company [*Versammlung*] remains, although many members here and there are devastated. David's military forces secured victory and remained intact even though some of his men were killed. God helps in many special ways, and not always in the same way for all people, for he wants us both to expect temporal help according to his will and to be willing and ready in obedience. Nevertheless, he maintains his gathered company, and help comes in many ways.

Help and deliverance for the congregation often occur through natural means, for God wants all men to recognize his presence in the Church. We should pray therefore for him to manifest his presence, even as Moses prayed that the Lord would manifest himself to his people so that the Egyptians might hear and know that he had visibly revealed himself.

And some help is beyond human understanding, in that it does not happen according to our thoughts, for God wants us to live in faith and trust in him, and to live and expect deliverance through the Lord *Christ*, even as he says in Isaiah 30:15, "In quietness and in trust shall be your strength." And from this statement a very important rule of life follows: we are to abide in God's commandments in expectation of the goal, even though reason cannot see how it will occur. So says Psalm 37:34, "Wait for the Lord, and keep to his way, and he will exalt you to possess the land; you will look on the destruction of the wicked."

And although there are many temporal gifts, for which we need help in this miserable life, and although all the gifts of grace are grounded on the grace that is freely given for the sake of the Lord *Christ*, nevertheless there are at the same time various rewards for saints who are obedient and patient. Jeremiah says that Ebed-melech, who gave him food in prison, will not perish in the great destruction of Jerusalem, but will be rescued. And the Lord Christ himself says in Matthew 10:42, "Whoever gives to one of these little ones even a cup of cold water because he is a disciple, truly, I say to you, he shall not lose his reward."

Even though these gifts are rewards, we must still confess that we have much sin, that God may justly punish us, and that we continually need forgiveness of sins through faith, for the sake of the Lord Christ, without merit on our part. As Jacob confesses, "I am not worthy of the least of all the mercy and faithfulness which you have bestowed on your servant" [Gen. 32:10].

As this mortal life does not last forever, for all men must by physical death proceed to another existence, it is necessary to know and firmly to maintain this: Although all temporal goods are taken from us, we are nevertheless not to allow the eternal promise of the Lord Christ and his grace to pass away, for the promise is sure and firm for all times and for all men who accept it with faith. When David was driven out, he had the comfort of knowing that his sins were forgiven out of grace, for the sake of the Mediator. And Job declares, 13:15, "Though he slay me, yet will I trust in him." Faith should always first contemplate and accept the eternal promise of the Lord Christ, the promise of grace, and should abide by it even though all physical blessings are taken away. The promise of grace is the eternal covenant, the eternal testament, for through it eternal salvation is given, for the promise is sure and firm for all times and for all men who accept it with faith. The divine oath is immutable, "*As I live, says the Lord God, I have no pleasure in the death of the wicked, but that the wicked turn from his way and live.*"

Here one might ask, Since promises are appended to the law, how are these promises to be understood? Answer: We should clearly know the distinction between law and gospel. The eternal promise of *Christ*, the grace about which the gospel preaches, shuts out all our merit and says *freely*, for the sake of the Lord Christ, God gives forgiveness, grace, and eternal blessedness. The law, however, requires that we be completely obedient, and the promises which are appended to the law are based on perfect obedience. Now it is obvious that perfect obedience in this life is not possible for us, and that in this life sin remains in us. For this reason we have no right to the promises which are appended to the law.

But when we are justified through faith in the Lord *Christ* and God is pleased with the beginning of obedience *for the sake of the Lord Christ*, then the rewards of that obedience follow, as these passages indicate: "As you pray, so will you receive" [*cf.* Lk. 11:9; Mt. 21:22; Mk. 11:24]; and, "Whoever gives to one of these little ones even a cup of cold water because he is a disciple, truly, I say to you, he shall not lose his reward." These promises are not empty, yet, as previously discussed, it is also true that the Church remains under the cross. More will be said about this later, and what should be stated further about the promises of the law will be mentioned under the heading of the Old and New Testament.[4]

4. See below, Article XVI.

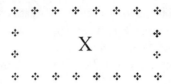

X

HOW MAN OBTAINS FORGIVENESS OF SIN
AND IS JUSTIFIED BEFORE GOD

Although the promise of Christ and of grace is very clear throughout divine Scripture, human reason is so blind that it does not behold the sun, the Lord Christ, and is always devising some merit and justification of its own. From the beginning, idols were invented; the distress of war called for a special sacrifice, and then the *cultus Martis* developed. Wives prepared special sacrifices in connection with birth, and out of this the *cultus Junois* developed. Later men invented invocation of the saints, such as St. George and St. Ann. The priests in Jerusalem imagined that we merit forgiveness of sins with a sacrifice. And later the blindness prevailed that the Mass and monkery merit forgiveness of sins.

Still later, the learned happened on to the word "justification." Some of them understood it only in terms of external morality, as one might understand worldly justice and declare that Aristides is a just citizen in that he conforms to the law; for according to the law *justification* means being uniform with the law. Some, like the Anabaptists and enthusiasts,[1] have desired to proceed still higher. They have imagined that they are justified and pleasing to God on account of some inner illumination and rapture. Many falsely praise such rapture, as one discovers in reading about Marcion, Priscilla,[2] and others, who practiced adultery and other gross vices

---

1. Those who tended to agree with the radical Anabaptists were often derided as enthusiasts, a term associated in the early Church with the Euchites of the fourth century A.D. in Mesopotamia and Syria. The Euchites boasted of having the Holy Spirit, rejected the sacraments and moral law, and advocated ascetic living. Anabaptist extremists frequently spoke of their emotional inspirations and direct revelations through the Holy Spirit.

2. Prisca and Maximilla were fanatical second-century prophetesses of Phrygia. They left their husbands to join Montanus, a former priest of Cybele who claimed that the Holy Spirit had invaded his body to proclaim through him the Christian truth. These chiliastic evangelists declared that the new Jerusalem was to be estab-

under the guise of the same rapture. Marcion led a deacon's wife to Cyprus, and she later returned to her husband and gave a good report about Marcion's immorality. In our own times many people knew Münzer and Storch,[3] who also boasted about a great rapture, but they were nevertheless adulterers and insurgents.

The devil and blind men continually storm against the truth in this important article about our Lord Christ and the grace which he brings with him. They rob him of his glory, destroy true invocation, and obscure true comfort for the frightened conscience. Note, then, the many ways in which one can be led away from the truth in this article. The Pharisees, Pelagians, monks, and Interimists [4] imagine that external morality is merit and justification. The enthusiasts and Anabaptists extol inner rapture and say that it makes them just and pleasing to God. These false paths lead away from the Lord Christ; they obliterate faith. But through God's grace the truth in this article was explained by the worthy Dr. Martin Luther and was uniformly preached in the churches of Saxony and repeatedly confessed, especially against the Interim and against Osiander [5] in 1552. I want to say that this singular doctrine, as it is known in

---

lished at Pepuza, and they called on believers to prepare themselves for the event by practicing asceticism. The association of the three occasioned rumors of immorality.

3. Nicholas Storch and Mark Stübner, two of the leading "heavenly prophets" from Zwickau, came to Wittenberg (1521-22) during Luther's protracted absence at the Wartburg and abetted the revolutionary reforms of Andreas Karlstadt, Luther's senior colleague at the University of Wittenberg. The Mass was altered and numerous vestiges of Roman Catholicism were violently destroyed. Storch and Stübner spoke of being blessed with an inner light and received visions about actions to be taken. Melanchthon could not decide whether they were led by the spirit of God or Satan. Associated with them in their fanatical activities was Thomas Münzer (see note, p. 83).

4. Interimist was a term of derogation denoting those who accepted the Augsburg Interim proclaimed by Charles V in May 1548 and the Leipzig Interim of Saxony, December 1548. The former was vigorously resisted by the German evangelicals, including Melanchthon, but the latter, which Elector Maurice enforced in Saxony, was accepted by many of them, including Melanchthon, who said that he could accept it so long as justification by faith was preserved; everything else, he said, could be regarded as nonessential. He was bitterly criticized for this stand. The interim ended when the Lutherans won toleration in the Peace of Passau, 1552, but criticism of Melanchthon continued.

5. Osiander, Andreas (1498-1552), was a leading German reformer and controversial figure who became an enemy of Melanchthon on account of the Augsburg and Leipzig Interim of 1548. Osiander was forced to depart from Nürnberg. Taking a post as professor at the new university at Königsberg, he published two works in 1550, De Lege et Evangelio and De Justificatione, which caused much controversy. While he opposed Calvinism and Romanism in line with Luther's thought, he ap-

the churches of Saxony, is certainly right. And I hereby repudiate whatever is contrary to the confession of the churches of Saxony.

Speaking first of external morality and worldly justfication, God certainly requires all men, whether born again or not born again, to live according to all God's commandments so far as external morality is concerned: in accordance with the first, to accept right teaching about God in external confession, and not to blaspheme God with idols or Epicurean words; in accordance with the second, not to make false oaths; in accordance with the third, to sustain and honor the true office of preaching and Christian churches; in accordance with the fourth, to be obedient to the authorities in all honorable things; in accordance with the fifth, to kill no one unjustly, to help sustain general peace in an orderly way; in accordance with the sixth, to shun all prohibited sexual relationships; in accordance with the seventh, not to steal; in accordance with the eighth, not to lie in the courts or otherwise.

This external morality is called worldly justification, and the word "justification" may be used when one speaks of this morality, this conformity with God's law in external works. And it is true that this morality or external justification is commanded and is necessary, and that God physically punishes immorality in this life and hereafter if the sinner is not converted again to God, for man is able out of his natural powers to maintain this morality to some degree.

But at the same time it is necessary to know that external morality merits no forgiveness of sins. It is not the justification by which man is justified before God, i.e. made pleasing to him. And it is by no means a fulfillment of the divine law; such morality is simply an external restraint. Adam and Eve covered themselves with fig leaves, and thus this restraint covered their inner impurity. Such restraint is born of reason, a movement in the will to keep the tongue, eyes, ears, hands, and feet still or to move in accordance with these thoughts.

These thoughts and movements are strong in some, weak in others. Scipio is firmer than Alexander in his resolve to avoid adultery. When these thoughts and movements are strong, one calls this virtue. But all virtues are very weak in this wretched human nature. And St. Paul is right in saying that such are only works of the law, not God's works,

---

parently went too far in asserting that justification by faith means not an imputation of faith but an infusion of actual righteousness or the divine nature of Christ. Melanchthon emphatically rejected this view, as the Saxon Confession of 1552 indicated.

merely works which we produce when we guide ourselves with the law. These thoughts are transitory; they are not life and joy and an overcoming of death; and doubt about God and impurity remain in the heart. Therefore, St. Paul says that righteousness [*Gerechtigkeit*] of the flesh is a transitory thing.

This is clear and easy to understand, and the Pelagians, papists, monks, and their like will be punished and repudiated if they imagine that external morality is a fulfillment of the divine law and that on account of his own works man is justified before God and merits forgiveness of sins. Such lies and abuses of the Lord *Christ* should be rebuked and avoided, and the true understanding of the divine law and gospel learned and sustained.

Note first of all the passage which John, after much reflection, wrote at the beginning of his book in order to distinguish between law and the Son of God. "For the *law* was given through *Moses; grace and truth* came through *Jesus Christ*" [Jn. 1:18]. Grace especially denominates forgiveness of sins and gracious acceptance by God, without merit on our part. Truth denominates true, eternal favor, not a shadow, and not a transitory thing, but eternal life, right knowledge of God, eternal wisdom and justification, that is, uniformity with God. After this life, in eternal blessedness, God will be all in all; he will shine clearly in the blessed, so that they will be full of light, justification, and joy, without any sin.

By Moses and the law come only shadows, external worldly morality and an external kingdom. But the Son of God became a sacrifice and merited *grace* for us, that is, forgiveness of sins, gracious acceptance by God, and eternal justification and blessedness. The Son himself in this mortal life brings about these benefits in us, so that we are turned to God and born anew; he gives the Holy Spirit and the beginning of blessedness, which will afterward be eternal blessedness in which we will have perfect justification, that is, uniformity with God. God will shine clearly in us and will be all in all. When John speaks of grace and truth, he includes everything that the Son has obtained and gives, both in this and in eternal life. He is not merely speaking of a weak beginning in this life.

St. Paul speaks similarly in Romans 5:15, ". . . much more have the grace of God and the free gift in the grace of that one man Jesus Christ abounded for many." Here he calls grace the forgiveness of sins, gracious acceptance by God; and he calls the gift everything that the Son of God effects in us when we are newly born through him and the Holy Spirit, and afterward to have eternal blessedness.

This is what our churches teach; they do not speak simply of acceptance, without any change in man, as Osiander does; they speak of all the divine benefits which the Son of God has won for us, which he bestows upon us and produces in us, namely of the forgiveness of sins; of gracious acceptance by God; of the imputation of righteousness; of the new birth in us, in which God himself is active through the gospel, comforting us, giving us the Holy Spirit, making us heirs of eternal blessedness now and giving us eternal blessedness after this life.

From the beginning God's promises proclaimed the Lord *Christ*, and we must now consider how we receive them. It happens in this way. When the eternal Son of God revealed the promise of grace and eternal salvation to Adam and Eve in these words, "The seed of the woman will tread on the head of the serpent," he at the same time began and instituted the office of preaching, through which he gathers to himself an eternal Church, punishes sin in all men, and proclaims the gospel of the Savior, grace, and eternal blessedness. In this preaching the Son is powerfully active in the faithful, as St. Paul declares, "The gospel is the power of God to salvation to all who believe" [Rom. 1:16].

The Son of God maintained the office of preaching through the prophets; when he himself became incarnate, he preached; and then he gave command to the apostles, saying, "As my Father has sent me, so send I you" [*cf.* Jn. 17:18; 20:21]; and, "You shall preach repentance and forgiveness of sins in my name" [*cf.* Lk. 24:47].

This preaching of the gospel, since it speaks of repentance and forgiveness, speaks first of what sin is, namely everything that is against God's law, and it expressly speaks of punishment of the great common but profound sin of *not believing in the Son of God*. For this reason the Lord *Christ* says, "The Holy Spirit will punish the world for the sin of not believing in me" [*cf.* Jn. 16:9], and *St. Paul* says, "The wrath of God is revealed, namely, through preaching, against the sin of all men" [Rom. 1:18].

And one should note that the office of preaching includes the part of the law known as *legem moralem*, the eternal unchangeable wisdom and rule of justice in God, a rule which is revealed to us because we are to know the nature of God and the nature of sin. For God wants sins to be known and punished, as previously explained.

And it is most certainly true, to speak quite bluntly, that no nation and no religion in all the world has fully taught the law, *legem moralem*, the law of external works, except the true Church of God. The heathen have all made great rents in it with their idols, immorality, and other vices, which they have not only practiced but have also sanctioned as right.

This is obvious confirmation that all other religions are untrue and rejected, for they have permitted and sanctioned gross sins. It follows that only the gathered company is the true Church of God in which true doctrine concerning the law has been maintained. Therefore, we should always teach the Ten Commandments in the Church in their true meaning, even as the Lord Christ, in Matthew 5, and the apostles preached them.

Although we may be secure, proud, and impregnable for a while, all men finally feel the judgment and wrath of God, for "God is a consuming fire." But before that happens, God wants to bring us to repentance. Therefore, when we hear the preaching of his word, we should recognize God's anger against our sins, and instead of rebelling, we should ask for conversion [*Bekehrung*], as Jeremiah pleads, in Jeremiah 31:18 f., "Bring me back that I may be restored, for thou art the Lord my God. For after I had turned away I repented." Obviously there must be an inner turning to God, for the divine oath clearly implies it: "As I live, says the Lord God, I have no pleasure in the death of the wicked, but that the wicked turn from his way and live" [Ez. 33:11]. Note that both repentance and life are included in the oath.

However, it is not only the *law* that should be preached, for God's unchangeable will and earnest commandment is that we at all times should also preach the *gospel* of his Son, grace and blessedness, and thus bring merciful consolation to the frightened conscience. Only through this preaching, not otherwise, does the Son of God gather an eternal Church. In this consolation of the gospel through faith we are to remain; we are not to seek the raptures of which the Anabaptists and enthusiasts speak. We also have the consolation that the office of preaching is not merely an empty voice, for the Lord *Christ* truly works through it; in this gathered company where the gospel is rightly preached are the predestined, and they are not to seek other sects.

Now when hearts tremble before the wrath of God, his unchangeable will and highest command is that we should believe that, *for the sake of his Son Jesus Christ,* who was appointed to be our Reconciler, graciously and *without any merit on our part,* he will give to us forgiveness of sins, justification, the Holy Spirit, and eternal life. As Paul says, "Grace and gift."

If we believe on the *Son of God,* we have forgiveness of sins; and

Christ's righteousness is imputed to us, so that we are justified and are pleasing to God for the sake of Christ. We are reborn through the Lord Jesus Christ; he speaks comfort to our hearts, imparts to us his Holy Spirit; and we are heirs of eternal salvation. And we have all this only on account of the Lord Christ, by grace, without merit, through faith alone. And this faith trusts in the Lord *Christ*, who is God and Man, for whose sake we wretched men will be received, as St. Paul says in Romans 5.

This is the consolation which God first revealed in his promises and then explained through the prophets, Christ and the apostles.

And although it may seem strange to human reason, the heathen, Pharisees, Mohammedans, Pope, monks, Anabaptists, and other secretaries storm against this in all sorts of ways. However, we should know that this consolation is a special divine revelation, and we should mark the testimonies to it in Scripture and with firm faith keep and console ourselves with it in all invocation. For this reason I wish to set forth a few important sentences.

Acts 10:43: "To him all the prophets bear witness that every one who believes in him receives forgiveness of sins through his name." This clearly says that forgiveness of sin and faith are bound to one another. When we come before God, we must first receive forgiveness of sins, which occurs through faith in the Son of God.

Romans 3:24 f.: "They are *justified by his grace as a gift*, through the *redemption which is in Christ Jesus*, whom God put forward as an expiation by his blood, to be received *by faith*." Now *to be justified* is to obtain forgiveness of sins, to please God, to be clothed with the righteousness of Christ, and endowed with the Holy Spirit. This occurs, he expressly says, *without merit on our part*, through faith in the Lord Christ, God and Man, because he bore for us the wrath of God. By speaking of blood, he includes the entire obedience and merit of the Lord *Christ*.

John 3:16: "For God so loved the world that he gave his only Son, that whoever believes in him should not perish but have eternal life."

Romans 4:3: "Abraham believed God, and it was reckoned to him as righteousness." *St. Paul* deliberately quoted this passage as evidence that the ancient Church of the first fathers taught as he. Romans 4 sets forth *St. Paul's* principal argument in this matter.

The promise of grace must be certain; otherwise we would have no sure comfort and there would be no distinction between God's Church and that of the heathen. If the promise were uncertain or empty, then salvation would rest on our fulfillment of the law. But we are all mired deep in sins, and are far from conforming to the law. So it follows that the promise of grace is not grounded on our merit, but on our Savior *Christ*, and must be received with faith. These are the words of *Paul:* "Therefore out of faith, without merit, so that the promise may remain firm" [*cf.* Rom. 4:13–14; Gal. 3:17–18].

Romans 5:1: "Since we are justified by faith, we have peace with God through our Lord Jesus Christ. Through him we have obtained access to this grace in which we stand." This sentence is clear and comforting, for Paul obviously says we are justified through *faith;* and that we may know how this happens, and what this faith is, he says, "Through this faith the heart has peace before God" [*cf.* Rom. 5:1]. Though we feel God's anger, as Hezekiah says, "Like a lion he has crushed all my bones" [*cf.* Is. 38:13], faith in the Lord Christ brings comfort and life.

Ephesians 3:12 speaks thus also, ". . . in whom we have boldness and confidence of access through our faith in him."

Ephesians 2:8 f.: "For by *grace* you have been saved through faith; and this *is not your own doing*, it is the *gift of God — not because of works*, lest any man should boast."

Faith should be based on these and similar passages which explain the preaching of the Lord Christ, the apostles, the ancient promises and passages in the prophets. Isaiah 53:11, "By his knowledge shall the righteous one, my servant, make many to be accounted righteous," is clear if one understands that *this knowledge* is *faith* in the Lord Christ *through the gospel.*

This having been established, we should consider how this truth is assailed, especially by the papists, who give false meanings to *faith, grace,* and *justification*. Therefore, let us look at their true meanings.

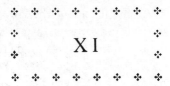

XI

OF THE WORD "FAITH" [1]

Faith does not mean merely knowing the story of Christ, for even the devils confess that the Son of God appeared and arose from the dead, and in Judas there was a knowledge of Christ. *True faith* is truly to retain all the words which God has given to us, including the promise of grace; it is *a heartfelt reliance on the Savior Christ, a trust that God for his Son's sake* graciously forgives us our sins, receives us, and makes us heirs of eternal blessedness. Romans 4 clearly shows that this is the meaning in the word "faith" when we say, "Through faith we are justified."

The promise is to be received in faith, and so faith is a reliance on the Savior, Christ. Whoever does not receive the promise does not believe all of God's word. Judas does not believe that God will forgive him his sins, but David and Peter believe not only the story, commandments, and threats, but also the promise of grace. I am not devising some new view in saying this. "I believe in the forgiveness of sins" means more than just believing that sins are forgiven others; it means, My sins are forgiven *me*. Not to believe this is to believe only the external history. The symbol includes not only the story but also the promises and the fruit of the promise. Obviously, when Paul says, "Since we are justified through faith, we have peace with God" [Rom. 5:1], he speaks of a faith which brings comfort and peace to the heart. This peace is not just knowledge, for the devils know, and it causes them to tremble and flee from Christ; they are certain that God will punish them. This faith, which receives the promise, says that God wants to forgive us our sins for the sake of the Lord Christ. It is a reliance on the Lord *Christ,* and it effects peace, as all true Christians know. It is not untrue to say that the Lord Christ himself effects this peace, or that the Holy Spirit does. God is present in this comfort. He is active, however, through the external word, and kindles

1. Melanchthon reverses the listing in his introduction and treats "faith" before "grace."

faith in the heart. But these are all together — the external word, contemplation of the external words in us, and the Son of God, who works through the external word, manifests the eternal Father, speaks comfort to the heart, and gives the Holy Spirit, which produces love and joy in God.

When one says, "*Through faith* we have forgiveness of sins, and are justified," this does not mean that we have forgiveness for the sake of this work which is called *faith;* but *for the sake of the Lord Christ* on whose obedience and merit the reliance is based. Faith is the means by which we behold the Lord Christ and by which we apply and appropriate his merit to ourselves.

To prevent erroneous interpretation, which is common in our churches, when one says, "Through faith we have forgiveness and are justified, that is, pleasing to God," it should be understood correlatively, that is, for the sake of the Lord Christ, not that the work, namely faith, is the merit.

And the power to revitalize, pacify, and comfort the heart is not the power of faith, but of Christ himself, who through faith works, comforts, and gives his Holy Spirit in the heart. But Christ wants to work through the gospel and faith, and not otherwise.

Let this be remembered, that there is a distinction between the meaning of worldy justification and *this* justification which is given through the gospel, as we will further explain in connection with the word "justification." [2] Worldly justification pertains to those purposes, and works in accordance with them, which die with men; but the comfort which *the Lord Christ* effects in believers is life, and it remains, as written in Romans 8:10, "Your spirit is alive because of righteousness." With this information we can answer the arguments of the papists, Anabaptists, and Osiander.

2. See below, p. 161 ff.

OF THE WORD "GRACE"

Grace in the above passages certainly means *gracious forgiveness of sins,* and *God's gracious acceptance out of mercy, for the sake of the Lord Christ, without any merit on our part.* And moreover, with the forgiveness of sins there is always the gift of comfort in our hearts, which is the Holy Spirit, given to us through the Lord Christ, as it is written in Romans 5:2, "Through the Lord Christ we have obtained grace and the gift"; and in Romans 8:9, "He who does not have the spirit of Christ does not belong to him." Therefore, we say that Christ gives the Holy Spirit in our hearts along with forgiveness of sins, and he produces comfort, life, and joy unto God. And we do not say that no change occurs in man with acceptance of the gift, as Osiander falsely insists.

The monks, on the other hand, have misused the word "grace" by saying that it makes man holy, so that they identify grace with themselves. Since we always find weakness and sin in ourselves, this is a lie. *Grace* is a gracious forgiveness of sins, and acceptance for Christ's sake, without any merit on our part, *freely* and *for the sake of the Lord Christ.* So says St. Paul in Romans 6:14, "You are not under the law but under grace." This is as comforting as if one were to say, Although you are weak and still have sin, nevertheless the law shall not condemn you, for you are under grace, that is, for the sake *of the Lord Christ, freely, without any merit,* you have received forgiveness of sins and gracious acceptance, and are pleasing to God. Thus St. Paul directs us not to a quality in us, but to the Mediator Jesus Christ. But this still stands; when we are comforted through faith, Christ produces life in us and gives his Holy Spirit. We need to remember all this about grace, lest the words of the monks lead us astray.

XIII

OF THE WORD

"Justification" and "To Be Justified" [1]

In a worldly sense it is obvious that justification means conformity to the law: Aristides is a just citizen, we say, meaning that he does what the laws command, and he does not act contrary to them.

To speak of complete, perfect justification of the law before God, such as that which angels have and men who are saved will have in eternity, is to speak of justification as conformity with God, which is as much as to say, with God's law; for God is thus as he gives himself to be known in the law.

This perfect justification in eternity means God himself is in the saved [*seligen*]. As St. Paul says, "God will be all in all" [*cf.* 1 Cor. 15:28; 12:6; Col. 3:11], that is, God himself is in the saved, and makes them like himself, so that they are entirely pure, without sin. As John says, "We will be like him" [1 Jn. 3:2]. St Paul speaks about this complete and perfect justification in Galatians 5:5, "For through the Spirit, by faith, we wait for the hope of righteousness."

Although in this mortal life believers have a spark, the gospel nevertheless preaches to us the justification of *Christ*, of the *Mediator* between God and us, and says that the Mediator's entire obedience, from his Incarnation until the Resurrection, is the true justification which is pleasing to God, and is the merit for us. God forgives us our sins, and accepts us, in that he imputes righteousness to us for the sake of the Son, although we are still weak and sinful. We must, however, accept this imputed righteousness with faith.

So now in this mortal life, that by which we are pleasing to God is the righteousness of *Christ*, which is imputed to us. We receive forgiveness of sins, and are pleasing to God for the sake of the Christ, namely on

---

1. *Gerechtigkeit und gerecht sein.* Melanchthon uses *Gerechtigkeit* to mean "righteousness" and/or "justification"; in this translation both English words have been used.

account of his obedience, as St. Paul says, Romans 5:19, "By one man's (namely *Christ's*) obedience many will be made righteous."

Thus we are clothed with a strange righteousness. Although our nature itself is still not uniform with God, nevertheless, as the Mediator Christ in his complete obedience is uniform with God and covers our sins with his righteousness, so we are justified, have forgiveness of sins, and are pleasing to God, for *Christ's* sake, whose righteousness is accepted on our behalf. And this we must accept *with faith*.

Certainly no man in God's court is without sin. As the Psalm says, "No one living is justified before God" [*cf.* Ps. 143:2]. And Job 9:2, "Truly I know that no man is justified before God," should be understood with reference to the complete fulfillment of the law. Moses says, in Exodus 34, "The innocent before thee is not innocent." [2] All men must come before God through the Mediator Jesus Christ, and must first receive forgiveness of sins and acceptance for the sake of the Lord Christ; that is quite certain. Thus righteousness means this imputed righteousness.

In all this Christ effects life in us, and gives us the Holy Spirit, and eternal righteousness is begun in us, as written in John's letter, "He who has the Son has life" [1 Jn. 5:12]. To have the Son is to receive him in faith; God gives us, for the sake of his Son, forgiveness of sins, and accepts us. The Son speaks this comfort to us and gives us his Holy Spirit, who kindles love and joy to God in our hearts, as written in the same letter, "By this we know that we abide in him and he in us, because he has given us of his own Spirit" [1 Jn. 4:13].

Now the Holy Spirit is a living divine motion in us, producing in us that which is akin to God, of which Jeremiah speaks in the thirty-first chapter, "I will put my law within them, and I will write it upon their hearts" [v. 33]. God is as he reveals himself in the law: wise, true, good, just, pure, and chaste; one who punishes sin. And when he says he wants to give us his law in our hearts, this signifies that the Son of God reveals to us the wisdom of the eternal Father through the gospel, that we may recognize the Father. He also gives us the Holy Spirit, who produces in us joy to God, cleanness of heart and other virtues, as the law teaches. Thus there is a spark of new obedience in those who are converted to God; but the faith that *for the sake of the Lord Christ* we have forgiveness of sins, and are pleasing to God, must always precede, and this faith must be grounded on the *obedience of the Lord Christ*, God and Man. When this

2. Verse uncertain, reference probably to Moses' veil v. 33-35.

comfort is in the heart, then we are the dwelling place of God and obedience is begun.

Thus in Romans 3:24 f. St. Paul directs us to obedience and the merit of Christ: "We are justified by his grace as a gift, through the redemption which is in Christ Jesus, whom God put forward as an expiation by his blood, to be received by faith. This was to show God's righteousness, because in his divine forbearance he had passed over former sins." *Are justified* means that we obtain forgiveness of sins, and are received by God into grace. This happens as *St. Paul* says, "on account of the blood of Jesus Christ" [*cf.* Eph. 2:13], and John also says, "*The blood of Jesus Christ* purifies us from all sins" [1 Jn. 1:7]. Thus faith is grounded on the obedience and merit of Christ.

This definition is also in the words of Paul. By *are justified* he means this comfort in the midst of true anguish, forgiveness of sins received through faith, and being pleasing to God for the sake of the Lord Christ. But the renewal that follows, which God effects in us, he calls *sanctification* [*Heiligung*], and these two words are clear and distinct.

Answer to Several Counterarguments

These words and the doctrine itself are further clarified in the following counterarguments, and it is reasonable to explain that the old mother tongue in the Church has been so obscured by the fancies of the monks that we must now struggle with the meaning of words such as sin, faith, grace, and so forth.

The first argument: Since the devils also believe [have faith], how then can belief [*Glaube*] ³ be that whereby a man is justified?

Answer: The devils believe only the history, they do not believe that the Son of God has come to them for good. Yes, they know that he will punish them in eternity, and for this reason they rage against God and against the Son of God. In hate, they blaspheme God among themselves, and they drive poor wretched men to idolatry, murder, immorality, and other vices.

However, we should firmly believe that the Son of God is sent to us for good, as expressed in the symbol, *Qui propter nos homines et propter nostram salutem descendit de coelis*, "who for the sake of men

---

3. Throughout this section Melanchthon uses *Glaube* to signify "faith," but often it could be translated "belief."

and for our salvation came down from heaven." John 1:9 says, "He enlightens all men"; and Isaiah 9:6, "A Son is given to us." Bernard [4] rightly says that we must not only believe that God will forgive the sins of others, but that he will graciously forgive us, each one of us, our sins. This belief brings the comfort that the heart experiences. Of this Paul says, "Since we are justified through faith, we have peace with God" [Rom. 5:1]. The devils in their knowledge do not believe that forgiveness of sins is given to them; they see nothing but wrath and punishment; and, therefore, furious hate follows. . . .

The second argument: Since it is quite impossible to be justified by knowledge only, and as faith is a matter of knowledge and thought, and not some power of will and heart, how then is a man to be justified through faith?

Answer: The faith of which St. Paul speaks when he says, "Since we are justified through faith, we have peace with God," is not only knowledge and thought but something in the will and heart, a burning reliance on the Son of God, an earnest, ardent desire and will to accept the precious treasure, forgiveness of sins and grace. It cries out to God, Dear Father [*Herzlieber Vater*]! As St. Paul says in Romans 8:15, "God has placed the Spirit of his Son in your hearts, which cries, '*Abba, dear Father!*' "

As far as heaven and hell are from one another, so far are we to separate this *true faith* from the *knowlege* that the devil and godless men possess. What true faith is, and how it shines in men, is learned only when, in the midst of great anguish, we are again quickened, and drawn out of the vengeance of hell. When David hears, "The Lord has taken away your sins" [2 Sam. 12:13], then he begins to believe, to recognize God's great grace, and the Son of God comforts his soul, indicates to him the Father's will through these words, gives at the same time his Holy Spirit, which makes in the will and heart the burning reliance on God's promise, and joy to God. Thus this faith [*Glaube*] is not simply a knowledge and thought that men by themselves produce: it is a light and joy which the Son of God produces through the gospel and the Holy Spirit. So speaks God in Zechariah 12:10, "I will pour out on the house of David a spirit of compassion and supplication"; that is, the Holy Spirit will give testimony in preaching and in the heart, so that we may feel comfort and recognize that we are in grace, and the Holy Spirit will produce joyful invocation in our hearts. So long as the heart is in flight before

4. St. Bernard of Clairvaux; see note, p. 68.

God, there can be no true invocation; but when it recognizes God's mercy through faith, then it flies back to God, calling on him and expecting his help.

Scripture speaks of this in 1 Peter 1:23, "You have been born anew, not of perishable seed but of imperishable, through the living and abiding word of God." When the Son of God, by means of the gospel, works this comfort in our hearts, points us to the gracious will of the Father, and gives us his Holy Spirit, then we are reborn, and have in us the divine light and the beginning of eternal life. In his work on the Holy Spirit, Athanasius says, "When the Holy Spirit is in man, there is the word, which speaks of the Son who through the gospel comforts the heart of man, indicates the Father's will, and bestows the Holy Spirit." [5] Gregory of Nazianzus says, "From the eternal light, God the Father, we receive light, the Son, through the Holy Spirit." [6] Faith is believing that all the words of God, including the promise of grace, are true; it is a heartfelt trust in the Son of God. It is light and trust which God produces in us, to bring comfort, life, and joy in God. Through this faith our hearts conclude that our own sins are forgiven and that we are pleasing to God *for the sake of Christ*, who gives us his merit and clothes us with his righteousness.

The third argument: Why say that we have forgiveness of sins and are justified *only* through faith? Surely many virtues must accompany faith, repentance and sorrow for sins, belief, good resolution, and hope.

Answer: The exclusive *sola* or *gratis* must be fully maintained, as will be explained later more adequately. It shuts out *all our merit*; it teaches that we receive forgiveness of sins and are justified *for the sake of Christ alone*, that is, we are pleasing to God, and the heart must receive this with faith. This great grace is given through the knowledge of Christ, as Isaiah says. This knowledge is the faith about which we speak. Here an order is established by God that makes a distinction between God's children and others. The children of God are those who thus recognize Christ and accept him with faith. There must be an *application* of the grace of Christ; and this *application* occurs through faith, and faith results from preaching, contemplation of the gospel, and the sacraments.

And it is true, as indicated in the explanation of the second argument,

5. Cf. *Nicene and Post-Nicene Fathers*, H. Wace and P. Schaff, eds. (Oxford and New York, 1893), IV, *Writings, Athanasius, Discourse Against the Arians*, III, chap. 25:24–25; II, chap. 15:18.

6. St. Gregory of Nazianzus (329–389). Cf. *Ibid.*, VII, *Fourth Theological Oration, On the Holy Spirit; Fifth Theological Oration, On the Son.*

that where true faith is, there at the same time are many virtues. However, they are not meritorious; they are not *causae justificationis;* they are not reasons why God accepts us. They result from faith; as indicated above, we receive grace and gift. As the sun has both light and the power to warm, and the two cannot be separated, so wherever there is true faith, a recognition of God's mercy, there also is love, invocation of God, and hope, and a will which willingly subjects itself to God and is obedient. These accompany faith as light and heat accompany a fire. Nevertheless, there is no merit in these virtues. Merit lies only in the faith by which we receive forgiveness of our sins, and is received *for the sake of the Christ.* This we receive in the word and through the word; the Lord Christ is active through the gospel.

Why must we firmly maintain Exclusivam: fide sola *or* gratis?

Answer: For five reasons. The first, so that Christ may be given his special honor, for *his* obedience *alone* is merit for us. On his account God is willing to forgive us our sins, receive us graciously, and make us heirs of eternal blessedness; and *our* wretched deeds, sufferings, and works *do not* merit this exalted grace.

The second reason is that God in his great mercy wants the grace which he has offered to men in his promise to stand certain, firm, and immovable, for the promise is called an eternal testament. This comfort is certain if it is grounded *only on the Son of God* and *not* on our merit. For this reason we say, *Only* through faith may the heart be assured that God is gracious, for the sake of Christ. If this depended on our merit, it would not only be uncertain, but the promise would be empty, for in this wretched life we always have much sin, ignorance, and transgression. *Paul* says, "Therefore, *out of faith, without merit on our part,* the promise remains firm" [*cf.* Rom. 3:28, 4:16; Gal. 2:16, 3:11-14].

The third reason is that there is no other means whereby we acknowledge and accept the Lord Christ and his grace except by *faith alone.* God's unchangeable counsel is that there be a clear distinction between the children of God and other men, that the Son of God be rightly known by the children of God; this knowledge is faith. Faith hears the preaching of the gospel, in which Christ and his grace are conveyed to us, and faith accepts. When we recognize God's mercy, the heart is revived and drawn out of hell. And therefore it is crude to say, *Fides apprehensiva et quietativa.*

The fourth reason: so that the distinction between law and the gospel may be clear. The law says that when we are as the law commands, then we are justified. But no man, with the exception of our Lord and Savior Christ, is as the law teaches. But when we *believe on the Son of God*, we have forgiveness of sins, and we are pleasing to God *for the sake of Christ*, freely, without any merit on our part, although our sinful nature is very unlike the law.

The fifth reason: so that we may be able to call on God. Without this Mediator, the Son of God, we could not approach God. If invocation depended on our merit, then the heart would flee from God. Therefore, the Lord says, we are to invoke in *his* name, that is, *in the faith* that he is the Mediator and High Priest who bears our prayer before God and that we are heard *for the sake of his merit*.

The fourth argument. Why do you say, "Not out of works"? Is faith itself not also a work?

Answer: When one says, "Through faith we have forgiveness and are justified," this, according to Paul, means *for the sake of the Lord Christ and through him* we have forgiveness of sins and are justified, or pleasing to God, but not on account of our works or virtues. Nevertheless, we must accept Christ, through faith, for God wants this Savior, his Son, to be known; and he wants to gather to himself an eternal Church through knowledge of the gospel, through which the Son of God himself works and gives comfort and life. He wants a distinction to be made between the heathen and us; therefore he must enlighten us with knowledge of the Lord and true faith. No distinction would be possible between us and the heathen if God saved men without knowledge of Christ and without faith! This we should consider diligently, and also know that we have forgiveness of sins, and are pleasing to God, for the sake of Christ the *Mediator*, who presents his obedience for us, and is our Intercessor, not on account of the worthiness of our virtues.

The fifth argument. Righteousness is uniformity with, or fulfillment of, the entire law, and to this belongs not only faith, but love and all the other virtues, so why say, *sola fide*, "by faith *alone*"?

Answer: It is legal language to say that righteousness is uniformity with the divine law or with God, or that it is the fulfillment of the entire law, or, as Osiander childishly says, Righteousness is that which makes us do right. All this is legal language. The blessed are justified, that is, one [*gleichförmig*] with the law in that God himself is in them and enlightens them, and gives to them his light, so that they are one with him, without any sin, for as Paul says, "God will be all in all."

In this weak life we do not have perfect righteousness. Therefore, the gospel preaches to us about forgiveness of sins, and says how a poor sinner may come to God, obtain forgiveness, and become pleasing to him. The gospel calls this an imputed righteousness, for the sake of Christ. *Christ's obedience*, accordingly, is the oneness with God which is received on our behalf, and with which we are clothed so that the wrath of God is not poured over us, and does not destroy our wretched nature.

Clearly, in this mortal life we cannot approach God and invoke him unless we first receive forgiveness of sins and are justified, or pleasing to God, on account of *Christ*, whose righteousness is accepted for us, and who clothes us. This occurs *only through faith*, when the heart in true anguish trusts on the Mediator *Jesus Christ*, God and Man; all the prophets, Christ himself, and the apostles teach this about invocation.

David states, "No man living is righteous before thee" [Ps. 143:2], but this is with reference to complete fulfillment of the law, and it teaches us to take refuge in mercy. In Psalm 6, he says, "Help me for the sake of thy mercy" [*cf.* v.4]. When the prophets mention mercy, let it be understood to mean on account of the promised Mediator and Reconciler, the Lord Christ.

Accordingly, Daniel petitions, "Not on account of our righteousness, but on account of thy mercy, and for the sake of Christ, hear me" [Dan. 9:18].

So also speaks Christ: "No one comes to the Father except through me," [Jn. 6:44]; "Come unto me, all you who are troubled; I will give you rest" [Mt. 11:28]; "What you ask in my name . . ." [Jn. 14:13–14; *cf.* Mt. 1:7–8; Lk. 11:10].

In Ephesians 3:12 Paul says, "We have boldness and confidence of access through our faith in him. . . ."

Hebrews 4:14–16, "Since then we have a great high priest . . . let us draw near to the throne of grace."

Let us consider these and similar testimonies and strengthen our hearts in the truth that we are justified, that we truly receive forgiveness of sins and are pleasing to God *for the sake of Christ, out of grace, through faith,* on account of the merits of Christ, and do not let ourselves make the error of Osiander, who speculates that we are justified on account of the essential [*wesentlichen*] righteousness of God in us. Just the opposite is obvious: man receives forgiveness and is pleasing to God on account of the merits of *Christ*, through faith.

As the words *are justified* mean "to be pleasing to God," so *righteous-*

ness must be understood as the imputed righteousness of which Paul speaks.

And yet it follows that when we are received through faith, the Son of God speaks comfort to our hearts through the gospel, enlivens us, snatches us out of the vengeance of hell, and gives us the Holy Spirit. Thus John declares, 1 John 5:12, "He who has the Son has life"; also 1 John 4:13, "By this we know that we abide in him and he in us, because he has given us of his own Spirit." So we are to keep a distinction between passages in the law and passages in the gospel about justification, for the gospel says, "We are justified for the sake of Christ." Here *justification* or *are justified* means to have forgiveness of sins and to be pleasing to God for the sake of Christ, through faith, and as we are accepted, it is true that then the Son of God is in us, giving the Holy Spirit, comfort, and life; nevertheless, man is pleasing to God *for the sake of the Lord Christ*, God and Man. This faith must light our way. . . .

Osiander's statement that "righteousness is that which makes us do right" is a legal teaching which deprives us of comfort; for we find in us all kinds of sins, transgressions, and ignorance. Only very weakly do we do what is right, and if being justified depended on doing what is right, conscience would be without comfort.

In contrast to this the Psalms declare, "Blessed are those whose sins are forgiven" [Ps. 32:1]; and, "Blessed are all who rely on the Son" [Ps. 2:12]. To be justified is to receive forgiveness of sins and imputed righteousness, for the sake of Christ, through faith. And the Lord Christ speaks comfort in our hearts, gives the Holy Spirit and life, as we have said so often.

The sixth argument: Solomon says, "Man does not know whether he pleases God or not" [*cf.* Prov. 21:2; 1 Chron. 6:36]. Then why say that we must believe that we have forgiveness of sins and are justified, that is, are pleasing to God?

Answer: The monks have ushered into the Church a frightful blindness; they stubbornly fight for an error, for they say that man shall always doubt whether he is pleasing to God. They falsely interpret the passage in Solomon, and yet recently, just six years ago, they established their devilish error in the Council of Trent. Over against this it is very necessary to know and to uphold the true doctrine of faith. Such blind error should be clearly and openly rebuked.

We boldly say that all men who are not converted to God and who persist in their sins against conscience certainly do not know that they are not in God's grace, and if they are not converted, they will surely fall into eternal punishment. First Corinthians 6:9–10 warns that, "Whores, idolaters, adulterers, and so forth, shall not inherit the kingdom of God."

Truly, all men ought to obey God and hear the Son Jesus Christ, for the divine voice states, "To this [my Son] shall you listen" [Mt. 17:5; Mk. 9:7; Lk. 9:35]. He punishes sin; to those who truly tremble before God's wrath and do not persist in sins against the conscience, to those who desire to have comfort and salvation, he will give forgiveness of sins and grace. Terrified consciences are obliged to believe that God gives to them for the sake of Christ, without merit of their own, forgiveness of sins, and that God receives them into grace through faith. They are not to remain mired in doubt. Doubt in the terrified heart is a deep, terrible anger against God, which blocks invocation, as the experience of true anguish shows. Christians are to understand this struggle in the heart.

Romans 4 indicates that we should not remain mired in doubt, "Because the promise rests *on faith, without merit.*" There Paul teaches that one must receive the promise with faith, that for him who does not receive it with faith, but remains in doubt, the promise is in vain. Likewise Ephesians 3:12: "Through him we have boldness and confidence of access through our faith in him."

Romans 5:1: "Therefore, since we are justified by faith, we have peace with God." Doubt is a deep anger against God, and finally plunges men into despair and hellish anguish and fury. And when man remains in doubt, there is no true invocation, for *St. Paul* asks, "How can they pray if they do not believe" [Rom. 10:14]?

When we repeat the Creed, saying, "I believe in the forgiveness of sins," we should understand that this means not only that the sins of others, of Peter or Paul, are forgiven, but that *our own* sins are forgiven. The passages about faith serve to strengthen this belief.

But the weak heart says, "Ah, I find much impurity in myself; how then can I be pleasing to God?" Answer: The faith in the men who are converted to God is not grounded on their own purity, but on the Son of God. They should hold to the promise written in Psalm 130:5, "I wait for the Lord, and in his word I hope." And the passage in Augustine is true, for he shows in his book on meditation that the entire certainty of trust depends on the noble blood of Christ.[7]

7. Cf. *Works of Aurelius Augustine*, III, *Donatist Controversy*, Marcus Dods, ed. (Edinburgh, 1872), *Answer to Letters of Petilian*, Bk. 1, chap. 7; *Fathers of the*

In summary, the papal teaching that one should remain mired in doubt is empty heathenish blindness, and a destruction of the gospel, the promise of grace, and true teaching about faith.

Solomon's meaning [in Proverbs 3 and 16] is, "Man is not to judge from external fortune or misfortune, whether he is in favor or disfavor [*Gnade oder Ungnade*], but out of God's word." Jereboam should not think that he is pleasing to God just because he has become mighty and rich. And David is not to conclude that God has rejected him because he is driven out of the kingdom; his heart is to judge according to God's word. This is in keeping with the passage in Solomon, and our teaching; one is not to judge from external fortune or misfortune but according to God's word.

The seventh argument: In 1 Corinthians 13:2 St. Paul says, "If I have all faith, but have not love, I am nothing." Also 1 John 3:14, "He who does not love remains in death." These and many similar passages are cited against the *Exclusivam: sola fide,* "by faith *alone.*"

Answer: These and similar passages say that love and a new obedience must be in us; that is true. However, love and new obedience do not merit forgiveness or cause a person to be pleasing to God. A person has forgiveness and is pleasing to God *for the sake of the Mediator alone,* whom one appropriates only by *faith,* and Christ gives his Holy Spirit, who is the flame of true love and joy in God. This single true answer explains many passages.

The eighth argument: In 1 Corinthians 13, St. Paul says that love is the greatest virtue. Now if it is greater than faith, then it appears to follow that one is more justified for the sake of love than for the sake of faith.

Answer: The reason we have forgiveness of sins and are justified before God, that is, pleasing to God, is *Christ alone.* He is many hundred thousands of times greater than all virtues, all angels, and all men, and this Lord *Christ* we must recognize and accept with faith.

Which virtues among themselves are greater or smaller is a teaching of the law, and has nothing to do with the comfort of faith. We should remember that all our works and virtues begun in this wretched life are very weak. All of them belong in the category of which Job declares, "I know truly that no man is justified before God" [*cf.* 9:2–3, 28]; however, the Son of God is our Mediator and Reconciler, and places before the eternal

Father *his* obedience. *For this Reconciler's sake* we are justified by grace, that is, we have forgiveness of sins and are pleasing to God.

Other related arguments I omit for the sake of brevity.

But all men should diligently consider the principal distinction between the doctrines of our churches and of the monks. For the sake of instruction and strengthening of true faith I will set forth three of the gross distinctions.

First, the monks and other papists say that our good works merit forgiveness of sins, and that man is thus justified before God on account of his own works and his fulfillment of the law.

Secondly, they say that since no man can know if he has enough good works for the forgiveness of sins and if he is justified, then all men should continually remain mired in doubt about whether they have forgiveness and whether they are pleasing to God.

Thirdly, they say that a man has the ability to fulfill God's law, and that our works and fulfillment of the law are merit for the forgiveness of sins and righteousness before God. Several also think that man has the ability to fulfill the law without the Holy Spirit. They are in the even deeper blindness of thinking that divine law commands only external works.

The gospel's true doctrine, which prevails in our churches, opposes these three views. First, we have forgiveness of sins *for the sake of the Lord Christ,* and are justified, that is, pleasing to God, *through faith, without merit on our part.*

Second, we are not to remain mired in doubt; we are to believe that God truly forgives us our sins and graciously receives us *for the sake of Christ.* And although doubt is innate in our weak nature, we should nevertheless counteract it with the gospel, through which the Son of God is active and gives us the Holy Spirit.

Third, it is quite obvious from the writings of all the prophets and apostles that God's earnest and unchangeable will is for our hearts and external members to be just, pure, and sinless. How otherwise can one say that divine law commands entire obedience in the heart and external works? It is also obvious that no man, with the exception of God's own son, Jesus Christ, in this mortal life has entire obedience toward God in his heart. Therefore, *St. Paul* notes, Romans 8:7, "The flesh is hostile to God; it does not submit to God's law, indeed it cannot." And for this reason the gospel says that obedience in this life is begun in us through Christ and the Holy Spirit.

Because several adversaries declare that trust belongs to hope and not to faith, it is useful to note some distinctions. For although all three, true faith, love, and hope, go together, as light and heat in a fire, there is nevertheless this distinction: the knowledge of God and of Christ, according to the entire symbol, light the way for all the virtues in us. This knowledge and trust in *Christ* is *faith*, which now receives forgiveness of sins and God's grace.

Hope is indeed an awaiting of future deliverance, namely eternal life, assured on account of the merits of the Lord Christ, not on account of our worthiness; it is awaiting the alleviation of temporal misery according to God's will.

Love toward God we will better understand in eternal blessedness when a great consuming love and joy in God will be in us, kindled in us by God himself. In this life, nevertheless, there must be a spark about which one should speak as much as possible. We usually explain that love toward God is keeping his commandments, in faith in Christ, and having joy in God.

Faith, however, must always light the way, and should contemplate the three persons in the divine majesty. All three persons, the eternal Father, the eternal Son, Jesus Christ, and the Holy Spirit, are the true God, who forgives us our sins, graciously receives us, and gives to us blessedness. This occurs on account of the Mediator, namely the Son *Jesus Christ*. He is called the eternal Word. God has revealed that through him all creatures have come into being and that through him comes the gospel, in which he himself speaks comfort to our hearts and shows us the eternal Father and his will. And the eternal Father and the Son give the Holy Spirit in our hearts, who produces love and joy in God, and invocation and other virtues, as written in Zechariah 12:10, "I will pour out on the house of David a spirit of compassion and supplication"; that is, the Holy Spirit testifies to the heart that we are in grace, and the Holy Spirit impels the heart to true invocation and obedience to God. Faith should contemplate all three persons, and for this reason we may so phrase our prayers:

"O almighty, eternal, true God, eternal Father of our Lord Jesus Christ, together with thy only begotten Son Jesus Christ and the Holy Spirit, Creator of all creatures, thou who art wise, true, good, just, pure, free, and merciful, and who gatherest to thyself among men for the sake of thy Son, and through thy Son, an eternal Church, I confess and I am heartily sorry that I am sinful and have often acted in opposition to thee. I pray thee, however, that thou wouldst forgive me all my sins and graciously receive me and make me righteous for thy beloved Son's sake, Jesus Christ, and through him, whom thou hast ordained to be our Mediator and Reconciler, I pray thee to guide and sanctify my soul and heart with thy Holy Spirit, that I may truly acknowledge and invoke the true God, eternal Father, eternal Son, Jesus Christ, and eternal Holy Spirit, and be obedient to thee. Gather unto thee always an eternal Church among us, and give us blessed government, nourishment, and households, and graciously guide and preserve me and my poor children, that we may happily serve in thy true Church in this life and in eternity be with thee and praise thee in eternal wisdom, righteousness, and joy."

XIV

OF GOOD WORKS [1]

When an anguished heart is turned to God through faith in the Christ and is comforted, then certainly God is in the heart and is active, although he may give to one a greater and to another a smaller light, or he may let himself be more clearly seen in one than in another. Nevertheless, this passage is true for all, "Whoever loves me will keep my sayings, and my Father will love him, and we will come to him and abide with him" [Jn. 14:23]. This occurs, as said above, and as St. Paul writes in Galatians 3:14, "The promise of the Holy Spirit we receive through faith." The Son comforts our hearts through the gospel, and points us to the gracious will of the Father, and the Holy Spirit is given through the word, that we may have joy in God and love to God. Accordingly, these follow: true invocation, a beginning of obedience, true fear of God, love to God, trust in God in all necessity, humility in the knowledge of one's own weakness, patience, joy in God, hope, confession, perseverance in confession, and earnest diligence. Such impulses [*Regungen*], which God kindles in our hearts and external members, are called good works.

It is boorish to imagine that good works mean only external deeds. Several crude people contend that the thief who was converted on the cross had no good work after his conversion. On the contrary, as soon as his heart was comforted through the word, "This day you will be with me in paradise" [Lk. 23:43], God himself was in the thief's heart, showed himself to him, became active in him, drew him out of the vengeance of hell, began in him eternal life, and produced the beginning of all virtues, so that the thief had repentance for his sins, acknowledged the Messiah, and had comfort through faith, love to God, joy in God, and assured hope of eternal life. He was willingly obedient in his sufferings to God, and so he had external good works. He made a public confession of

1. Melanchthon includes Of the Difference Between Deadly and Other Sins in this article.

his sins, confessed the Messiah, rebuked the other thief, and publicly invoked Christ the Lord. While the other apostles trembled and were silent and scattered, this thief, hanging there in the air, became an apostle and preacher for many thousands of men. I say all this as a reminder that good works, light and virtues, in one's heart and externally, mean obedience.

For the sake of simplicity, however, I will speak of good works, or new obedience, in accordance with these five questions. Whoever wants to speak more sharply of it may do so.

The first question: Which works should one teach and do?

The second question: How are they possible?

The third question: How are they pleasing to God if sin still remains in us in this life?

The fourth question: Why should we do them?

The fifth question: What about the distinctions in sins?

The First Question

The clear answer to the first question is that one should teach and do those works which God has included in the Ten Commandments, and these should be understood as Christ, the prophets, and apostles explained them, as previously discussed.

The Anabaptists say, one should not direct people to the commandments and the law, for they are the evil claws of the devil, who would like to lead men away from God's word. But the Ten Commandments, rightly understood, are God's eternal unchangeable wisdom, which he has graciously revealed to and through the voice of his Church. The true and full understanding of the divine law has not remained with any people on earth, except those in the true Church of God. We would heartily thank God that he maintains his wisdom and word in his Church.

And God's earnest will is that both faith and works be guided by his word, for he says, Ezekiel 20:19, "I am the Lord your God; in my commandments you shall walk." This is repeated many hundreds of times in the writings of the prophets and apostles.

These divine services are the only works which he has commanded. They are to be performed in faith. And men are not to invent new divine services, such as the papists and monks have invented in the prohibition of marriage, Masses, and invocation of saints, and as the heathen have done with their idolatries. To ward off and to rebuke such horrors, God maintains the voice of his Ten Commandments in the Church, a voice which should forever rebuke the sins still in the saints, and testify to the works which are divine services.

The Second Question

The answer to the second question is that the works are possible for us through the Son of God and the Holy Spirit, for both are sent from the eternal Father to help us miserable men. As long as a man does not have forgiveness of sins through faith in Christ, he cannot call on God. Man must first acknowledge Christ and through faith receive forgiveness of sins; then immediately Christ gives his Holy Spirit in the heart, so that it has joy in God, and calls on and wishes to be obedient to him.

We should daily consider our weakness and our foes, the devils, and, on the other hand, the great love of God toward us, for he has sent his Son *Jesus Christ* and the Holy Spirit to our rescue, to bring us again to eternal righteousness and salvation. Christ is called Immanuel, that is, God with us, or God by us. Through him we have forgiveness of sins and are justified, that is, pleasing to God. He is truly the head of the Church, our king and high priest, actively preserving us. He sustains us amid the destructions of the governments of the world and the temptations of the devil, even as he preserved and stood by the three men in the fiery furnace at Babylon. The text [Dan. 3:25] clearly says that the fourth by the three is God in this person, the Son of God. He gives us his Holy Spirit, that we may have strength for true obedience and wisdom for a true understanding of his teaching and counsel.

We should call on God for deliverance and help, as many passages indicate. John 15:5: "I am the vine, you are the branches. He who abides in me, and I in him, he it is that bears much fruit, for apart from me you can do nothing." Luke 11:13: "How much more will the heavenly Father give the Holy Spirit to those who ask him?" Psalm 50:15: "Call upon me in the day of trouble." . . . [Melanchthon also cites Rom. 2:12, 13 and Gal. 3:14].

Christian teaching is not like philosophy, which glories much in its own strength [*Fleisch*] and say nothing about invoking God. The gospel calls us to God, punishes our sin, gives comfort, points us to Christ, and says that the Son of God truly wants to be with us, to preserve, enlighten, and strengthen us with the Holy Spirit for the obedience that is pleasing to God.

We should acknowledge this presence and activity of God, by us and in us, and ask and give thanks for it, as Jacob says, "The Lord, before whom my fathers, Abraham and Isaac, walked, and the angel, who rescued me from all evil, will bless us" [Gen. 48:16]. This angel is the Lord Jesus Christ, who is with his Church and will help it. For the sake of brevity I will stop with this reminiscence, but each one should further consider this teaching.

The Third Question

There are three parts to consider in this question: How is the new obedience, or how are good works, pleasing to God? First it is necessary that we who are converted believe [*glaube*] that we have forgiveness of sins, and are justified, that is, are truly pleasing to God, for the sake of Christ, God and Man, by grace, without any merit on our part, through faith; that is to say, God graciously receives us on account of the obedience and merits of our Lord Jesus Christ, through faith, as clearly expressed in Romans 3. For we are not justified on account of the law, but for the sake of our Lord Jesus Christ, through faith.

In the next place, we should know that many sins still remain in us all in this mortal life, many evil tendencies, ignorance, doubt, and false security. Our hearts do not burn with love to God. Consequently, we do not have that full obedience which should be in us. On account of these sins and at the same time on account of actual sins, we should feel pain so that we may not be proud, like the Pharisee who boasts of his holiness in the eighteenth chapter of Luke.

In the third place, we should know that God's earnest and unchanging will and command is that we begin to be obedient. He has given us the Son and the Holy Spirit and he desires obedience in the faithful, for the sake *of the Mediator Jesus Christ*, as written in 1 Peter 2:5, "You shall offer spiritual sacrifices acceptable to God through Jesus Christ."

Both knowledge of our sins and humility and, on the other hand, knowledge of the great mercy of God and consolation are necessary; we must know first how a person has forgiveness of sins and is justified and then how his works are pleasing to God, even though our initial obedience is very weak and we still have much impurity, which we should not deem insignificant.

Ancient scholars and later the monks disputed this article, and asked:

How is man pleasing to God? The monks have directed people to their own works. Some speak grossly about their works, some exaggerate. They deem their own works fitting and say that when we have grace, that is, when we have infused love, we are pleasing to God. Or they say that man is justified and pleasing to God, *novitate*, through the new obedience, or as Osiander says, *justitia essentiali*, through the essential righteousness of God in us.

But then they also say that if we do not feel this, but see evil tendencies in ourselves, that we should remain mired in doubt and that this doubt is true humility before God.

All these teachings of the monks are departures from Christ and deprive the converted of true comfort. Therefore, it is necessary in this article to maintain clear instruction. Throughout the writings of the prophets and apostles this article is simple and clear, as David says in Psalm 32:5, "I said, 'I will confess my transgressions to the Lord'; then thou didst forgive the guilt of my sin." Certainly there is sin and much uncleanness in us, which we are not to deem insignificant; however, we are to confess it in true terror before God, and we are not to be proud like the Pharisee who says that he is pure, good, and righteous, but that the tax collector is a stinking dirty person.

On the other hand, we should have this comfort and not remain mired in doubt, for we should believe that God truly forgives us our sins, *for the sake of Christ*, God and Man, clothes us with the righteousness of the Christ, and accepts us through faith, freely [*gratis*], without any merit on our part, and certainly not on account of any infused love or newness, nor on account of the divine activities in us in this life, of which Osiander speaks in his *justitia essentiali*, but on account of the obedience and merits of the Christ, who is the Mediator and Reconciler. Although divine activity and light are in the reborn, the obedience of Christ is immeasurably higher than such activity in the saints, and the same obedience of Christ is the reconciliation. This faith, therefore, which relies on Christ's reconciliation, must always light the way, and be awakened in all invocation. Thus the converted man, *is justified, for the sake of the Lord Christ, by faith alone, gratis, sola fide*, not on account of his new virtues.

The prophets Moses, Job, and Daniel all come before God in confession of their own sins and in reliance on the mercy which is promised on account of the Mediator. As Moses says, "Before thee no man is innocent" [*cf.* Ex. 34:7]; and as Job says, "I will defend my ways to his face, but he will be my salvation" [Job 13:15]! And Daniel prays, "Be gracious to us, O Lord, not on account of our righteousness, but *on account of the Lord*" [Dan. 9:18], namely Christ.

In these entire Psalms, 32, 51, 130, and 143, this doctrine is repeated and clearly expressed, "Enter not into judgment with thy servant; for no man living is righteous before thee" [Ps. 143:2]. This is the confession, and at the same time, the comfort, "Be gracious to me for the sake of thy truth, for thou art gracious and true, and hast spoken of thy gracious promises to us" [*cf.* Ps 4:1; 51:1; 119:132].

St. Paul explains this doctrine at length in Romans 5–8. He laments his sins within himself, as an apostle instead of a convert, and preaches at the same time the comfort: "You are not under law but under grace" [6:14]; likewise, "Now there is no condemnation for those who walk in the Lord Christ" [8:1].

Colossians 2: "In Christ you are made perfect" [*cf.* Col. 1:28, 4:12]; namely, that in this weak life through Christ the cleanness is begun in us, and through him will be given entirely in eternal life. At the same time we are perfected in this life, in that we are pleasing to God for the sake of Christ and are clothed with his righteousness, which is imputed to us.

And Galatians 5:5: "Through the Spirit, by faith, we wait for righteousness, in which we hope"; that is, we hope in eternal life to be entirely pure, without any sin and without any death; but in this time we are pleasing to God *by faith*, and this faith is a light of the Holy Spirit in us. About faith he frequently says that we thereby are justified and have grace by God. Romans 5:1: "Since we are justified by faith, we have peace with God." And Ephesians 3:12: "We have boldness and confidence of access through our faith in him."

After we are snatched out of hell's vengeance and given the Holy Spirit, then the good works should follow, which in the faithful also please God, for the sake of the Lord Christ. We should also believe that our invocation and service are pleasing to God, not on account of our own worthiness, but on account of Christ. Nevertheless, they are still not a fulfillment of the law.

The Fourth Question

Why and to what purpose should one do good works? First, it is necessary to know that our good works, or our commenced obedience, is not a meriting of forgiveness of sins, not a fulfillment of the law, not a righteousness on account of which man is accepted by God, and not a meriting of eternal salvation. With the forgiveness of sins through faith we become heirs of eternal blessedness!

This is grounded on the full teaching of Christ, the prophets, and the apostles about law and gospel; for as David says, "No one living is justified before thee," from which it is clear that our works are not a meriting of eternal salvation.

However, that we may not remain mired in hell, the Savior, the Son of God, Jesus Christ himself says, "O death! I will be a poison to you, and O Hell! I will be the spoiling of you" [cf. 1 Cor. 15:54 f.]. In John 3:16 he says, "For God so loved the world that he gave his only Son, that whoever believes in him should not perish but have eternal life." And the divine oath is quite certain, "As I live, says the Lord God, I have no pleasure in the death of the wicked, but that the wicked turn from his way and live" [Ezek. 33:11]. These important words are to be understood in the context of the entire divine teaching; namely that we, for the sake of Christ, without any merit on our part, through faith assuredly have forgiveness of sins, and are born again through the word and Holy Spirit, and are justified, that is, are pleasing to God, and are made heirs of eternal blessedness. Grace and the gifts are bound together.

Having said this, the answer to the question, "Why and to what purpose is one to do good works?" is, "On account of obedience, for which end God created all rational creatures." This is the principal answer, out of which others follow. God's eternal unchangeable will is that all rational creatures be obedient to him, and for this purpose he sent his Son, Jesus Christ, so that he might restore us to this obedience. And by no means is one to think that the Son of God, Jesus Christ, bore God's great wrath, and poured out his blood that men might continue in their raving madness and depravity. He was sent that he might take away sin and death, and give righteousness and eternal blessedness.

Inasmuch as we are obliged to obey God, and inasmuch as Christ restores us to this obedience, it is obviously necessary that obedience is to begin in the heart and in external works.

Some would not permit the words, "necessary, obliged, and obedience," saying they are words of the law and signify compulsion through fear, as when one is frightened into not stealing for fear of the gallows. But such an understanding would be unwarranted, for "necessary" and "obliged" here signify divine eternal unchangeable wisdom, righteousness, and order, in that rational creatures should be obedient to God, as they were created for this purpose.

Christ and *St. Paul* say "are obliged"; in Romans 8:12, "We are obliged not to live after the flesh" [*cf*. Mt. 5:18–20; 6:24; Gal. 5:16–25; Rom. 7:12, 15].

"As I live, says the Lord God, I have no pleasure in the death of the wicked, but that the wicked turn from his way and live," is an oath that requires conversion. Clearly, therefore, we are not to continue in sin against the conscience. More about this in the article on Christian freedom.

We must also know that the conversion to God in this life must occur before physical death, as St. Paul indicates in Corinthians 5:3, "We long to put on our heavenly dwelling, so that by putting it on we may not be found naked"; and this passage in the Revelation of John is well known, "Blessed are those who die in the Lord" [Rev. 14:13], that is, in the knowledge, true faith, and invocation of the Lord Jesus Christ. Yes, such must be converted to God before physical death.

Also it must be obvious that if conversion to God does not happen, and the heart continues in sin against conscience, that there is no true faith that desires or receives forgiveness of sins. The Holy Spirit is not in a heart in which there is no fear of God, but instead a continuing defiance. As clearly expressed, 1 Corinthians 6:9 f., "Whores, adulterers, etc., will not inherit the kingdom of heaven."

Although obedience is for the glory of God, and not principally for fear of punishment, nevertheless God has revealed terrible punishments respecting it, so that we may know his will and earnestly desire to show obedience. He wishes us to flee the punishments, for he has no pleasure in our miserable ruin. David should have abstained from adultery for the glory of God. He should also have considered the eternal and temporal punishments that would follow. . . .

On the other hand, God has added special promises to obedience. "Whoever gives one of the least of these even a cup of cold water because he is a disciple, truly, I say to you, he shall receive his reward" [Mt. 10:41]. Now, it is true, as often said, those who turn themselves to God receive forgiveness of sins and are justified, out of grace, *gratis*, without any merits on their part, by faith alone. But other gifts, which follow forgiveness of sins, which follow faith, in this life and in the future, are richly given when faith and obedience are stronger. The

Church . . . and all of us . . . need physical and spiritual help for protection against the devil and temptation.

Special sins merit and provoke special punishments, as did David's adultery. On the other hand, where faith and obedience are stronger, God so much the more graciously mitigates and gives more gifts. He gave prosperity to Laban for Jacob's sake; and he spared the widow of Zarepath because she divided her food with Elijah; and Ebed-melech was protected in the destruction of Jerusalem, for he had given help to Jeremiah. The Psalmist says, "Blessed is he who receives the poor, for God will give him help in evil times" [Ps. 41:1].

All this happens for the sake of the *Lord Christ*, for the maintenance of the Church, for the exercise of faith, for a testimony to the presence of the *Lord Christ* with us. As Paul says, "All promises are firm for the sake of the Lord Christ" [*cf.* Heb. 6:17 f.; 8:6 f.]. And we are earnestly to exercise daily faith and obedience for alleviation of deserved punishments and for all sorts of help, guidance, and protection. We poor miserable men can hardly imagine the dangers that daily beset us. We are like a small child who falls into a den of wolves and with three or more wolves standing round does not understand his great danger; but if the child stays alive (and I know of such a case), then obviously God has preserved it. Just so the Son of God preserves and protects his weak Church and children. We should acknowledge and ask for such protection and in our invocation exercise faith and obedience.

The Fifth Question

It is highly necessary to know that there are distinctions in sins, that some sins remain even in the saints in this life, and that some sins grieve and repel the Holy Spirit, causing some men to fall from grace, who, if not again converted, fall into eternal punishment. After the first disobedience Adam would have remained in eternal punishment if he had not again turned to God when the promise was graciously revealed.

Paul sets forth a distinction when he states in Romans 8:13, "If you live according to the flesh you will die, but if by the Spirit you put to death the deeds of the body you will live." Likewise, Romans 6 sets forth the distinction between sins that prevail and those that do not.

From these and many similar passages we should know with certainty when a man acts against his conscience, that is, consciously and willingly against the command of God, even though he previously has been holy and in God's grace, if he nevertheless grieves and repels the Holy Spirit, he is then not in God's grace, and if he is not again turned to God in this life, he will come to eternal punishment. Some, like David and Manasseh, were again turned; some, like Saul, were not. According to 2 Peter 2, Matthew 12, and 1 Corinthians 10, thousands fall from grace.

Here also corrupted understanding of one or more articles of faith should be discussed. Although a person in this case does not act against conscience, but out of misunderstanding, if he will not allow himself to be instructed, earnest faith often degenerates into Arianism and idolatry. *Paul* says that fundamentally true faith must be maintained among the saints, even though some chaff becomes mixed with it, even as foolish opinions have often become mixed with the views of important men like Augustine and Bernard. Nevertheless, believers should be inclined to be instructed; the wanton ignorance, pharisaical blindness, of many bishops and rulers is inexcusable. We are all obliged to learn and receive true doctrine, and this remains unchanged, "No other foundation can be laid except the Lord Jesus Christ" [*cf.* 1 Cor. 3:11]. And John 3:18 says, "Who does not believe is already condemned."

Thus sin prevails if one consciously acts against God's command, and also if one persists in error. Such overriding sin is deadly sin; on account of it man is cast into eternal death if he is not converted.

Saints in this life, even though their faith is right, may nevertheless still have many sins, which, however, are not sins against conscience. For example, along with the initial fear of God may come a foolish security; the heart may not recognize and mourn its sins as deeply as it should. Faith and reliance on God may still be weak, and much doubt may remain. The heart may not burn with love of God; and many inordinate flames and desires may still be present.

Such impurity in us should not be deemed insignificant, as the Pharisees and monks have taught. It certainly is sin, as we have said. However, as long as we do not will to follow these evil tendencies with action, but painfully strive against them and believe that these sins are forgiven for the sake of *Christ*, and that we are clothed through the *Christ*, we remain holy; and the Holy Spirit is in us, ruling us, and giving light and strength to our hearts, to strive against the sins, as Joseph through the Holy Spirit strove against adultery.

Significantly, *St. Paul* says that we are to slay the activities of the flesh through the Holy Spirit. In this he makes a distinction between heathen morality and obedience in the saints. Scipio keeps his external members under control so that he does not touch a noble young maiden who is married to another.[2] This is a work of reason, in which there is no true invocation of God, no knowledge of the Mediator *Jesus Christ*, and no knowledge of why faith and obedience are pleasing to God.

Joseph acts similarly, but in Joseph the word of God enlightens, guides, and strengthens him with the Holy Spirit; he earnestly thinks he should be obedient to the glory of God, and he knows that he is pleasing to God for the sake of the promised Savior; he appeals to him and asks for help that he may not be seduced into breaking a commandment.

In their calamities Stephen, Laurentius, Polycarp, and Agnes, are magnanimous and joyful, for the living word of God and the Holy Spirit strengthen them, so that they have joy in God, call on God, know why they are pleasing to him, and how they are to be obedient. They also know that he gives them strength and power, and that he desires to impart to them his wisdom, righteousness, and joy; and they know why, and how, he gathers to himself, out of great mercy and for the sake of his beloved Son, an eternal Church.

These men understand this passage, "O death, I will be your death" [Hos. 13:14; *cf.* 1 Cor. 15:54; Heb. 2:14]! They feel that God produces comfort and joy in them, and does not let them sink into and remain mired in anguish. We should consider this in daily prayer when the heart asks: Will God hear us if we are unclean sinners? For the sake of *Christ* we are heard, and the Lord *Christ* produces this comfort in us through his gospel and Holy Spirit, as the passage says, "I will pour out on the House of David the spirit of grace and supplication" [Zech. 12:10].

Notwithstanding, this rule remains unchanged; those who continue in sins against conscience are not pleasing to God, for the divine oath requires conversion, "As I live, says the Lord God, I have no pleasure in the death of the wicked, but that the wicked turn from his way and live." Likewise, 1 Tim. 1:18 f., "Wage the good warfare, holding faith and a good conscience." This and many similar passages clearly indicate that men who again fall into sin, against their conscience, that is, who consciously follow their evil tendencies with action, as Eve followed the devil, fall out of grace, and those who are not converted again fall into eternal punishment.

Although much more might be said about this, I do not wish to make this writing too long, and I entreat each reader to ponder all the articles

2. See note above, p. 67.

of this introduction. According to the way the Son of God has spoken, we should pray that the Holy Spirit be given to us; and, as the eternal Father has graciously said he will give the Holy Spirit to those who ask, I heartily beseech him to enlighten and guide me and all who call upon him with his Holy Spirit, for the sake of the Lord Christ. Amen.

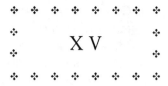

XV

OF ETERNAL PREDESTINATION AND REPROBATION

When men, who have neither God's word nor faith, behold the misery of human life on earth, when they note that all men have frailties and that all kinds of misfortunes come to both evil and honorable men, then reason questions whether there is any group among men that is particularly pleasing to God, and whether there is a Church of God. To combat this common temptation we should contemplate the testimonies in which God from the beginning has revealed himself, namely all his mighty works, the exodus from Egypt, resurrection of the dead, and all the other miracles which have occurred for the strengthening of the faithful. Let our hearts firmly believe God's word, and be reassured that God himself is gathering an eternal Church among men through the gospel. . . . To bring this about, God revealed his promises and has had them preached throughout the world, and there have always been children of God, those who have received the promises in true faith. But those who did not or do not believe are condemned, as declared in John 3.

But man wonders in his heart if he has been called to salvation[1] and asks on what basis he is chosen.

Despite contrary disputations, an unchangeable truth is that we should draw conclusions about God's nature and will from his word, namely through his only begotten Son Jesus Christ revealed through the prophets and apostles, and outside of God's word we should not invent a single thought about his nature and will.

With this basic tenet, we can now say that the source of sin is in our rejection, that is, whoever is not turned to the *Lord Christ* is certainly rejected, as Scripture, John 3:18, attests, "Whoever does not believe is condemned already." Psalm 2 and Deuteronomy 18:19: "Whoever will not heed him, I will root him out." And likewise Hosea 13, "Corruption is by you; only through me is your salvation" [*cf.* v. 4].

1. *Seligkeit* is here translated as "salvation," but generally it has been translated as "blessedness" elsewhere.

On the other hand, only *God's mercy, for the sake of Christ,* is the source of being chosen to eternal salvation. For this reason the Son of God is sent, and grace revealed; otherwise no one would be saved [*selig*]. If the Savior and grace had not been revealed to Adam and Eve, they would have remained in eternal death and wrath. With this revelation is the unalterable command that we accept the promise with faith, as stated in Psalm 2 and in John. "God so loved the world that he gave his only Son, that *all who believe in him* should not perish but have eternal life" [Jn. 3:16], and Romans 4 says, "*By faith, without merit on our part,* so that the promises may be sure" [*cf.* v. 3–6, 16].

And undoubtedly the highest and most earnest commandment is that we listen to the Son of God and believe him as the eternal Father says, "This one you shall hear" [Mk. 9:7; Lk. 9:35]! Also in John 16:8, "The Holy Spirit will convince the world of the sin . . . of not believing in me."

Assuredly all are elected for eternal blessedness who, through faith in the Lord Christ, in the conversion in this life receive comfort and do not fall away before their death; for thus says the text, "Blessed are the dead who die in the Lord" [Rev. 14:13].

We should not invent ideas about God's will outside of his word. Election [*Erwählung*] to eternal salvation is not on account of the law, but *for the sake of Chirst through faith;* and as we previously said about forgiveness of sins and righteousness, so we say now about election, namely that we have forgiveness of sins, the Holy Spirit, and eternal salvation for the sake of the Lord Jesus Christ, out of grace, through faith, and thus we are also predestined to eternal blessedness for the sake of the Lord Jesus Christ, out of grace, without any merit on our part, and not on account of the law; we are, however, finally to be found in this faith.

This comfort is genuine, for it is quite certain that *we are all obliged to believe* the Lord Christ.

However, two temptations arise from our anxiety: the first stems from merit and the enormity of sins; the second, from a question about whether the promise is offered to *all* men. To combat the first temptation, we should be comforted by the fact that blessedness is given for the sake of the Lord Christ, without any merit on our part, *gratis;* and grace is stronger than any sin, as written in Romans 5:20, "Grace is stronger and mightier than sin." We should strive finally to believe that the Son of God is mightier than all the might of devils and sin.

Yes, one might say, the promise belongs to those whose names are written in God's book, David, Peter, and some others, but perhaps it does not belong to *me?* Is the promise offered to *all?* Here we should firmly conclude that preaching is *universales*, both the preaching of punishment and the preaching of grace; God is just; he is no "respecter of persons." He has offered his promise to *all* who will turn to him and seek comfort in the Lord Christ. Note the passages which offer the promise to *all.*

John 6:40: "This is the will of my Father, that *all* who believe on the Son may have eternal life."

Matthew 11:28: "Come to me, *all* who labor and are heavy laden, and I will give you rest."

John 3:16: "That *all who* believe in him will not perish."

Romans 3:22: "The righteousness of God through faith in Jesus Christ to *all* and for *all* who believe."

Romans 10:12: "The same Lord is Lord of *all* and bestows his riches upon *all* who call upon him."

First Timothy 2:4: "God desires *all* men to be saved." This is to be understood as meaning as far as his will is concerned, which he has graciously explained in his word. We should not put contradictory wills in God, *contradictorias voluntates.* To *all* who tremble before his wrath and seek comfort in *Christ, to each and every one*, grace and blessedness are offered and promised. "Come to me *all* you who labor," and, "All who call on the name of the Lord will be saved."

Consider also the delightful passage which says that "God is no respecter of person" [*cf.* Acts. 10:34; Col. 3:25]. And the passage in Isaiah 42 praises Christ and says that in him there will be no favoring of persons, that is, in him all men are equal [*cf.* v. 1–8]. God is irritated by *all* sin, whether in David or in Saul; and his mercy extends equally to *all* who seek refuge in his mercy for the Savior's sake, whether this be Manasseh or David; his divine wisdom includes all ranks on an equal basis.

Since the divine promises proffer grace to *all* who are terrified, we should include ourselves in the *all*, and should reflect that the greatest sin is not willing *to believe in the Lord Christ*, and not willing to receive his grace. The second Psalm says, "Kiss the Son" and likewise, "Blessed are those who trust in him; receive him that his anger may not come upon you," and so forth [*cf.* v. 12]. Note how the Canaanite woman included herself among the Israelites [*cf.* Mt. 15:21–28; Mk. 7:24–30]; even so, like the dogs, we may find refuge in Christ.

"Yes," we might say, "but I cannot believe that God gives me his Holy Spirit!" True, but we should know that God gives his word even to us, and that he wants to give us the Holy Spirit, just as he gives us his word. Inasmuch as he has called us, we should accept his word and Holy Spirit. Having heard the gospel, we should not consciously continue in sin or remain mired in doubt, foolishly thinking, I will wait until I feel God's miraculous rapture upon me. These are the words of enthusiasts and Anabaptists. The heart should trust itself with God's word, and immediately the Son of God himself will work in us and strengthen us with his Holy Spirit, and at the same time we should beseech him to help us, for Christ says, "How much more will your Father give his Holy Spirit to those who ask him!" And the terrified man in Mark 9:24 pleads, "I believe, O Lord, help my unbelief." These passages also belong here: "The gospel is the power of God to salvation to all who believe therein" [Rom. 1:16]; and Rom. 15:4, "Through the consolation of the Scriptures we shall have hope." We should sustain ourselves with this gospel, acknowledge God's will, and not strive against it nor wantonly remain in doubt.

This is the intent of the words in John 6:44, "No one comes to me except the Father draws him," for they are immediately followed with, "*Everyone* who has *heard* and *learned* from the Father comes to me." If we *hear* and *learn* the gospel, and do not wantonly cast it out of our minds, if we comfort ourselves with it, then the Son himself will work in us. Chrysostom says that "God draws, but he draws *those* who are *willing*." [2] This means whoever does not scorn the teaching and does not wantonly push it away, but desires to hear it, seeks comfort in it, and cries to God, even as Jeremiah cried, "Turn me, O Lord, so that I will be turned" [cf. Jer. 31:18; Lam. 5:21], and as David did, asking, "O Lord, create in me a clean heart, and teach me thy righteousness" [Ps. 51:10].

So, it is very comforting and true that only those who are called are numbered among the predestined, that is, among those who listen to and learn God's word, for "Those whom he has chosen, he also calls" [cf. Num. 16:5; Rom. 8:30; 2 Thess. 2:13–14; 1 Pet. 1:2]. Now we are called, and we should not despise the calling, but thank God for placing us in this group, where we can hear and acknowledge the Lord *Jesus Christ*. Having received the gospel, we should turn to God, and comfort our-

---

2. Cf. *Homilies on St. John*, 5 (Jn. 1:3–5), 10 (Jn. 1:11–13), 45 (Jn. 6:28–40), 46 (Jn. 6:41–53); *Homilies on First Corinthians*, 2 (1 Cor. 1:4–5).

selves through faith in the Savior Jesus Christ, through whom we are pleasing to God, and ask for strength to persevere to the end. This is said for the comfort of those who are called. It is not necessary for us to dispute why the heathen have been left so long in blindness. They are *themselves* the cause of their blindness, for God originally revealed his promises, established his Church, and made himself known among the heathen, in Egypt and in Babylon. Afterward he revealed himself through the apostles' preaching. God adorned his Church in Israel with Elijah and the other prophets. In all kingdoms it has been known. However, like the Jews, many have scorned God and have entirely lost the teaching of the gospel through their own evil and ingratitude. We should tremble before such examples of wrath, and earnestly learn the truth and live in fear of God and in prayer.

XVI

OF THE DIFFERENCE
BETWEEN THE OLD AND NEW TESTAMENTS

For the word "testament" the Hebrew language uses this word, "covenant," or "promise," or "obligation"; and the Old Testament, or the Old Covenant, properly speaking, is the promise in accordance with which God gave a certain country to the stem of Israel. He established a worldly government, bound it with his own laws and ceremonies, and promised the people help and protection, all so that this country and government might be a lodging place for the divine promises of the Savior Christ, of the true Church of God, and afterward of the Lord Christ himself, after his birth through the Virgin Mary.

And the establishment and maintenance of this land and government is a special gift of God and a witness that God himself is gathering a Church among mankind; he himself protects and preserves it.

After the Flood, even though the people scattered and powerful kings waged great wars, causing much destruction, God graciously led *Abraham* out of Chaldea and promised a Messiah to his children. God promised them land and a government that should last for two thousand years, until the Messiah appeared and preached and visibly accomplished his office, a government in which the divine promise of the Messiah would be sustained and explained, in which prophets would be raised up and mighty works occur as testimony of the teaching, in which there would always be a small company of those predestined to eternal blessedness, in which there would be a true Church until the Savior Messiah had visibly accomplished his office.

With this government was the special gift of the law, the Ten Commandments, or *legem moralem*, which God openly renewed with testimonies because the blindness of the raging world was so great that the doctrine of the law had become extinct. Therefore, God in his special counsel set before the entire world his law, that we might know it, and know that *it is God's eternal unchangeable wisdom*.

Let each one ponder how great and glorious have been the gifts and testimonies from God, which may still be testimonies to all men. The prophets and their successors instructed the people concerning the law and the ceremonies, saying that men obtain forgiveness of sins, are pleasing to God, and are saved *through faith in the Messiah,* and not through law; they explained the promises, as may be seen in the Psalms and prophets, and they taught why the government was established and maintained.

However, the New Testament is the promise in which God said that he would send his only begotten Son, and through him, on account of *his obedience,* without any merit on our part, would give to believers forgiveness of sins, grace, the Holy Spirit, eternal righteousness, and blessedness.

The word "testament" implies a promise concerned with death, and this promise of grace is just such a testament. For the Savior has confirmed it with his death, as stated at length in Hebrews 9.

Although this promise of grace was revealed soon after the fall of Adam, and thereafter was preached, it is nevertheless call *new.* We should retain old and new in accordance with the times of both kingdoms, the temporal and the eternal. The worldly was ordained for this temporal life, at the end of which the Savior was visibly to appear. The eternal kingdom began through the Resurrection, and the new kingdom is to be full of splendor, for this temporal life will entirely cease, and after the resurrection of the dead, the entire Church will live in eternal wisdom, righteousness, and joy with God.

The worldly kingdom is call the *old promise* because it grows old and ceases, but the promise of grace is eternal. It is also called the *eternal testament* because it remains with us even though we lose all our physical goods. As Job says, "Even though he slay me, yet will I trust in him" [13:15].

Here once more it is necessary to know the difference between law and gospel; and likewise, the distinction in the law itself, as stated above.

It is certainly true that men have in all times been turned to God and saved; Adam, Eve, Seth, Enoch, Noah, Abraham, Moses, Samuel, David, Elijah, and Daniel received forgiveness of sins, and were justified; that is, they were pleasing to God, received the Holy Spirit, and were made heirs of eternal blessedness *for the sake of the promised Savior, through faith* in the promised Savior, without merit on their part, not on account of the law, or their wonderful morality in the law, the Ten Commandments, church ceremonies, and civil orders. This is clearly stated in Romans 4 and Acts 15, and throughout the prophets. The Son of God produced life in them through the promise, and gave them his Holy Spirit.

What purpose, then, has the law served? Answer: God wanted to give this great gift to men so that there would be a school of his doctrine and promise in a particular people and land. He himself ordained an elaborate government for this people to which belong law, the Ten Commandments, church ceremonies, and civil order; and obedience has served to maintain this physical government.

Moreover, all this served as a reminder of God, for in the Ten Commandments is a much higher and more necessary wisdom than in transitory laws. They apply in all times, so that one may know God's nature, what sin is, and which works always constitute *divine service*.

However, the unlearned priests and many unintelligent among the people have continually dreamed that sacrifice and eternal morality merit the forgiveness of sins and eternal blessedness; they have not had true knowledge of the Messiah. Like the blind heathen, they have invented their sacrifices. The Mohammedans, godless Jews, papists, and monks are still stuck fast in this blindness. Pope and monks extol their sacrifice of the Mass and orders as merit for forgiveness of sins. This frightful blindness and idolatrous sin are often rebuked by the prophets. Jeremiah 7:22 f., "I did not speak to your fathers or command them concerning burnt offerings and sacrifices. But this command I gave them, 'Obey my voice, and I will be your God, and you shall be my people.' " Likewise, Psalm 50 and Zechariah 7–8.

XVII

OF CHRISTIAN FREEDOM [1]

We can see that the Church is laid under the cross, and has great persecution from devils and tyrants in this world; Pharaoh had the children of the Israelites slain; thousands of saints were driven out of Babylon with Daniel, and so forth. Now, when the powers in this world hear about "Christian freedom," they scoff, and regard Christians as absurd fools, and think: It is empty talk, like the disputes of the Stoics.

Freedom is often misused by savage people who wish to dignify their worldly disorders with the name "Christian freedom." Therefore we should learn what Christian freedom really is. *Christ* himself speaks of it, saying, "If the Son makes you free, then you are truly free" [Jn. 8:36]. For rough guidance, I will first remind the reader that when he hears the words, "Christian freedom," he should think of the perfect freedom which will come after this mortal life in eternal blessedness, when God will be in all the saved, who will have eternal joy in God without death, without poverty, and without sorrow. This is eternal freedom, about which the Son of God discourses; it is begun in this life in the soul and heart through the Son of God with the gospel and Holy Spirit; and it remains even though the body is still subject to death and various persecutions.

To speak more clearly about Christian freedom, I have often divided it into four stages.

The first stage is the stage of freedom and deliverance, through the Son of God, *Jesus Christ*, from our sins, from the wrath of God, from eternal punishment, and from the frightful judgment of law on our sins. For *this purpose*, out of great mercy, the Son of God was sent, so that, in turning to God, we might receive this gracious deliverance through him, and be justified, that is, please God, for the sake of the Mediator, without merit on our part, *gratis*, through faith. This Mediator is presented to us

1. In Melanchthon's list of articles in his introduction, Of Christian Freedom comes much later.

195

so that we may have forgiveness and be justified through him, and not through the law. So speaks *Paul*, Galatians 3:13, "Christ redeemed us from the curse of the law, having become a curse for us." And Romans 6:14: "You are not under the law but under grace."

The second state is inseparable from the first. Upon receiving forgiveness, we are rescued from eternal death, and the Son of God produces *life in us*, through the gospel, and gives the *Holy Spirit*, which produces in our hearts comfort, strength, and joy. Stephen, Laurentius, and Agnes felt comfort and joy in death; and this comfort and joy is the beginning of eternal life in us. Herewith should be included all divine strengthening for obedience, all assistance, and all protection against danger from devils and tyrants. For example, Saul, Cato, and Brutus fell into great anguish when they were pressed by their enemies; they knew no comfort in God or in men, and they slew themselves. But the three Israelites stood happily in the fiery furnace in Babylon, and the Son of God visibly stood by them [*cf.* Dan. 3:25]. This presence of God in us and by us, strictly speaking, is the second stage of Christian freedom, about which this stands written in John 14:23: "If a man loves me, he will keep my word, and my Father will love him, and we will come to him and make our home with him."

Let each one contemplate the grace and gifts which this freedom embraces; deliverance from sins, from God's wrath, and from eternal punishment, gracious forgiveness of sins, righteousness, and God's presence in us, and *all* this *for the sake of the Lord Christ, out of grace*. Those men who, in their conversion through faith, receive this freedom are mentioned in 1 Timothy 1:9, "The law is not laid down for the just," that is, the law exists always, for it is God's eternal wisdom, but it does not afflict and condemn him who is justified *through faith* in the *Lord Christ* and is pleasing to God. Moreover, he has comfort, divine help, and strength so that he stays obedient to God. Joseph was strengthened through the Holy Spirit so that he did not fall into adultery.

The third stage is external: it is freedom from two parts of the law of Moses, ceremony and civil law. These ceremonies and civil laws were ordained only for a particular time for the government of Israel. With that government they ceased and came to their end, as the prophets previously announced, and as clearly expressed in Acts 15.

Although this is clear and easy to understand now, one must nevertheless be reminded that many men in our times, like Thomas Münzer [2] at

2. See note above, p. 83.

Mühlhausen, Strauss,[3] and other foolish men, have claimed that the law of Moses should prevail in worldly tribunals rather than imperial law.

For this reason we should know this rule: Wherever they are, Christians should use the laws of the land, which conform with natural justice; they are not bound to Moses or to one particular form of worldly government. For Christian holiness is in having God present in one's heart, the word and the Holy Spirit, true knowledge and invocation of God, joy in God, truth, chastity, and a good will so that other men are not unjustly injured. In summary, this holiness in one's heart is the beginning of eternal life and holiness. It is in keeping with the last chapter of Isaiah, in which God repudiates the external sacrifices of calves with these words, "He who sacrifices a lamb is like him who breaks a dog's neck" [Is. 66:3].

And we should distinguish the external natural life of eating and drinking, and likewise the civil life of holding property, being rich or poor, noble or not noble, even though the natural and civil life are works of God, from holiness in the heart. God's will is that we recognize this distinction, and learn how every aspect of life is to be ruled. God is now gathering to himself an eternal Church from all sorts of kingdoms, and he permits us in civil life to use the rational laws which are common to each kingdom, even though all laws are not equal in all kingdoms, as the days are not all equally long in all countries.

Here we might ask why freedom from law is only freedom from the ceremonial and civil laws of Moses, and not also from the Ten Commandments. Answer: So far as the meriting of forgiveness of sins and justification by God is concerned, the freedom extends to all the law; true believers are free from the law, from ceremonies, from the civil laws of Moses, and from the Ten Commandments; that is, none of our works, ceremonies, or civil customs, or works of the Ten Commandments *merits* forgiveness of sins; none of this is the reason man is accepted before God and received in grace. We receive forgiveness of sins and righteousness is imputed to us, so that we are pleasing to God, only for the sake of the Lord Christ, through faith.

However, the Lord Christ was sent not to strengthen sin but to take sin away, and to give again eternal righteousness and life. This eternal right-

3. Jakob Strauss (*ca.* 1482–1533), German reformer, attracted large crowds by his open-air preaching. He advocated abolition of the Mass, pictures, and oil and chrism in baptism. He wanted Mosaic rules to prevail, permission for priests to marry, taxes to cease and simple water baptism to be adopted. He was associated with Karlstadt, and was blamed for much of the social and religious unrest among the peasants in 1524.

eousness and life in us is the presence and activity of God, who reveals his nature, and that he is as he explains his will in the law. Therefore, light and holiness in the converted person are an obedience, already begun in accordance with the Ten Commandments. The Ten Commandments pertain to the heart and eternal righteousness, that is, to uniformity with God. But the ceremonies and civil customs are only external forms which will not apply in eternal life; there one will not sacrifice oxen nor hang thieves.

This important distinction should also be noted carefully: Ceremonies and civil customs were past orders, established for a certain time, as the worldly government in Israel was to last only for a certain time, from the exodus from Egypt to the last destruction of Jerusalem, 1,582 years. But the law, which is called the Ten Commandments, or *legem moralem*, is the eternal unchangeable wisdom and righteousness in God, which he has imparted to us. As he created us to be like him in eternity, the law cannot be effaced, as a writing on the wall, for the order that the rational creature should be obedient to God stands forever. If the rational creature is not obedient, then he shall be destroyed, or be in eternal punishment.

Here these important questions arise: If this law is eternal, how could Adam have been received again? How can we be free of it? How can we be pleasing to God, if we are far from being what we should be? Answer: No creature has been able to answer these questions, but the Son of God has graciously revealed to us an answer. Adam argued with himself, saying: God's righteousness in unchangeable; God's righteousness also demands that the disobedient be destroyed or remain in eternal punishment, like the devils. It follows then that men also must remain in eternal punishment.

No creature could help Adam overcome this argument, only the *Son of God could be his Mediator*. It is true that God's righteousness in unchangeable, that God remains thus throughout eternity, and that he has no pleasure in sin. However, in all laws there is an understanding that one should be obedient or willingly bear punishment; *omnis lex obligat ad obedientiam, vel ad poenam voluntariam*. Now the Son of God says that he who is innocent will take our punishment on himself. Thus mercy and justice come together; God accepts his only begotten Son's obedience *for us*, and is merciful to us. And because the punishment is paid, God's justice remains; he has made an equal and higher payment for our sins, and is victor over sin and punishment.

So Adam has a solution. God's righteousness is that we be obedient or suffer punishment. But the Son of God has offered himself for us, and Adam understands that he is again received. Thus we are freed from punishment, for the Son of God has taken it on himself. Thus we are pleasing to God, for the sake of the Lord Christ, even though we are still not as we should be; for the Son of God has taken the punishment from us, and presented to us his righteousness.

We shall know and contemplate this lofty wisdom in eternity. But even in this life we are in some measure to make a beginning in contemplating God's grave wrath against sin and the mercy and the love of God for us in the Son.

This explanation provides the answer to other questions. How are we free from the law which is called *lex moralis?* Answer: We are free from it, *quoad justificationem et condemnationem, non quoad obedientiam*,[4] that is, we are not justified through the law, but through the Son of God. The law does not condemn us if we trust on the Son of God; but still we are to be obedient to God, for God does not desire sin; he has ransomed us so that we may again practice obedience, and he tells us why our weak obedience is pleasing.

This freedom is only for the men who in true conversion to God receive comfort through reliance on the Son of God. Where there is no conversion to God, no faith in Christ, there is no freedom. Instead, the heart experiences terror and feels punishment.

With this simple answer I will stop, and pray the Christian reader to think further about this high wisdom.

We should also carefully consider the speech of *Christ* in which he says, "I have not come to destroy, but to fulfill the law" [Mt. 5:17]. This fulfillment should be understood in a fourfold manner. First, the Lord Christ fulfills the law in that he himself is perfectly righteous and entirely keeps it. Second, he fulfills the law in suffering punishment for us. This punishment has to be paid, and his suffering is a payment for us because he is innocent. Third, he fulfills the law with his activity in us, for he himself is active in us through the gospel and Holy Spirit, making us like himself and giving us eternal life, and only in eternity will full obedience be in us. Fourth, he fulfills it in that he explains the Ten Commandments and says what sin is; he does not give freedom to act against these commandments, which are called *lex moralis*.

The fourth stage of Christian freedom is freedom from the precepts of

4. With regard to justification and damnation, not with regard to obedience.

men in church regulations, about which Paul speaks in Colossians 2:16, "Therefore, let no one pass judgment on you in questions of food and drink." That is, no man has the authority, outside of the word of God, to command works as divine services, and consciences should be informed that human precepts and church regulations do not merit forgiveness of sins or justification before God. It is no sin not to keep the precepts of men in church regulations, about which more is said later.

XVIII

OF THE LETTER AND THE SPIRIT

The "letter" refers to any command, teaching, or work without the Holy Spirit, for thoughts without the Holy Spirit do not live in the heart; they are merely written on the brain, like something painted or knitted on externally. The "Spirit" means the *Holy Spirit of God himself in us*, effecting life, light, and joy in us, so that the heart truly experiences fear of God, comfort, faith, prayer, and strength in tribulation. Origen spoke of the "letter" as a knowledge of history, and of the "spirit" as a knowing of the meaning, as when one understands that the paschal lamb signifies the Messiah.[1] But even this knowing is also a "letter," if the Holy Spirit is not in the heart. Here, however, one should be careful. The Anabaptists boast much about the Spirit, and reproach us, saying that because of the letter we violently strive about the office of preaching and the administration of the sacraments. At this point, we should know that the Holy Ghost is given through the gospel, and that we should not despise the external preaching and administration of the sacraments. Yes, the Son of God, the eternal Word of the eternal Father, imparts comfort to us through the external word in our hearts, and thus gives his Holy Spirit. Athanasius says, "The Holy Spirit is thus in men by means of the word." [2]

1. Cf. *Ante-Nicene Christian Library*, A. Roberts and J. Donaldson, eds. (Edinburgh, 1869), *Writings of Origen, Origen de Principiis*, chap. 1.
2. Cf. *Nicene and Post-Nicene Fathers*, H. Wace and P. Schaff, eds. (Oxford and New York, 1893), IV, *Writings, Athanasius, Discourse Against the Arians*, III, chap. 25:24–25; II chap. 15:18.

XIX

OF THE SACRAMENTS

This word "sacrament" now commonly refers to the external words and forms [*Geberden*] which Christ instituted as signs to signify his promise and grace. We say that there are two sacraments, baptism and participation in the body and blood of Christ [*Niessung des Leibs und Blutes Christi*]. For these there are words and forms, which Christ himself commanded and appended to the promise of grace to remind us and to attest that the promise of grace is given and applied to those men who use these external signs, as divine doctrine instructs us.

First, we should consider why in each case God appended external signs to his promise, how we should use them, and how blind men slip from right use into idolatry.

For many reasons, from the very beginning God set up external signs pointing to his Word. Adam, Abel, Seth, and Noah sacrificed lambs by divine revelation to signify the future Savior whom God himself would sacrifice for mankind. God prescribed the sign of circumcision as a continual reminder of the sacrifice of the early fathers. The Son of God, Jesus Christ, commanded that baptism and his Supper be kept. Why were these external signs instituted? Answer:

The almighty God himself graciously revealed that he is the God and Creator of all creatures; he revealed how mankind was created for eternal life, wisdom, righteousness, and joy, how man fell, and how God wants to gather again to himself an eternal Church for eternal blessedness, for the sake of his Son. For this purpose he revealed his promise with clear testimony, and established signs, for he wants his word openly to be known and *his* Church recognized and distinguished from all other peoples. God wants his word and Church in the light and openly to be known, for he wants men to accept grace and to be saved through the preaching of the gospel in his Church, and in no other way. All who are destined for salvation must become members of his true Church, as Paul says, "Those whom he has predestined, he also calls" [Rom. 8:30].

For this reason the sacraments are signs and pledges of divine grace, the application and appropriation of grace, which is borne in the promises. Whoever uses the sacraments which the Lord Christ has given to us in such a way that he begins to understand, should know the promise, believe that it and the grace are given not only to others but to him, for his benefit, and that the use of the sacraments is a reminder and a testimony of the gracious will of God and the promise of grace, and is a pledge and application to him. With this faith we should use the sacraments. Thus Paul teaches, Rom. 4:11, "Abraham was not justified through circumcision; but circumcision was the seal of justification"; that is, Abraham bore this sign on himself by God's command, as a reminder, testimony, pledge, and application of the grace promised through future descendants.

But this understanding permits blind men to slip into thinking that these works merit forgiveness of sins and justify us before God. The heathen so kept the sacrifices, and the Arabs, Egyptians, and at present the Jews and Mohammedans have kept circumcision, besides inventing more idolatries. Thus the papists and monks have misused and perverted the benefits of the body and blood of Christ by trying to gain forgiveness of sins for the dead and the living, and by selling this work, as the Pharisees and heathen sold their sacrifices. More is said later about these errors. . . .[1]

The Anabaptists also destroy the right understanding and the right use by saying that the sacraments are only signs of good works; baptism, they say, means that we are to suffer much, and the Lord's Supper means that we are to be good friends with one another. In these discussions they say nothing about the promise, faith, and comfort. However, true doctrine directs us to the promise and says, "Use the sacraments as signs of divine grace to yourself, and believe that for the sake of Christ God is gracious to you, and attest this with the sacrament, as if he gave you a special voice or signs out of heaven, as he gave to Gideon or Hezekiah."

As to the number of the sacraments, it is obvious that baptism and the Lord's Supper were ordained by Christ. Therefore, it is definitely God's will that they be kept in the Church. If sacraments are the words and external forms commanded by God, then these are sacraments.

Absolution is a word ordained by the Lord Christ in these words:

1. See below, Article XXII.

"Whatever sins you forgive shall be forgiven" [*cf*. Mt. 16:19; Jn. 20:23]. Since absolution is an application of the promise to one or more persons, many call it a sacrament. Whoever does not wish to call it thus, but prefers to call it a service of the Church, or the keys, well satisfies me. The papists quarrel about confirmation and unction. They themselves confess that these are not necessary works, so that the blessings which are spoken over the oil are obviously idolatries. For this reason we should not hesitate to reject anointing, and to be no longer involved in false and blasphemous opinions. Moreover, invocation of dead men is attached to this, which also is idolatrous. The apostles used balsam with the sick, as a physical medicine, and without doubt some earlier prophets were doctors, and had *donum sanationis*, but we can only counterfeit this with dead ceremony.

Ordination will be discussed later; it is a public witness and proclamation of the call to the office of preaching, and the calling belongs in the necessary offices of the Church. That is, when the Church needs pastors, God commanded that the Church, or the important persons in the Church, call qualified men to this office. We should examine them to determine whether they are pure in the doctrine, and afterward we should publicly testify to the calling and invoke God for the maintenance of the Church. We should acknowledge this great gift of God, and give thanks that the Lord Christ, through the preaching of this person whom we selected, will be effective, for Romans 1:16 says, "The gospel is the power of God." It is clear that the calling and ordination of the preacher are offices of the Church, and that they thus may be called. But the papists call their ordination a sacrament, and they speak only of their ceremonies, in which they have mingled many errors; they say nothing about the office of preaching, but much of their sacrifice for the dead and living. That is not right, as hereafter is said. Likewise, they attach to their ordination obligations that are not right, persecution of true doctrine and prohibition of marriage. For these reasons it is obvious that we cannot seek ordination by the papal bishops, for they are persecutors, as Paul says, "If anyone is preaching a contrary gospel, let him be accursed" [Gal. 1:8].

Let us in the true Church of God recognize that God has proffered the calling, and in it be very diligent in assisting studies so that we may have qualified persons, may seek qualified persons, and truly maintain the examinations, instruction, and visitations.

Let these necessary works be earnestly commanded by the Christian rulers if they want God to mitigate punishments and to give gracious rule, for Christ declares in Matthew 10:42, "Whoever gives to one of these little ones even a cup of cold water because he is a disciple, truly, I say to you, he shall not lose his reward."

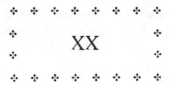

XX

OF BAPTISM

The words of Christ in Mark 16 show that baptism is an external sign and blessing of divine promises in the New Testament: "He who believes and is baptized will be saved" [v. 16]. Therefore, when we are baptized, the promise is written and painted on our body.

Since such external signs also have their private significance, so the holy baptism signifies repentance [*Busse*] and forgiveness of sins through *Christ*, or as *St. Paul* says, "rebirth," and as *Christ* in John 3:5 says, "New birth through water and the Holy Spirit." When we are immersed in the water, this signifies that the old Adam and sin in us are dead. This happens in those who are anguished, when the terrified conscience experiences God's judgment and wrath on sin. When we are drawn out of the water, this means that we are now washed and renewed through water and the Holy Spirit, and are awaiting a new and eternal righteousness and life, which *Christ* has obtained for us.

Two things signify the right use of baptism, the external sign and the promise. "He who believes and is baptized will be saved" [Mk. 16:16]. Likewise, the words which one uses in baptism, "I baptize you in the name of the Father, of the Son, and of the Holy Spirit"; that is, through this external sign I testify in the place of God that you are reconciled to God, and received by God, which is by God the Father, the Son, and the Holy Spirit. The Father, however, receives us for the sake of the Son, and gives us the Holy Spirit, through whom he will renew, quicken, comfort, and sanctify us. In these words are the glorious comforting promises of God and the sum of the entire gospel.

Therefore, the true use of holy baptism is lifelong, for it enables us to be certain that through *Christ* God is reconciled to us and will forgive us our sins, and that he has established baptism as a sign and blessing of this covenant. Although we afterward fall into sin, nevertheless the divine convenant remains firm for all if they again turn with right faith, seek comfort, and reform themselves.

We will more fully understand the fruit and power of baptism as we diligently contemplate the words of the divine promise, exercise our faith therein, and strengthen ourselves therewith in all sorts of temptations, in the anguish of death, against the devil and sin.

And as circumcision was a permanent [*ewiges*] sign which was not to be performed more than once, so whoever is once baptized shall not again be baptized.

The second commandment teaches that we are not to misuse the name of God, nor slander the right use of God's name. Now the Anabaptists repudiate the first baptism, saying that in it the name of God was uselessly, falsely, and wrongly invoked and pronounced over them.[1] Now this is to blaspheme the name of God. For this reason Anabaptism is a frightful, evil error and blasphemy of the divine name. Besides, if the Anabaptists extended their errors, much more perplexity would be added to the world.

Of the Baptism of John and the Apostles

Both of these baptisms are external signs and testimonies of the New Testament. And there is no distinction between the baptism of John and that of the apostles, except that the baptism of John signifies and points to the *future Christ;* the apostles' baptism points to the Christ who *has arrived and has been revealed.* Both baptisms are of one and the same office, and require faith in the Savior Christ; both those who are baptized by John and those baptized by the apostles are equally sanctified [*geheiligt*] and saved. However, John says, "I baptize you with water unto repentance, but he who will come after me will baptize you with the Holy Spirit and fire" [Mt. 3:11]. Here John distinguishes, not the offices or the ceremonies, but the person of the servant from the *person of Christ;* he wishes to indicate that *Christ himself is the Savior and Lord* through whom baptism has divine effect and power, the one who gives life, righteousness, the Holy Spirit, and eternal salvation, and that he,

---

1. Melanchthon thought the Anabaptists were slandering the right use of God's name when they rejected infant baptism. The Anabaptists subscribed only to a believer's baptism, one in which the person consciously chose to receive this external sacrament as a sign of an internal conversion wrought by the Holy Spirit. They did not think that infants could make such a responsible choice and that infant baptism, therefore, was invalid.

John, is a servant who presents only the external sign, water, and preaches the word. Such an external office of baptism and preaching is equal in John and the apostles, and equally effective in those who have faith in the promise of *Christ*.

It is true, however, that after the Resurrection of Christ, more and clearer examples are introduced in which the baptism of the Holy Spirit is given, as in the history of the apostles.

XXI

OF THE BAPTISM OF CHILDREN

St. Paul ordered and commanded with great seriousness and diligence that we should prove the spirits [1] — and Christ established the rule in Matthew 7:16, "By their fruits ye shall know them." This is a sure indication of a heretic's false and godless doctrine. Therefore, we should certainly take heed of such signs in the Anabaptists, for they repudiate the baptism of young children. . . .

However, in the teaching of the Anabaptists we find all sorts of hateful, terrible errors, lies, and blasphemy, for they teach wrongly not only about baptism but about many other important articles of the entire Christian doctrine. They say that Christians cannot participate in governments, be princes or lords, and so forth; they advocate having nothing as their own but everything in common, no swearing of oaths, and so forth. Thus they teach tumult against the orderly governments. From this and similar cases it is clear that they absolutely do not know what Christian righteousness or life is, know absolutely nothing of the knowledge of *Christ* or *faith*, and fancy that Christian existence [*Wesen*] is only an external monkery.

The new Anabaptists at Münster teach still more hatefully and shamelessly. A married person may abandon the other if the other is not willing to accept the sect. In addition, they are entirely possessed by the devil; they drive out and presume to blot out orderly authority, they imagine and teach shamelessly that before the last days a kingdom of Christ will be on earth in which only the saints will rule, and all the godless will be eradicated and extinguished.

These are nothing but terrible errors, seditious doctrines, Jewish fables, stains, and black diabolical marks. Moreover, we can know and prove

---

1. That is, ascertain the true motives and convictions of those who declare they have the Spirit of Christ, for they may have another spirit.

such fanatics. Because the Anabaptists now publicly teach against the Scripture, they should be condemned and driven out.

Many frightful, terrible doctrines of the devil and errors against the entire Holy Scripture are in their articles in which they forbid baptism of young children. For example, they say and teach that there is no original sin. This is a birthmark of the devil, who is a liar and a murderer; they do not know about the highest and most necessary article of Christian doctrine nor about the Holy Spirit. They do not know the nature of either sin or righteousness, for they believe that only the gross external vices and depravities are sins.

This being so, that the Anabaptists teach out of an evil spirit, the devil, we should not let their teaching excite us into yielding that established doctrine of the Christian Church, that we should baptize young children, and that this baptism is Christian.

In order to show that infant baptism was practiced in the early, pristine Church, I will set forth several testimonies from antiquity.

Origen, commenting on the sixth chapter of Romans,[2] writes, "The Church received from the apostles this doctrine that we should extend baptism to young children [infants], for those who were entrusted with the mysteries of divine things well knew that all men have original sin and innate desires which must be washed away by water and Spirit."

In these words Origen confesses and teaches both that we should baptize infants and that through baptism they obtain forgiveness of sins, that is, that they are reconciled to God.

Cyprian writes that the council [of Nicaea] considered the assertion that we should not baptize children before the eighth day, and that the council concluded one should baptize them, without waiting a specified period of eight days.[3]

Augustine, speaking of baptism, in Book 4, against the Donatists,[4] sets forth a very fine, clear word about the baptism of infants when he says, "This article about infant baptism, which the entire Church maintains, was not established in the councils, but, on the contrary, has always been maintained in the Church. Therefore, we rightly believe that it was begun by the apostles themselves and established as a custom. Likewise,

2. *Commentary on the Letter to the Romans*, in *Patrologiae Cursus Completus: Series Graeca*, J. P. Migne, ed. (Paris, 1857–66), XXIV.
3. *Ante-Nicene Fathers*, A. Roberts and J. Donaldson, eds. (New York, 1890), V, *Epistles of Cyprian*, No. 58.
4. *Works of Aurelius Augustine*, III, *Donatist Controversy*, Marcus Dods, ed. (Edinburgh, 1872), Bk. iv, chaps. 5, 6, 24.

what the sacrament of baptism effects in young children we can truly judge from the circumcision which was commanded for the early people of God."

These and similar passages clearly indicate that from the beginning the entire Christian Church has kept infant baptism as Christian and right. Such we should diligently note; for some impostors wish to depress the unintelligent, saying that the ancient fathers taught against infant baptism; this, however, is doing them a gross injustice.

All God-fearing men should note that it is very dangerous, and no one should dare to initiate a doctrine, which has absolutely no testimony in the early Christian Church.

However, we will here set forth *more reasons out of Holy Scripture* why we should baptize young children. My first reason is this:

It is certain that the kingdom of God, the gospel, and the promise of grace have to do with children. It is also certain that outside the Church (where neither word nor sacrament is) there is no redemption and no forgiveness of sins. Therefore, we must bring children into the body of the Church, and present them with the external sign, which indicates that forgiveness of sins and the promise belong also to them.

That the promise and the kingdom of God pertain to children is certain, for Christ himself says in Mark 10:14, "*Of such* is the kingdom of heaven." Likewise, "It is not the will of my Father who is in heaven that even one of these little ones should perish" [Mt. 18:14].

These passages must not be rendered insipid with some fabricated comment to the effect that Christ is only admonishing us, as there is no promise in the above statement, and that we should not become like children as to naïveté and such. This comment is alien, far-fetched, and empty, for it is certain that Christ is speaking about children and little ones who are very young or infants. And Christ says, "Their angels always behold the face of my Father who is in heaven" [Mt. 18:10]. Therefore, he indicates that they please God and will be protected by angels; and Christ still more directly declares, "It is not the will of God that one of these little ones should perish."

These passages clearly give the valuable comfort to the Church that children will be saved, and we are diligently to put these comforting passages into the minds of youth so that they may keep them throughout their lives and learn to comfort themselves with the divine promise.

The baptism of infants also confirms the law of circumcision, as the Lord God says, "I will be their God" [Jer. 31:33]. There God indicates that he will be gracious to these whom he calls to circumcision, and he commands the young children to be circumcised. Surely no one can deny that we should not exclude the young children from the gospel and God's kingdom.

In the second place, it is certainly true that outside the Church, where there is no gospel, no sacrament, and no true invocation of God, there is no forgiveness of sins, grace, or salvation, as among the Turks, Jews, and heathen. For God wishes to give us such gifts only through his Church and through his word and sacraments. Therefore he says, "He who is not reborn of water and the Holy Spirit cannot enter into the kingdom of heaven" [Jn. 3:5]. This clear statement indicates that outside the Church, where there are no sacraments — where, indeed, there is persecution of the sacraments — God gives no salvation.

Similarly, in Ephesians 5, St. Paul teaches that the Church is "a people purified by God's word and baptism." From this it is clear that there is no church outside of God's word and baptism.

And still clearer is this passage of St. Peter in Acts 4:12, "for there is no other name under heaven given among men by which we must be saved." For this reason it is certain that there is no salvation outside the Church, that is, among those over whom the name of Christ is not invoked.

It follows from all this that we should and must baptize little children. For certainly the promise of eternal life belongs to children, and this promise does not belong to anyone outside the Church, where there is no salvation. Thus we must bring children into the body of the Church and must make them members of the Church through baptism. Whoever diligently considers this argument will discover that it is firm and fixed.

The second argument is very strong and clear. Those over whom the name of Christ is not invoked and who are marked by no sacrament are certainly not in God's Church. Now some children must be a part of the Church; therefore, it is certain that over them the name of Christ must be invoked and that they must be baptized.

The Anabaptists, nevertheless, are so outrageous that they would make a part of the Church a people over whom the name of Christ was not invoked; [5] but this sentence is unchanging, "There is no other name by which one is saved except the name of Jesus Christ" [cf. Acts 4:12]. He over whom this name is not invoked is no member of the Church of God. Since such invocation and blessing occur in baptism, it is frightful that

5. The Anabaptists did not regard external baptism as absolutely necessary, so long as a person had the Spirit.

the devil exercises such rage and does not want the name of Christ to be invoked over young children nor for them to be blessed through baptism.

The third argument: Children need forgiveness of sins; they carry with them the misery of human weakness and inborn disobedience. Now God has commanded the Church to forgive sins, and to impart such forgiveness through the sacraments. From this it follows that one has a duty to impart forgiveness to children through baptism.

The fourth argument: To whom the promise belongs, to them assuredly belongs also this sign. To whom the purchased good belongs, to the same belongs also the bill of exchange. Now it is quite obvious that the promise of eternal life and the merit of the death of Jesus Christ belong to children. From this it necessarily follows that to children also belongs the sign.

The Lord Christ, the Son of God, died not only for adults but for children as well. Because this sublime redemption belongs to children, and because Christ wants us to impart it through the gospel and the sacraments, it is certain that the sign belongs also to children.

The deceitful and poisonous devil in the Anabaptists asserts that in infants there is no sin, so that the Son of God was not a sacrifice for children. To avert such a murderous error, we should not deprive children of the sign of the grace of Christ.

The fifth argument: Baptism is definitely commanded for all, without distinction. "He who is not born again by water and the Spirit cannot enter into the kingdom of heaven." This passage concerns *all* men, as the true, natural meaning of this statement shows. From this it follows that we should and must be baptized, and contempt for baptism is obviously against this passage which is drawn from St. John.

Adults should diligently consider these related reasons in order to quicken their own faith, that they also are accepted by God through baptism. God bound himself and promised that he, the eternal Father of the Mediator *Jesus Christ*, would be gracious to us, would save us for the sake of his Son *Jesus Christ;* as soon as we are accepted, he wants to give us his Holy Spirit to effect in us new righteousness and eternal life.

And as the elders consider their own baptism in this manner, they should hold dear the baptism of children, and thank God that he accepts children through baptism into his Church and grace. In accordance with the command of Christ in which he said, "Let the children come unto me, for of such is the kingdom of heaven," they should bring their young children before the Lord Christ for baptism, so that they may be brought into the body of the Church, so that God may accept them, give them forgiveness of original sin, and begin purification in them.

In the faith that God assuredly accepts children, adults should invoke God over the children, commending them to God with earnest prayer, and afterward, as the children learn to speak, commending to them invocation of God and the Lord Christ, and thus continually nurturing and training them in the teaching of the gospel.

But the Anabaptists cry out against this *Christian advice and comfort.* First, they say that where there is no faith, baptism is useless. As children have no understanding of doctrines, they have no faith; therefore, for them baptism is not useful.

Answer: The Holy Spirit is given to children through baptism and in baptism, and in them is active in accordance with their capacities. So he was in John, in the womb of Elizabeth. Although there is a distinction between the old and the young, in that the old take note of their actions, nevertheless the inclinations to God in the old and the young are activities of the Holy Spirit.

But the opinion that God is active in the young only if they are brought before him, through baptism brought into the body of the Church, is no invention. Children in the Church are saved, as *Christ* clearly says, "It is not my Father's will that one of these children should perish." Likewise, "Of such is the kingdom of heaven"; that is, forgiveness of sins, grace, activity of the Holy Spirit, new righteousness and eternal life, for all this is included in the words, "kingdom of heaven."

And it is entirely certain that without divine activity no man can obtain eternal life, as expressed in John 3:5, "Unless one is born of water and the Spirit, he cannot enter the kingdom of God." Likewise, Romans 8:14, "Those who are led by the Spirit of God are the children of God." And 1 Corinthians 15 says that flesh and blood which are destroyed in death cannot have eternal salvation, that we must be renewed through Christ, who is life and light, as John says.

There is no such grace and activity in the children of the heathen, Jews, and Turks, for among them is persecution of God and Christ, and on this account God's name is not invoked over their children. In these words, "Let the children come to me; of such is the kingdom of heaven," are two things. First, Christ says we should let the children come to him; and he adds, *of such,* that is, *of the same* as we bring to Christ, is the kingdom of heaven, not of those who persecute and despise God and his Son Christ, the gospel, and baptism.

Because children are certainly saved in the Church, two things assuredly follow: that we should baptize them and that God then accepts them and gives them the Holy Spirit, which is active in them according to their capacities. As proclaimed in the gospel, the Holy Spirit is given when we receive baptism; John 3 and Titus 3 clearly call baptism a bath of new birth through the Holy Spirit.

Baptized children are a large part of true Christianity, and are truly God's people, Church, and saints. Adults should diligently consider this, so that children already accepted in baptism may with greater earnestness be instructed, guided, and preserved, that they may not be snatched from God by the cunning of the devil, by their own want of foresight, or by evil companionship.

Second, the Anabaptists cry: We should do nothing without a command. Now we discover no command in the gospel about infant baptism; therefore, they say, we should not baptize infants.

Answer: It is true that we should do nothing without command. However, it is obvious that all that pertains to baptism pertains to the kingdom of Christ. John 3:5: "Unless one is born of water and the Spirit, he cannot enter the kingdom of God." These words are a command, from which no one is exempted; it concerns all, young and old. And all reasonable persons know that such words, which are *negative*, are very strong.

This also is true: All that truly follows from God's word and command is also called God's word and command. Above I have indicated that it follows from God's word that grace and eternal life are promised to children, and so it follows incontestably that they must be brought into the body of the Church through baptism. This blessing of grace and promise simply does not exist outside the Church of God; it is not for Jewish or Turkish children, or for any other people among whom God and his Son *Jesus Christ* are despised or persecuted.

Here the other above arguments may be repeated, out of which it follows that we should impart baptism to children. Because they need forgiveness of sins, the Church should impart to them forgiveness through baptism. However, this lie adheres to the Anabaptists; they think that original sin is nothing, which is a great error.

Third, the Anabaptists cry: Baptism is a covenant in which one obligates himself to kill evil lusts and to suffer austere living and forbearance.

However, children still cannot understand and do such. Therefore, they say, baptism is not useful for children.

Answer: This talk of the Anabaptists is nothing but blindness. Baptism is first and foremost a testimony of divine grace toward us, and a covenant through which God promises to us his grace. That is first to be seen. When the servant says, "I baptize you in the name of God, the Father, Son, and Holy Spirit," it means: "I certify with this work by the mandate of God, that God, the eternal Father, forgives your sin for the sake of his Son, Jesus Christ, who also accepts you, and wishes to begin in you a new light and righteousness and eternal life, through his Holy Spirit, who also accepts you." Those who would properly understand the words in baptism are not to interpret them as saying, "I baptize you to a strenuous life, to forbearance, and so forth."

All this, which is indicated for the preservation of infant baptism, I pray the God-fearing will diligently consider in order to strengthen themselves against the many-sided errors of the Anabaptists. Also I pray that God, the eternal Father of our Savior *Jesus Christ*, will preserve all God-fearing hearts, that they may not fall into Anabaptism or other errors; that he will root out all scandals which wretchedly oppress his poor Church that the blood of our Savior Jesus Christ redeems, and that he will graciously enlighten, teach and guide us. Amen.

XXII

OF THE SUPPER OF CHRIST THE LORD

We indicated above that God has always bound to his word and promises certain external signs which serve to bolster thought and memory so that we can retain and think about the word. At the same time faith is awakened through the word and such divine memorials.

After the Son of God appeared, and renewed his gospel, and commanded that it be preached in all the world, he ordained these two delightful [*lieblichen*] ceremonies to serve as memorials. Baptism reminds us that we are baptized into the death of our Savior Jesus Christ, washed of our sins, and resurrected to pure eternal life.

And this ceremony is more pleasing than circumcision was in previous times, which for good reasons was ordained as a special work. Because God promised a descendant through whom we would be delivered and blessed, the sign on this member was ordered, although the heathen saw it only as a curious spectacle. But clearly baptism, if it occurs with earnestness and invocation of God, is a beautiful ceremony.

This custom of keeping the Supper of the Lord in the gathered company, along with preaching and prayer, is much more delightful than the slaughter of oxen was in previous times.

We should see that this remembered Supper is rightly kept, as commanded in God's word, and for the purpose appointed. Four points then become important. The first: What is administered and how? The second: For what purpose are the body and blood of Christ eaten? The third: Who are admitted to such participation? The fourth: What about the sacrifice of the Mass and the misuses which undercut its institution?

Of the First

How to observe the Lord's Supper is expressed in *St. Paul*. Christians should have public, honorable gatherings. God has had such for his

Church from the beginning until now; Adam, Noah, Abraham, Isaac, Jacob, and afterward the Levites preached in the tabernacle. God has always upheld such gatherings so that his doctrine and preaching might not be from some corner, but be publicly proclaimed before all creatures, kings, and princes and publicly attested and passed on to successors.

And although the world often attempts to exterminate such a beautiful, holy congregation,[1] where in the public office of the gospel God is praised and invoked and the people instructed, nevertheless it is wondrously and continuously upheld. As one time is purer than another, so through special gifts of God it is often renewed, as worship was often renewed through the prophets.

In such a gathering there must also be a public ceremony, through which faith is exercised and acknowledged, and with which the divine promises may be remembered, and God invoked and thanked. This work was instituted so that a Supper might be kept in which we preach about the Son of God, his sufferings and Resurrection, about his promise, grace, and rule, and in which we speak his word over the bread and wine, and distribute such among the congregation. With this bread and wine he gives *his body and blood* to us, and thereby attests that he accepts us, makes us his members, grants us forgiveness of sins, and that he has purified us with his blood, and will abide in us.

And such participation is not a heathen memorial, or a spectacle such as one might keep for Julius, or for those who are dead and have nothing to do with us. The living Son of God, *Jesus Christ*, our Savior, is truly present and active in this participation [*Niessenden*], attesting through it that he will abide in us.

How this work was instituted and originally administered is expressed at length in 1 Corinthians 11, where *St. Paul* points out that we should have public, honorable gatherings in which to keep the Supper together.

Of the Second

As to the fruit and uses [*Nutzen*] of this participation, it is very necessary to say that for those who are without fear of God and without conversion who consciously live in evil and are without faith, that is, without true reliance on Christ, such a Supper *is not useful;* it contributes *to their punishment*, as *St. Paul* earnestly teaches.

1. *Versammlung* has also been translated "gathered company," or "gathering," to avoid awkward phrasing.

True faith should accompany the participation, for this order of Christ is a testimony, appended to his promise, as said previously about the sacraments. The Son of God himself says, "This is the cup of the New Testament" [1 Cor. 11:25], that is, the sublime promise in which God vows to take away sin and death and begin eternal justification and eternal life through the Mediator, whom he sent for this purpose.

As frequently said, we must accept this promise with faith. Therefore, faith must be present in the use of the sacraments to exhibit to us the promise. This participation should take place for the awakening and the strengthening of faith in those who have turned from sin and seek consolation in Christ. They should participate believing that Christ truly accepts them, because he makes them members of his body, and that he truly wishes to forgive them their sins, for which he died on the cross.

Therefore, external participation in the Supper points to the word and promise, to the Son of God, who died for us and arose again, and now listens to his Church and members of his body, whom he wants to bless. In this Supper the heart and the faith should behold, and, in conversion and amendment, seek comfort *in Christ*.

The foremost benefit of participation is that of which Christ speaks when he says, "Do this in remembrance of me"; that is, not as a heathen, but as a believer, which is to say, we should remember that the Son of God died and arose for us in order to take away sin and eternal death, that he gives eternal righteousness and eternal life, and attests that he will abide in us, and that we should accept all this with faith. This certainly is the meaning of Christ's words, which we should carefully consider to inform ourselves as to why this participation should take place, and why the foremost fruit should be such an awakening and strengthening of faith.

Other benefits also follow, reminding us to give thanks for such grace. The necessary custom is maintained for bringing the Church together in a public, honorable gathering where preaching, teaching, and invocation of God should take place. Through this participation Christians confess their faith.

With this common participation we obligate ourselves to manifest friendship, love, fidelity, and helpfulness to one another as members of one Lord and Savior, *Jesus Christ*. Of this obligation *Paul* also speaks, "Because we all partake of one bread, we are one body" [1 Cor. 10:17]. After participation, therefore, whoever offends another's conscience offends the body and blood of Christ.

Of the Third

Who is permitted in this holy participation? With the present information about uses, this is easily understood. St. Paul says, "Each one is to examine himself and accordingly to partake; and whoever takes it unworthily, takes it to his own condemnation" [1 Cor. 11:28 f.]. From this we can conclude that no one should participate who consciously lives in evil, that is, who is not converted, who has no regret for his sins, who does not desire forgiveness, and who has no faith and reliance on *Christ*.

The servants of the gospel who openly sin, by persecution of divine truth, magic, adultery, and murder, are not permitted. As the ancient Church maintained the ban, which was highly necessary, it should again be enforced with earnestness.

However, those who have turned from sin, who have remorse and terror, participate in order to strengthen their faith. They understand that through this order the promise of Christ is actually applied and ascribed to them as members of the body of the Lord Christ, for Christ attests in this that he makes us members. Terrified consciences should not participate trusting in their own purity or holiness; they should acknowledge their weakness and trust that God is gracious to them *for the sake of the Mediator Christ*.

St. Paul speaks of preparation and worthiness when he says, "Each one is to examine himself." Because such examination is part of the participation, it is not the custom to bring young children who are not yet instructed in God's word.

Of the Fourth

Contrary to the usages, of which I have spoken, many frightful misuses unfortunately have arisen which are to be avoided and shunned, as *St. Paul* says, "Shun idolatry" [cf. Eph. 5:5].

Now this rule is to be carefully noted; sacraments, that is, divine orders or divine ceremonies, are sacraments and divine works only if they are kept in accordance with the institution and intention for which they were established. For example, if one were to carry baptismal water about and pretend that the Holy Spirit were therein, this would be idolatry. Likewise, if one were to arrange baptism for the purpose of helping against leprosy, that would be magic, not baptism. Therefore, the present circumcision of the Jews and Turks is no longer a sacrament; instead, they mock God with it.

Servants of the gospel and the laity should participate at the same time. Christ did not say that some special persons, such as priests, should sacrifice for the living and the dead, or that the Supper merits forgiveness of sins for them, or that we should make a spectacle out of it by carrying the bread about and placing it before the people for adoration.

These are all devised works, undertaken by clerics partly out of error and partly as a deliberate fraud. In such misuse, when the sacrament is perverted, there is no sacrament, only frightful idolatry. And as God always has severely punished idolatry with great wars and changes of realms, there is no doubt that the cruel raging of the Turks is inflicted now as a punishment for the idolatry in the Mass, the invocation of the dead, and all the shameful immorality which accompanies impure celibacy. May God the eternal Father of our Savior, Jesus Christ, root out all errors and protect and sustain his forsaken Church!

Although many other writings have disputed about these things, I want nevertheless briefly to indicate why the papal Mass should be shunned and abolished.

This error, that the priest's sacrifice merits forgiveness of sins for himself or others, living or dead, obviously contradicts the article of faith that we have forgiveness only through faith and trust in Christ, as this passage clearly says, "The just live by faith" [cf. Rom. 1:17]. Because this article assuredly is true, and because no human work to the contrary is to be established or tolerated as if it merited forgiveness of sins, so it is quite certain that the sacrifices of the Mass are wrong.

In Hebrews 10 it is written that Christ through his sacrifice, which occurred only once, has perfectly sanctified the saints. Therefore, no other sacrifice is necessary to purify men; the faithful become pure and holy on account of the *single* already-accomplished sacrifice that Christ *himself* made by his death (if they apply the same sacrifice to themselves through their own faith, that is, if they trust thereon). The sacrifice of the priest should not be placed on a par with it.

Second, there is absolutely no command that miserable men should sacrifice the Son of God; he alone is the High Priest, who sacrificed *himself*, as the Letter to the Hebrews says. No one else has had the power, not even the most holy, to come before God without the Mediator reconciling the first wrath against sin.

Indeed, no creature can fathom this marvelous divine counsel; God wanted to be reconciled through *no person other than his only Son, Christ*. This definitely indicates that God harbors against sin a gravity of wrath that cannot possibly be appeased by any angel or man. But also this places before us the great love in God toward mankind.

Even though these matters are unfathomable, we should contemplate the single *sacrifice of Christ*, whereby he appeased God, in order to learn of God's wrath against sin, and on the other hand to learn of the great grace which is ours in Christ if we accept it and trust therein. The merit of Christ's sacrifice is imparted to us, through our *own faith*, and not through some other way which *Christ* has *not* commanded. There is no command for us to sacrifice the Son of God. And it is assuredly wrong to produce a sacrifice without the express command of God.

For this reason we should keep the Supper of Christ as it was instituted. With the sermon or exhortation, we should speak in prayer the words of *Christ* about the Supper, reminding ourselves of the sufferings of *Christ*, and afterward the entire sacrament should be administered to those who seek comfort and manifest improvement; with it they should strengthen their faith and firmly conclude that the living Son of God receives them and makes them members of his body. This is the usage proclaimed in the gospel, and this work was originally so kept in the Church. To go beyond this reception and make a spectacle out of it is vain idolatry, for a sacrament is only a sacrament in its instituted usage.

For whoever desires to know, until the third century there were no private Masses in the Church, and the canons of the Mass were not the same [as now]. Although the old scholars often use the word "sacrifice," they do not mean that priests sacrifice the Son of God, and that this work of the priests merits forgiveness of sins for others. As any rational person can easily determine, what they call sacrifice includes all that prayer, faith, participation, and giving thanks include. One ancient custom was to bring to the gathered company much bread and wine for the welfare of the poor; this was also called a sacrifice.

Especially is it an open lie and idolatry to offer the sacrament as a sacrifice for the dead, for it was instituted only for the exercise of faith in the living.

Because the word "sacrifice" is so mentioned many times in divine Scripture and by so many scholars, I want to give a brief report of it.

XXIII

DISTINCTION BETWEEN CEREMONIES, SACRAMENTS, AND SACRIFICES

Several ceremonies, such as baptism and participation in the Supper of Christ, are decreed so that God may give us something. Such ceremonies are attached to the divine promises, and usually are called sacraments.

But other works, in which we perform or give to God our merit, obedience, and veneration, such as patience in suffering, almsgiving, and chastity, are called sacrifices, for sacrifices are works which we bring to God to manifest our obedience. We keep them for the eternal God whom we invoke, and with them we serve him.

There are, however, two kinds of sacrifices. First, there is a sacrifice that is the payment for sin, which atones for sin, a sacrifice for others that obtains for them forgiveness of guilt and eternal punishment. It is a sacrifice that reconciles divine wrath, averts displeasure, and atones for eternal pain and guilt.

The second is a sacrifice which is called a sacrifice of thanks [*Dankopfer*]. It does not merit forgiveness of sins; it is a work of obedience through which those whom God has reconciled give thanks for grace and forgiveness.

I am not imagining two kinds of sacrifices; they are clearly to be seen in the Letter to the Hebrews. The entire letter teaches that in all the world only one single sacrifice is an atonement for sin. Therefore, it follows that *all* other sacrifices are sacrifices of thanks in which we manifest our obedience.

Although there are sundry sacrifices in the law of Moses, they can all be included under these two kinds of sacrifices. Several are called sin-sacrifices, for the sake of what they signify and not because they merit forgiveness of sins. They signify the noble, costly, future sacrifice, *Christ*.

However, with reference to the law and external nature, one might obtain a certain forgiveness of sins through such sacrifice, in that a person so reconciled might not be excluded from the synagogue or the Jewish community. Such sacrifices in the Scriptures are called sin-sacrifices, guilt-sacrifices, and burnt sacrifices. Others are called food-sacrifices, drink-sacrifices, sacrifices of praise, first fruits, tithes, and the like.[1]

Otherwise, there truly has been only one sacrifice for sins, namely the *death* and the *blood of Christ*, as the Letter to the Hebrews, chapter 10:4, teaches, "For it is impossible that the blood of bulls and goats should take away sins." And soon thereafter the letter speaks of the obedience and will of Christ, and says, "In whose will we have been sanctified through the offering of the body and blood of Jesus Christ once for all" [Heb. 10:10].

In John 17:19 f. *Christ* himself indicates that his death and blood is a sacrifice for us: "And for their sake I consecrate myself, that they also may be consecrated in truth. I do not pray for these only, but also for those who believe in me through their word." Behold, these are the words of our Mediator and High Priest with which he offers himself for all of Christendom and the Church, and for them he makes a very comforting prayer! These words we should never forget.

Isaiah, the prophet, sets forth the law of Moses in such a way that we know it is not the sacrifices of the law of Moses, but *only* the *death* and *blood of Christ* which is an atonement for sin. In chapter 53:10 he says, "When he makes himself an offering for sin, he shall see his offspring, he shall prolong his days." This is as if he had said there is another sacrifice at hand, which will truly take away sin. Therefore, the daily sacrifices of the law of Moses did not take away sin, nor deliver from eternal death.

St. Paul has still more clearly laid out the passage in Isaiah when he says, in Galatians 3:13, "Christ redeemed us from the curse of the law, having become a curse for us." Likewise, Romans 8:3, ["sending his own Son in the likeness of sinful flesh and]' for sin, he condemned sin in the flesh"; that is, he took away sin, was punished, and made atonement through his sacrifice for sin, for in the Hebraic language sacrifice for sin is also called "sin."

Certainly there is no more than one sacrifice which takes away sin, for the sin-sacrifices in the law were so called only for the sake of what they signify, the one sacrifice on the cross, *Christ*. Therefore, since *Christ* is revealed, since he has come, they are abolished, for they were only the shadows of the true reconciliation, as St. Paul declares, "Therefore, since the truth, Christ, is revealed, they have ceased" [cf. Heb. 10:1, 9–14].

1. Also commonly called "thank offerings," "burnt offerings," etc.

Of the Sacrifice of Thanks [*Thank Offering*]

Now let us talk about the sacrifice of thanks, or sacrifice of praise, in the Scripture. When Christians render such sacrifices, they are truly and purely preaching the gospel, faith, prayer, thanks, patience in trouble and affliction, and confession of the gospel; in general, all the good fruits of the faith of the saints are sacrifices of thanks.

These sacrifices of thanks are now not a satisfaction or atonement for sins, nor are they sacrifices which one can perform or apply for another. They do not merit forgiveness of sins *ex opere operato*, that is, without fear of God and without faith.

Therefore, there is no sin-sacrifice and no atonement for sin in the New Testament, except the dearest, highest *sacrifice, the death and blood of Christ*. All the others in the New Testament are sacrifices of thanks. First Peter 2:4 says, "You are a holy priesthood, to offer spiritual sacrifices." Since St. Peter uses the words, "spiritual sacrifices," he indicates not only that the slaughter of oxen and he-goats in the law but also that all other external good works, *ex opere operato*, without Spirit and faith, are not spiritual sacrifices. *Spiritual* here means the light and living activity of the Holy Spirit in the heart.

The thirteenth chapter of the Letter to the Hebrews also talks about this spiritual sacrifice, "Through him then let us continually offer up a sacrifice of praise to God" [v. 15]. The apostle clearly says that the sacrifice of praise is the fruit of the lips which confess his name, that is, which preach the gospel, pray, and call upon God. These thank-and-praise-sacrifices are empty and comfortless when performed merely as works, *ex opere operato*, for God is pleased only *through faith, for the sake of Christ*, as the little words "through him," that is, through Christ, indicate.

But it is very comforting for Christians to know in their hearts that all their works, tribulation, and sufferings are costly, noble sacrifices which please God, and that through them God is also glorified and praised.

Many beautiful passages in the Psalms and prophets mention such sacrifices. Psalm 50:14, "Offer to God a sacrifice of praise; namely, call on him in time of trouble"; likewise Psalm 51:17, "The sacrifice acceptable to God is a broken spirit."

Second, we must know that in the New Testament worship is not just external forms and showy works, but is a divine light, faith, fear, comfort, and joy in God in the heart; and the beginning of eternal life and suitable works follow the divine light and life in the heart, as the prophet says, "I will put my law within them, and I will write it upon their hearts" [Jer. 31:33]. And Christ says in John 4:23, "The true worshipers will worship the Father in spirit and in truth." Therefore, the ceremonies and sacrifices of the law of Moses are abolished, for the New Testament demands spiritual sacrifices of the heart, that is, true faith, true fear of God, and from this the external, true fruit of faith.

The New Testament has no sacrifice or divine service whereby I can for myself or for another merit forgiveness of sins through some mechanically performed work (as they call it, *ex opere operato*). This passage is definitely against it: "The worshipers will worship the Father in spirit and in truth." On this account it is a hateful, cruel, pharisaical teaching and error that anyone, through mechanically performed works, without heart and faith, should merit forgiveness of sins.

As the Bible and history of the entire Scripture clearly indicate, when the Israelites in such pharisaical error had prepared unnumbered sacrifices, altars, and divine services to obtain grace and forgiveness of sins, the prophets opposed and with all their power endeavored to root out such pharisaical teaching.

In Psalm 50:13 God rejects sacrifices, preferring to have sacrifices of praise and invocation. "Do you think that I eat the flesh of bulls? . . . Offer to God a sacrifice of thanksgiving."

Isaiah 1:11: " 'What to me is the multitude of your sacrifices?' says the Lord."

Jeremiah 7:22: "For in the day that I brought them out of the land of Egypt, I did not speak to your fathers or command them concerning burnt offerings and sacrifices. But this command I gave them, 'Obey my voice, and I will be your God.' "

As the prophet says that the Lord did not speak with their fathers concerning sacrifices, and as it is certain that throughout the law of Moses there is much about sacrifices, Jeremiah must be reproving the hypocrisy of external sacrifices, *ex opere operato*, which God does not require, for he wants to have the heart.

By similar pharisaical error, unnumbered divine services of Masses for souls and other Masses have been adopted in the Church, and priests have blasphemously taught that such are pleasing to God and merit forgiveness of sin for themselves and others merely for the sake of performance, *ex opere operato*.

They have taught that through the same Masses we partake of the sacrifice of Christ on the cross. But, on the contrary, each *through his own faith*, not through the Mass or the work of another, must partake of the death and sacrifice of Christ, *without merit*, and *out of grace*, not for the sake of any work.

This, then, is evident, that true participation in the Supper as instituted is a covenant, through which the Son of God gives to us and accepts us in grace, and therefore it is not a sacrifice. We must, however, accept the proffered grace with true faith and trust in the divine promise, and from this faith and trust follow true invocation of God and the Mediator, Christ, and thanksgiving for redemption and other gifts.

There follows confession of the gospel, harmoniously manifested, with each other at the Supper of the Lord *Christ* to set others a good example, confirm them in true teaching, and encourage them to improve.

The preaching of the gospel and Christian exhortation should also be heard with this ceremony. These works of the heart, as they follow after the ceremony, are sacrifices of thanks, and pertain to the passage in Hebrews 13:15, "Through him then let us continually offer up a sacrifice of praise to God, that is, the fruit of lips that acknowledge his name."

For these works which followed the ancients used the word "sacrifice," and later through a misuse it was drawn into the ceremony. Nevertheless, we are definitely to keep the distinction between the external work and the true worship of God in the heart, without which the ceremony is neither useful nor fruitful to anybody, as previously said, "The true worshipers will worship the Father in spirit and in truth"; that is, with the Holy Spirit producing true desires in the heart, as written in Romans 8:26, "The Spirit helps us in our weakness."

Clearly the teachings of the papists about their application and sacrifices of ceremonies are frightfully empty errors, and far from the worship of God; on the contrary, they anger God the more. All pious men should beseech God to purify the Church and to root out all idolatry so that the favored may rightly invoke the eternal God in true trust in his Son *Christ*.

However, some will dispute and assert that it is the art and nature of every sacrifice to be done for another, and for another to partake of it. Romans 12 indicates that this is false. "Each will receive a reward according to his work"; likewise, "Each is to prove his work," and, "The just shall live by faith." The parable of the wise and foolish virgins also points to this.

Such divine services are works required of Christians, for as *St. Paul* says, "We are debtors" [Rom. 8:12], also, "Woe to me if I do not preach the gospel" [1 Cor. 9:16]! If our works in themselves are not enough, if *faith in Christ* must make them acceptable, what would it be but pharisaical, inflated arrogance if we considered our work a payment for sin not only for ourselves but also for someone else? Therefore, Christ says, in Luke 17:10, "So you also, when you have done all that is commanded you, say, 'We are unworthy servants! . . .' "

Psalm 50 calls the prayers and invocations of the prophets in the day of trouble [*Anfechtung*] a sacrifice, likewise, the giving of thanks, a sacrifice of praise. Now to thank God for rescuing us from anguish and distresses is not a work that can be imparted to someone else, and cannot be applied to our own undertaking. Therefore, it is false to say that the nature of every sacrifice is that one participates in someone else, for *only* the one sacrifice, Christ on the cross, is a sacrifice which happened for others and is imparted to others. The others are sacrifices of thanks, and do not assist any further than other good works and fruits of faith. Therefore, they are not to be considered as sacrifices if they are done for the good of others to obtain forgiveness of sins.

Someone might here say, "Nevertheless, do we not pray for others?" Answer: Prayer is another matter, for when we pray, we do not bring a work to God as a payment for someone else; instead, we seek to receive something from God. God has promised to give us and others that for which we pray; for this reason a distinction here is easy.

In prayer we bring before God, not our works as sacrifice or payment for sin for others; we want to obtain something through the Mediator Christ, and the Lord himself says, "Whatever you ask the Father in my name, he will give it to you" [Mt. 7:7; Lk. 11:9]. To come before God, in faith in Christ, and not for the sake of our work, is a very different thing from coming before God with the merit of our own works, intending to impart the works to someone else.

For this reason we should not concede the teaching that our good works can be imparted and applied to others to obtain for them grace and forgiveness of sins, for it is written, "The righteous shall live by faith" [Rom. 1:17].

Further, we should know that, on account of the sins of some, divine punishment and plague fall on others in this life. But for the sake of the virtue of a few pious men God frequently spares others, and staves off temporal punishment, as many passages and examples indicate.

As Jeremiah 49:12: "For thus says the Lord: 'If those who did not deserve to drink the cup must drink it [will you go unpunished]?'"

Likewise, Isaiah 33 points out that for the sake of some God-fearing and pious men God will bless country and people with good rulers, with temporal peace, and other things. "He who walks righteously and speaks uprightly, who despises the gain of oppressions, who shakes his hands, lest they hold a bribe, who stops his ears from hearing of bloodshed and shuts his eyes from looking upon evil, he will dwell on the heights; his place of defense will be the fortresses of rocks; his bread will be given him, his water will be sure. Your eyes will see the king of his beauty; they will behold a land that stretches afar" [v. 15–17].

Here God promises, among other things, that for the sake of a few God-fearing men, the government shall quietly move forward, and general peace shall be maintained.

There are also examples of others being punished on account of the trespasses and sins of a few. On account of David's sin, the people were punished, and for the sake of a few righteous, pious people God was willing to spare all Sodom. On account of Naaman God bestowed blessing and fortune on all Syria. Therefore, we should know that God widely extends both reward and punishment, so that we may become even more zealous in good works.

However, in such and similar passages of Scripture we are to know, first, that all this is not related to the chief article, or to the question about how we are *justified* before God. That is, the good works of others, of the saints and the pious, *do not help* to reconcile the godless and unrighteous to God, or to obtain for them forgiveness of sins, but to those who *through Christ* are now pious and holy, they are occasions for good in all sorts of gifts, for the faithful and the Christians are members of the body of Christ.

Second, we have no right to impart our works to someone else, for that is to trust in our works contrary to the gospel; it shall be left to God to reward Christian obedience in common or in particular. However, the Christians can pray for their brothers and others; for they do this not on their merit, but in faith, and on the promise of grace in Christ.

From this we can well understand how much of the application or impartation of works, which the monks have much too highly extolled, we should maintain. As far as justification before God is concerned, there is no application *without faith*. Faith, however, uses the instruments of the word and the sacraments as they give evidence that each one through his own faith, and not through the work of someone else, has received the treasure of the grace of Christ. That is enough about Mass at this time.

XXIV

OF PENANCE [Busse] [1]

It is thought that some of the old scholars counted penance among the sacraments, so that the teaching about penance might be more easily carried on by the Christians.

Here, first of all, the heretics are to be condemned, the Novatianists and Cathari, who taught and, contrary to all Scripture, said that those who fell after receiving baptism could not obtain forgiveness of sins. The heresy developed because they did not know what sin or righteousness by faith is. The Cathari were deluded, knew nothing about original sin, and they thought they were made pure through their works. In this dream they remain, and understand nothing about the gospel, which points out that we need forgiveness of sins throughout our entire life.

So first let us bring forth the passages of Scripture which indicate that those who fall after baptism can obtain forgiveness of sins, and that if they are again turned to God, the Church is to impart to them comfort and absolution.

Numerous examples are in the Old and New Testaments. David, and Manasseh, and Peter, as he was denying Christ, obtained grace. Moreover, Peter again fell later, and was rebuked by *St. Paul,* as the Letter to the Galatians indicates. Many in the church at Galatia fell, and were brought again to penance by St. Paul. *St. Paul* commands that the sinner, who was banished, 2 Corinthians 2, be received again after penance. In Ezekiel 33:11 it is written, "As I live, says the Lord God, I have no pleasure in the death of the wicked." Such fine preaching is everywhere in the prophets, admonishing those who have fallen to penance.

This passage in Ezekiel is especially comforting, for in his promise the Lord God takes an oath ("as I live"). As God swears, the conscience should be more joyful and comforted, for it hears not only the divine promise, but also the faithful oath of the sublime Majesty.

1. See also subsection in Article XXV, p. 237.

When the Novatians teach that if poor sinners fall after receiving baptism they cannot obtain forgiveness of sins, they accuse God himself of lying, and reproach him for perjury. To the anguished heart and conscience God's oath is a very great comfort because it shows that God wants us to have faith in him. Those who say that such words in the *Old* Testament are of no use, in view of the *New* Testament, introduce false glosses. This word of the prophet has to do with the true people of God, the entire Christian Church. As there has been *one* holy Christian Church in *one* faith and spirit from the time of Abel, so in the Old *and* New Testaments there has been *one* forgiveness of sins.

Further witnesses in the New Testament should be noted. Christ says, Matthew 18:15, "If your brother sins against you, go and tell him his fault, between you and him alone. If he listens to you, you have gained your brother."

Christ clearly indicates that he is speaking of those with whom such rebuke brings improvement, and that he is speaking about those who have fallen after previous holiness and recognition of the gospel; and he indicates that they are to be expelled from the Church and damned if they will not listen.

When St. Peter asks how often he should forgive his brother, Christ answers, seventy times seven [*cf.* Mt. 18:21–22].

This indicates that those who have fallen can obtain forgiveness of sins. If *Christ* wants Christians and the Church to forgive, then he himself will also forgive, as he said a little earlier, "even so you have gained your brother."

The entire Christian Church daily prays, "Forgive us our debts," indicating that even the sins of those who fall after baptism may be forgiven.

Galatians 6:1: "If a man is overtaken in any trespass, you who are spiritual should restore him in a spirit of gentleness." Since *St. Paul* commands that those who have fallen be allowed to come to penance, this indicates that their sins may be forgiven them.

In Luke 15:7 Christ says, "Just so, I tell you, there will be more joy in heaven over one sinner who repents than over ninety-nine righteous persons who need no repentance."

In Revelation 2:5: "Remember then from what you have fallen, repent and do the works you did at first." These passages are clear enough.

However, the Novatian heretics draw upon two passages above all others; one being in Hebrews 6:4, "For it is impossible to restore again to repentance those who have once been enlightened. . . ."

Although the passage appears hard, nevertheless if the Christian's heart and conscience are rightly instructed, he will definitely have comfort, for the entire Letter to the Hebrews should be abandoned before this absolutely necessary article, which is clearly grounded in the words of Christ and the apostles, is allowed to fall. Ancient scholars write that the Letter to the Hebrews was not made by *St. Paul* but by one of the disciples of the apostle.

Now if we know from other clear passages of Scripture that those who have fallen after baptism may obtain forgiveness of sins, we should not insist on the words of a single passage, but explain the same according to the principle of other Scripture.

The ancients have sought various interpretations of this passage, but in the true original, in the Greek text, it reads, without subtracting from its meaning, thus, "It is not possible for those who again crucify and despise Christ . . . to be restored in repentance."

It can and is to be understood to mean that those cannot be restored again in repentance who abandon and curse the gospel, who toss to the wind their baptism and doctrine about repentance. This is the true interpretation of this passage, and it is not contrary to the doctrine of penance, for such cannot be restored in penance as long as they disavow the gospel and crucify *Christ* anew.

If this explanation is not sufficient for anyone, let him interpret this passage about public blasphemers. For these are violent, frightful words, which say, "They crucify *Christ* again, and hold him up to contempt" [Heb. 6:6]. This is not the usual sin of weakness, but open, frightful blasphemy. The obdurate [*Verstockte*] and the Epicureans are such blasphemers. Against their own conscience they persecute God's word and the truth, defiantly despise all admonition and penance, and moreover celebrate their wisdom and take pleasure in laughing at God and divine things.

Further, it is also an empty argument when some allege that blasphemy will not be forgiven, and that, therefore, no sin will be forgiven. The Lord *Christ* clearly indicates that other sins will be forgiven in Matthew 12:31, "Therefore, I tell you, every sin and blasphemy will be forgiven men, but the blasphemy against the Spirit will not be forgiven." Also in 1 John 5:16: "If one commits a mortal sin, for him I do not say that you should pray."

About blasphemy we want to say more shortly, but we want first to mention the passage in Hebrews 10:26, which reads thus, "For if we sin deliberately after receiving the knowledge of the truth, there no longer remains a sacrifice for sins, but a fearful prospect of judgment."

This passage is not contrary to the teaching about repentance either, for the apostle does not want those who have fallen not to come to repentance, but he is placing the reconciliation and grace which we obtain through Christ over against other sacrifices or other payment and satisfaction. If we have known *Christ* and the *gospel*, and if we have not kept this treasure, then necessarily the frightful punishment of judgment must follow, for if we do not have *the one* sacrifice, then neither work nor sacrifice is of any avail. He does not say that those who have fallen in sin may not again come to Christ or to his sacrifice, but says there is no other to be found, and if one does not come again to Christ, there is nothing else except to wait for judgment and eternal wrath.

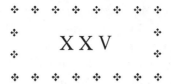

XXV

OF SIN AGAINST THE HOLY SPIRIT

St. Augustine understands sin against the Holy Spirit as the obstinacy of those who are bitter enemies, despisers, and persecutors of the gospel, to such an extent that they will not finally do penance and despair of God's grace. His reason is that this sin struggles against grace. Other sins, as great as they are, will be forgiven if we ask for and desire grace. But those who persecute the gospel of Christ, or despair, thrust grace away. Augustine also speaks in agreement with the word of Christ when he says, "Whoever speaks against the Holy Spirit . . . (that is, finally to thrust away the word of grace which is preached and established through the testimony of the Holy Spirit) . . . that is a sin which will not be forgiven." [1]

This explanation of Augustine is Christian and in conformity with the Scriptures. In accordance with recognized truth, we should not consider every sin as one against the Holy Spirit or as one which will not be forgiven. This is the reason I pointed out many passages in Holy Scripture which indicate that several such sins will be forgiven. We should not consider every persecution of doctrine as a sin which will not be forgiven, because Manasseh and Paul both obtained forgiveness.

We should carefully note two things. First, it is definitely certain that all the sins of those who have faith will be forgiven, for the forgiveness of sins and the grace of Christ are not only offered to some but to all, as the text reads, "All who believe in him will not perish" [Jn. 3:16]. Likewise, "Where sin has become strong, grace is even stronger" [Rom. 5:20]. Also in 1 John 2:2: "Christ is the expiation for our sins, and not for ours only but also for the sins of the whole world." Therefore, if anyone says that such a costly sacrifice, Christ, has not paid for his sins, he reviles Christ. Also this is contempt for God and his grace when we consider the

1. *Works of Aurelius Augustine*, III, *Donatist Controversy*, Marcus Dods, ed. (Edinburg, 1872), *A Treatise Concerning the Correction of the Donatists*, chap. xi.

kingdom of sin stronger and mightier than the kingdom of *Christ* and *grace*. Therefore, we should quite assuredly hold that all sins will be forgiven for those who believe.

Second, the highest commandment is that we listen to the Son of God and believe him. This commandment compels us to turn to Christ no matter how great our sin previously.

Now I come to the second part, for man also is to know that the Scriptures speak of a sin which will not be forgiven, which John the apostle calls, "a sin unto death" [*cf.* 1 Jn. 5:16]. What kind of sin this is, and in whom, is not for us to judge. However, it is dangerous to pursue persecutions and blasphemies of Christ and the gospel. Nevertheless, we should conclude that the sin which will not be forgiven is not in those who come to repentance and turn again to the gospel.

From this we can learn that no man is turned away from penance by a threat from Christ. The threat affects only *those* who do not again come to Christ and to faith, for grace and forgiveness of sins are offered to *all* who come again to Christ and to faith. So let us keep in mind, then, what this sin is and in whom it is, for this sin which will not be forgiven is only in *those* who do *not* again turn to repentance and faith. Many passages of Scripture indicate this.

St. Paul says in Titus 3:10 f., "As for a man who is factious, after admonishing him once or twice, have nothing more to do with him, knowing that such a person is perverted and sinful; he is self-condemned."

Also, Romans 11:7 f.: "The rest were hardened, as it is written, 'God gave them a spirit of stupor, eyes that should not see and ears that should not hear.'"

These passages speak of the frightful delusion of those who are scorners and hardened persecutors of the gospel, who continue in the Cain-like poisoned bitterness and rancor of their hate and rage against the truth. Neither sermons nor admonitions, supplications nor entreaties, help; and, although they are overwhelmed in their hearts and conscience by the public attestation of the Holy Spirit in Holy Scripture and miracles, they do not cease justifying their godless doctrine and life. Pharaoh was not moved by such high divine miracles; he proceeded furiously to storm against the Israelites, and so did the Jews against *Christ* and the apostles. Such persecutors of the divine truth who act against conscience are blasphemers, of whom the words in Matthew 12 speak.

In my opinion this is a useful and correct reading of the words of

Christ, which follows when we place the above-mentioned two parts over against one another. As it is certain that *all* sins are forgiven those who believe, it follows that sin against the Holy Spirit is only in *those* who are not willing to come to *Christ*, to accept the gospel through faith.

Because the Church has the scriptural comfort that all sins are forgiven those who believe, and also the commandment with regard to sin to bind and to loose, the Christian heart and conscience should not first dispute which are the sins that will not be forgiven, but should obey God's word and command, and listen to the sermon about penance, and in accordance with it seek grace. If we do this, then such sin is not in us, as *St. Paul*, 1 Timothy 1:15, says, "The saying is sure and worthy of full acceptance, that Christ Jesus came into the world to save sinners." Enough about this item.

Of Penance [2]

Now I come again to that which I undertook to say about penance. It is not necessary to quarrel about the word *poenitentia*, or penance, for according to the use of the Church it means "conversion" [*Bekehrung*], or "renewal" [*Erneuerung*]. The Latin word [*poenitentia*] means "repentance" [*Reue*], and agrees well with the word *contritio*, which is called repentance and terror in the presence of God's wrath. The Holy Scripture calls the entire matter *poenitentiam*. The scholastics divided it into three parts: repentance, confession, and satisfaction. I will say later how much of these three parts is to be retained. However, to speak more correctly about it, let us divide penance [*Busse*] into two parts.

The first pertains to *contritio*, or repentance and terror before God's wrath against sin; the second pertains to faith in Christ. If anyone wishes to add the third part, namely the Christian life, which is a fruit of penance, I shall not oppose it. I make faith in Christ a part of penance, so that the thought of penance always brings to mind faith in Christ. If we treat forgiveness of sins, we must be concerned with the doctrine of faith in Christ, without which there is no forgiveness of sins. The scholastics speak about penance, however, and make absolutely no mention of faith in Christ, and for this reason they have taught terrible errors.

We will now speak first about contrition, which is genuine, earnest terror before God's wrath against our sin, anguish and pain because we are in sin and have angered God.

2. See also Article XXIV, p. 231.

The Scripture speaks of this part when the Gospel says, "Do penance (or repent), for the kingdom of heaven is near" [Mt. 3:2]. Likewise, John 16:8: "The Holy Spirit will chastise [strafen] the world on account of sin." Also, 2 Corinthians 7:9: "I rejoice . . . because you were grieved into repenting." Romans 1:18: "For the wrath of God is revealed from heaven against all ungodliness." Also, Joel 2:13: "Rend your hearts and not your garments." Isaiah 57:15: "I dwell . . . with him who is of a contrite and humble spirit, to revive the spirit of the humble. . . .'" And Isaiah 66:2: "But this is the man to whom I will look, he that is humble and contrite in spirit, and trembles at my word." Also Psalm 34:14: "Depart from evil." The Psalms have many examples; Psalm 38:4: "For my iniquities have gone over my head; they weigh like a burden too heavy for me." Proverbs 9:10: "Fear of the Lord is the beginning of wisdom." And the Scripture always places fear of God and faith next to one another, "The Lord is gracious to those who fear him, and who hope in his goodness" [cf. Ps. 33:18; 147:11; 31:19; 103:11, 17].

These and similar passages indicate that genuine, heartfelt repentance and acknowledgment of sin is necessary in conversion [Bekehrung], and that such acknowledgment should enlarge so that we not only acknowledge the sins which we have committed externally, but also see the unbelief and the most profound sins which lie deep in the heart, such as contempt of God and impatience against the will of God.

For this reason there is no true penance in the unholy self-satisfied hypocrites who go about without any anguish in their hearts, trusting and building on hypocritical forms and works of monks, thinking afterward that they are without sin. Christ sternly rebukes this security of the hypocrites and false saints when he says, Luke 13:3, "Unless you repent you will all likewise perish!"

Sincere terror and anguish of heart occur in this way. The eternal God, having resolved in his wonderful counsel to save and to deliver mankind once again from eternal death through his Son, in the beginning instituted the high and holy office [of preaching] to proclaim his word, to rebuke the sin of man, and to point out God's wrath against sin, which he shows in this life with many cruel plagues. Accordingly, God punished the sin of Adam and Eve, and afterward, Cain's, and so forth. On the other hand, he also gave the patriarchs a comforting promise about the Deliverer [Erlöser].

This office is maintained throughout the prophets, and is explained in the New Testament, and it extends to the entire world. John the Baptist clearly announces that the godless are damned to eternal fire and eternal punishment. At the same time that he calls for repentance, he gives comfort to those who turn, saying, "Behold, this is the Lamb of God who takes away the sin of the world" [Jn. 1:29]! And later Christ preaches still more clearly about eternal punishment for sin in those who do not turn, and says, in Matthew 25:41, that their judgment will be, "Depart from me, you cursed, into the eternal fire." For this end he commands the apostles to preach in all the world. For this reason also St. Paul says, Romans 1, that through preaching God's wrath is revealed against the sin of all men [cf. v. 16–18].

God has allowed his law to be preached in these punishments so that the world may always know this judgment on sin. Through such a voice he punishes and condemns forever all the disobedience of men, contempt of God, doubt, blasphemy, and vice. He also rebukes the world through the voice of the gospel if we do not honor and receive the Son of God with faith. Through this voice God produces terror and recognition of sins in those who do not despise this sermon.

John 16:8 says, "The Holy Spirit will chastise the world on account of sin," that is, with his voice he will act and judge sin in the heart, so that the world may acknowledge God's wrath, truly tremble and feel the despair that eternal death would bring, if the heart were not comforted again through the knowledge of the great grace which the Son of God, the Mediator, has obtained for us.

Accordingly, in penance knowledge of sin and terror before God's wrath in the heart must come through the divine law and judgment on sin. To this, however, the comfort and the second part must be added, namely faith in the Son of God, *Jesus Christ,* who merited, obtained, and promised us forgiveness of sins. This faith comes through the voice of the holy gospel, or the promise, in which the Holy Spirit is also active.

And this faith is not only knowledge of history, or law, it is the true, definite confidence in which each and every Christian truly trusts that his sins are forgiven him, *without any merit on our part, out of grace, for the sake of Christ.* Without faith no one can obtain forgiveness of sins, as the passages will indicate which we will shortly relate.

This faith makes the difference between the repentance of Peter and Judas and that of David and Saul. Repentance and sorrow did not help Saul and Judas, the informer, for they did not have faith in the promise of grace. The repentance in David and Peter did not bring death and condemnation, for they had faith in the promise of grace, through which they obtained forgiveness of sins and received comfort. If we knew this teaching about faith, we could then distinguish between childlike and slavish fear. Here we do not need to dispute much about contrition and attrition, about whether repentance proceeds from love or from a slavish fear of punishment. The two, childlike and slavish fear, are mingled in the greatest saints and true children of God. However, it is plain that slavish fear is in the heart when there is no faith in *Christ*, and that childlike fear toward God is in *the heart* when there is faith in Christ, faith which lays hold of the promise of grace, and in the midst of terror lays hold on grace.

From this we can easily perceive that we give sufficient and better instruction about honest contrition and true repentance and sorrow than the monks. Moreover, they err frightfully in saying that we obtain forgiveness of sins through the merit of our contrition, for the sake of our repentance and our sorrow. Many terrified hearts and consciences would despair, and perish in their sins, if they should think in the great anguish of death and final struggle that they did not have forgiveness of sins inasmuch as their repentance and sorrow, their weeping and tears, were not quite enough.

Further, as disputations and unending snares of conscience have resulted from the doctrine that we merit forgiveness of sins with our repentance, even though the contrition or repentance proceeds out of love toward God and not out of fear of damnation, no one can say for certain that it proceeds out of love. Accordingly, they have allowed innumerable wretched, miserable consciences to remain mired in anguish and despair. To this day they still speak and write about this in their books so obscurely that no one can learn or comprehend for certain whether they themselves understand it or not.

We teach and clearly say that repentance and sorrow belong to honest penance. We also clearly say that repentance and sorrow *do not merit* God's reconciliation, that is, forgiveness of sins, and that we do not obtain grace for the sake of our repentance or heartfelt anguish, but that there must be faith, that is, confidence, that our sins are forgiven *without any merit on our part, for the sake of Christ.*

And it is not enough that I believe in general that God forgives sin. Even the devil believes that. He well knows that in the Church there is forgiveness of sins. But each one among us must conclude for himself that *his own sins* are really forgiven. We are speaking about this faith, the faith in my and in your heart, through which each one *for himself* partakes of the grace of *Christ*.

Passages

Acts 10:43: "To him all the prophets bear witness that everyone who believes in him receives forgiveness of sins through his name."

This is a very clear passage showing that *for Christ's sake* we obtain forgiveness of sins, and that we should assuredly rely on *Christ through faith*.

Romans 5:1: "Therefore, since we are justified by faith, we have *peace with God through our Lord Jesus Christ*"; that is, we have a happy and peaceful conscience.

However, what if someone said, "I know that Scripture says we must be justified *through faith*, but you should prove that we are justified *'without merit.'* " Answer: In the extreme struggle conscience yearns for comfort. The heart in all men says that according to the natural law, God is good, gracious, and merciful, and that he also forgives the sins of some. On that point, however, consciences are troubled. Does God forgive sinners and those who are unworthy? Will my sins and yours be forgiven even though we are unworthy?

Therefore, it is necessary to keep in mind the passages which clearly indicate, first of all, that the promise of grace pertains to all men, and second, that *without merit on our part*, we who are sinful and unworthy will be forgiven *through Christ*.

Romans 3:24 f.: "They are justified by his grace as a gift, through the redemption which is in Christ Jesus, whom God put forward as an expiation by his blood, to be received by faith."

This sentence clearly sets forth *gratis, without merit*. This does exclude good works, or fruits of faith, but indicates that we obtain forgiveness of sins *not for the sake of our worthiness* but *for the sake of Christ*, so that the promise may stand strong and sure. Therefore, we should rest assured that we do not obtain forgiveness of sins and grace for the sake of our penance or our work, but *for the sake of the Lord, Christ*.

Ephesians 2:8 f.: "For by grace you have been saved through faith; and this is not your own doing, it is the gift of God — not because of works (lest any man should boast)."

Romans 8:3: "For [God has done] what the law could not . . . ."; that is, we could not fulfill the divine law, so the law always accuses us. Therefore, we cannot set our worthiness over against God's wrath and earnest judgment; we must obtain grace and forgiveness *through the Mediator, Christ.*

Romans 5:2: "Through whom we have access to the Father, to this grace."

And the sentence in Romans 4:16 is especially to be noted, "Therefore the promise is obtained through faith, without merit, so that it may remain strong and sure." If reconciliation should be given to us on account of our merits and penance, then the promise would be uncertain and empty because we never satisfy the law.

To this also belong passages from the prophets and Psalms. Psalm 32:5: "I said, 'I will confess my transgressions to the Lord'; then thou didst forgive the guilt of my sin."

Psalm 143:2: "For no man living is righteous before thee." These and similar sentences clearly teach that we obtain forgiveness and grace *not on account of our merits,* but *purely and simply out of mercy.*

So we now know that we must obtain forgiveness of sins through *faith in Christ.* And faith *does not* rely on our work; it sustains itself on the Mediator *Christ.* Only through this faith are hearts strengthened and delivered from anguish and terror and snatched from the jaws of death and hell. In such strengthening and saving comfort of the gospel we are resurrected with Christ from the dead and renewed through the Holy Spirit.

Therefore, *St. Paul* says, 1 Corinthians 15:56 f.: "The sting of death is sin, and the power of sin is the law. But thanks be to God, who gives us the victory *through our Lord Jesus Christ.*"

Up to now I have spoken about contrition, repentance, and sorrow, and about faith in *Christ,* and for this reason have all the more preferred to set forth the two foremost parts which belong to penance, in order to point to the summation of the entire Scripture, namely that all Scripture teaches two things, law and gospel. All the sermons of the prophets and the books (of the law) treat two things, the threat of the divine law and the promise of *Christ.*

If *through Christ* we are reconciled to God, then should follow the Christian life, fruits of faith, and good conscience, as John the Baptist says, "Bear fruit that befits repentance" [Lk. 3:8]. Also, Romans 8:12: "So then, we are debtors not to the flesh, to live according to the flesh. . . ." And, therefore, because no man can perfectly fulfill the divine law, Christian consciences should always and before all things establish and maintain this one foundation, that persons are justified and accepted by God *for the sake of Christ,* and that the works following are pleasing to God because the person now is reconciled with God through *Christ,* the Savior. This having been said, let us talk about confession and satisfaction or compensation.

XXVI

OF CONFESSION

Confession and satisfaction [*Genugthuung*] originally developed from several ceremonies of public penance. In the beginning the Church would put under the ban those who were living in open blasphemy and sin, and would not receive them again until they had confessed in the presence of their spiritual shepherd, humbly sought absolution, and promised to improve themselves. Then a satisfaction was laid on them, that is, a public punishment, as an example to others, to protect them from similar sin and blasphemy, and to demonstrate the sincerity of the penitent. From such ceremonies confession and satisfaction developed.

First we will speak about confession. We are not commanded to relate and enumerate all our sins one after the other, for nothing about this is found in Scripture. Besides, such counting is impossible, just as Psalm 19:12 says, "Lord, who can discern his errors?" Also the canonists themselves admit, especially the intelligent ones, that such counting is not commanded in the Holy Scripture.

So one finds that at Constantinople confession was entirely eliminated for a long time because a deacon in the private confession had disgraced a woman. Now, if it had been commanded by God, men would not have had the power to eliminate it.

Experience has shown that many pious hearts and consciences have suffered great torture and torment because they were taught and cruelly frightened by the thought that if they so much as omitted to confess one sin, they would be damned. Therefore, it is very necessary to say that any such commandment, canon, or teaching about the enumeration of sins is no more than a human precept.

On the other hand, it is necessary to keep absolution in the Church. It serves as a special dialogue to promote good discipline, especially to examine and instruct the unlearned. It is improper to allow the unconfessed to come unexamined to the sacrament, as the pastor does not know what they believe, what they know about Christ, or whether they have promised to repent. The spiritual shepherds are obliged to discover these matters, and for this reason the people are obliged to confess such. To accomplish this we keep the special dialogue, but nevertheless, we should not burden the conscience with a counting of sins.

However, someone might bring up the common argument that the judge cannot release anyone unless he first knows what to release from; if the people are to be absolved and released, the sin must first be related so that a decision may be given.

Answer: There is a twofold power in the Church or in the spiritual leaders in the Church. First, there is the office of preaching, or the pastoral office, through which the gospel is taught, the sacraments administered, and forgiveness of sins announced to everyone. Priests have no command to hear all sins by name and to judge them, but only to announce forgiveness of sins and grace through absolution; and this also appertains to those who repent over hidden sin, known only to the individual, or to sin which has been forgotten. Therefore, it is not necessary to enumerate all sins in order to give a decision.

There is another power in the Church which is but an external recognition that the Church may condemn some on account of open blasphemy. Such a judgment should not be spoken except with prior recognition of what has happened, for we should not condemn or expel anyone from the Church unless he be convicted of sin. Also, we should release no one from sin unless we have previous knowledge of the matter and know that the person has repented. This is not a judgment about secret anxiety in the heart, but about external conduct and activity. This distinction with regard to the administration of the sacraments and external jurisdiction should be diligently marked, for the office of preaching and the administration of the sacraments have to do with conscience.

That common and particular sins are forgiven through the power of the gospel, these passages show:

John 20:23: "If you forgive the sins of any, they are forgiven."

Matthew 18:21: "How often shall my brother sin against me, and I forgive him?" . . . Matthew thus speaks about forgiveness, with which God himself is pleased.

For this reason we should highly esteem absolution in the confession, which is spoken particularly to each one. It is very comforting and useful to God-fearing hearts and consciences to hear in this way that the promise is appropriated and applied to *them*.

Some cry out against absolution and say that men do not have the power to forgive sins. That is true, if the absolution, or word of comfort and gospel, is not spoken in the name of God. However, the gospel is a divine commandment, to all in common, and to each in particular, to forgive sin. The servants of the Church, in that they administer the sacraments, also forgive sin. When I say, "I baptize you," this is said in the same way as, "I forgive you your sins." Through the sacraments are administered the mysteries of God and the gospel, and the seal and security is that the treasure of the gospel belongs to us. It is not enough to believe that some obtain forgiveness of sins; everyone should believe that he himself obtains forgiveness of sins. As Christ says, "Your faith has saved you" [Lk. 7:50].

Also, St. Paul, Romans 5:1, "Therefore, since we are justified by faith, we have peace with God."

Other questions about confession are easily answered, but we should know that this word confessio, or admission of sins, often used in Scriptures, means, I confess, or admit, my sins to the Lord; that is, I acknowledge my sin before God. Such acknowledgment is accompanied by great terror and anguish if we recognize the sin in our hearts and seek grace and mercy.

Psalm 51:3: "For I know my transgressions, and my sin is ever before me."

Psalm 38:3: "There is no soundness in my flesh because of thy indignation; there is no health in my bones because of my sin."

Also Psalm 32:5: "I will confess my transgressions to the Lord."

Such confession is in reality heartfelt repentance and sorrow, for it is an earnest confession of the heart if we acknowledge sin and God's wrath, and tremble in anguish. These passages indicate that true repentance and sorrow are a great earnestness and anguish in the heart. Where there is no such terror, there is no true penance, but people without such fear are, as St. Peter says, like irrational animals.

OF SATISFACTION [*Genugthuung*]

In the early Church those who had been in open sin and blasphemy would not be received without prior punishment, which they called *satisfaction,* or *compensation.* Although the custom was abandoned long ago, the word *satisfactio,* or *compensation,* remains, and has caused much disputation.

The ceremony of public penance in the Church was an external discipline and punishment, ordained as external punishment in the secular government of men is ordained. Such discipline was entirely external; it had nothing to do with conscience. But as with so many things, some unlearned people made this external thing a necessary service of God, and baselessly imagined that such satisfaction is necessary in order to obtain forgiveness of sins before God.

I will say shortly how much of this should be kept, but at this point, I think it useful to root out false doctrine and error, as they are dangerous and pernicious to conscience; therefore, I will note the distinction between forgiveness of guilt before God and forgiveness of pain and punishment, for confusion about these have done great injury.

First, when we speak of satisfaction, we are not speaking of a payment such as one might connect with the seventh commandment, which says, "You shall not steal." We are obliged to make satisfaction for injury and for goods taken that are not our own; this is commanded by God and belongs to repentance and sorrow and good resolution, as Isaiah 1:16 says, "Cease to do evil," and so forth.

However, our opponents say that works here, which are not required, are *satisfactions* with which one pays for and discharges the pain of purgatory and the particular punishments which God here inflicts for each and every sin. The monks say that because of his mercy God will forgive guilt, but because of his justice, he converts the eternal pain of damnation into the transient pain of purgatory. They add that a part of the pain may be remitted through the power of the keys; for a part, however, *satisfactio*, that is, compensation, must be made. That is the sum of their dream.

This much of what they say is true; guilt before God is not remitted on account of our satisfaction. But when they say that eternal pain is converted into the transient pain of purgatory, that is an error. It is an error to teach that the eternal pain is transmitted for the sake of our satisfaction. They have very foolishly asserted that we must pay for eternal death with works which God has neither taught nor commanded.

We, however, do not separate eternal pain and guilt; we become rid of both *without merit on our part through faith in Jesus Christ*. Through faith we are delivered from the guilt of sin, from eternal death, and from God's wrath *for the sake of Christ*, according to 1 Corinthians 15:56 f., "The sting of death is sin . . . but thanks be to God, who gives us the victory through our Lord Jesus Christ." Also Romans 6:23: "The gift of God is eternal life in Christ Jesus our Lord."

If we have received comfort and have obtained forgiveness of sins through faith, we are delivered from eternal death, as the apostle says, "Now, since we are justified by faith, we have peace with God" [Rom. 5:1]. Therefore, whoever would take away eternal death with his satisfaction shames and blasphemes Christ!

Second, although forgiveness of guilt and transmission of eternal death should not be separated, one should separate forgiveness of guilt before God and transmission or alleviation of temporal punishment here on earth.

It is true that even the saints in this life must bear various plagues; the first being the common necessity and anguish, into which all mankind was thrust through the fall of Adam, namely death, sickness, persecution in the world, and injury in common destruction.

Although Isaiah, Daniel, and John the Baptist are children of God, nevertheless in the flesh they are troubled and mired in death, on account of sin, as it stands written in Romans 8. And God especially intends to press and torture highly gifted saints for these reasons:

The first: The world is deluded, and thinks that God does not rule or that he is not seriously angry over sin; the world regards plagues in general as natural things, and with a sense of security, contemptuously dismisses the destruction of kingdoms. But God wants his Church to recognize sin, death, and divine wrath. The saints know that such misery comes to pass in the world because God is angry over sin, and because all must share death, for the flesh of all is sinful. Because they recognize God's wrath, they tremble, call on God, become clean, and exhort themselves through plagues to more constant penance and invocation. They do not become fat and lazy.

The second reason why the saints are more plagued is that their sufferings must be a testimony that life and justice will follow in the next life. It is obvious that God was with Isaiah, as the miracle shows; so as he is cut and torn to pieces by Manasseh, the king of Judah, we may conclude that another life and justice must follow, for God would not let his own come into the hands of tyrants if he did not intend to judge hereafter.

The third reason is that God wishes to show that he, rather than we, is strong and mighty, and that he is powerful in our weakness. Why God so deeply humbles the wise people in his Church so that they lie under the feet of worldly power and insolence, and are trampled under foot by kingdoms like Egypt, Babylon, Rome, and Turkey, is a wisdom understood nowhere except in the Christian Church alone.

Second, in addition to common plagues, God punishes the sins of some saints with special plagues. On account of adultery and manslaughter David is severely punished. His sons killed one another; Absalom stirred up tumult, put his father to flight, and disgraced women. Many people were slain. This afflicted and haunted the mighty man David.

The victorious king of Babylon, who was famous for his wisdom and great deeds, was greatly humiliated, becoming mad and wandering about for seven months like a beast.

The histories of kings have often shown that war and destruction have been caused by idolatry, immorality, and murder. For this reason the saints should ponder whether they do not themselves deserve the particular punishments which come to the Church.

Psalm 89:32 f. speaks thus about the punishment that comes upon the chosen. "I will punish their transgression with the rod and their iniquity with scourges; but I will not remove from him my steadfast love." And St. Peter says, "Judgment, or punishment, begins in the house of God" [1 Pet. 4:17]. And Jeremiah sets forth a very ardent sentence in chapter 12:7; "I have given the beloved of my soul (that is, my people) into the hands of her enemies."

These passages and examples indicate how highly necessary it is to distinguish temporal punishment in this life from forgiveness of guilt and eternal death.

Concerning such temporal punishment which God inflicts, let it be known that the power of the keys can neither inflict such punishment nor take it away.

In the second place, although the common sorrow of the saints has its source in sin, they should know that their particular sorrow does not always have its source in their particular sins and is not necessarily a sign that God is angry with them. John and Paul and many similar ones were beheaded; the old man Isaiah, who ruled honestly and ably for eighty years, was sawed into pieces; Jeremiah, who for forty years guided the people in the most important matters, was finally stoned. God himself admitted to Job that he was not being punished on account of his sins.

These and similar examples teach that the sorrows of the saints are not always punishments of their particular sins but are singular works with which God exercises them, and in their weakness he wishes to manifest his strength. He also places them before us that we may learn that life and judgment will follow this life. Although some plagues, as David's, are punishments for particular sins, we should know that in general all trouble is visited upon us that we may be drawn to penance and invocation and that faith may be exercised and strengthened, as I will discuss later under the topic of trouble and the cross.

Third, let it be carefully noted that general and particular punishments are alleviated by our improvement, as Isaiah 1 clearly indicates. And in Zechariah God says, "Return to me, and I will return to you" [Zech. 1:3], that is, I will again give you peace, nourishment, and well-being. Here also belongs the sentence, "Alms deliver from sin" [cf. 1 Pet. 4:8], that is, they obtain forgiveness or alleviation of temporal punishment in this life.

It is essential that in the Church we teach and preach that punishments and plagues are sent on account of sin and that they are alleviated if we do penance. But here we are speaking of genuine, righteous penance, not of childish, silly satisfaction and compensation, which our opponents say are useful even if they have committed mortal sin. The stupidity and godlessness of this doctrine is easy to determine, for certainly the service or work of the godless does not please the Lord God, as Psalm 5:4 says, "For thou art not a God who delights in wickedness."

Fourth, the *satisfactiones scholasticae* annul both the gospel and the law and foster higher esteem for the precepts of men than for the gospel. In their teaching about satisfactions they assert that something takes place which is over and above what the law requires, inasmuch as the law is already fulfilled through other works. It is highly necessary that in the

Christian Church this be clearly and correctly explained: not even by the highest work of the saints is the law fulfilled.

With their works they annul the gospel, for they teach that for the sake of our satisfactions or compensations God makes allowances for eternal pain and death, allows temporal punishments, and so forth. Thus there is the danger that the unlearned will believe that through such satisfactions and compensations sin and guilt may be forgiven.

These *satisfactiones* also strengthen the idea that the precepts of men and monks are divine services, whereas Christ's teaching in Matthew 15:9 must always remain firm: "In vain do they worship me, teaching as doctrines the precepts of men." It is necessary, therefore, not to regard such precepts of men as if they were divine services.

From this let it be carefully understood that the conscience is not to be burdened with satisfactions and compensations. In the first place the Christian has the keys and the command to forgive sin and to teach forgiveness of sins through *Christ*, without our work or merit; but the Christian does not have a command to impose satisfactions or punishment. It is also false that eternal death will be converted to temporal punishment on account of our satisfactions and compensations. And again, the teaching about satisfaction basically annuls the teachings of the law and the gospel and causes reliance on the precepts of men. Let Christians realize that it is not through the false works of satisfaction, but through genuine penance and work which God *obligates* us to do that temporal punishment and plagues are alleviated. Therefore, we should admonish the people to Christian conduct, so that through our penance temporal evil may be alleviated.

At this point someone might say, "Shall we let the flesh indulge in every sensual pleasure? Shall we not restrain ourselves with work, fasting and similar exercises? Shall we cease being chaste, moral, and temperate?" Answer: Anyone who loves God's word already knows the answer. I have often said that penance should bring about a new obedience to God's commandments. Where earnest obedience does not follow, there is neither repentance nor faith. According to a passage in John, those who remain unchanged, who continue in sin against their conscience, are damned. "He who commits sin (namely against his conscience), is of the devil" [1 Jn. 3:8].

God has commanded us to eat, drink, and work with moderation; to discipline the body; to give no cause for unchastity with food, drink, or leisure; to keep the body which God has given us from the corruption of reveling or immorality; and to place no obstruction on our calling or our invocation through revelry. These are God's commanded works. Obedience and diligence with regard to them are always to follow, and these commands are not to be bound to a certain day or to certain food. They are continually to be observed. This is commanded hundreds of time in the Holy Scriptures.

Christ says, "Take care that your hearts be not laden with revelry" [cf. Lk. 21:34]! Matthew 17:21: "The devil yields not except through prayer and fasting," that is, through prayer that is earnest. From the idle heart that lives in pleasure and intemperance comes only an indolent, shameful prayer. Moses says that when the people had eaten and drunk their fill, they then made themselves a calf about which to dance. Experience shows that idleness, sensuality, intemperance, and degradation produce adultery, insolence, murder, folly, impiety, and all sorts of vice. Hosea 4 says, "Harlotry, wine and gluttony take away the heart" [cf. Hos. 4:1 f.]; that is, they delude and bring impiety and folly, so that evil follows. And St. Paul, in Galatians 5:19 ff., says, "Drunkards, adulterers, and so forth, will not inherit the kingdom of God."

These and many similar passages clearly show that God has commanded us to maintain discipline with regard to the body's eating and drinking and other desires. Diligence in this is not a work of superfluity, but necessary, just as prayer and almsgiving are commanded works that are necessary. We do not need to seek out or pile on special cases for almsgiving; God sends misery enough to heads of households; there true and sincere almsgiving can and should take place. We can and should give alms to poor orphans, sick persons, poor but upright maidens, pastors whose wives and children suffer hunger, poor students, and poor pious citizens whose work has suffered from divine punishment, and whose livelihood [Nahrung] is thus threatened. It is God's will that some be rich and some be poor, that those who are able help the poor, as Christ says, "I was hungry and you gave me food . . ." [Mt. 25:35]. This obliges us to help according to our ability, with loans, gifts, and advances, so that the servants also may maintain their necessities of life and livelihood, as distinctly indicated in 2 Corinthians 8. We should urge people to such necessary almsgiving, not to a spectacle of almsgiving in which they are judged for splendor, as in earlier times they were to perform many Masses.

Some also quote the sentence of St. Paul in 1 Corinthians 11:31, "But if we judged ourselves truly, we should not be judged." This they interpret to mean that if we lay on ourselves punishment and compensation, then we will not be punished by the Lord; therefore, through our compensation, they say, pain and punishment are remitted. Answer: St. Paul in that passage is not speaking about compensations or works which we are not obliged to do; he is speaking about genuine penance. Judgment in this passage is a hearty condemnation of sin that occurs in true repentance and sorrow, and in penance throughout life.

I said above that temporal plagues and punishment are alleviated through repentance and works we are obligated to do. This is useful to teach; as Isaiah 58:3–8 does, when he repudiates the precepts of men, and requires the works which God's command obliges us to perform. "Behold, in the day of your fast you seek your own pleasure, and oppress all your workers. Should such a fast be pleasing to me?" Further, about true fasting he says, "Share your bread with the hungry. . . . Then shall your light break forth like the dawn." Hence the prophets teach in many places, as in Micah 6:8, "Will the Lord be pleased with thousands of rams? . . . He has showed you, O man, what is good; and what does the Lord require of you but to do justice,[1] and to love kindness, and to walk humbly with your God?"

Here they bring up this excuse, saying that sin merits punishment, therefore, that sin will not be forgiven unless enough is done to satisfy the punishment. Therefore, if through penance the sin is forgiven, then the penance in itself is a compensation for the punishment.

Through this they want subtly to embellish satisfaction, but it is not true that sin is forgiven only if enough is done to compensate for the punishment through our works or sorrows. God promises alleviation and forgiveness of temporal plagues and punishment for those who ask everything in grace and turn themselves. The example of Nineveh indicates this. Further, alleviation of plagues and punishment is obtained by those who do penance [Busse], not for the sake of their compensations or sorrow, but out of grace, according to the divine promise, "Turn unto me and I will turn unto you" [Jer. 31:18].

For their doctrine they also draw on the example of David. David, they say, even though his guilt before God was forgiven, nevertheless was inflicted with punishment, so that rebellion against him was incited, and his entire country was set against him. After forgiveness of guilt (they

1. Melanchthon says, "to keep God's word."

say) Adam was nevertheless inflicted with natural death and other punishments, as compensation.

Concerning this example I have said that God often sends punishment and plagues; however, the power of the keys has nothing to do with these punishments. Also, it follows, not that such punishment is averted through the work of satisfaction or compensation; but, as said above, it is alleviated through true Christian penance throughout one's life. Also, I said above that the tribulations which are sent by God to the saints are not always punishment for previous sins but an exercise of their faith.

When the old scholars, or church historians, make mention of satisfaction, they are speaking about the external ceremony of public penance which was used at that time. Their opinion was not that the ceremony or the work should merit forgiveness of pain or guilt of purgatory or anything else; they knew that it was an external ceremony of the Church, established by men, to frighten others away from sins and depravity, and to ascertain whether the penitents really intended to improve themselves. St. Ambrose clearly says it is enough for public penance to occur once in a lifetime. These words show that this kind of satisfaction is not necessary for salvation, or to obtain forgiveness of sins. Besides, it would have to be repeated many times.

Out of this old ceremony of the Church developed indulgences, which are nothing more than remission of punishment and release from such *external* ceremonies and *public* punishments. After that, some hypocrites and deceivers, who were unlearned and wicked, clothed such remission of punishment and indulgence with magnificent words and made it into an annual affair, saying that it alleviates all pain and guilt, etc.; and that there should be a regular treasury for the extra good works, for the rich superfluous merits of all converted men, living and dead, and that they should be distributed for God at a price fixed by the Pope and bishops. Consequently, many errors, deceit, and fraud have accompanied remission of punishment, as the God-fearing and learned can easily observe. The real basis and truth about indulgence, or remission of punishment, in the beginning was nothing other than the dispensation and relaxation of the old canons of satisfaction, and as the years passed, the indulgences declined, along with their canon. The ceremonies, called satisfactions, were human precepts and were of no help for the alleviation of pain or guilt before God. The newly invented indulgences, or remission of punishment, help very little for the forgiveness of pain and guilt; they are an empty fraud and falsehood.

XXVIII

OF THE POWER OF THE CHURCH, OR OF THE KEYS

In Scripture the word "keys" refers to a household government. Accordingly, the gospel and the power of the Church refer to a gracious, motherly household government, where punishment is meted, not through a fist, but only through God's word in sermon and ban. So we call the power of the Church the keys, because the power of the Church and the keys are one and the same thing.

In contrast, we refer to worldly authority or government as "the sword" because it exercises physical punishment with the sword. And there is a vast difference between worldly dominion and this command, service, or office, which is called the *keys, or government, of the Church.* Worldly dominion is a command to keep external justice, discipline, and peace, to protect person and goods and to use physical punishment on the disobedient. To this belong subjects and sovereign, that is, power to rule, goods and property. And if it proceeds tolerably in its order, as David, Jehosophat, and a few more pious rulers managed, it is a great gift from God, of which we will speak at the end of this book. But for the time being we want only to draw the distinction between these two offices.

On the other hand, the *keys* are a command of God to preach the divine word, to administer the holy sacrament, to forgive sin in general and in particular, to ordain servants of the Church, to banish the disobedient if they persist in open depravity, and to absolve and release them if they turn and desire absolution.

These six items, as related, are the necessary and true offices of the Church, or service of the keys. They have to do with spiritual things, God's word, the sacraments, justification, the office of preaching, and punishment of sin through God's word and the ban, not through physical power. Therefore, the preachers or bishops in such service do not need physical power and a following, great principalities, sovereignty, etc.; it is a service which should proceed in God's command, name, and power, and be concerned with eternal things, justification and blessedness or eternal punishment. Nevertheless, the preacher, or servant of the Church, must have obedience and the power to command.

Here we might question whether the bishop, that is, a truly Christian preacher or pastor, has power to command, to make laws, and how far all this extends. Answer: First of all, it is highly necessary that we learn to extol the keys and the service of the Church, and to honor the Church with true, heartfelt thankfulness as the greatest gift that God has given, because by it he sent his only begotten Son, *Jesus Christ*, to the lost human race, and through its service has directed us to eternal life again, which he effects through this his word and command. I therefore say that as we truly owe God earnest obedience, we are obliged to be obedient to the divine word, as pronounced in the service of the minister, in the sermon, in the punishment of sins, and in the ban. Disobedience is a sin which deserves eternal wrath. So far we are obliged to obey the minister, and so far has he power and might to command, yet not only to command, for *God* works through him, giving blessedness to the obedient and a curse to the disobedient.

However, all this is still not a dominion which has power to command anything beyond God's word or to make and require new laws as divine services. The service of the Church is not like worldly tyranny or kingly might, for the might of tyrants is unrestrained, and has no definite rule.

The bishops, or the servants of the Church, have a strict order, which is quite definite, in which they are obliged to remain; and, if they assert another, or contrary, doctrine which is beyond their office, we are obliged to abandon, to curse, and to treat them as exiled.

Is it also not kingly power, for although kings have some fixed laws, they may, however, as masters, have sovereignty, a following, and property, and make useful laws for physical peace and protection of goods.

It is usual in the world, always has been, and probably always will be, for the worldly wise [*Weltweisen*] who have no understanding of the gospel and no fear of God to make the office of the Church into a kingly domain like that of worldly powers. They see that the Church is not without divine law, but even so they want to rule, to have power to make new laws to exalt the authority of their station. And they think that if the Church has no kingly power, it is a miserable, weak government which has no authority, no force, and no obedience, and is merely an array of confusion. So it appears in the eyes of the world and to reason. If we take away from the Church the kingly might to command and to compel, the Church seems to be very weak and little. The true Church has always had just such a form, from the time of Shem, Abraham, Isaac, and Jeremiah to the time of *Christ* and the apostles. However, it is definitely not weak and little, for God is in the Church, powerfully and mightily working in her and sustaining her against the gates and power of hell.

Therefore, we must put worldly thoughts out of mind, and look on the rule of the Church as *God* ordained it, and as he has always maintained and guided his true Church beyond worldly wisdom. And this school is not the place to dispute what the wise rulers, Solon, Augustus, or the philosophers, like Plato or Aristotle, disputed *in politicis*, which has its place in worldly government and is wisdom.

The true Christian Church is a marvelous government, which proceeds from and must be maintained through God's word, the power and might of the living Son of God, and the Holy Spirit. This is clearly expressed by *St. Paul* in Ephesians 1 and 1 Corinthians 12.

The following passages speak of this: Luke 10:16: "He who hears you hears me, and he who rejects you rejects me, and he who rejects me rejects him (the eternal Father) who sent me." Hebrews 13:17: "Obey those who rule over you. . . ."

These passages and similar ones are earnest commandments, which teach us that we should be obedient to pastors, in their office, if they carry out God's word and exercise punishment accordingly. It is God's earnest will that with all humility and obedience, we honor these in their office, and help to maintain them. However, these passages do not give the pastors or the bishops a power to produce any new kingdom outside the gospel.

Having said what the government of the Church is, and that it is not tyrannical or kingly power, and having said that we are obliged to give obedience to the high and worthy office in which the divine word is preached, we will now briefly set forth several rules which will serve to explain these articles.

The first rule: If the pastors, bishops, or servants of the Church teach something that is contrary to the word of God, then all listeners are obliged to reject such. And if pastors or bishops continue in their error, the Church should abandon the same erroneous preachers or bishops. This rule is commanded in God's word. Acts 5:29: "We must obey God rather than men." Galatians 1:8: "But even if we, or an angel from heaven, should preach to you a gospel contrary to that which we have preached to you, let him be accursed." Now if untrue teachers are accursed, obviously we should not follow nor be obedient to them. A "ban" is not a trifling curse; it is a real anger of God in which he permits punishment to come upon the cursed. When Saul was cursed, his fortune came to an end. About this we will speak further later.

The eternal God says of *Christ*, "This is my beloved Son, listen to him" [Mt. 17:6]. This command leaves no room for any other; therefore, we should not be obedient to untrue teachers or bishops contrary to this commandment.

Also Christ says, "Beware of false prophets . . ." [Mt. 7:15]. These and similar passages we should note to comfort the conscience against the poisonous slanders of those who reproach us, saying we are disobedient, and cause schisms and dissensions. On the contrary, we should point out that all men are obliged by divine command to abandon untrue teachers and bishops as accursed. Of this, more later.

The second rule: The bishops or shepherds of souls have no power to command new divine services, as the Pope has done in forbidding priests to marry, and in making a distinction in foods, and the like.

In these and similar items are three errors which it is necessary to rebuke. The first, that such works are asserted as meriting grace. This is a great error contrary to the doctrine of faith. The second error is that some of the learned see that the first error is too gross, and wishing to speak more subtly of it, say, "Although these works do not merit grace, they are nevertheless divine services which God deems as a very special honor." This is also an error, for Christ clearly says, Matthew 15:9, "In vain do they honor me with the precepts of men." The third error is that they make of them necessary works and teach that it is a sin if one even without scandal breaks such commandments. However, the gospel forbids keeping such works as necessary, as we hereafter will discuss further in the chapter about the precepts of men.[1]

The third rule: What power do the shepherds of souls or true bishops have? Answer: A Christian shepherd of souls has power to determine the time for good order and *lectiones* [lections], as a schoolmaster must maintain an order so that the youth may know when they should assemble and what is useful at various times to read. The difference between human nature and the beasts is that the human reason understands order, and in all works should maintain suitable order and measure, but the beast knows nothing about order.

1. See below, Article XXXIV.

And, it is reasonable that the most beautiful order should be in the Church, where we are engaged in the important, earnest work of explaining to the people by divine command God's word concerning eternal life; where God is invoked, and so forth. This is why *St. Paul* commanded everything in the assembly to be done in an orderly and polite fashion. In accordance with this opinion certain holidays are established. On Sundays we come together for preaching, divine invocation, and the sacraments. This is also the reason for various holidays such as *Natalis Christi, Circumcisio, Annunciatio, Pascha, Ascensio,* and *Pentecoste.* Because we cannot relate the entire history of *Christ* nor all the parts of the Christian doctrine in one day, we must divide it into several festivals, as one might divide school lectures, and such festivals are pleasing in that they mark historical time and aid the memory.

Christ suffered and died and should have risen about the time we observe Easter. For this reason God ordained in the Old Testament the ceremony with which the paschal lamb was to be kept. The Church has followed, preaching the Passion and Resurrection also about the same time, and calling the day pascha, for the sake of the commemoration. For the purpose of teaching and remembering the exodus out of Egypt pascha has been maintained up to this 1,548th year, 3,058 years. Such a praiseworthy custom is to be kept to exhort the people concerning the true Pascha of the sufferings and Resurrection of Christ. To despise it, or to put it aside, as many of today's saints have done, is a gross barbarity.

There are, however, external orders which we are not to regard as required, nor to observe as if we merit grace though keeping them, or as if God deems external work a special honor to him; or as if it is necessarily a sin to work on a holiday, even without scandal and without impediment of the public sermon and assembly. From this it is easy to understand how extensive is the power of the shepherds of souls to establish order.

On the other hand, this is quoted, "Who hears you, hears me!" [Lk. 10:16]! Also, "They sit on the seat of Moses; what they tell you to observe, you should observe" [Mt. 23:2–3]! Out of these passages they would conclude that they have power to make laws and that such laws must be kept, to which an answer is given above. These sentences talk about the mandate of the office to carry forward God's word. This does not give them a power beyond God's word, to produce new laws and other teachings or regimentations. For this reason the sentence says, "They sit on the seat of Moses"; for if they teach alien things, outside the divine law, they sit not on the seat of Moses, but make for themselves individual thrones of power and dominion without God's command.

The fourth rule: True shepherds of souls or bishops have jurisdictions in which we are obliged by divine command to give obedience, to summon open sinners, and if they do not improve after admonition, to expel and exclude them from the Christian gathering and ceremonies, by means of the word, without physical violence, as *St. Paul* does in expelling the immoral Corinthian. In this judgment we are obliged by God's command to be obedient to the shepherd, for *Christ* has thus commanded this judgment in Matthew 18. And it is highly necessary that this be earnestly done in the churches. And such a ban is not to be dismissed as an ineffective human word, for because it is commanded by God, he will cause real punishment to fall on the cursed; as many examples indicate.

When Ambrose cursed Stilicho's secretary, the secretary was possessed by the devil, and was not sound again until Ambrose prayed for him; then he became better. And after the secretary said to him that from then on he would fear and obey God, Ambrose absolved him again.

For this reason we should not think that intercession and the curse of the Church are trifling, for these sentences remain true: Genesis 12:3, "I will bless those who bless you, and him who curses you I will curse." God keeps his word, whether we esteem it or not. So it finally happens that cruel punishments follow upon a just curse, as Psalm 109:18 says: "He clothed himself with cursing as his coat, may it soak into his body like water, like oil into his bones!" Therefore, one must greatly esteem and earnestly fear the true ban and curse of the Church.

I have said, however, that this punishment happens through the word and the sermon, not through physical coercion with fist and sword. Only the worldly power should punish with fist and sword. It is very necessary to note this difference, so that we do not make the Church into a worldly kingdom, as did Thomas Münzer, and later, in 1534, the Anabaptists at Münster. In their opinion preachers should wield the sword, and force acceptance or kill those who will not accept their teaching. That such is erroneous and that the preacher is forbidden to do this, the following passage in Matthew 20:25-28 proves: "You know that the rulers of the Gentiles lord it over them, and their great men exercise authority over them. It shall not be so among you; but whoever would be great among you must be your servant, and whoever would be first among you must be your slave, even as the Son of man came not to be served but to serve, and to give his life as a ransom for many."

These words are a clear command that the office of the apostle was not to prepare a new kingdom and wield the sword, but only to preach the gospel and suffer for its sake, as Christ himself did. John 18:36: "My kingdom is not of this world." Second Corinthians 10:4: "The weapons of our welfare are not worldly." Second Corinthians 4:5: "We do not domineer over your faith, but are servants for your joy" [cf. 1:24]. Second Corinthians 3: "The gospel is an office of the Spirit, through which souls obtain eternal life" [cf. v. 6].

John preaches, and God works through the sermon. This office does not hinder Trajan in his external honorable rule; it allows Trajan to maintain justice and worldly punishment and to conduct war. All such are physical things and do not belong to the office of the apostle.

According to this information it is entirely clear and certain that the papal laws are wrong which say that Christ not only entrusted the office of preaching to the Pope, but also gave him sovereignty and dominion over all worldly kingdoms, to establish and depose kings, and that, for this purpose, the Popes must have great countries and people so that they may have a following to compel opponents with the sword. Under this pretense they have drawn to themselves land and people, and have set up a heathenish kingdom and laws and idolatries for the maintenance of such a kingdom.

All this was depicted in the suffering of Christ the Lord when he was crowned with thorns and dressed in purple. In such a manner the Popes and bishops have long driven the true Church, suppressed the gospel and true service of God through their worldly kingdoms, and domineered in their singularly idolatrous anti-Christian kingdom. I mentioned this to remind God-fearing men to shun the anti-Christian government of the Pope and the bishops, and not to share in their tyranny.

The fifth rule: It is true that the office of the apostle is not to wield the sword; also it is true that it is an impediment if an apostle or a pastor wants to wield the sword or worldly government and be a pastor at the same time; therefore, such is forbidden in the old councils.

Along with this we should know that [John] Wycliffe's error nevertheless should be repudiated, for he said that pastors are not to have property.[2] This error comes from the monks' imagining that there is great

---

2. John Wycliffe (1328–1384), in On the Pastoral Office (1378), maintained that the pastor's duty was to purge the Church of immorality and feed the people on the spiritual word. He urged frugality as a proper way of life for pastors, and declared that they should distribute all other possessions to the poor. In On Divine Lordship

holiness in not having property. On the contrary, above we showed that ownership is a divine order, established in the seventh commandment, and every saint may use this order just as he does food and drink, which also are divine orders.

Also let it be further known here that churches and lords are obliged to give the pastors and shepherds of souls their maintenance, as Christ commanded, "To the worker belongs his wage" [cf. Lk. 10:7; 1 Tim. 5:18]. What then a pastor saves, or otherwise honorably inherits, or has for himself, his wife, and child, that is his own. And in this case no distinction is to be made between the pastors and other Christian heads of families.

Yet in this evil world pious pastors will probably remain poor, as they always have been. In contrast to them are the godless priests, with their great possessions, who have imagined themselves in the service of God, as it seems useful for the enhancement of their possessions, pomp and power.

Of the Vocation of Pastors and Shepherds of Souls

Because bishops who have title and name are persecutors of the gospel, they do not wish to sanction our pastors. Therefore, some debate whether our shepherds of souls can be in the office when they have not been sanctioned or consecrated by bishops. A basic Christian answer to this is necessary.

Although the name and title of the bishops and the custom with regard to the consecration be kept, it is nevertheless basically invalid to create in the unintelligent a hallucination. The *persecutors* of the gospel are *not bishops,* and should be regarded as exiled [cf. Galatians 1:6–24]. The ceremony of the consecration, as customarily practiced by bishops, is wrong and full of error, in the same way as Masses for the dead and the consecration and transubstantiation of the bread.

But there is a true way of maintaining the vocation and confirmation, or consecration, of preachers. St. Paul ordered Titus to arrange for and to ordain priests here and there in the cities. From this it is clear that true shepherds of souls are commanded, when preachers and shepherds of souls are needed, to obtain in the churches qualified persons and to ordain

---

(1375) and *On Civil Lordship* (1376) Wycliffe argued that men possess goods and offices only as stewards of God, to whom everything belongs. Bad stewardship then became justification for depriving a person of his property or office. Cf. *Advocates of Reform,* Matthew Spinka, ed. (Philadelphia, 1953).

and confirm them with laying on of hands and prayer. Consecration is this, and nothing more than, a confirmation of the one chosen after a judicial examination of his doctrine. It is done by several persons of the Church laying their hands on his head, entrusting him with the office according to divine order, and praying that God may give him the Holy Spirit, rule him, and that God through this preaching and administration of the sacraments will be strong, as it stands written, "The gospel is the power of God to salvation to all those who believe" [Rom. 1:16].

And the command of St. Paul that Titus should arrange for priests applies not only to those with the title "bishop," but to *all* Christian shepherds of souls.

Hieronymous [St. Jerome] remembers that according to divine right there is no difference between bishops and other priests, and his words are given in *decret. distinctione XCIII.*[3] Therefore, if a Christian shepherd is requested to send a virtuous priest from another church, there is no doubt that he has power to confirm him, and in many cases is obliged to do so.

The passage of *St. Paul* in the Letter to Titus absolutely does not apply to the persecutors of the gospel, called bishops or canons, who should be regarded as exiled. Confirmation is not to be sought from them.

Further, it should be known that the Church in the time of the apostles and for hundreds of years maintained the custom of selecting bishops from a gathering of leaders from all ranks, priests and laymen, known for their Christian faith and good habits [*Sitten*]. Two or three bishops from the nearest cities sufficed to ascertain the doctrine of those chosen, and then to confirm them. The gathered company had to choose and give consent, and the bishops had to inquire about doctrine and hold the ceremony of confirmation with the laying on of hands.

Cyprian often describes this custom, especially in the fourth epistle to Cornelius, in which it is clear that the people above all have power to choose qualified priests, and to reject the unqualified. Augustine announced the same in his first epistle, and there are many such clear passages in the old councils.[4] History also is revealing. Ambrose in Milan and Athanasius in Egypt were chosen by a Christian gathering of all ranks.

---

3. Cf. *Nicene and Post-Nicene Fathers*, H. Wace and P. Schaff, eds. (Oxford and New York, 1893), VI, *Principal Works of St. Jerome, Letters* 52, 146.

4. Cf. *Ante-Nicene Fathers*, A. Roberts and J. Donaldson, eds. (Grand Rapids, Mich., 1957), V, *Epistles of Cyprian*, 40, 41, 42, 44, 51, 61, 67. Also *Works of Aurelius Augustine*, III, *Donatist Controversy* Bk. 3, chaps. 16, 17, 18.

In the decrees and in history it is easy to see how the Pope gradually changed the original old customs and established the capital as the only place of selection, reserving confirmation for himself. This was not customary in the ancient Church, as clearly proved by the writing of the bishops in the Orient to Pope Damasus, who sought to have them obtain confirmation at Rome.[5] They answered in all sincerity that they did not wish to burden their churches with new and unreasonable encumbrances, that they wished instead to maintain themselves as in the time of the apostles, and in accordance with the decisions of the Council of Nicaea, that at any time two or three bishops from the nearest cities would suffice for the selection of a bishop. From this it is clear that it is not necessary to seek confirmation from the Pope. This epistle is found in Theodoret.[6]

Clearly the Church has power to choose qualified persons for the care of souls, and to entrust to them the office of bishop.

Such selection by the Church is grounded in the following sources. In Matthew 18:17 Christ says, "Tell it to the church." In this text he regulates judgment in the Church, giving the highest power *not to any one* rank alone, but to Christians of *all* ranks. These should judge the teachings. From this it clearly follows that the highest authority of establishing and of deposing stays with the Church.

This text also states, "Where two or three are gathered in my name, there am I in the midst of them. What they bind on earth shall be bound in heaven, what they loose on earth, shall also in heaven be loosed" [Mt. 18:18 ff.].

Here Christ speaks obviously about forgiveness of sins, and puts this responsibility on the congregation. This means that the Church has power

5. Pope Damasus was Bishop of Rome, 366–384. For this controversy over papal authority see *Patrologiae Cursus Completus. Series Latina*, J. P. Migne, ed. (Paris, 1878–90), XIII, 581, 586. The struggle revolved around Damasus and Ursinus, who were elected bishops by opposing factions in the Church, and eventually it led to bloodshed. Ursinus, though opposed by Emperor Valerian, brought about a schism, and the question of secular and ecclesiastical jurisdiction was left unsettled. Whether bishops and priests were subject to the Roman See was not clarified.

6. Theodoret (*ca.* 393–458), Bishop of Cyrrhus in Syria, a stormy opponent of paganism and heresy in the fifth century, became involved in the Christological controversy between Nestorius and Cyril of Alexandria. His writings against Cyril were condemned by the Council of Constantinople in 553. Apparently he abandoned his Nestorian views in the latter part of his life. For the controversy to which Melanchthon refers, see *Nicene and Post-Nicene Fathers*, III, *Theodoret, Ecclesiatical History*, chap. 8; *ibid., Letters*, 113–133, 146, 152, 157, 181.

to commit such an office to certain persons and also that the Church cannot be without such an office to announce forgiveness.

First Peter 2:9: "You are a royal priesthood." These words pertain to the *entire* Church in that all the saints are consecrated by God to this office if they are called to it by the gathered company.

Ephesians 4 contains the foremost passage about the office; God built the Church, and it is led by *Christ* in heaven, who bestows gifts on it, namely servants, prophets, apostles, preachers, shepherds, and teachers.

With these words *St. Paul* declares that the Church must have a ministry and an office, as he also says that a certain doctrine should be maintained and that everyone is not to invent out of his own imagination a special religion, as the heathen did when they daily made new gods. God wants an office and ministry to be in the Church, and he maintains such. Because a ministry is necessary and must be maintained, it follows that the Church has the power and is obliged to choose qualified persons as often as necessary, in this case, if the titled bishops and their supporters are persecutors, and will not give to the Church qualified shepherds.

For these reasons which are well grounded and corroborated, the Church shall and must choose and confirm qualified shepherds if the titled bishops and their supporters are persecutors. And from this it is clear that the ordination, if it occurs through our churches and shepherds, is right and Christian.

XXIX

OF THE CHURCH

Under the previous heading something was said about the keys, that is, about the offices, through which the Church and God's people are ruled spiritually. To know the offices, namely the divine office of preaching, administration of sacraments, and punishment through the ban, is to understand what the Church is; it is the gathered company [*Versammlung*] in which such divine offices are rightly exercised.

Because hypocrites who persecute the word of God often decorate themselves with the word "church," I wish to give a short, clear Christian statement concerning it.

First, it is known and obvious that in divine Scripture *the church* is often used to indicate only the saints, that is, those who please God, who commonly are called "living members of the head and Savior, Christ," who also have external signs to distinguish them from other people, such as the true gospel, the right use of the sacraments, confession of true doctrine, and invocation of God with trust in *Christ*. Along with these are testimonies that God has accepted them, that he rules and manifests his power through them, as he has always given testimony of himself to his people with great deeds of wonder, as in the case of Moses, Samuel, Elijah, Elisha, Daniel, Peter, Paul and others.

Thus Ephesians 1:22 f. speaks about the Church, that is, about the gathered company of those who please God, exclusive of the godless, "And he has made him the head over all things for the church, which is his body, the fulness of him who fills all in all." According to Ephesians 5:27, "The church has no spot or wrinkle. . . ." And 1 Timothy 3:15 says, "The church of the living God, the pillar and bulwark of the truth. . . ." Surely such a promise that the truth is and shall remain in the Church pertains only to those who please God and *not* to the godless.

Thus speaks the Apostles' Creed about the Church, "I believe in the holy, universal church, the communion [*Versammlung*] of saints." And this article is placed in the Creed with good reason, for it reminds us, as we behold the world, in which the greater part is godless, and in which the godless have the greatest rank and power, that we should not despair nor think that God has entirely forgotten the human race and is finished with his Church, or that no one need call on God or hope in his grace which is promised to the Church.

This article in the Creed gives us comfort against this temptation by attesting that God will always have a people, and in all times will keep what he has promised to the Church. Whoever prays and seeks forgiveness of sins in faith in *Christ* and follows the gospel is a member of this people, in every time and everywhere. There stands the word *catholica*, "universal Church," as a reminder that God's people are bound only to the gospel which the universal Church confesses, not to the precepts of men, to Rome or Antioch.

Above all *the church* means "God's people," those who confess the holy gospel and follow it, who rightly use the sacraments, those born again through the Holy Spirit. John 1:13 says, "Those born of God . . ."

Because the opponents cry out that we are speaking about an invisible church, and seeking a subterfuge, I want to say something about the visible church.

The *visible* church is a gathered company of men who confess and obey the gospel, who have been reborn through the Holy Spirit. Hypocrites mingle in such a gathered company, and are included in the confession of true doctrine with the saints if they keep and confess true doctrine.

Therefore, the visible church was in the time of Zechariah, Mary, Simeon, Hannah, Joseph, Elizabeth, the shepherds and whoever was in like confession with them. Nevertheless, with them was mixed a great host of godless priests and others who were also in the office of preaching and the government.

The Church was in the time of Eli, Elijah, and Elisha; nevertheless, a great number of unholy people were mingled with them.

There are, however, two kinds of unholy people. Some confess true doctrine, although they do not fear God, and continue in sins against their conscience. At Corinth, the disciples of St. Paul, although they were of *one* confession, were not all holy, and all did not remain in the new birth.

Such are called dead members of the Church; they are admitted to the offices of the church and to the use of the sacraments if they do not continue in open disgrace and evil, for which they are to be punished through the excommunication and ban. For all that, so long as they remain in office, the office and divine word are still valid, and the saints may use their service, preaching, and sacraments. This is to be remembered, so that we may reject the error of the Donatists, who caused great dissension and murder by the false pretense and assertion that true preaching and sacrament are void if the servants who preach or administer the sacraments are not holy. The Donatists asserted that each individual must separate himself and shun such shepherds.

But that this opinion of the Donatists is wrong is entirely clear from the following passages. In Matthew 13 *Christ* compares the Church to a fishing net in which there are good and bad fish. He also says that there will be weeds in the Church until the resurrection of the dead. Before the end of the world the Church will be as in the time of Noah.

These passages clearly indicate that many unholy people are and will be in the Church until the resurrection of the dead. If our faith depended on the merit of persons, we would be very uncertain, for *Christ* says, "There will be holy and unholy servants in the church" [*cf.* Mt. 13:24–30, 36–40]. As human eyes do not see into another's heart, we cannot distinguish hypocrites from saints, and we would always doubt whether we had obtained what is promised by the gospel and the sacraments if the gospel and sacraments were void and ineffective in the service of hypocrites.

We should regard God's eternal unchangeable promise as fixed and effective, whether it is spoken through St. Paul or Demas.[1] Therefore, *Christ* directs us from the sacraments to himself, "*Who hears you, hears me!*" This is as if he had said, "It is not *your* word, and it does not depend on *your* merit; it is an eternal divine command, by which I wish to be effective." Therefore, it is necessary, as often said, for these servants of God's word not to preach their own invented lies.

Augustine, who wrote rightly and usefully against the Donatists, also tells us that the laudable Emperor Constantine had the dispute examined twice and finally himself heard it and issued a Christian prohibition against the error. Such is found in Epistle 166,[2] in which Augustine also argues that our faith would be entirely uncertain if God's word were

---

1. For Biblical references to Demas, companion of Paul and Luke, see Col. 4:14; Philem. 24; 2 Tim. 4:10.

2. *Works of Aurelius Augustine*, Marcus Dods, ed. (Edinburgh, 1875), *Letters*, II, 166.

void and ineffective in the service of hypocrites. *This* sentence of Christ is quoted, "The Scribes and Pharisees sit on the throne of Moses" [Mt. 23:2], in which Christ reminds us that if hypocrites are in the service, nevertheless the service is not void if they preach the commanded word and do not set up their own throne and their own doctrine. This is enough to comfort the conscience against the Donatist error.

Human weakness being what it is, defects in customs can hardly be prevented. The shepherds are fathers of families; they are poor and hard pressed, and sometimes become impatient, and they are ungraciously used by their enemies among the people. Some others are light-minded and have more desire for social gatherings than is good.

If such persons teach rightly and truly, we should have much patience with them, for true teachers carry a great burden. This is described in the story of Noah, when the rogue Ham brought disgrace upon his father, who was merely lying there [*cf.* Gen. 9:20–27].

The Lord Christ washed the feet of the disciples, and commanded us to do likewise, meaning that we must be loyal and friendly with one another. We wash the feet of one another, as we endure the one who breaks the moral custom, as we soothe, expiate, and with diligence compensate as much as possible. Seldom are two who share an office equal in ability, and for this reason one must be patient with the other, offering his hand if peace is to prevail and something be accomplished.

Jonathan supported his father Saul, and improved him as much as possible. Examples of this are often described in worldly government. Themistocles manifested toward Aristides much unfriendliness; nevertheless, when the necessity arose and they had to be together in government, Aristides manifested no spite, but diligently helped with the work and knew how to give way to Themistocles.

God particularly requires that we treat his gospel with consideration, and therefore honor the servants who preach rightly, as we would honor our father and mother. For this reason it is wrong, on account of a little defect in custom, to cause controversy in the Church.

However, if the shepherds of souls have obvious blemishes, such as lack of discipline and adultery, if they practice wanton violence and lodge dishonorable people, then the Christian authority is obliged to punish them as it does other subjects, for God commanded the authority to use physical punishment. The Church, that is, the foremost members, should admonish such a vexatious person in an orderly manner, and if improvement does not follow, should punish him with excommunication. That should be done. When it is not done, however, God's word and sacraments nevertheless remain valid, even when administered by such servants.

Up to now I have spoken about the visible church in which the doctrine of the gospel is pure and right use of the sacraments is kept without open idolatry. Although many hyprocrites or ungodly people are now in this visible company and make this same confession, where there is true doctrine, some saints and heirs of eternal life who truly acknowledge and invoke God must also be present. In the time of Abraham, or the apostles, although their listeners were not all holy, there were nevertheless some who confessed true doctrine, always some children of God.

This should be noted very carefully, for it is a great comfort to know where to seek God's people and where there are always some children of God. The Apostles' Creed clearly shows that this is so, "I believe in one [eine] holy universal [gemeine] Church, the communion of saints." This article indicates that there are and always will be some saints and heirs of eternal life.

And these are not to be sought under the titles of pope or bishop, but where the gospel is truly acknowledged and taught, be it in churches or schools, city or village. Persecutors of the gospel are not the Church; they are called heathen, Jews, Turks, tyrants, pope, or bishops. This word of Christ must endure, "My sheep hear my voice" [Jn. 10:16]! Therefore, the Church, or the true people of God, is bound to the gospel. Where the gospel is truly acknowledged, there are some who are holy.

As also this most beautiful passage in Isaiah 59:21 says, "This is my covenant with them, says the Lord: my spirit which is upon you, and my words which I have put in your mouth, shall not depart out of your mouth, or out of the mouth of your children, or out of the mouth of your children's children, says the Lord, from this time forth and for evermore." This comforting passage teaches not only that there will always be a true Church and people of God, but also shows where and how it will be, namely where the correct, true doctrine of the gospel rings out.

Close by the visible church are other people who are godless, who teach falsely, persecute the true people of the gospel, or are supporters of untrue doctrine. As in the time of Jeremiah or of Judas Maccabaeus, or of Christ, the high priests, Levites, and the principal and greatest part of the Jewish people were against divine doctrine and persecuted the prophets, Christ and the apostles.

This group, even though it might control the government and keep some ceremonies, is nevertheless not the true Church and is not a part of the visible church. It is to be regarded as a foe and banned, and the people are obliged to separate themselves from it and to shun their untrue doctrine and idolatry.

Therefore, it is necessary to make a distinction between the evil people, who nevertheless remain in the true confession, and the other Caiaphas-swarms who persecute true doctrine. We should shun and abandon this Caiaphas-swarm. When the bishops in Asia followed the poison and error of Arius, the people were obliged to separate themselves from them.

And now, if Pope, bishops, and other high prelates persecute the true Christian doctrine and continue to murder pious Christians, not otherwise than as Caiaphas, Nero, Maxentius, and others did, we should assuredly forsake them as exiled and no longer consider them as members of the Church; and no one should participate in the errors which they retain in the Mass, in the worship of the saints, and in various idolatries when using the sacraments. But even baptism is to be received from them in the places where they retain their office and power. However, as in the time of Caiaphas, when circumcision by his godless group persisted [and bore] the divine promise which served for the children's salvation, it [baptism] is to be received not as the servant's but as God's work.

In Israel the priests and Levites were often persecutors; nevertheless, the prophets and their hearers who were the true Church received circumcision by the priests and brought their offering to the temple. St. Paul also says that Antichrist is to rule in the Church, that is, the Pope and bishops.

However, clear commands show that the people are obliged to abandon the accursed. Galatians 1:8: "If anyone is preaching to you a gospel contrary to that which you received, let him be accursed." Matthew 7:15: "Beware of false prophets!" First Corinthians 10:14: "Shun idolatry." Matthew 10:33: "Whoever denies me before men, I also will deny him before my Father who is in heaven."

These are enough to remind us that we should abandon the persecutors of Christian truth and doctrine and not help them to strengthen their idolatry and tyranny.

If the Pope, bishops, and their supporters insist that *they* are the Church and the rulers of God's people, and that we are obliged to support them and to be obedient; if they boast that they cannot err, these false, invented speeches can easily be overturned with the information which I have given. It is impossible that the people of God are those who openly condemn so many articles of Christian doctrine and unjustly put people to death to validate their idolatry. Because this is so obvious, it follows that one is not to strengthen them but to abandon them. If they say, however, that they cannot err, then let God's word and the early Church be the standard; then each and every God-fearing man can easily discover that they do err.

If they also assert that the Church is bound to the titled bishops, and that all of them could not err, this also is untrue, for the Church is bound to *God's word*, and *not* to the Pope or bishops; and God has always maintained a spark in some. There have always been some who have kept the foundation, as *St. Paul* says [*cf.* 1 Cor. 3:10 f.], that is, the articles of faith, and who have not approved but rebuked open idolatry. And although such persons have not been in the government as bishops or prelates, somewhere there have been such preachers or schoolmasters or fathers of families.

Of the Marks of the Church

The really true Church, the people of God, which we have called a visible church, has the external marks of a pure doctrine of the gospel and right use of the sacraments. Along with this, some persons also give evidences of the Holy Spirit, with virtues and special works of wonder through which the name of *Christ* is glorified. Although some of the same things happen among the heathen, they are not intended to glorify the name of the Savior, whom God sent to us, *Jesus Christ.*

Some create still more signs, such as obedience toward the bishops and uniformity in the precepts of men. I have often said to what extent we are obliged to obey shepherds of souls, and I will later make a report about the precepts of men, from which it will be easy to understand that uniformity in the ceremonies, if established without divine command, is not necessary, as Augustine wrote to Irenaeus.

And this is clear from many sentences in St. Paul, Romans 14:17, "The kingdom of God does not mean food and drink but righteousness and peace and joy in the Holy Spirit; he who thus serves Christ is acceptable to God and approved by men." About this more under the heading about the precepts of men.

Of the Gift of Interpretation in the Church

I have often said that it is very harmful to portray the Church of God as a worldly kingdom. In worldly rule the highest authority has the power to interpret laws, to soften and to sharpen. And the subjects are obliged to receive the interpretations, for it is the opinion of true authority to which God gave the power to decide and to command. However, in the Church the interpretation of the Scripture is not a power; and it does not follow that since bishops have interpreted something, their authority impels us to keep it. Interpretation is *a gift of the Holy Spirit,* not limited to bishops or to those of any other special rank. And this rule of *St. Paul* holds true, "The natural man does not understand what the Spirit of God effects." There is true understanding when the *Holy Spirit* has shed his light in the heart. John 6:45: "You shall all be taught by God."

As it is obvious that many bishops are godless, we cannot say positively that their positions prevent them from erring. It is possible for the saints to fall into error; the church at Galatia departed from the doctrine of *St. Paul.*

There is a great difference between these two: interpretation by power and interpretation by gift. A king has *power* to interpret his law, but St. Stephen had the *gift* to interpret the prophets. These things should be distinguished, and the papal and episcopal power should not be embellished with pretexts [*Farblein*].

XXX

OF THE KINGDOM OF CHRIST

The gospel clearly indicates that the kingdom of Christ is not an external but a spiritual kingdom; Christ the Lord has gone to heaven and sits at the right hand of God and pleads for us. The power of his kingdom is that he reconciles all his faithful believers to the Father and unfailingly gives them the *Holy Spirit*, comfort, and strength. Here in the Church on earth all who call upon him are sanctified and enlightened more and more in the knowledge of God; he protects them, and on the Day of the Last Judgment will raise them from the dead to eternal life and glory, as described in this brief but very consoling sentence, "No one will snatch my sheep out of my hand" [Jn. 10:28].

The apostolic office of preaching was established to obtain this unutterable treasure of *Christ*, as St. Paul calls it in Ephesians 3. Through it God calls all men to the knowledge of *God* and *Christ*, and through the word of the gospel God wishes to give his Holy Spirit. In the meantime, before the Last Day of Judgment, Christianity and the Church must suffer persecution, and the evil people will remain mingled among the pious in the Church.

So conclude the Scriptures about the *kingdom of Christ;* and so speaks the gospel of it. Therefore, the Anabaptists teach an odious, frightful error in imagining that before the Last Day of Judgment Christianity and the Church will be a worldly, magnificent kingdom on earth in which only the saints will rule and wield the sword, blotting out all the godless and capturing all kingdoms.

Concerning this, let us refer to several passages of Scripture about *the spiritual kingdom of Christ*, not only to refute such teaching of the Anabaptists and other enthusiasts, but also to have such sentences for consolation and to arouse us to various exercises of faith, prayer, and patience in temptation. A worldly kingdom of Christ is a Judaic dream and an odious error; it comes from the devil and does great injury. Those who do not know or believe that the kingdom of Christ is spiritual lose all the comfort of the Scripture and the gospel; they cease to pray, lose faith, and succumb to external forces; they do not understand that the great treasure and power of the kingdom of Christ is forgiveness of sins, and that God reconciles us and is gracious; they cannot comfort themselves in death and resurrection, expecting only physical goods and a physical kingdom on earth; they cease entirely to believe and become carnal.

Here is evidence from Scripture that the kingdom of Christ is spiritual: John 17:2 f.: "Thou hast given him power over all flesh, to give eternal life to *all* whom thou hast given him. And this is eternal life, *that they know thee the only true God*, and *Jesus Christ* whom thou hast sent."

There the Lord *Christ* clearly indicates that his kingdom and glory is eternal life. He goes further, indicating that eternal life is not a dominion over the world, but a right knowledge of the true God and our Lord Jesus Christ.

Romans 8:26: "Who is at the right hand of God and who indeed intercedes for us." Isaiah 11:10: "In that day the root of Jesse shall stand [as an ensign to the peoples]; *him* shall the nations seek."

These passages pertain to the priesthood and kingdom of *Christ*, and indicate that *both* are to be *spiritual*. Christ did not produce a worldly government; he returned to heaven; there he is our high priest and king, lord in heaven and on earth, interceding for us, hearing the prayers of Christians on earth, sanctifying, protecting, and strengthening through his Holy Spirit all who call on him. As *St. Paul* says, "*Those* whom the Spirit of God moves are the children of God" [*cf.* Rom. 8:16]. Likewise in Jeremiah 31:33, "I will put my law in your heart." This action of the reign of Christ will not be understood if the Judaic dream of a physical kingdom, money, and lust is forced on the people.

Romans 8:17 ff.: "We are heirs of God and fellow heirs with Christ, provided we suffer with him in order that we may also be glorified with him. . . . For in this hope we were saved. . . . For those whom he foreknew he also predestined to be conformed to the image of his Son. . . . For thy sake we are being killed all the day long; we are regarded as sheep to be slaughtered."

These passages indicate that the dominion of the reign of Christ will not be in *this* life, that instead the Church will suffer tribulation and persecution.

Matthew 16:24: "If any man would come after me, let him deny himself and take up his cross and follow me." John 16:33: "In the world you have tribulation; but be of good cheer, I have overcome the world." And 2 Timothy 3:12: "Indeed, all who desire to live a godly life in Christ Jesus will be persecuted." Clearly the Church here on earth must suffer persecution until the end of the world.

Colossians 3:3 f.: "Your life is hid with Christ in God. When Christ who is our life appears, then you also will appear with him in glory." First John 3:12: "Beloved, we are God's children now; it does not yet appear what we shall be, but we know that when he appears we shall be like him, for we shall see him as he is."

This passage also indicates that the glory of the kingdom of God will not be a worldly kingdom, but spiritual, in which we will arise from the dead, and live with *Christ* in eternal glory.

St. Paul clearly says that the Antichrist is to rule until the Day of Judgment. Then *Christ* will come and the kingdom of Antichrist will be destroyed. For this reason neither Christianity nor the Church will possess the kingdoms of the world, but will suffer still greater danger, tribulation, and persecution. In 2 Peter 3:3 f. it is said, "First of all you must understand this, that scoffers will come in the last days with scoffing (following their own passions), and saying, 'Where is the promise of his coming?' " Therefore, there will always be some enemies who will persecute the Church and Christians. And Daniel says that the beasts will be cast into the fire when *Christ* appears, indicating that kingdoms and godless tyrants will remain until the Day of Judgment [Dan. 7].

John 20:21: When Christ sends forth the apostles, he gives them no command except *to preach* and *to teach*. "As the Father has sent me, so send I you." Christ was sent to preach about the Father, not to establish a worldly kingdom, as he himself says, "My kingdom is not of *this* world" [Jn. 18:36]. In Luke 22:25 f. he forbids lordship to the apostles: "The kings of the Gentiles exercise lordship over them; and those in authority over them are called benefactors. But not so with you." Also in Matthew 5:39, "Do not resist one who is evil," that is, do not use the gospel to establish a new kingdom, or journey with the sword and power. The apostles were sent *to preach* and *not* to take possession of kingdoms.

For this reason St. Paul says, "The gospel is an office of the *Spirit*," that is, the gospel offers spiritual and eternal goods, not dominion over the world.

Second Corinthians 10:14: "The weapons of our warfare are not worldly but have divine power to destroy strongholds. We destroy arguments and every proud obstacle to the knowledge of God. . . ." Also,

2 Corinthians 5:20, "So we are ambassadors for Christ." Also, 2 Corinthians 6:4, "As servants of God, let us commend ourselves in every tribulation." Also, 2 Corinthians 4, "We are not to be lords over your faith" [cf. 1:24].

As the apostles were commanded only to preach the gospel, the doctrine of the Anabaptists and their ilk is a devil's doctrine, for they say that before the Day of Judgment the kingdom of Christ must be established on earth with physical pomp, and that in this there will be neither godless men nor hypocrites, that only the saints will rule, and that they will forcibly subdue all the godless. The devil has again and again raised up in the Church this Judaic dream and fable, for (as history shows) from early times there have been enthusiasts, chiliasts, and Pepuzianists.[1]

Here let us indicate some passages of Scripture which teach that good and evil will be mixed in the Church until the Last Day of Judgment.

Luke 17:28 f.: "Likewise as it was in the days of Lot — they ate, they drank, so will it be on the day when the Son of man is revealed. . . . In that night there will be two men in one bed; one will be taken and the other left." Also, in Matthew 13:30, 39, 41, Christ says about the tares, "Let them both grow together"; and soon thereafter, "The harvest is the end of the world." Also, "The Son of man will send his angels, and they will gather out of his kingdom all causes of sin and evildoers. . . ."

These passages and similar ones indicate that the evildoers, or the hypocrites, will not be separated from the true saints until the Last Day of Judgment.

This, too, is to be pondered. All bishops, pastors, and shepherds of souls are commanded, without physical compulsion, to expel those who notoriously sin or blaspheme. Men cannot see inside the heart, or judge concerning secret sins, so St. Paul says, 1 Timothy 5:19, "Never admit any charge against an elder except on the evidence of two or three witnesses." Those who cannot publicly be overcome with witnesses should not be separated from the others. Before the Last Day of Judgment it is impossible to establish a kingdom or church in which there will be no godless hypocrites.

Therefore, Christian pastors and shepherds should perform their office, diligently and faithfully teach the gospel, and commend to the care of God Christians who in the next life will be completely purified and live in

---

1. A term that was sometimes applied to the followers of Montanus because their special revelations predicted that the new Jerusalem would be established at Pepuza. See note, p. 150.

peace, honor, and joy. In the meantime, in this life the Church will always have within it many evil, godless people of the world who will possess the Church and the dominions of this world and who will cruelly persecute the saints and the kingdom of Christ until *Christ himself* comes from heaven. Nevertheless, despite enemies and despite persecution, the Lord Christ wonderfully preserves his Church, and the devil cannot blot it out. Such a kingdom is the kingdom of Christ on earth!

And this is certain, that even though such a new church should be on earth, nevertheless neither the bishops, teachers, nor preachers should undertake to establish such a church or new kingdom with the sword, without a new, clear command from God. However, no new word or command should be expected, for *Christ* will give no command which is contrary to the gospel.

But the Jews and Anabaptists draw on the prophets Isaiah and Jeremiah, who, in speaking about the kingdom of the Messiah, Christ, use words as if they were speaking of a worldly kingdom! The first answer to this is that the gospel and the writings of the apostles explain the prophets. As the gospel says that Christ's kingdom is to be spiritual, that it signifies eternal and spiritual goods, and that it should not be a dominion or sovereignty of the world, but will suffer persecution, then we should interpret the prophets according to the gospel. And the apostles themselves in Acts understand everything which was promised about the kingdom of David, as spoken about the *spiritual* kingdom of Christ, and about the *Church*, which must suffer tribulation and persecution on earth. *Christ* himself rebuked the apostles when they had Judaic ideas about taking possession of the kingdoms of the heathen.

Second: The prophets themselves, although they use words which pertain to a physical kingdom, nevertheless point out that Christ's kingdom is to be spiritual. For Daniel 9:26 clearly says, "that the Messiah or Christ shall be killed, and rejected by his own people." And Isaiah 53:10 says, "When he makes himself an offering for sin," and so forth. Therefore, he will establish no worldly dominion in this life. Besides, the prophets announce with clear, significant words that Christ's kingdom is to be everlasting. No worldly kingdom, however, can be eternal on this earth. Therefore, the words which the prophets use that sound as if they pertain to a physical kingdom actually signify a *spiritual* kingdom, and should be interpreted *spiritually*.

This spiritual eternal kingdom of *Christ* commences on earth in the Christian Church through the divine word, Spirit, and faith, and it lasts hereafter eternally. The prophets speak in the meantime in such a way that they do not distinguish this life here on earth in the Church (which the Scripture also calls the "heavenly kingdom") from the eternal life in the future.

They do distinguish it when they say that the Church in this life is to suffer persecution, as the Second Psalm says, "The kings of the earth set themselves, and the rulers take counsel together, against the Lord and his anointed" [2:2]. Also, Psalm 116:15, "Precious in the sight of the Lord is the death of his saints." And Psalm 72:14: "And precious is their blood in his sight." Also Isaiah describes how the Church here on earth must suffer poverty and tribulation when he asserts, in chapter 30:20, "And though the Lord give you the bread of adversity and the water of affliction, yet your teacher will not hide himself any more. . . ." There Isaiah clearly indicates that the Church shall be maintained under all sorts of temptation and tribulation.

Daniel sets down clear words about the persecution of the kingdom of Christ and the Church before the Last Day of Judgment when he says in the eleventh and twelfth chapters, "And those among the people who are wise shall make many understand, though they shall fall by sword and famine, by captivity and plunder, for some days" [11:32]. "At that time your people will be delivered, *every one* whose name shall be found written in the book" [12:1].

Christians should comfort themselves with these and similar passages, and realize that the kingdom of Christ is spiritual. They should earnestly invoke their Lord in time of anguish and seek comfort in him, thus exercising their faith. These passages sufficiently refute the Judaic dream of the kingdom of *Christ* on earth, where none but saints shall rule.

OF THE RESURRECTION OF THE DEAD

The article about eternal life and resurrection of the dead is one of the most sublime in the entire Christian doctrine of the gospel. In the New Testament it is clearly proclaimed, and often repeated and cited.

Christ obviously preaches about it in Matthew 25, saying that the righteous will have eternal joy, and the godless, eternal torment and pain. And in John 5 and 6 Christ says, "For this is the will of my Father, that every one who sees the Son and believes in him should have eternal life; and I will raise him up at the last day" [Jn. 6:40]. And the apostle *St. Paul* gives a sublime sermon about this article in 1 Corinthians 15. It is very useful for Christians to have such clear, definite passages through which to strengthen piety and faith.

As the passages in the New Testament are well known, we want to indicate several excellent passages in the prophets of the Old Testament.

Isaiah 26:19–21 says, "Thy dead shall live, their bodies shall rise. O dwellers in the dust, awake and sing for joy! For thy dew is a dew of light, and on the land of the shades thou wilt let it fall. Come, my people, enter your chambers, and shut your doors behind you; hide yourselves for a little while until the wrath is past. For behold, the Lord is coming forth out of his place to punish the inhabitants of the earth for their iniquity, and the earth will disclose the blood shed upon her, and will no more cover her slain."

This sermon of Isaiah clearly speaks about the dead rising, the holy having joy and eternal salvation, and the godless, eternal torment; and it also speaks about the persecution of the Church in this life. One must diligently ponder such excellent, truly apostolic sermons of the prophets.

Your dead, he says, will live; he calls the saints of God the dead; therewith he indicates that the Church for God's sake suffers tribulation and persecution, just as if he had said: Your children who are killed for your sake, you will see again. Further, he says that eternal life is to be full of rejoicing. The saints will have eternal joy, for they will be without sin, without weakness, without death, without fear of the devil. They will know the unutterable wisdom, the heart of the Father and the superabundant goodness of God, and they will live forever, and in spiritual gardens and meadows fresh with dew they will blossom in eternal rapture and joy.

The prophet comforts those who must suffer in the meantime, saying that the Church must be hidden for a little while. The saints and the pious will be maintained in the Church by the word and the Spirit of God until the Last Day. After that, he announces the punishment of the godless and the resurrection when he says that the earth will no longer cover her slain.

Isaiah 66:22–24: "For as the new heavens and the new earth which I will make shall remain before me, says the Lord; so shall your descendants and your name remain. From new moon to new moon, and from sabbath to sabbath, all flesh shall come to worship before me, says the Lord. And they shall go forth and look on the dead bodies of the men that have rebelled against me; for their worm shall not die, their fire shall not be quenched, and they shall be an abhorrence to all flesh."

There the prophet describes both the eternal tribulation and pain of the godless and the joy and rapture of the saints and believers, and announces that eternal life will be as if every day were a sabbath. All the saints throughout eternity will praise God and give thanks to him. Everlasting life and glory will be an eternal heartfelt joy in God, an eternal adoration and thanksgiving, and we will fully know the great goodness of God and eternal justification of creatures; and there will be no sin and no death.

Isaiah 65:17–20: "For behold, I create new heavens and a new earth; and the former things shall not be remembered or come into mind. But be glad and rejoice for ever in that which I create; for behold, I create Jerusalem a rejoicing, and her people a joy. I will rejoice in Jerusalem, and be glad in my people; no more shall be heard in it the sound of weeping and the cry of distress. No more shall there be in it an infant that lives but a few days, or an old man who does not fill out his days, for the child shall die a hundred years old, and the sinner a hundred years old shall be accursed."

There may be a passage in the prophets clearer than this second one, but this beautiful, excellent sermon of the great Isaiah announces that the entire creation shall be renewed and that the saints and the children of God shall have joy, and that weeping shall no longer be heard.

These are little words, but they speak about great things: sin and death will cease; the old and young children will live eternally. Sinners of a hundred years, that is, those who have persisted in their sins, without repentance, will suffer the punishment of eternal damnation.

Because these sentences clearly attest that before the resurrection and the Last Day the Church is to suffer tribulation and persecution, and after the resurrection, in the renewal of all creation, heaven and earth, is to be glorified, the prophets obviously testify that the kingdom of Christ on earth *will not be a physical kingdom*, as the Jews and Anabaptists fictitiously imagine.

Isaiah 25:7–8: "And he will destroy on this mountain the covering that is cast over all peoples, the veil that is spread over all nations. He will swallow up death for ever, and the *Lord God* will wipe away tears from all faces, and the reproach of his people he will take away from all the earth."

This passage announces also that death and sin shall cease, and that the children of God shall be rescued from all reproach, from all wailing and weeping, that is, from sin, death, and the fear of the devil, and finally from all evil. By the covering that he mentions, he means death (for they used to sew and cover the dead with cloths); the same covering, that is death, is to be taken away completely.

Also, Isaiah 24:21–23, "On that day the *Lord* will punish the host of heaven, in heaven, and the kings of the earth, on the earth. They will be gathered together as prisoners in a pit; they will be shut up in a prison, and after many days they will be punished. Then the moon will be confounded, and the sun ashamed; for the *Lord of hosts* will reign on Mount Zion."

Isaiah 35:10: "And the ransomed of the Lord shall return, and come to Zion with singing; everlasting joy shall be upon their heads." The Lord Christ is called "eternal Father" by Isaiah in the ninth chapter, that is, a beginner of eternal life.

Daniel 12:2: "And many of those who sleep in the dust of the earth shall awake, some to everlasting life, and some to shame and everlasting contempt." Hosea 13:14: "But I will ransom them from hell, and save them from death. Death, I will be to you a poison; hell, I will be to you a pestilence." Ezekiel 37:12: "Behold, I will open your graves, and raise you from your graves, O my people." Here also belongs the passage in Ezekiel 33:11: "As I live, says the Lord God, I have no pleasure in the death of the wicked, but that the wicked turn from his way and live."

Here belong all the passages in the prophets which speak about the kingdom of Christ and eternal glory.

The Sixteenth Psalm speaks thus about Christ: "My body also dwells
secure, for thou dost not give me up to Sheol, or let thy godly one see
the Pit" [16:9 f.]. David is talking about *Christ* and including the members of Christ, namely all believers. The better people well knew the
promise that the blessed seed, Christ, is to trample the head of the serpent
and destroy the kingdom of the devil.

Psalm 22:26: "The afflicted shall eat and be satisfied; those who seek
him shall praise the Lord! May your hearts live forever!" Psalm 34:21:
"Misfortune will kill the godless." Inasmuch as all goes well with the
godless in this life, it is certain that the prophet is speaking about the
punishment in the *next* life.

Again he says, in Psalm 116:15, "Precious in the sight of the Lord is the
death of his saints," because after this life they will have comfort and joy
and eternal life. Here also the passage in Psalm 34:19 belongs: "Many are
the afflictions of the righteous; but the Lord delivers him out of them
all."

In Psalm 49 the prophet observes, on the one hand, the godless who are
rich in this world and for whom all goes well, and, on the other, the holy,
or pious, for whom on this earth all goes wrong, and he says that this will
be reversed after death. Of the godless he says, "They lie in hell like
sheep, death gnaws them; in hell they must remain." Of the holy and
pious he says, "But God will ransom my soul from the power of Sheol,
for he will receive me" [Ps. 49:14 f.]. The prophet also observes the
godless and believers in Psalm 4:7 f.: "Thou hast put more joy in my
heart than they have when their grain and wine abound. . . . In peace I
will both lie down and sleep." All the passages in the prophets about the
eternal kingdom of Christ belong here.

Job 19:25 ff.: "For I know that my Redeemer lives, and at last he will
stand upon the earth; and after my skin has been thus destroyed, then
from my flesh I shall see God, whom I shall see on my side, and my eyes
shall behold, and not another." This is a very beautiful passage announc-
ing that we in this flesh, and in this body, which we now have, will be
resurrected, and that our body and entire nature will be renewed [*ver-
neuet*], as *St. Paul* teaches. The same passage says that the nature of
eternal life will be knowledge, bright and clear, of God and all creatures.

Exodus 3:6: "I am the God of Abraham, and the God of Isaac, and the
God of Jacob. . . ." From these words Christ the Lord concludes in

Matthew 22:32 that Abraham, Isaac, and Jacob are living, "for God is not a God of the dead, but of the living."

From all the divine promises and examples given to the fathers, we can conclusively say that there is to be another and eternal life. All such divine promises, which God gave to the fathers, indirectly include resurrection and eternal life. God made glorious promises to Abraham, Isaac, and the other patriarchs, saying they should obtain comfort and treasure, joy and rapture in God. To Abraham he says, "Fear not, I am your shield and your reward" [Gen. 15:1].

In this life the greatest, most sublime saints have misery and sorrow of heart, and it appears as if God has forsaken and is paying no attention to them. For this reason, it is certain that another life must follow, where God will delight the saints with eternal comfort, with the glory and joy of eternal life. On this all the saints stand, and suffer all the tribulation, misery, and wretchedness of this life, and wait in patience for the unending treasure and unutterable comfort of eternal life.

Genesis 4 . . . indicates that God is holding back future judgment and revenge over Cain and all the godless, and that some sins which are not punished now will be punished in the next life. . . . A general judgment in which all sins shall be revealed and punished, therefore, must come.

Cain's judgment was a prefiguration and symbol of the Flood and the frightful punishment of Sodom and Gomorrah. St. Peter, the apostle, in 2 Peter 2, says that God set such examples before all the godless.

The divine promise in Genesis 3 declares that the serpent's head shall be trampled and the kingdom of the devil destroyed, that is, that death and sin shall cease and be taken away. For this the nature of man must be renewed.

The great patriarch Jacob, in Genesis 49, foretells the champion [Helden] who shall be the Savior of mankind. The chief fathers and patriarchs well understood that the promises of the blessed seed, Christ, should not be understood in terms of a physical kingdom, but in terms of the spiritual kingdom of Christ, eternal justification, and eternal life. To be sure, they also saw that the Church, the people, and children of God would have to struggle in this life and be exposed to sin, weakness, misery, and sorrow, even as Adam was when he saw before his eyes the frightful murder of Abel.

God called on Abraham to kill and sacrifice his own son. The chief people noted in this a prophecy that the blessed seed, Christ, would become a sacrifice and suffer, and have no physical kingdom on earth.

While still living, Enoch and Elijah were taken from this life to God, because God wanted to give visible evidence of the eternal life. For if they were nothing after this life, then they would not be with God; to be with God means to dwell in a new, divine, eternal life.

Now open examples are clearer than divine words or promises would be alone. Without any doubt, the holy patriarchs and afterward the prophets based many exhortations on such examples and promises of God.

That there is another eternal life after this one is shown also by the angels who talked with Abraham and other patriarchs. By doing so, the angels signified that we shall be their companions, participating in eternal life, for they protect and preserve us.

In Numbers 24:17 Balaam craves to die the death of the righteous. "I shall see him, but not now; I shall behold him, but not yet."

XXXII

OF BEARING TRIBULATION AND THE CROSS

I have said that the Church in this life must suffer persecution and carry the cross, but let us take a further look. We must teach and preach diligently about this in the Church, so that Christians in tribulation, temptation, and anguish may have comfort. Concerning this comfort of Christians we must know four things.

First, it is highly necessary that hearts in anguish be reassured that the tribulations are not without God's counsel and permission. The heathen and the Epicureans think that God has nothing to do with such things, that they happen only according to natural law, or by blind fortune, without the foreknowledge of God. On the contrary, we should know that God beholds the sufferings of his Church; he determines in himself why they are ordained, and how far they shall prevail, as seen in the story of Job.

In Lamentations 3:37 ff. Jeremiah says, "Who has commanded and it came to pass, unless the Lord has ordained it? Is it not from the mouth of the Most High that good and evil come? Why should a living man complain?"

To this pertain all passages about the foresight of God. Matthew 10:27: "Not a sparrow falls to the ground without your Father's will." Acts 17:28: "In him we live and move and have our being." Psalm 100:3: "He has made us and not we ourselves." Psalms 94:9: "He who formed the eye, does he not see?" Psalm 33:15: "He fashions the hearts of them all, and observes all their deeds." And in 1 Corinthians 11:31 f. St. Paul says, "But if we judged ourselves truly, we should not be judged. But when we are judged by the Lord, we are chastened. . . ." There he clearly says that tribulation is sent to us by the Lord.

And in Hannah's song in 1 Samuel 2:6, this is written, "The Lord kills and brings to life; he brings down to Sheol and raises up."

Second, Christians should not only be certain that God beholds the sufferings of his Church, knows and ordains and wills that we be humbled, but also that he does not punish us out of displeasure or to ruin us, but to call us to repentance and to exercise our faith. Tribulations are reminders that we should turn to God, not flee further from him.

This is the greatest and foremost consolation for Christians, for in great temptation and anguish the first thought in the heart is that God is angry, and is punishing. When the heart does not apprehend that God is punishing us out of grace, that he does not condemn us, but with fatherly concern exercises our faith, then temptation and anguish become still greater, and man finally despairs. Therefore, the gospel speaks about tribulation as a mark of grace.

Scripture often mentions this comfort, as in 1 Corinthians 11:31 f.: "But when we are judged by the Lord, we are chastened so that we may not be condemned along with the world." Proverbs 3:12: "Whom the Lord loves, he chastens." Hebrews 12:6: "The Lord chastises every son whom he receives." Psalm 98: "It is good, Lord, that thou dost humble me" [cf. 94:12]. Revelation 3:19: "Those whom I love, I reprove and chasten." Isaiah 28:9 f. notes that the rod makes pious children. "Whom will he teach knowledge, and to whom will he explain the message? Those who are weaned from the milk, those taken from the breast?" that is, the comfortless and the poor. Isaiah 26:16: "O Lord, in distress they sought thee, they poured out a prayer when thy chastening was upon them." Nahum 1:7: "The Lord is good, a stronghold in the day of trouble; he knows those who take refuge in him." Jeremiah 31:19: "And after I was instructed, I smote upon my thigh. . . ." Matthew 5:3: "Blessed are the poor in spirit for theirs is the kingdom of Heaven." Luke 6:21 f.: "Blessed are those who mourn . . ." and "Woe unto you who laugh. . . ."

Tribulations are a part of the law, for they are punishments which the law threatens. As the gospel teaches right use of the law, namely that the law is given to humble us so that we will seek Christ, it teaches that the punishment of the law and the tribulation are not sent to ruin us but to exhort us to penance, and to remind us where to seek comfort.

Many passages of Scripture which have a general meaning also belong here. St. Paul says in Romans 11:32, "For God has consigned all men to disobedience, that he may have mercy upon all." Consigned to disobedience means not only to be subjected to all kinds of tribulations, but also to eternal damnation. Nevertheless, the gospel says that the law lays such terror and burden upon us not to ruin us but to bring us to the rich grace of *Christ*. Ezekiel says as much, "I have no pleasure in the death of a sinner."

Moreover, there are many passages in Holy Scripture which announce that the Christian Church and all the saints on earth must suffer and must be exercised and alarmed so that true fear of God and faith toward God may be increased in their hearts.

Second Peter 1:6 f.: "Though now for a little while you may have to suffer various trials, so that the genuineness of your faith, more precious than gold which though perishable is tested by fire. . . ." Second Corinthians 1:9: "We felt that we had received the sentence of death; but that was to make us rely not on ourselves but on God (who raises the dead)." Second Corinthians 4:16: "Though our outer nature is wasting away, our inner nature is being renewed every day."

Romans 5:3 f.: "Suffering produces endurance, and endurance produces character, and character produces hope. . . ." James 1:2: "Count it all joy, my brethren, when you meet various trials." In Genesis 22:12 God says to Abraham, "Now I know that you fear God. . . ."

Christians must keep these and similar passages of Scripture in mind, and cling to the words of divine promise and comfort, for all tribulations are indications of the gracious, fatherly divine will. God does not send tribulation to destroy and damn us, but rather that he may admonish us to penance and exercise our faith. Such comfort fortifies the Christian heart against despair and teaches us why the cross and tribulation are useful.

Third, there is a great weakness in human nature which causes us to think that God assails us too severely and lays too much on us. Therefore we are often impatient, and murmur and grumble against God, as if he were pressing us too hard. We think that God's judgment and works are not just when the godless and tyrants live in all pleasure, superabundance, and pomp, and we dwell in misery, poverty, and wretchedness.

We should warn Christians that they must not persist in such sorrow of heart and impatience toward God, which Satan seeks to increase, for it is a great sin against the first commandment; God requires obedience, according to these words of St. Peter, which are a commandment, "You shall humble yourselves under the mighty hand of God" [1 Pet. 5:6]!

Here we should cite those passages in the Scripture which speak about the suffering that comes particularly upon the Church and the children of God. These same passages indicate that God requires and wishes to have obedience. Therefore, we should receive this excellent consolation: First, that God commanded Christians and the Church to be obedient. Also, because tribulation is an acceptable sacrifice and service of God, we should not think that temptation is an indication of divine anger, or that God sends us sufferings because he wants to disown us, but that we may be conformed to our head Christ, and manifest to God an obligated service. Third, as the church on earth must suffer misery and wretchedness, the tribulations cannot be signs of anger, for God loves the Church and remembers to deliver it, even as he raised Christ from the dead.

The reason, however, why the Church and the saints on earth must suffer tribulation before all others is that the kingdom of Christ is finally to be a renewal, an eternal new righteousness and new life. Here on earth, in this life, even in the greatest saints, there is still weakness and sin. As God wishes the flesh and the old Adam to be slain, he has for this reason inflicted us with all sorts of tribulation, frightful punishments, and natural death, that afterward we may be clothed with a new body and be made glorious in the new eternal life that is without death and without sin. In this life he wishes to exercise the faith in our hearts, as *St. Paul* says, Romans 8:10: "Although your bodies are dead because of sin. . . ." Romans 6:6: "Our old self was crucified with him so that the sinful body might be destroyed. . . ."

Someone might interject human reason at this point and say that inasmuch as the saints are holy, it is not reasonable that they should have tribulation. Answer: Christians, or the Church, are indeed just and holy, but only because God esteems them just for the sake of *Christ*. According to the flesh the saints are still weak and sinful. Therefore, God lays a burden and discipline on them in the form of tribulation, death, and the cross.

Concerning this, someone might insist that according to reason, what happens to the pious and just ought at least to be reasonable; that is a true word of Moses and the law. The gospel, however, everywhere explains the law and teaches that in this life the saints, on account of the sin and weakness that remain in them, are subjected to death. And, therefore, while the Church before God is pure and holy for the sake of *Christ*, it will finally have to be fully redeemed.

We also want to set forth several passages about persecution of the Church, for from the beginning of the world God's children have been persecuted by the devil and the world.

First, by all means the greatest examples are those of the Lord *Christ* himself, and of the entire Church from the beginning of the world, Able, Abraham, Isaac, all the people of Israel in Egypt, and all the apostles and prophets. These sublime examples are intended to comfort and admonish us that the Christian Church must be conformed with the likeness of Christ. Therefore, the God-fearing will suffer persecution and the Church will have tribulation.

On account of this, as great and bitter as the temptations and anguish are, we should not be faint-hearted, but should know that the Church is descended from her Lord *Christ*, who is her true principle, and we should consider Abel, yes Christ himself, all the prophets and apostles, who were persecuted and killed. St. Paul, Romans 8, says that we must become like Christ, the Son of God. In 1 Peter 4:17 the apostle says, "Judgment begins in the household of God." Also, "Be not astonished when tribulation comes upon you; everything happens to test you; but rejoice that you participate in the suffering of Christ" [1 Pet. 4:12 f.]. *Christ* himself says in Matthew 16:24, "If any man would come after me, let him take up his cross and follow me." Second Timothy 3:12: "Indeed all who desire to live a godly life in Christ will be persecuted. . . ." Psalm 126:5 f.: "Those who sow in tears will reap with shouts of joy!" Psalm 118:18: "The Lord has chastened me sorely, but he has not given me over to death." Psalm 116:5: "Precious in the sight of the Lord is the death of his saints."

In these passages this excellent comfort may be found. The Christian's temptation and tribulation are an acceptable sacrifice before God, for sacrifice means a gift or service of God, which happens particularly to the glory of God, and is accepted by him. As Psalm 51:17: "The sacrifice acceptable to God is a broken spirit; a broken and contrite heart, O God, thou wilt not despise." Romans 12:1: "Present your bodies as a living sacrifice. . . ."

God also requires obedience, so that we may be patient in tribulation, which pleases him as heartily as the highest, noblest sacrifice and service of God. Therefore, we should not think that we are rejected by God, still less should we murmur against him, as if he had entirely forsaken us. We should consider the usefulness and fruit of the cross and tribulation as pointed out above, so that we can joyfully display patience and obedience, as *St. Peter* says, "Rejoice that you share in the tribulation of Christ" [1 Pet. 4:13]!

Obedience in itself is good, for God orders us to be obedient in patience. As *St. Paul* says, "Be patient in tribulation" [Rom. 12:12], and in 1 Corinthians 10:10, "Do not grumble as the Israelites grumbled."

Second, the cross and tribulation bear fruit in exercising and strengthening us in faith and drawing us to penance.

It is also comforting that tribulations are a divine service and an acceptable sacrifice, for no higher title can we give to any work than that it is a sacrifice, holy and acceptable to God. However, our tribulations do not become a sacrifice until we contemplate the wishes of God and suffer because we are obedient to God and believe that our sufferings for the sake of *Christ* please God.

However, we are talking here not about tribulations or sufferings which we ourselves create, like the hypocrisy of the monks, but those tribulations which come or will come upon us without our choosing — sufferings which come by the destruction of nature, or those which result when Satan, tyrants, and other evil men plague us. For this reason *St. Peter* clearly says, "Be patient according to God's will!" that is, do not plague yourselves. It is a heathenish error for us to choose our works and fancy that they must be an acceptable sacrifice, as the priests of Baal did when they stabbed and cut their own bodies. As God requires obedience in tribulation, and desires that we patiently bear his will without grumbling, we should guard against such impatience and bitterness toward God and take comfort in those Scriptures which say that God's will is for the Church to bear and suffer tribulation and temptation.

Third, it is necessary to know that we should in faith invoke God in all tribulations and temptations. Therefore, we should not only note that such do not happen by blind chance, without God's permission, and that they are not signs of wrath, and that impatience or grumbling against God is sin, and that God requires obedience; we should also bear the tribulations in a Christlike way in the *faith* that God is near us, will forgive sin and mitigate the punishment. Psalm 34:18: "The Lord is near to the brokenhearted." Also, that he will help and save us, not according to our thoughts, but according to his divine wisdom and counsel.

The foremost fruit of tribulations is that through anguish and necessity we acquire motivation for exercising our faith, for earnestly calling on God. In the comfort and strength that follow we note that God is near us and that he truly cares for us.

In this way the light of divine knowledge becomes ever brighter in our hearts and faith grows in us. As the example of King Manasseh in 2 Chronicles 33:12 f. shows, and as the text says, "When he was in distress he entreated the favor of the Lord his God . . . and God received his entreaty. . . ." Manasseh acknowledges that the *Lord* is God. Psalm 50:15: "I will deliver you, and you shall glorify me"; that is, at the time you will acknowledge me even more fully. Psalm 69:32: "Let the oppressed see it and be glad; you who seek God, let your hearts revive." Note the strong, sure, rich comfort that God is close to his own. In 2 Corinthians 1:3 ff. *St. Paul* gives us a very beautiful word: "Let us give many thanks to God for his gift (that is, for the strong, rich comfort) which he has given us through many people," that is, that God's superabundant goodness may be ever more clearly and widely known.

So we should bear tribulation patiently for these two reasons, God's commandment and the divine promise. God's commandment orders us to pray and patiently expect help, as the Fiftieth Psalm says, "Call upon me in the day of trouble; and I will deliver you." And Psalm 4:5: "Offer right sacrifices, and put your trust in the Lord." Also, in Matthew 7:7: Christ says, "Ask, and it will be given you." And in Luke 18 he orders us to pray always. In 1 Thessalonians 5:17 St. Paul says, "Pray without ceasing!" Philippians 4:6: "Have no anxiety about anything, but in everything by prayer and supplication with thanksgiving, let your requests be made known to God." And Psalm 55:22: "Cast your burden on the Lord, and he will sustain you."

Such commandments to pray, with which he exhorts us, should incite and stir us all the more securely to invoke him.

Thereafter, we should also look on the divine promises. John 16:23: "Truly, truly, I say to you, if you ask anything of the Father (in my name), he will give it to you." Matthew 7:11: "If you then, who are evil know how to give good gifts to your children, how much more will your Father who is in heaven give good things to those who ask him?" And in the Psalms there are innumerable comforting promises, as when the prophet says, Psalm 10:14, "Thou art the helper of the fatherless!" Also, Psalm 50:15: "Call upon me in the day of trouble; I will deliver you, and you shall glorify me."

The true exercise of faith and the highest and holiest divine service of Christians is to perceive the general need and the danger and temptation in the Church and state, both of which the devil vehemently hates, and with valiant, steadfast faith ask God to rule his Church and save it from false doctrine, error, hypocrisy, and lying. The governments of the world should maintain good order, peace, and tranquility; give us a favorable climate; ward off all the insolent, wild wantonness of the rabble; and maintain Christian discipline, virtue, honor, and honesty; so that his divine name may be hallowed, glorified, and honored, his kingdom increased and strengthened, and that of the devil destroyed.

Through such exercises faith, right knowledge of God, and all sorts of fruits of the Spirit grow in the heart. That was the highest divine service of Abraham, Joseph, David, Daniel, all the early fathers, prophets, and apostles.

In the monkish idleness, hypocrisy, security, and pleasures of this life, faith in the heart expires, for if we are not accustomed in necessity to turn to God and heartily invoke him for help, then the heart becomes indolent and cold, and the devil easily steals upon us and blinds us to our own weakness and flesh, so that people think that God does not receive them and that things happen in the world without God's agency. For this reason the Scripture says that men in good, easy times become blind and godless; they lose this exercise and reason for seeking help and deliverance from God, as Moses says in Exodus 32:6, "The people sat down to eat and drink and got up to play." Deuteronomy 32:15, "My people waxed fat, grew thick, became sleek," and Hosea 7:5, "The great lords rage from wine."

There is, unfortunately, in the Church, in worldly government, and in households so much wretchedness that there are always pressing reasons to pray and to call on God; however, those who are drunk and full of good fortune, security, and pleasure do not notice such.

The philosophers have highly praised the virtue of patience in tribulation. Natural reason teaches that a man should be strong and firm so that sorrow or temptation will not move him to act against his reason and do something injurious, either to himself, as Cato, Antony, and many others did in committing suicide, or to others.

But Christian patience is a much higher virtue, and we will properly understand this if we reflect on what evil impatience brings.

In the first place, all those who allow the devil to embitter them with impatience, who give way to the flesh, and who mumble and become angry against God, allow faith and obedience to God to depart (which is frightful). Impatient, angry, embittered hearts think that God does not pay attention to them, that there is no point in praying, or in waiting and expecting comfort and help. In truly great temptations the heart will impatiently grasp at blasphemy, despondency, and human comfort and assistance, against God's commandment, just as King Saul sought out the witch. Such frightfully heavy sins against the first table come from impatience. A little patience, however, often produces much good.

Thereafter, contrary to the second table, impatience incites bitterness, poison, hate, and envy toward one's neighbors (often toward the innocent), and it also engenders fury, violence, death, and vengeance. From this, as history shows, often spring discord, strife, quarrels, war, tumult, bloodshed, confusion of government, wretchedness and sorrow. Coriolanus, to avenge himself, attacked his own native land as an enemy. Scipio [1] acted more worthily and with a more princely spirit. He scorned several rabble-rousers and moved outside the city, away from the eyes of the mob, so that he gave his enemies no cause for greater bitterness. He could have protected and avenged himself with force, but for the good of the government he put aside personal injury and burden. Scipio acted more worthily than Marius and many others who avenged themselves and caused so much damage.

Thrasibulus at Athens made a law that those who had triumphed in the commonwealth should forget what they themselves in the time of stress had to bear, and for the sake of the general welfare, not make additional demands. This was a worthy, princely thought. However, Marius, when he returned to Rome, tyrannically executed and strangled all the leaders of the opposition, and much trouble followed. Fierce dispositions and impatience cause endless, deadly injuries. Many men commit suicide in impatience. . . .

Christian patience is a great necessity: first, that we may not fall against God in disobedience, but stand fast in true faith. Second, that peace and unity in the Church and governments may be maintained. Also, that we ourselves, each in his own heart, may be more satisfied. Therefore, through the apostles the Holy Spirit often exhorts us to patience, as *St. Paul* does in Colossians 3:15, "And let the peace of Christ rule in your hearts," that is, faith in your heart, which knows that we should be obedient to God and expect help and comfort from him. If we do seek revenge but wait patiently, we prepare neither tumult nor war.

Accordingly, Isaiah 30:15 says, "In returning and rest you shall be saved; in quietness and in trust shall be your strength." That is, God helps those who are patient, who await help and comfort from him, who do not

---

1. Publius Cornelius Scipio Africanus the Elder (237–183 b.c.), grandfather by adoption of Scipio the Younger, was the renowned Roman general who defeated Hannibal at Zama in 202. His championship of Hellenism and his leniency toward conquered Carthage, whose culture he did not wish to destroy, brought him into disfavor with his political rivals in Rome. For a number of years he retired from public life, dying finally on the coast of Campania. For a note on Scipio the Younger, see above, p. 67.

get angry nor murmur against God, who do not cause an alarm in their impatience, nor seek forbidden help, nor undertake the comfort of human revenge. And Psalm 4:4 teaches: "Be angry, but sin not."

For this reason we are to accustom ourselves to bear tribulation patiently, that we may thus exercise faith, and especially that we may not act rashly in anger or impatience, when hot swift emotion provokes a desire for revenge. In such cases it is an exalted, noble Christian virtue not to seek our own profit or glory but to consider the Church, the nation, the people, and their welfare, lest thirst for revenge be the cause of many injuries.

XXXIII

OF PRAYER

With the word "prayer" we instinctively think of invocation and thanksgiving, and for this reason we divide Christian prayer into these two parts. *Invocation* means sincerely to ask something of God; *thanksgiving* means to praise, glorify, extol, and acknowledge that he repeatedly gives comfort and assistance, and finds pleasure in such well-doing.

These two parts often are together in Scripture, Psalm 50:15: "Call upon me in the day of trouble . . . and you shall glorify me. . . ." Also *St. Paul*, Philippians 4:6: "With thanksgiving let your requests be made known to God." But first we will say something about invocation or petition.

We should consider these five parts in Christian prayer: first, the God we invoke; second, God's commandment; third, divine promise; fourth, comprehension of the promises in faith; and fifth, the necessity of coming before God.

First, we should contemplate what we invoke, and we should separate our prayer from that of the heathen by contemplating that the true God is he who revealed himself through the *Lord Christ*, and by his word and miracle.

Second, we are to consider God's command because God has commanded us to call upon him. His command tells us that not only murder, adultery, and theft are sins, but that it is also a grave sin not to pray, not to wait for comfort, not to give thanks for innumerable blessings, and not to show him the worship which he demands.

So we should not maintain our weakness or retain our unbelief against God's command, even though since Adam's fall we are all born with doubt as to whether God pays attention to us or hears our prayer. *Those who remain in doubt*, or despair of God's goodness, cannot pray, for as long as the heart thinks, "My invocation is to no purpose," there can be no prayer. Such darkness and blindness in the heart make it impossible for people to find refuge in God.

For this reason we should remember God's command, and say to ourselves, "We are indeed obliged to be obedient to the commandments of God. He has ordered, he has enjoined us to call on him in necessity, and he has not enjoined without purpose. Without doubt he will hear those who obey him, and he will punish those who do not. I am to honor God; I must not scorn or lightly toss his command to the wind."

We should also keep such commands of God despite thoughts of unworthiness, for some, if not entirely godless, may think, "Although God favorably hears some, he nevertheless does not hear me; for I feel like a sinner, unworthy." Such thoughts thrust us back; by our unworthiness we are frightened away from God. We should, however, obey God's commandment to us, for we would be very silly to argue that we are not worthy to obey the divine commandments not to steal nor kill. This would be as if a vassal were commanded by his Lord to do his daily work and excused himself, saying, "I am not worthy to obey your orders. . . ." *We are not free to pray or not to pray; we are obliged to pray.* We should think not that we are either worthy or unworthy, but that God has commanded us to pray. . . .

Here are some of the Scriptures in which God has given us his command to pray.

Matthew 7:7: "Ask, and it will be given you; seek, and you will find"; and the Lord Christ adds, "for everyone who asks receives." In Luke 18 the Lord gives a parable about praying always and not losing heart. Matthew 26:41: "Watch and pray that you may not enter into temptation." First Timothy 2:1: "First of all, then, I urge that supplications, prayers, intercessions, and thanksgivings be made for all men." First Thessalonians 5:17 f.: "Rejoice always, pray constantly, give thanks in all circumstances; for this is the will of God in Christ Jesus for you." Psalm 50:15: "Call on me in the day of trouble."

These passages belong to the second commandment, for sincere Christian prayer is the holiest divine service.

Third, we should esteem the divine promises, which so clearly say that God will hear us, and that our prayer will not be in vain. The same is often repeated in Scripture. John 16:23: "Truly, truly, I say to you, if you ask anything of the Father, in my name, he will give it to you." Luke 11:13: "How much more will the heavenly Father give the Holy Spirit to those who ask him!" Psalm 50:15: "Call upon me in the day of trouble; I will deliver you, and you shall glorify me."

Divine goodness and mercy are unutterably great. God not only commands us, but also, through his fatherly goodness and gracious promises, entices us to pray. If we look at our own hearts in comparison with the sublime divine love in the heart of the Father, we must confess that we are harder than any stone, iron, or diamond, that we are so adamant against God's earnest command that we cannot truly see the gracious promises, and are so cold, rotten, lazy, and sullen that we can neither invoke nor pray.

Tauler spoke well when he said, "We are ever more eager to take; but God is a thousand times, indeed times without number more ready and sincerely willing to give; for he wishes indeed to be God, and to keep his promise." [1]

Fourth, *faith* also belongs with true prayer; for through faith *in Christ* we are reconciled with God; otherwise our weakness is so great that when we would invoke and pray to God, our first thought would be that God does not hear sinners. Therefore, we should remember that through *Christ* we are reconciled and justified before God. If we now do penance, acknowledge our sin, and believe the gospel, which declares that through *Christ* our sin is forgiven, then shall we assuredly remain firm in the knowledge that God is gracious and that our sin is forgiven, even though we still experience sin and evil tendencies in ourselves.

Therefore, the *Lord* Christ says, "Truly, truly, I say to you, if you ask anything of the Father in my name, he will give it to you." This is as if he should say, "You cannot stand before God my Father in your own purity or worthiness; you need a Mediator and High Priest. Therefore, take refuge in me, and do not doubt that you are pleasing to God for my sake."

We should think of God's promises as promises to *Christ himself*, and that God assuredly hears his Son Christ. This is a true, strong divine comfort against our unworthiness. For this reason we should include, "Through Jesus Christ, our Lord," in all our prayers.

If Christian prayer is to occur, there must first be faith in Christ, namely that *through Christ* we are justified, have forgiveness of sins, and know for sure that our prayer pleases God *for Christ's sake*. When faith is present we wait with assurance for the help and comfort which God promises.

Because God has expressed his will in the gospel, saying he certainly

1. This was a common thought in Tauler's sermons, first published in Leipzig, 1498. For a critical text, see *Deutsche Texte des Mittelalters*, XI, *Johann Taulers Predigten*, F. Vetter, ed. (Berlin, 1906). Cf. Sermon 83.

will accept us, forgive us our sin, and give eternal life, we should conclude that such is certain, and conquer doubt, not trifling with stipula-
tions such as, "if you will," or, "if I am worthy." It is true, we are
unworthy; however, *for the sake of the Mediator* we are accepted out of
grace, and God has sworn, "As I live, says the Lord, I have no pleasure in
the death of the wicked."

Here it is not necessary to dispute about eternal divine foresight, for
we have God's commandment that we are to believe the promise, and are
not to judge concerning God's will or imagine thoughts contrary to the
promise. Also, we are not to seek God's will outside his word, or without
the word. And I have already said that the divine promises offer grace not
only to some but to all.

To bear tribulation in time of physical danger is to obey God, and we
should know that God wants to have such obedience, and wants, moreover, to comfort and to help us in his time. In all prayer there should be
generalis fides, that is, a general faith that *through Christ* our sins are
forgiven; that our prayer is pleasing to God and will be heard *for the
sake of Christ;* and that our prayer is not in vain, for through it we will be
delivered or our difficulties mitigated. And this faith, which does not rest
on any human condition, always brings peace to the heart.

However, if in faith we ask to be delivered from a specific burden, then
we should expect help and rescue, but we should also add, "If it pleases
God; if God esteems us to be blessed with it," etc. Thus we should
prepare the will to obey, and at the same time expect deliverance, but
with this distinction, "if it pleases God."

David prays in this manner when he asks God to help him regain his
kingdom, from which Absalom had driven him. "If I find favor in the eyes
of the Lord, he will bring me back, but if he says, 'I have no pleasure in
you,' let him do to me what seems good to him" [2 Sam. 15:25–26].

In the Gospel the leper says, "Lord, if *you will*, you can make me clean"
[Mt. 8:2; Mk. 1:40; Lk. 5:12].

And Christ says, "Father, if you will, take this cup from me" [Mt.
26:39]! St. Paul, Romans 8:26: "We do not know how to pray as we
ought." That is, our weak flesh, as it is in anguish, asks for deliverance
and shuns obedience; however, the Spirit directs us again to divine obedience and to patience, and although Christ also sighs for deliverance, he
nevertheless does not struggle against God's will, but trusts in God and
his holy will.

There are several excellent examples of such prayer and faith. In Matthew 15, that of the Canaanite woman; Matthew 8, that of the centurion of Capernaum. They do not speculate about whether Christ will help; they conclude in their hearts with the greatest strength and certainty: If I come to *Christ*, he will help me. There faith is so strong and great, the longing of the heart so fervent, and the supplication so compelling that an encounter takes place. Christ speaks of such strong faith when he says, "If you say to this mountain, cast yourself into the sea . . ." [*cf.* Mt. 17:20; 21:21; Mk. 11:23].

These are individual, highly special examples, about which we can say little either in teaching or preaching (as Dr. Martin Luther says). It is enough to teach that the faith without any rationalization should conclude that our prayer pleases God for the sake of Christ, and obtains mitigation, even though the physical necessity is not entirely taken away. We should nevertheless specifically indicate the physical necessity, whether war, hunger, sickness, or affliction of children, for God uses all sorts of necessity to exercise our faith, so that we may learn to call on him. The chief reason why God sends tribulation to the saints is that when they obtain comfort and help in time of danger and necessity, they may note that God is not far from his Church, but near, as Jeremiah says.

So a Christian heart should be prepared to suffer patiently God's will, for this really means to kill the old Adam, and through faith to remain firm, not doubting that God will help. Although in asking for something by name, we add, if it is God's will, we should nevertheless not give way to lack of strength, but in faith and in patient humility should wait and endure to the end, without turning our eyes from God's promise. . . .

Christ says to the centurion in Matthew 8:13, "Be it done for you as you have believed." Also, he commands the master of the school to believe that his daughter will again live.

These examples are presented so that we also may pray in full trust and strong faith, and so that faith may be exercised through such invocation and supplication. Our obedience is in such prayer in that we rely on his will and set God the Lord neither time nor limit as to how he is to help or deliver. As *St. Paul* says in Ephesians 3:20, "God is able to do far more abundantly than all that we ask or think." We should know that God can order and ordain according to his divine wisdom wonderfully and graciously beyond all our thoughts. The Lord God leads his saints in unusual, wonderful ways, so that they, as St. Paul says, may learn to acknowledge God's will and not put their trust in themselves, that each may walk in obedience to God, according to his calling, letting God rule and guide, help and avenge. Thus God guided Abraham, Isaac, and Jacob, Moses and David.

And God would have us know that he marvelously leads and guides his children and the holy Church on earth, beyond all thoughts of men, as Psalm 4:3 says, "Know moreover, that the Lord wonderfully leads his saints," that is, he helps his saints not according to human but according to divine counsel and will. Thus says *St. Paul*, 1 Corinthians 10:13, "God is faithful, and he will not let you be tempted beyond your strength, but with the temptation will also provide the way of escape, that you may be able to endure it."

Therefore, says St. Paul, we are not to desist nor to refrain from prayer. . . . Even though we do not immediately obtain what we request, we are nevertheless not to cease, as Christ teaches in Luke 18 in the parable about the judge and the widow.

Fifth, in Christian prayer we should lay before God and earnestly ask for what we desire. A useless rigmarole or prattle of wind is not a Christian prayer. Prayer is a divine service in which we show that we acknowledge God as our *Lord* and *Father* and believe that he is merciful and gracious, that he sees and accepts us; that God does not sit idly by in heaven, but unfailingly, freely bestows rich gifts and abundant comfort on his Church on earth.

For this reason we should ask something of God, and present our need to him, or give thanks for his divine benefit. For thus God wants to be acknowledged; that is, with honor and glory to his divine name. Such is said in the song of Mary in just a few words, "He has filled the hungry with good things . . ." [Lk. 1:46–55]. So says the Lord Christ, in Matthew 7, "Ask, and it will be given you; seek, and you will find; knock, and it will be opened to you." However, the Scriptures of the prophets and apostles sufficiently indicate that we are to ask for both spiritual and physical gifts.

We should get rid of the thoughts taught by ignorant hypocrites, that physical gifts are not worthy of our asking. God wants to be petitioned for the benefits of government, for good climate, and for good harvest.

So we should contemplate all sorts of danger, both of the body and soul, and invoke God for refuge and protection. *St. Peter* says in 1 Peter 5:8, "Your adversary the devil prowls around like a roaring lion, seeking some one to devour."

There is immense power, strength, and quick cunning in the devil, which he employs to seduce and lead us astray with false doctrine, error, heresy, and poison. He captures our hearts with unbelief and blinds us with security. He cheats us, under the appearance of holiness, with false worship, hypocrisy, and lies. He presses forward and provokes difficulty, sorrow, and impatience, often for flimsy reasons; and he hurls us into all sorts of wretchedness. Human thoughts and words can hardly describe a spirit so embittered, poisoned, and enraged against God, Christ, and his Church, or how great are his strength and cunning, for without ceasing he watches to harm the Christian Church, especially if we are weak, lazy, and indolent.

We should diligently take to heart how much immeasurable wretchedness, sorrow, misery, anguish, danger, and trouble; how many strange, cruel, frightful accidents; how much sickness, poverty, murder, war, and misfortune can come to men in this life on earth.

We should pray not only for our own necessities, but for the necessities of the whole Church. The apostles admonish us to beseech God to protect the Church from heretics, corruption, and such assaults of the devil, so that many may be sustained and come to the gospel.

First Timothy 2 commands the apostles to pray for the authorities, governments in the world, and so forth. We should ask God to give universal peace to maintain good government, worship, honor, and discipline; and to grant us nourishment and other physical gifts. All this is included in the Lord's Prayer.

A Short Explanation of the Lord's Prayer

Our Father who art in heaven!

That is, eternal Father, thou who art truly close to thy Church and thy children, look on them, and hear their prayer!

I

Hallowed be thy name!

That is, grant that men may know thee as the true living God and Father; that thy word may be preached purely, through which thy divine glory may be rightly and truly known; that men may learn to acknowledge thee in faith, call on thee in time of necessity, and rightly serve thee in Spirit and truth.

The first petition in the Lord's Prayer concerns the first and most important commandment in the Decalogue, for we pray that God's glory and pure Christian doctrine may be maintained and that the Church may always prosper. Here "name" means true knowledge of God.

II

Thy kingdom come!

That is, enlighten and rule us by thy Holy Spirit, that we may truly believe thy word. Begin thy kingdom in us so that we also may be heirs of eternal life and riches.

Thus the second petition speaks about the fruit of the gospel, that God may rule and lead us.

III

Thy will be done, on earth as it is in heaven!

That is, grant that all men on earth may be obedient to thee; grant that the true shepherds and bishops, kings, princes, and lords, all authorities, teachers, and preachers, and all subjects and attendants may diligently and faithfully execute their offices, be obedient to thee, and walk in a way that is pleasing to thee, even as the angels in heaven are pleasing and obedient to thee.

This third petition includes all the spiritual things that may be useful for the glory of God and the salvation of men. And the petition for physical gifts follows.

IV

Give us this day our daily bread!

That is, grant us our nourishment; give us temporal peace through diligent God-fearing authority; grant us refuge and protection, happiness and prosperity in government, good morality among our youth, and well-being in all things in this life.

V

Forgive us our debts, as we forgive our debtors!

This petition indicates that faith should be in all prayer, faith which believes that we have forgiveness of sins *through Christ*, which lays hold on Christ as our High Priest and Mediator. Thus we know that we have an entrance to the Father *through him,* and that *for his sake* we will be heard.

In this petition the entire holy Christian Church and all the saints confess that they still have sin in themselves. But there is also this comfort; as Christ himself orders us to ask for forgiveness of sins, there is no doubt but that he will forgive us.

"As we forgive our debtors" is also included, but Christ is not saying that for the sake of our forgiving we will be forgiven. Our forgiving is an obedience which should follow. It is included here because our forgiving should be a reminder that God both has and will forgive us.

VI

Lead us not into temptation!

That is, beloved Father, let us not be ruined by difficult temptation; defend and protect us in the presence of the cruel, frightful stratagems of the devil, that we may not come into error and delusion, sadness and unbelief, and then despair of thy grace and goodness.

VII

But deliver us from evil. Amen!

This is a general conclusion for all the petitions; it asks for deliverance from all the weakness, sin, wretchedness, and misery of this life. In short, let us ask to be delivered from the sorrow of this life and to be given eternal righteousness and eternal life. Amen.

In a very brief way the Lord's Prayer, a precious prayer which the *Lord Christ* himself has given to us, teaches us that we should pray for both spiritual and physical goods, for the office of preaching, for the universal Church, for governments, for universal peace, and for present and future needs.

When we speak this noble prayer, we should open our eyes and behold not only the frightful raging of the devil but also the daily gifts and benefits by which God sustains us, so that we may learn sincerely to pray, and in each petition of the Lord's Prayer to include our present necessity. These are truly Christian exercises of faith and services acceptable to God.

The prophet Zechariah comprehends the treasure which we have through *Christ* and the gospel and the nature of divine service when he says, "I will pour out upon the house of David the spirit of grace and supplication" [Zech. 12:10]. The spirit of grace is the spirit of adoption, which we receive *through Christ*. It assures us that we have a gracious God and are pleasing to him. The prophet also indicates how we are justified before God and what is the most exalted, noblest, and holiest divine service. For the spirit of prayer is to call on God in time of need, to thank him joyfully, and to confess his word cheerfully.

So far we have spoken about invocation and petition, but we should also know that we should always be thankful for divine benefits. We daily receive from God innumerable benefits which we do not even know about. We would be faced with innumerable dangers and could expect countless misfortunes and injuries from Satan if God did not protect us with his might. Therefore Paul says, "We must thank God always for everything" [1 Thess. 4:18]. In 2 Corinthians 1 he says that many should pray for him so that many will give thanks that God has protected and sustained him. He indicates that this is a divine service which the Christian should always practice.

XXXIV

OF HUMAN PRECEPTS IN THE CHURCH

We have already discussed many great things — true knowledge of God, forgiveness of sins, faith, the new obedience which the Holy Spirit produces in our hearts, the Church, the sacraments, future life, and suffering in this life.

The secret wisdom which God has revealed to his Church through his word is vastly different from the wisdom which comes from reason, such as one finds in philosophy, medicine, and government. And although such wisdom of reason is praiseworthy, we should not throw the two together as the papists, monks, and Anabaptists do.

There are various grades and kinds of customs. Some are commanded by God, of which we spoke in connection with divine law. Some are for worldly authority, to establish and maintain general peace or morality, as a magistrate's command that no weapons be carried in a city. Some are external manners and rules concerning special days and exercises, such as a bishop might order in a church or a schoolmaster might use to regulate young people, their hours of assembling, times of reading, and so forth.

These human ceremonies are the lowest grade in human customs. Although they are serviceable in an external sense for discipline, for teaching, for guiding, and for introducing virtue, we should be careful about how highly we esteem them. People usually thrive on these external rules, and out of an inborn blindness make great holiness and merit of them. In this error, men everywhere throughout the history of the world have fabricated and accumulated ceremonies.

The heathen saw that at a certain time and with a certain sign the early fathers sacrificed a lamb or small ox, and those who came afterward took up the work without understanding why; they imagined that the work was a service by which God is reconciled, and that the costlier the sacrifice, the holier and more meritorious the work. For this reason great lords often uselessly slaughtered and sacrificed hundreds of oxen, and even men, thinking that human sacrifice was nobler.

With such examples, the Christian reader might ponder the degree to which human blindness goes astray in thinking that external rules, invented by men, are divine services and reconciliation. From this follow still more errors, quarrels, and greater darkness. To avert this, we should carefully instruct the people in just what human precepts are to be kept in the Church.

And this article is not concerned about commandments connected with worldly dominions which are specifically designed to protect life and property and to maintain a worldly kingdom; it is concerned with church ceremonies, commanded by bishops, established by custom, and regarded as works of special holiness, such as distinctions about food and clothes.

Although the philosophers cry out and protest that we have made a shambles of ordinary human laws, caused disdain of episcopal authority, brought destruction of praiseworthy customs, and created impudence and dissatisfaction, nevertheless all God-fearing men must know and firmly hold that the light of the gospel, in which God has revealed his own *Son Jesus Christ* for the salvation of men, should be considered higher than all human things, episcopal authority, or peace.

Some people have insolently misused this article but this is no reason to suppress the truth; we should rescue the truth and refute the misuse, concerning which I want to set forth three rules.

The first rule: If the bishops or worldly authorities command us to do something contrary to God's command, then we are obligated to consider the divine command higher and not obey the human command. When the king of Babylon ordered the golden image to be worshiped, all men were obligated to shun such worship and confess the true faith [*cf.* Dan. 3]. When the high priests forbade the apostles to preach the gospel, they were obligated to scorn such prohibition and to fulfill the office entrusted to them by *Christ.* Acts 5:29 gives us this rule in just a few words: "One must obey God rather than men."

Now consider some episcopal laws which compel sin, such as the commands to keep the idolatrous Mass and to invoke dead men. In the same category is the law about celibacy, which forbids priests to marry. For the most part, it cannot be maintained without frightful sin, for God created men to be fruitful. And *St. Paul* commands, "Let each one take a wife to avoid fornication" [*cf.* 1 Cor. 7:29]. All should know, whether priests or laymen, that if they discover that marriage is necessary for them, they are obligated to get married, despite papal prohibition.

However, the tyrants who do not wish to bear God's order persecute the innocent and create discord, and the fault is not with the God-fearing who make use of God's order. This is comforting to remember when worldy-wise philosophers complain that we have brought discord through our changes. The tyrants who persecute divine truth and order must give a reckoning for it.

The second rule: Some works that are commanded are in themselves adiaphora, that is, nonessentials [indifferent things]; such are the rules about not eating meat, wearing a long or short dress, and the like — if not commanded or prohibited in God's word. While such external works in themselves are nonessentials, false teachers always create an erroneous situation by enacting them into laws. The papists make seven such errors.

Seven Errors Which the Papists Enact into Their Laws

1. The first error is their assertion that we merit forgiveness of sins with these works. This is a crude pharisaical absurdity, which confuses the doctrine of faith and grace. If we think that we merit forgiveness of sins through such works, we rob the *Lord Christ* of his glory. When false trust in these miserable works ensues, or doubt, true faith is blotted out.

This is why *St. Paul* strives so earnestly to abolish circumcision and other ceremonies of the Jews, so that faith will not be blotted out of the Church: for we have forgiveness of sins and are justified, or received by God, *for the sake of Christ, out of grace, not* out of our merits or those of another. *St. Paul* reminds us to be on our guard lest through the precepts of men we blot out the true light of the gospel. There is absolutely no doubt that this pharisaical error should be rebuked with the greatest earnestness.

2. The second error which adheres to human precepts is more subtle: Some see very well that one plays the fool too crudely if one claims for our miserable works an honor such as the forgiveness of sins, which belongs only to the Son of God. So, because the hypocrites nevertheless want such ceremonies to be highly esteemed, they embellish them by saying that although they do not merit forgiveness of sins, they are a special cultus, or divine service, because God pays attention to them and

wants to be honored by them, and that as a special honor they please him. For example: Although the Nazarite ceremony of not drinking wine does not merit forgiveness of sins, it is nevertheless a good work, pleasing to God and a special honoring of God. This embellishment is a shameful, gross deception, which we must see in order to ward off the cunning stratagems and sophistries of the devil.

We must strive against this thing, for the hypocrites think that their works, which God has not ordered or instituted, are equal to the works which in God's word were instituted through Moses. The works in Judaism are divine services, for they have God's word; but the works which are commanded only by the precepts of men are like heathenish works which are without God's word. Therefore, they are not divine services.

We must diligently consider God's word, for God will not suffer us to invent our own divine services without his word. The heathen have had many beautiful customs and exercises, which they esteemed as holy divine services; but because they were deluded, and wanted to establish their own devotions without God's word, they continually introduced many filthy works, sacrificed dogs, pigs, asses, and men, made images, and worshiped the priapus. Such absurdity follows when we relax the rule that divine services are only those works which God has commanded. This rule is clearly seen in Matthew 15:19: "Vainly do they honor me with the precepts of men." And in Colossians 2, St. Paul rejects the holiness which we ourselves invent and elect, such as forbidding some foods, not for the sake of the body, but because such work is regarded as a special holy honoring of God.

3. The third error is that the hypocrites go still further, and make perfection out of these works; they boast about the lives of the monks and their unclean celibacy, and they set these invented hypocrisies above the callings and works which God has commanded.

4. The fourth error is that they make essential things of all this, and teach that it is a mortal sin, a revolt against the Church and God's people, not to keep these hypocrisies. For this very reason these precepts should be repudiated. The kingdom of *Christ* rests in confession and faith in God's word, right use of the sacraments, good conscience, and the activity of the Holy Spirit in us; is it not bound to a conformity with human ceremonies.

This is sufficiently shown in Colossians 2:16, 20: "Therefore let no one pass judgment on you in questions of food and drink or with regard to a

festival or a new moon or a sabbath. . . . If with Christ you died to the
world, why should you again be laden with laws, as though you still
belonged to the world?"

5. The fifth error follows from the foregoing in that we Judaize Christianity and obscure the gospel, faith, grace, and true divine service in all
kinds of ways. The papal decrees openly boast that inasmuch as Judaism
had ceremonies, rules about foods, and so forth, the bishops for the
preaching of the gospel had to establish new ceremonies of even greater
holiness.

Therefore, they instituted the prohibition of marriage, the spectacle of
penance, pictures, idols, and all sorts of other injurious hypocrisies, under
the pretense that Christians are the heirs of the people of Israel, and that
the priests of the Levitical priesthood had special sacrifices and grades to
distinguish them from other members in the Church. This error is rebuked in the letters to the Galatians and the Hebrews. And it should
be noted that this infatuation and absurd imitation has caused much
harm.

6. The sixth error is that the bishops assign to themselves a power
which they do not have. For if the false, idolatrous opinion prevails that
such works fabricated by men are great holiness and divine service, then
the bishops hold sway; for to them belongs the right to make laws, and
they proceed accordingly to invent new divine services, Mass sacrifices,
worship of the sacraments, worship of the saints, and prohibition of marriage; and they teach that whoever does not keep such is eternally
damned, because, they say, God has bound his Church to the episcopal
laws, and we are obliged to obey them.

That this error has brought hundreds of thousands of men into despair
and eternal wrath is easy to understand, for the prohibition of marriage is
tyrannically thrust upon the priests and has become a source for sin and
eternal harm.

There are many more items through which conscience is violated because people think that the bishops have power to impose such commandments on the Church, that the Church is bound to obey them, and that
the people are no longer God's people if they do not obey these commandments.

7. The seventh error is that injurious division and discord follow when
we consider these human commandments necessary. In an earlier time the
churches separated and quarreled because they disagreed about a date for
Easter. The Greek and Latin churches disputed about using leavened or
unleavened bread in the Lord's Supper. Papal decretals anathematized all

who taught confession contrary to the papal commandments. And so on.

For the sake of all, or some, of these seven errors, the precepts of men are defended by the hypocrites, as their old and new books show. Although some gross errors are subtly embellished and disguised, the notion that this obedience is necessary to strengthen the bishops' unrighteous power is always there. . . .

In general we can conclude this about human ceremonies. Although they are nonessentials, if they are intended to maintain or strengthen the aforesaid errors, preachers are obliged to expose them. They should not consent to a burdening of the Church with false divine services or snares of the conscience.

Because such hypocritical commandments are both punishable and invalid, those who know better should chastely remind others and root out the superstitions by acting contrary to them. In Matthew 15 the apostles were quite right not to keep the Pharisees' rule about hand washing.

Spiridon,[1] the holy bishop in Cyprus, furnishes a good example. During a fasting period a foreign guest came to him. Having made no advance preparations, and in haste to feed his guest, who was tired and hungry, he commanded his daughter to put some pickled meat on the table. Seeing the meat, the guest said that it was not his custom to eat meat at this time, for he was a Christian. To which Spiridon answered, all the more reason he should eat the flesh, because Christians are not made holy or sinful by a distinction of foods.

If our opponents say that we make unnecessary changes by the abolition of fasts and similar human ceremonies, remember these two passages from *St. Paul:* In Colossians 2:16 he says, "Let no one condemn you on account of food and drink"; and in 1 Timothy 4:1 he calls the prohibition of food a doctrine of the devil. There are so many errors in these matters that all reasonable men are required to strive against them.

St. Paul would not even keep the ceremonies of Moses, so that by his example he might turn others from error and bring about an understanding of true divine service. He did not want to strengthen error. Now in our day, when our opponents say it is a great sin not to keep the fasts and similar human ceremonies, they but confirm their multitudinous errors.

1. Spiridon, or St. Spyridon, a bishop of Cyprus, suffered in the persecution under Diocletian in 303–04, was active in the councils of Nicaea (325) and Sardica (343), and became the center of many early legends. *Cf.* Socrates (Scholasticus), *Ecclesiastical History,* Bk. I, chap. xii, and Sozomen, *Ecclesiastical History,* Bk. I, chap. xi, in *Nicene and Post-Nicene Fathers,* 2nd Series, Henry Wace and Philip Schaff, eds. (Oxford, 1891), II.

Pygius[2] writes that it is a much greater, more frightful sin to be married than to commit immoralities against God's commandment. He makes a great show about maintaining obedience and unity in the Church. But is this statement of Pygius not an unchristian, Epicurean, injurious statement? Yet with these hypocritical pretexts our opponents now embellish their hypocrisy, tyranny, and immorality. Therefore, it is without doubt right for us to speak, write, and point out examples of true confession and doctrine. But with such contrary examples we should give instructions about faith in Christ, true divine service, and freedom in human ceremonies.

The third rule: The foregoing two related rules seek to counteract error, and instruct the conscience so that it may not be imprisoned with snares or beguiled with false divine services. However, this does not mean that there is to be no order at all, for in 1 Corinthians 14, St. Paul says that everything in church should be done with discipline and good order.

In schools there are set times for lessons and exercises, and from the beginning of the world there have been set fasts, lessons, ceremonies, and rules, instituted by men and maintained by God's people, but not contrary to divine command. For example, when a blessing was spoken over someone in ordination or something else, they laid hands on his head. This custom was used in the time of Jacob and Moses, and later by the priests, Christ, and the apostles, and it is still used in ordination.

The difference between human beings and beasts is that man has reason and was created for orderly living. God has given him this light, or ability to understand order, and we should not live without order, like wild animals. There can be no peace where there in no order. For this reason, fasts, Sundays, and other holidays are established so that the people might know at which times they should come together.

We should keep these ceremonies in the Church as they are established for true doctrine and divine service, but not as marks of holiness or necessary works. The errors which I mentioned above should be suspended, particularly to maintain order. Except in case of scandal, it is not a sin to discontinue these human ceremonies. Later I will tell how scandal is to be distinguished.[3]

---

2. Albertus Pighius (*ca.* 1490–1542), a Dutch Roman Catholic controversialist who took part in the diets of Worms and Regensburg. He strongly defended the papacy and appealed to tradition as a basis of knowledge alongside Scripture. His chief work, *Hierarchiae ecclesiasticae assertio* (Cologne, 1538), is a defense of the Church and its ways.

3. See below, Article XXXV.

Gerson [4] and others disputed much about these ceremonies and sought ways to help the conscience; however, our instruction is at the same time comforting to the conscience and serviceable for good order and peace. As long as we know that such ceremonies are not marks of holiness, and are not necessary, snares of the conscience do not come from these precepts.

Nevertheless, because one knows that they should serve for good order and that we should avoid scandal, especially in the Church where true doctrine is extolled, only the most excellent and useful customs should be retained. Modest people do not like to give an evil example, they are much more inclined to maintain good order and discipline, especially in what concerns the Church, so that in the publicly gathered company, which God instituted, we may learn of him, call on him, thank him, and do all things well.

Orders in themselves remind children and uneducated people of God's works and our Savior *Jesus Christ.* The story of Christ is told through holidays: In winter we observe the birth of Christ, for he was born about this time; in the spring we observe the festivals of the suffering and Resurrection of our Lord Jesus Christ, for about this time the same things occurred; and so forth.

Such festivals paint the story in the minds of the people, and are an eternal reminder which admonishes the people to learn and diligently to listen to the divine deeds and doctrine, so that they may be turned to God.

Accordingly, every Christian father should accustom his children to useful ceremonies, should teach them to pray, to read or speak a piece of Christian doctrine in the morning and evening, and as they go to and from the table.

Such orders, when used rightly, are extolled by *St. Paul* in Galatians 3:24, "The law was our custodian to instruct and to lead us to Christ"; that is, ceremonies and other disciplines were given to us for remembrance and restraint until we should come to the true knowledge of *Christ.*

4. Jean Gerson (1363–1429), a French nominalist theologian, Chancellor of Notre-Dame and the University of Paris for many years, is known especially for his conciliar views. He tried to heal the Great Schism (1378–1417), asserting the superiority of a General Council over the Pope. At the Council of Constance (1414–1418) he helped condemn John Hus, and also drew up the Four Articles of Constance, for which he is sometimes called the father of Gallicanism. As a reformer in the Church he urged a renewal of prayer, sacrificial living, obedience, and charity. He spent the last ten years of his life at Lyons writing. *The Mountain of Contemplation* (1397) and *The Power of the Church* (1417) are among his principal works.

Where there is no order, neither is there discipline, and then we cannot teach the people.

From this we can understand how to exclude the errors I mentioned and why some useful ceremonies should be kept for good order.

Of the Death of the Old Adam and Chosen Exercises

Our opponents want to embellish the precepts of men and monkery with earnest preaching about patience in suffering and about true terror in the wrathful presence of God. This suffering and terror St. Paul calls "death of the old Adam." In Romans 12:1, he says, "Present your bodies as a living sacrifice." Second Corinthians 4:10: "We carry in the body the death of Jesus!" Romans 8:13: "If by the Spirit you put to death the deeds of the body you will live."

But note that there is a great distinction between this death, of which St. Paul speaks, and chosen human exercises. Death of the old Adam means: Patience in suffering or affliction or earnest terror in the face of the wrath of God against sin. This patience is commanded by God, and is a necessary divine service for all true Christians. It is much more pleasing to God, as Psalm 51:17 says, "The sacrifice acceptable to God is a broken spirit; a broken and contrite heart, O God, thou wilt not despise."

Other works are also commanded: moderation in eating and drinking, becoming labor, and curbs to keep the body in check, so that it does not become lewd. For it is absolutely certain that where there is easy living, idleness, banqueting, and much eating and drinking, we become wild, forget invocation of God, seek sensual pleasures, and become inflamed with inordinate desires and lusts. Moreover, it is obvious that we do not pray, study, or ponder great things, or persevere, when we are seldom sober. Also, we cannot have the time for necessary things if the best and most of our hours are turned to sensuality.

The injuries which follow from this are too numerous to mention. But I ask the reader by himself to think about this and then consider the earnest commandments of Christ.

Luke 21:34: "But take heed to yourselves lest your hearts be weighed down with dissipation and drunkenness and cares of this life. . . ." Matthew 17:21: "The devil cannot be driven out except by prayer and fasting . . ." that is, sober, earnest prayer. Also, in Ephesians 6:4, *St. Paul* says, "You parents, bring your children up in the discipline and instruction of the Lord." We should discipline young people to live honorably, temperately, and chastely, to look forward to an honorable occupation, and to be accustomed to learning and praying.

These passages are commands pertaining to necessary works, which are to be continued always throughout all of life.

It is true, however, that the order, measure, and time are variable. As the schoolmaster apportions lessons and exercises to his students, so should everyone be free to arrange exercises for himself on his children, according to opportunity. This apportionment is called a chosen exercise. As the order of a school is a good work — not that in itself it is a mark of holiness or a service of God, but on account of the general commandments in which God shows that he wants youth to be instructed, which cannot happen without order — so order in your house is a good work on account of the general commandment to be moderate. The particular time in itself is not a mark of holiness or divine service, as the monks in their hypocrisy boast.

When *St. Paul* says that he chastises his body, and keeps it under control, this means he gives it no reason to sin or to hinder him in his office and prayer [*cf.* 1 Cor. 9:27]. This is a general command; the time and manner are for each to set according to opportunity.

There are very great differences among people. Youth and idlers who live without care and anguish should reasonably have more chosen exercises to keep them disciplined. And there always have been and still are people who act like the ass; they allow themselves to be beaten, but do not go forward any faster. These are the lazy ones who seek easy lives, in spite of divine commandment; they burden themselves with the easiest exercises or works.

Then again, there are some who already have too much care and work, who would have more if they were able to endure it.

Also, there are some who nevertheless could and want to keep some commanded exercises, as they are strong and not too highly burdened and have fear of God. St. Paul reminds us of this limitation: We should not make a meriting of grace and divine service out of selected ceremonies, and we should not cause harm to the body. For we are also commanded to give due honor to the body; it should not be overburdened either with gluttony, immorality, and wanton danger, or with damaging hunger and far-fetched, unnecessary hardship in work. God's will is for us to know that life, body and soul, health and mind, are divine works and gifts and his image. Therefore, he has commanded that the body should not be killed or inordinately and wantonly destroyed and wasted.

This is the meaning of another passage in St. Paul, 1 Timothy 4:8, "While bodily training is of some value; godliness is of value in every way." Here he makes a distinction between commanded and uncommanded order. Commanded works are very useful, and he includes them all in the word "godliness," that is, fear of God, penance, true belief, invocation, patience, chastity, temperance, truth, and diligence in vocation, so that we may serve God's glory. These virtues are useful to all; in this life God gives in return for them increase of spiritual gifts, good counsel, comfort, purity, success in vocation, peace, and nourishment, and rich reward in eternal life.

On the other hand, physical exercise has some value. But this is a little item that pertains to definite measure and manner, such as the days on which we should eat no more than one time. We should esteem such limitation as much less than the commanded works, and should not make general laws out of them. Each one may choose for himself his opportunity, time, and order.

And as St. Paul significantly says, "They have some value," that is, if we use them without error, without hypocrisy and without injury to the body, so that neither through excess nor disorder do we give reason for immorality or hinder prayer or necessary business; then such order is not punishable; it serves for something; not that a certain custom is a merit or a mark of holiness but that order in itself is required in this life.

Although it is desirable that people live orderly lives because human nature is created so to live and because order contributes to good health, advancement in business, reasonable peace, contemplation, and prayer, nevertheless many people are so barbarous, especially in Germany, and indulge in so much eating, so many parties and various disorders, from which so many illnesses and obstacles follow, that we reasonably ought to complain.

However, we cannot reform disorder and barbarity with church laws, for we immediately make hypocrisy out of them. But understanding preachers should charge the people with divine commandments about temperance and other virtues, and thereby politely exhort the fathers of families to maintain a respectable order among his domestics.

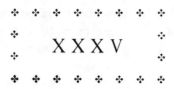

XXXV

OF OFFENSE [SCANDAL]

The word *Aegerniss* means an offense in someone else's heart which turns him from the gospel, causes him to strive against it, or makes him follow someone else's untrue doctrine or example. The word *scandalum*, strictly speaking, means a blow in the snare [*ein Schlag in der Falle*], as when an animal is captured in a mousetrap or wolfpit. The Church uses the word *scandalum* to indicate something that hits a man and then grips him.

There are two kinds of offense. The first is a pharisaical offense, or wrath and fury without reasonable motive that ensues when one preaches true doctrine and abolishes known idolatry. There are many enemies of the divine word who, on account of profit, power, or prestige, do not want to have their erroneous customs rebuked. And consequently they fight and persecute God's word and servants. This fury we call a pharisaical offense, so that we can tell which offenses the true servants of God should shun, and which they should not.

And although the entire history of God's people furnishes examples, we need only to see the example of *Christ* and the apostles and examples in our time for useful instruction and comfort.

Since the apostles preached the saving work through which God revealed himself to the world, namely the Resurrection of *Christ* and the holy gospel, which says that we are saved out of grace *for Christ's sake*, and may abandon the ceremonies of Moses, the priests and worldly-wise philosophers among the Jewish people became vehemently angry. As the wrath of such important, earnest people must have an honorable appearance, the aforesaid priests pretended good reasons.

First of all, they saw that great dissensions followed the preaching of the apostles, and they said that no logical person could behold such dissensions without great pain.

Second, they knew that the law of Moses was given by God, and they held, therefore, that it must remain until the end of the world, so they complained severely that the beautiful divine services were abandoned.

Third, they said that it was very painful and wretched to expect the destruction of well-ordered governments and stations, as the apostles were saying.

Fourth, that the priests were the orderly power and had a great following, while the apostles and their hearers were unimportant little people who appeared to be in an unnecessary rebellion against the ordained power. All this made prestige for the priests and Pharisees and oppression for the apostles.

Although the apostles did not want destruction, they esteemed God's command and honor higher than the peace, contentment, pomp, and circumstance of the priests, despite the unreasonable anger of the priests and Pharisees. In the spirit of the first and second commandments with respect to all human counsels and physical goods, they said, "One must obey God rather than men!"

From these words the first rule may be taken. We are obliged to confess divine truth, avoid idolatry, and perform commanded works; and we must not be deterred, even though the opponents become more violent, scandalous, and furious, and dissensions follow on account of their unreasonable hardness.

In our times, as the eternal God out of his great and unutterable mercy has again caused the light of his holy gospel to shine clearly among us, and has caused many errors and idolatries of the papists to be rebuked, the great prelates have grown angry, for they do not wish to be rebuked by unimportant persons and they are anxious lest true doctrine bring about a diminution of their high rank or loss of goods. They conceal their errors with colorful excuses, and cry out that we have caused dissension, departed from the orderly power of the Church, and abandoned the Catholic Church.

Although such blasphemies trouble reasonable men not a little, we should nevertheless maintain that we shall not act contrary to or allow true doctrine to decrease even though the opponents are greatly angered and cause dissension and persecution.

Here we should be armed with this clear passage, 1 Corinthians 10:14, "Shun idolatry!" We should not acquiesce in idolatry, whether peace or discord, death or persecution, follows. Matthew 10:33, 35 says, "Whoever denies me before men, I also will deny before my Father who is in heaven. . . . For I have come to set a man against his father and a daughter against her mother! . . ."

It is very necessary for us so to protect true, well-founded, pure doctrine, and not bewilder the conscience with falsehood or sophistry.

Until now we have spoken about pharisaical offense. But there is a second type of offense of which Christ spoke in Matthew 18:6, "Woe to the man who causes offense!" This refers to a punishable offense, which we should earnestly seek to avoid.

A punishable offense centers in untrue doctrine, or bad example, that turns others to evil or frightens them away from the gospel. Such offenses always have been and always will be. They encompass all false doctrine, heresy and idolatry; all the precepts of men which cannot be kept without sin; and the evil deeds which attract others to sin or frighten them from the gospel. Now consider how many men and sins belong in this category!

The first originator of offense was the devil, when he deceived Eve; his cunning trapped man. The Fall gave the devil a basis for new sins. He boasted victory over God, cruelly tore these creatures from God, and caused blasphemy. Many terrible sins among all mankind followed in the wake of this, and for one large part, eternal damnation.

Here let each and every God-fearing man reflect that in one sin, so many sins, offenses, and injuries always lie hidden. When David committed adultery, tumult followed; Absalom violated his father's legitimate wives, and many people were killed. Who can relate the offense? First of all, the devil had his triumph against God in that, through Absalom's tumult, he brought many men into eternal damnation. He violated the holy wives, and without doubt brought sorrow of heart. All David's pious subjects suffered affliction, and without doubt the young nobles who were Absalom's companions practiced on many the wantonness of their pleasure.

I have given these examples to remind us to live in piety and to remember that great offense and many sins often come from a single sin.

This is still to speak only of evil deeds. False doctrine also gives rise to many serious injuries, such as those which have followed the errors of Arius, Mani, and Mohammed. Also, papal doctrine has caused much injury. What a great idolatry invocation of the dead is! What sin and injury the prohibition of marriage has produced! How the idolatrous Mass has been bought and sold! In our times: What great injury the error of the Anabaptists has done; at Münster they would have prepared their own kingdom! The devil, who first of all overthrew Eve, continually pushes his wantonness to injure the Christian Church; he will continue to do so until the Son of God, in a public judgment, casts him into eternal punishment and pain. We should reflect on these examples and note the warning of Christ when he says, "Woe to the man who causes offense!" These words are spoken of the terrible injuries in the entire world.

Of Offense in Indifferent Things

The preceding is said about pharisaical offense, so that God-fearing people will have no hesitancy about teaching and doing necessary works, even though the poisonous Pharisees cry that it is offensive. A pious priest should be married if it is his necessity, even though the Pharisees fume.

What about works which are not necessary, such as eating meat on a day when it is prohibited? Answer: The true doctrine about genuine worship should always first be preached. Where the people still have no instruction, then it is right, not immediately to break the custom in indifferent things, for then we might turn away from the gospel those intelligent people who are anxious lest the gospel make people savage, and might also give occasion to some wanton people to stretch freedom much too far. Therefore *St. Paul* says that we are to treat the weak with consideration, and assist them, so that they may grow in faith. It is much more laudable and better to advance the gospel with modest, sensible conduct than to hinder it with unnecessary, useless audacity.

However, where people are reasonably well instructed, there are still obstinate people who admit that their doctrine is wrong and nevertheless will not suffer useless ceremonies to be abolished.

These give all sorts of offense, for their example strengthens the enemies of true Christian doctrine, and makes the unlearned doubtful; for they think that if this doctrine were true, then the learned people who understand would eat what we others eat. Thus they depress the Holy Spirit in pious simple people. That is not a trifling matter. Eusebius, in his fifth book, tells about a severe persecution of the Christians at Lyons.[1] A pious nobleman, named Attalus, and his wife, Blandina, were tortured, because they confessed the Christian faith. They were frequently taken from prison and punished in the town square to compel them to abandon their faith. At this time there was a husband among the Christians who practiced strict fasting, and would not eat meat or drink wine. Attalus had a vision that he should tell the man to stop his fasting, and eat

---

1. Cf. *Nicene and Post-Nicene Fathers*, 2nd Series, H. Wace and P. Schaff, eds. (Oxford, 1891), *Ecclesiastical History*, Bk. V, chap. 1.

common, natural food like others, because he was giving offense by causing simple people to think that a distinction of food is necessary holiness.
When Attalus pointed this out, the man obeyed the revelation.

. . . If people do not want to understand true doctrine, and keep their
false customs out of hate for the doctrine, they reveal themselves as
enemies and should be considered as enemies, as persecutors, whom God
in time will judge.

There are also many who, understanding true doctrine, nevertheless
firmly keep their previous custom, seeking therein not the glory of God
but an exalted status for themselves; or who feign to be great lords, and
do not want to appear unstable by accepting something new. In brief, the
world looks for many but finds few who truly seek *God's glory*.

We can easily understand why those who do not seek God's glory in
this matter, but only a status for themselves, act with so much evil. By
their example they strengthen the enemies of the gospel, and only pretend
to seek God's glory. Let each one search his own heart and be mindful
that he does not act against God, for he has commanded all of us to honor
his gospel and to help in the extension of true doctrine.

There are some who do not seek a status for themselves and are not
despisers of God. They would like to promote God's glory, for they have
considered how injurious an offense it is to strengthen the enemies of the
gospel, to hinder the course of true doctrine, to oppress the preachers of
true doctrine, to create doubt in the minds of simple people, and to cast
down the Holy Spirit.

If we read the signs correctly, we would see that the people themselves
long for laudable practices and manners, and would courageously and
firmly keep them. . . .

All of us should truly seek to promote God's glory and the extension of
the gospel. And while much more could be said about offense, this should
be remembered: . . . All sins produce cruel and difficult offenses, all
sins trespass the second commandment. To speak evil things about God or
godly doctrine, to mock or to sneer at the same, is particularly an offense
against the second commandment.

But all sins give occasion for such mockery of God. First, the devil
mocks, for he has gained a victory against God's will and against Christ,
be the sin secret or public; and be it secret or public, more sins and
punishments follow, creating public offense and insult to the Church, and
tribulation for the pious.

It is public injury when the true Church is dishonored, the pious afflicted, and doctrines considered very trifling. For example, when David's adultery was reported, the godless mocked, and said, "Is this the man who pretended to such great holiness?" Many came to doubt his doctrine.

All this is easily understood in our times, for unfortunately we have many examples. Many in public places, great and small, give occasion by their open vice for the blaspheming of our Church, bringing all pious men great tribulation and causing others to question staying with us. And there are many poisonous people who tear open these wounds with great exultation, so that not our person but the doctrine confessed in our churches, that is, the holy gospel of God, is injured.

Now the second commandment of God says, "Whoever takes the name of God in vain will be punished." Likewise, God says, 1 Samuel 2:30, "For those who honor me I will honor, and those who despise me shall be lightly esteemed."

Many men wonder why refined, discreet people often fall into misery and disgrace, and in this passage we find the reason; they previously dishonored God's name, and produced offense.

We, who confess the gospel, are especially to consider how severely God is angered if we give the gospel an evil name. For such sin God cast aside the high priest Eli and his sons, as the text says, 1 Samuel 2:17, "Thus the sin of the young men was very great in the sight of the Lord; for the men treated the offering of the *Lord* with contempt."

As God was angry with those who gave reason for speaking evil of the sacrifice, you should not doubt that God is seriously and fearfully angry with *those* who give reason for, or support, blasphemy or contempt of the gospel. We must, therefore, be careful in doctrine and customs, so that we do not incur the anger of God with offensive doctrine or injurious examples.

XXXVI

OF WORLDLY AUTHORITY

The physical life has orders [*Stande*] and works [*Werke*] which serve to keep the human race, and are ordained by God, with certain limits and means. By this order we should know that this human nature is not created without the distinct counsel of God, and that God in this way lets his goodness shine on us to sustain and provide for us.

Matrimony is first, for God does not want human nature simply to run its course as cattle do. Therefore, God ordained marriage, Genesis 2 and Matthew 19 and 1 Corinthians 7, as an eternal, inseparable fellowship of one husband and one wife.

Furthermore, Leviticus 18 has decreed which persons may be married and which may not. In these places especially we find the essential doctrine about matrimony, which is a very lovely, beautiful fellowship and church of God, if two people in true faith and obedience toward God cheerfully live together, together invoke God, and rear children in the knowledge of God and virtue.

That this order was created by God, and established and praised by his divine word, and that in those who truly believe it is a holy divine service, is certain from many testimonies in God's word, as Matthew 19, 1 Corinthians 7, 1 Timothy 2, and Hebrews 13 show.

On the other hand, whoever destroys matrimony as ordained by God, as do the Turks, or prohibits it, as some have done, including the Popes, certainly acts against God's command, and his prohibition should be considered and avoided as a doctrine of the devil. Besides, it is obvious what immorality against God and injury to the entire human race has followed out of the prohibition of marriage. This is said about the first order in physical living.

Still more orders and works are decreed for the protection and maintenance of this life; namely authority, justice, punishment, just wars, division of property, fair exchange in buying and selling, borrowing and paying; and also many useful arts, numbers, measures, distinctions of time with the course of the sun, which make our year, agriculture, medicine, architecture, and so on.

If these beautiful orders were everywhere maintained, if all rulers sought God's glory and the improvement and protection of the people, if judgments were true and just, if no falsehood were used in buying and selling, we could hardly complain about these useful, wholesome orders and works.

However, the devil and human evil have introduced so much filth into them that there have been innumerable injurious devilish tyrants, like Caligula and Nero. And the human mind begins to wonder whether the governments are of God or not.

For this reason there have been a great many frantic and bewildered souls, like Marcion, the Manicheans, and the Anabaptists, who have repudiated and blasphemed authority, worldly government, judgment, and punishment as nothing but sin against God, and have argued that whoever has an office, such as a king, prince, judge, soldier or servant of the court, cannot be saved.

Also many others, like Celsus,[1] Julian,[2] and Marcellinus,[3] have blasphemed the gospel as being opposed to governments. In the gospel it is written that we are not to exercise our own vengeance; these words have been falsely interpreted as applying to the punishment which God commended to the authorities.

Because quarrels frequently develop from this article, and do much harm, the people should be correctly instructed. A true understanding of this article will also serve to show that these gifts of God, government and judgment, are given by God to be beneficial to mankind, as are the light of the sun, winter, and summer; and also that we may thank God for such beautiful order, and seeing in it God's will and commendation, may be obedient to him! All this serves for peace and respect toward laws and governments.

1. See note, p. xlix.

2. Julian the Apostate (332-363), Roman Emperor from 361, was a staunch opponent of Christianity and a champion of paganism, which he attempted to revive throughout the Empire. His own ideas were rooted in Stoicism and the Eleusinian mysteries, into which he was initiated. He considered the doctrine of Resurrection particularly dangerous to the state.

3. Probably Pope Marcellinus (296-304) who became an apostate during the persecution under Diocletian, repented, and was then beheaded. He enlarged the catacombs of Rome, but otherwise not much is known about him.

First, however, we should note that the person and the order should be separated. People could come together in matrimony for something other than *the sake of God* — for money, for example. Although the person misuses the order, nevertheless the condition in itself is right. Accordingly, in speaking of authority and government, the person is to be distinguished from the office.

Diligently consider that the orders unite all human groups and that they are arranged for the knowledge of God, good custom, peace and unity, law, judgment, and punishment. Persons such as lords and office-holders should maintain such laws, judgment, and punishment; and subjects, who by their obedience exercise morality, should not shatter the peace. This is called *politica societas*, or politics.

This order is what the prophets and apostles behold as God's creation, which they honor, obey, and serve, to help maintain peace, as Daniel did in Babylon, although they may curse and sharply rebuke the rule of a person like the King Belshazzar or the tyrant Nero. It is essential, first of all, diligently to note this distinction.

Secondly, after I briefly reflect on what the order is, then I will show that the same order is God's work and creation for the entire human race, as are the light of the day and the course of the sun, summer and winter. God not only gave men light, namely, understanding of natural law through which we know that we should make and keep order in governments, and are obliged to obey natural law as God's will; he also gave and maintains sovereignty, government, judgment, and punishment. They are God's work, just as making the earth fruitful is his work. Although there have been and will be many filthy tyrants, nevertheless in his time God will again raise up a man to regulate the broken governments. Such were Nebuchadnezzar, Cyrus, Solon, Themistocles, Fabius,[4] Scipio,[5] Augustus, Constantine, and Theodosius.[6]

Likewise, as one obviously sees, murderers cannot finally escape punishment, and, although they sustain flight for a long time, they fall finally

---

4. Fabius is such a common Roman name that this reference is obscure. Melanchthon could be referring to Quintus Fabius Maximus Verrucosus (d. 203 B.C.), whose delaying tactics harassed Hannibal; he is included in Plutarch's *Lives*. It might also be a reference to Junius Fabius Maximus, prefect of Rome, 286–287.

5. Probably Scipio the Elder.

6. Theodosius I, called "the Great," Roman Emperor (379–395), fought off the barbarian attacks on Britain and quelled revolts in Africa. He recognized Christianity as the only legal religion in the Roman Empire, opposing Arianism as well as paganism. At Ambrose's demand he showed his obedience to the Church by doing penance for the massacre at Thessalonica in 390.

through a wonderful providence of God into their deserved punishment, so that all men may see that God himself earnestly accepts and supports government.

Yes, whoever knows something about ruling and considers all great changes in the world must confess that ruling is full of wonderful works of God, which openly testify that he maintains governments. Many wise rulers among the heathen have confessed, said, and written as much.

But on the other hand, the devil, from the beginning a murderer, prepares all sorts of disorder and murder through pride, hate, and avarice, drives to immorality, and so forth. And human nature is in part deluded, and full of evil, in part weak; indeed, the devil is so mighty that even the Son of God calls him "the prince of this world." And God inflicts punishments, as in the case of Absalom, who in frightful insurrection rose up against his father, David, and of the Turks, who now rage and cause murder over much of the earth.

But as long as God will maintain the human race, he will also maintain some sovereignty, laws, judgment, justice, and punishment, occasionally graciously and quietly, occasionally more severely and disturbingly, even as in one year the earth is more fruitful than in another.

Human reason cannot adequately understand the great strife of God and the devil in this. Nevertheless, we must distinguish life and death, good and evil, and know that good order is God's work, and to the extent that order is maintained, it is maintained through God daily. God always gives some wise, just, true judges and rulers, so that the devil may not ruin the entire world at once, for God wills to sustain this world for a certain time, for the sake of the chosen Church, and for no other reason.

Note further that when we say authority, government, and politics are of God, such does not mean that God allows sin to happen, that he inflicts it and does nothing through his own powerful works to prevent it. We should not think that God just inflicts the office of the judge, for the truth is that it is an order created by God, just as the order of summer and winter, and is daily sustained by God, as much good remains therein. Clearly the word of God commands and establishes it as a good work, and we will say more about this later.

Having said that the office [of worldly authority] is God's creation and work, I will now indicate some passages in the prophets and apostles which clearly confirm this article. God did not reveal this article in vain; he wants us to know and to honor this his work and activity so that our hearts may be obedient in this order not only to men but to God.

In Proverbs 16:11 Solomon says, "A just balance and scales are the Lord's order and work." This is a very good passage, which significantly speaks about the established order in this life, or politics, as God's work. When one speaks of buying and selling, he includes other items also, like judgment and authority, for they go together.

In Proverbs 8:16 Solomon speaks about divine wisdom, which speaks of itself thus: "By me kings reign, and rulers decree what is just." Here Solomon clearly teaches that governments are a work of divine wisdom. Daniel 2:21: "God removes kings and sets up kings." Psalm 144:9 f.: "O God, who givest victory to kings! . . ." These words are quite clear. Inasmuch as God assists kings, ruling is a divine work, and this order is not a sin, but good and pleasing to God.

Psalm 82:6: "I have said, you are gods . . ." that is, I, God, have established you in governments, have commanded you through my word, and you are to be gods, that is, to act as my divine representatives, to maintain the people in the knowledge of God, to keep the peace, to uphold discipline, to judge rightly, to protect the pious, and to punish the evildoers. All these are divine officeholders with power to command, and for this reason God imparts to them his own name, as his representatives.

Second Chronicles 19:6: "Consider what you do, for you judge not for man but for the Lord; he is with you in giving judgment." Romans 13:1 f.: "For there is no authority except from God, and those that exist have been instituted by God. Therefore he who resists the authorities resists what God has appointed."

Truly these are important words and sentences, pertaining to great things, quite particularly and fundamentally to government. And authority is highly praised by the Holy Spirit in the excellent preaching of *St. Paul*. Without doubt the Holy Spirit will punish the erring thoughts of all men who will not acknowledge that government is *God's* gift and work. Yet, along with true order, judgments, and reasonable laws, men often see disorder, oppression, wantonness, immorality, and other vices of rulers; and they think that rule comes only to the proud and bold, to the one who is stronger than the others and able to subdue them, and that God's justice has no bearing on it. But we are told that the Holy Spirit punishes such erring, Epicurean thoughts, checks the absurd spirits of the monks, and strengthens and comforts holy authority; consideration and pondering of this word will prove very beneficial.

Above all, he says, authority is of God. We are not to think that it is just a part of destiny, that it is a fixed *order of God*, so called that we may know that it is a creation and work of God, as day and night are ordained. He also indicates that government is an order, and that order is God's work, while disorder, immorality, murder, and oppression are works of the devil and tyrants, of members of the devil, seeking to destroy God's order.

Much useful doctrine is included in these words of St. Paul, which to treat just now would be too long, as there are other . . . [things about governments to be considered].

First Timothy 1:8: "The law is good; and was given for the unjust." These words are not about the ceremonies of Moses, but about the common law, which concerns all the world, for all are concerned about the teaching of virtue and the punishing of vice. "The law was laid down for the profane, murderers, fornicators, . . . such to restrain and to punish" [cf. 1 Tim. 1:9]. Obviously, authority is here included as an essential part of the law, as the head or the arm is a part of man's body. If law is God's will and work, so also are authority and government.

These related testimonies are definite and clear . . . but I will set forth one final passage to indicate specifically that God has established authority. In Genesis 9:6 God renewed the prohibition of murder, and said, "Whoever sheds the blood of man, by man shall his blood be shed." Here God himself decrees that a man has this office to kill the murderer. And there is no doubt that with the same words God established worldly authority, which he began again through Noah; for his words to Noah were not in vain.

All this clearly shows that authority and government are a good work, created and maintained by God, estabished and confirmed in his word, and pleasing to him.

Now I have spoken about the office, and distinguished the office from the person. However, we must learn that not all persons are virtuous, and keeping in mind what God's order is, we must also note the purpose for which God gives some virtuous persons, for some virtuous persons are especially raised up, endowed, and inspired by God. God sent Samson, David, Cyrus, Scipio [the Elder], and others who were called heroes, to establish justice and law, to punish tyranny, and to alter kingdoms. When the Persians became tyrannical and would have gobbled up the little nation of Judah, the Church of God, God raised up Alexander. Afterward, when the Greeks in Egypt and Syria became far too wanton, the kingdom fell to the power of the Romans.

And in exalted, praiseworthy rulers we can see that governments are the work of God, for he has endowed these men with particularly divine gifts. When monarchies go in a certain order, we should observe that such changes in government are not without God's counsel and judgment.

To counteract this, however, Matthew 5 and Romans 3 are quoted to prove that the gospel has forbidden revenge. "You shall not take revenge, but make room for anger" [*cf.* Mt. 5:22, 39, 44]. Answer: There is a great difference between one's own revenge, and the office which God has ordered.

Now it is clear from the indicated passages that God has commanded, decreed, and established the office. Moreover, it is entirely certain that Matthew 5 and passages elsewhere all forbid *individual* revenge, hate, and vindictiveness. But there the gospel is not about external rule; it presents a penitential sermon which applies not to government but to every person; it shows that our hearts are full of disobedience toward God, that the obedience which should be in us is not there.

"You have fallen by sin into death, and you shall sorrow" [*cf.* Rom. 3:9-19]. If one's companion spies on you, as Julius and Pompey did, if he does something that fills your heart full of bitterness and hate so that you would like to blot him out, nevertheless you should be patient. If he has done you an injustice, let it be revenged by whom God has commanded.

The disobedience of personal revenge *Christ* rebukes as disorder, and on account of it he will not abolish the orderly punishment of authority. Indeed, God speaks of the office of authority when he says, "Vengeance is mine; I will repay" [Rom. 12:19]. Authority is the hand of God, ordained in this office. Therefore, punishment via judgment and just war is a commanded work of God. More is said of this in other places.

In the third place, on the basis indicated, namely that authority and government are good works decreed, commanded, and established by God, we can establish much useful doctrine. And let this be *the first rule:*

As a true saint [*Heiliger*], a member of *Christ* may use other orders of God, such as food, drink, arithmetic, measures, and matrimony to exercise in such works his obedience toward God; he may also use the authority of government, courts, the law of inheritance, and punishments without feeling that such works are against God. A saint, a member of Christ, may be a prince, a judge, or a servant of the court; he may seek redress in the courts, sue and reply; and he may serve in just wars according to his calling.

That members of Christ may so act is indicated by what *St. Paul* says, "All of God's creatures are good, and with thanksgiving to be received" [1 Tim. 4:4]. Worldly government is part of the good order given by God, and we may use it as we do food and drink.

The sermon of John to the soldiers in Luke 3:14 also shows this: "Rob no one by violence or by false accusation, and be content with your wages." Here the soldier is told, if he is converted, how he may fulfill his office with a good conscience, namely by doing as much as the office requires.

So the Psalms and prophets often say the kings will truly invoke and glorify God, from which it is quite clear that kings and governments also may be holy, and members of Christ. Psalm 102:21 f.: "That men may declare in Zion the name of the Lord, and in Jerusalem his praise, when peoples gather together, and kingdoms, to worship the Lord." Likewise, Psalm 47:9 f.: "The princes of the peoples gather as the people of the God of Abraham. For the shields of the earth belong to God; he is highly exalted!"

Here the Psalm speaks especially about sovereignty, saying that much good follows if the princes rightly acknowledge God and serve him. When Jehosophat, Hezekiah, and Josiah reigned, the people had true religion, good protection and justice; they saw the miracles of God which gave these kings victory and peace. The princes were pious and God was honored, that is, the people came to the knowledge of God, and saw that great benefits were bestowed on them by God for the sake of the God-fearing princes; and they praised these gifts with thanksgiving.

Examples also support this rule. Good rulers were not only in Israel but also in the heathen kingdoms. Joseph was in Egypt, Daniel and other saints, in Babylon. Christ praised the captain in Matthew 8, and Cornelius was praised in the Book of Acts. God showed him and his servants a great miracle — the visible sending of the Holy Spirit, declaring that heathen and worldly rulers would also be heirs of eternal life and members of *Christ*.

We have many stories of soldiers who accepted the gospel and remained in their calling, experiencing wonders through the Holy Spirit in them: Attalus, in the time of the Emperor Severus; and Asterius, a noble Roman, in the time of Emperor Valerian; Mauricius in the time of Maximian; and many others.[7]

7. These three martyrs are obscure. Eusebius mentions an Attalus, in the time of Emperor Marcus Aurelius (161–180), as having borne a Gallic witness in the persecu-

And mark well that the works of these orders, that is, works in the government, courts, and wars, are true services of God if knowledge of *Christ* and a faith are present. If the heart believes that God has received us for the sake of his Son, we then may fulfill the calling of our office, to the praise of God and to the good of our neighbor.

Because these worldly works do not have the glamour of ceremonies and monkery, much disorder in the government occurs: those who lack understanding become confused and do not keep such works as a divine service. Rather, they consider monkishness much higher and holier; often good, useful rulers are afflicted with this error.

These errors are often rebuked by the prophets, for the Israelites expected their sacrifices to make them holy, and they neglected to do the other necessary works of justice, discipline, punishment, etc. Therefore Isaiah announces in his first chapter that God has no pleasure in sacrifices; he requires, instead, improvement in living, justice in the courts, and protection of widows and orphans. Then will he again be gracious to them.

In Zechariah 7 the prophet rebukes the people who pretend to great holiness through fasts, and tells them that God has no pleasure therein; rather, let them judge justly and cease oppressing widows and orphans.

There are many such passages, for the rule is often repeated that ceremonies invented by men are not divine services. God wants to be honored with the works which he has commanded and sanctified with his word. This rule is often mentioned in this book, as a reminder that we should diligently try to live according to God's word and abide in true obedience.

However, because this means fear of God, patience, and toil, we forsake the necessary works and true divine service, and seek softer works. Living as an idle monk is much more placid than living as the father of a family, a burgomaster, or a soldier. However, intelligent people should know that works of divine service are those which God has decreed, and that God has bound together the human race with various bonds in which

tion at Lyons; Septimus Severus was Emperor from 193 to 211. Asterius, Martyr, was a Roman senator of high rank whom Rufinus says was a martyr at Caesarea in Palestine in 262 (Rufinus, *Opera omnia, Historiae ecclesiasticae*, Bk. 7, chap. 13, in *Patrologiae Cursus Completus. Series Latina*, J. P. Migne, ed. [Paris, 1878–90]). Valerian was Emperor from 253 to 260. Mauricius was one of forty-five martyrs at Nicopolis in Armenia, possibly as late as 307, during the rule of Maximian, who had ruled jointly with Diocletian. Some ancient writers mention him as a martyr under Licinius, 319–323.

his knowledge shines, and in which he wants us to exercise faith and love.

The soldier should manifest his faith by struggling for the maintenance of true Christian doctrine and knowledge of the *Savior Christ;* in danger he should call on God, and he should strengthen others with his confession and his invocation. He should show love by his readiness to risk his life for the protection of good governments, peace, all virtuous women, and all children. In all callings, in all acts toward one's neighbors, confession and invocation of God as well as love and fidelity should shine forth.

Thus when Abraham was needed as a doctor for great lords, he spoke to them of the true knowledge of God, prayed for them, and served them with his medicine. Nebuchadnezzar, Darius of the Medes, and Cyrus, upon hearing Daniel speak of true divine service, were converted to God. The Christian wife Helena thus moved her lord, Constantius [Flavius Valerius], to protect the Christians, and their son Constantine embraced the gospel.

Such examples are many. We are to consider them and to regulate our lives so that the confession of true doctrine and invocation may be reflected in our calling and our obedience toward God proved in the works in which we are obliged to serve our fellow men. This can be done in each person's occupation as father, burgomaster, schoolmaster, merchant, and as neighbor toward neighbor.

The second rule: Christians are not bound to the laws of Moses, except when they are the same as natural laws. Christians may use reasonable laws, Roman or any other. And each and every citizen should keep the reasonable law of his government, as each is obliged to be subject to *his own* ruling authority, not to a foreign government.

France has its own laws of inheritance; Germany keeps Roman law. Any difference here should be considered by a Christian as he would consider that in the summer Rome has a shorter day than Denmark. Such externals should not be mingled with the spiritual eternal essence in the heart, for they have absolutely nothing to do with it.

This rule is therefore set forth, for it has often been reported that some erring people have wanted to bring Moses into the courts, and have caused an uproar thereby. Strauss and Thomas Münzer [8] wanted to free the people from usury. I know that this question has plagued many con-

---

8. See notes, pp. 83 and 197.

sciences: Should a thief be hanged? If so, why did Moses make a distinction between stealing by night and stealing by day?

In order that pious people may not be left in uncertainty, this rule should be remembered; each person is to maintain the reasonable laws of his governing authority, and nobody is to manufacture an authority out of his own fantasy, or to resurrect Moses or the old dead laws of Sparta or Crete. Such meddling is injurious and often inflammatory.

By "reasonable laws" I mean those which are in accord with the natural [sense of] right [*Recht*] that God has created in men so that we honor virtue and punish vice. This rule *St. Paul* also sets forth in Romans 13. If the laws honor and protect vice, so as to maintain public usurers who are unjust, they are wrong; however, if the laws punish vice, they are right, even though the measure of punishment in accordance with the customs of the land be sharpened or mitigated. The Germans are a savage people and punishments are few, but they are also sharp. . . .

That the judge should maintain present reasonable laws is based on the obligation of each person to be subject to authority. The law in particular is the authority, and, as said above, there is a distinction between the person and the office. In the kingdoms of the heathens Joseph and Daniel divided inheritance not according to the law of Moses, but according to what was accepted as right in those kingdoms.

That such variations in law have nothing to do with the gospel, anyone can conclude who understands that the gospel does not set up a new worldly kingdom or political society, but brings grace and new light [*Licht*] of God into the heart that believes, and begins in the soul a new obedience, eternal life, fear of God, trust in God, and patience. We should serve the general good in the government where we are. But enough is said about all this in the articles on the kingdom of Christ and Christian freedom.

The third rule: Deliberate disobedience against the worldly authority, and against true or reasonable laws, is deadly sin, sin which God punishes with eternal damnation if we obstinately continue in it. Faith in God cannot be present in one's heart at the same time as a design to act contrary to the open commandment of God.

I set forth this third rule because many dreamers have written that worldly commandments do not bind us to eternal punishment, for man can punish no one eternally! Such fantasy is found among the sententious. God has subjected the world to governments, and punishes disobedience eternal because his divine law is wantonly violated and despised, which says, "You shall be obedient to your authority."

And this third rule is clearly expressed in *St. Paul*, Romans 13:5: "Therefore one must be subject, not only to avoid God's wrath but also for the sake of conscience." These are clear words, showing that obedience is necessary, that disobedience hurts the conscience, and that God condemns it.

This statement of *St. Paul's* is the bulwark [*Mauer*] of all governments, for all sensible people understand that by this earnest commandment God binds them to obedience in all reasonable things. No such passage is found among the heathen. For this reason governments are more highly honored and preserved through divine doctrine than through all the heathen writings, although in the latter much good discussion about this may be found. However, here in *St. Paul* is the chief statement which fixes obedience for all sensible people in relation to governments.

In these rules, however, I have been speaking about right or reasonable laws, for *St. Paul* speaks about office, not about persons. The office, namely right or reasonable laws, is God's order. *St. Paul* is not speaking about a Nero who might command idolatry. Such unjust laws are *not* the office, are not God's order; they are confusion and disorder proceeding from the person and the devil's pressing him to blasphemy, unchastity, and murder.

Here an unalterable rule applies: "We should obey God rather than men." For this reason, if an authority commands us to act against God, we should not obey, but should act like the three men in Babylon who refused to worship the idols or countenance idolatry, even though King Nebuchadnezzar had proclaimed a frightful command regarding it [Dan. 3].

As the worthy soldiers connected with the tyranny of Saul, 1 Samuel 22, would not murder the innocent priest Ahimelech, the other priests, and their pious wives and children, even though Saul had commanded them to do it, so are we to act now. If the great lords command us to keep untrue doctrine and idolatry, we should not obey such commands. We should not assist in the murdering of the innocent or of Christians on account of their confession of the gospel, as many of the learned do by remaining silent because of fear. Such murder, along with such hypocrisy, will receive the terrible punishment of which *Christ* speaks in Matthew 23:35, "that upon you may come all the righteous blood shed on earth, from the blood of innocent Abel on . . . ," for the Son of God will judge, and will hurl all the godless into eternal punishment.

The fourth rule: Until now I have said in general that the office is of God, and that we are obliged to obey. Now the question is: What distinctly is the office, or what is a justly decreed work? What are rulers required to do?

Aristotle left a very plain sentence which should be engraved in the heart of every ruler: *Magistratus est custos legis,* "the authority is the hand and upholder of the law." From this we can readily understand that the work and office of worldly authority is the use of physical punishment to maintain external discipline, justice [*Gericht*], and peace, in accordance with the divine commandments and reasonable laws of the land.

This is generally understood concerning the office. When we think about authority, princes, or lords, we often picture a man holding in one hand a tablet of the Ten Commandments, and in the other a sword. The Commandments are above all *the* works which he [the ruler] is to protect and maintain by external discipline. Indeed, they are the guidance decreed by God, as the source from which all doctrine and well-written justice flows, and all laws should be regulated by this.

Special books in jurisprudence and philosophy have been written about other aspects of ruling, such as the constitution and maintenance of justice, divisions of property, methods of punishment, and so forth. As rulers may and should study these, I will not speak further about it.

I will consider only two questions, because they are currently being discussed. First: Is worldly power obliged to forbid, to abolish, and to punish external idolatry, blasphemy, and false divine service, or to establish true doctrine and true divine services, as they are given to the Church of God through his word?

This fundamental answer should be noted. Worldly power does not merely serve to satisfy the stomachs of men, like a herdsman who drives his cattle to the meadow, thinking only of food for the beasts; worldly authority serves above all to enforce the two commandments to maintain morality and peace. It is obliged, with all earnestness, zeal, and determination, to punish adultery, incest, and impurity contrary to nature, even though these depravities do not concern the peace. Worldly authority is obliged to maintain external discipline according to *all* the commandments. External idolatry, blasphemy, false oaths, untrue doctrine, and heresy are contrary to the first table. For this reason worldly authority is obliged to prohibit, abolish, and punish these depravities, idolatries, and blasphemies. This is clear from the passage in 1 Timothy 1:9: "The law is laid down for the lawless, the disobedient, the despisers of God. . . ." Here the apostle is saying that we are obliged to forbid and punish Epicurean talk and all sorts of blasphemy. Psalm 2:10: "Now therefore, O kings, be wise; be warned, O rulers of the earth." Psalm 24:7: "Ye princes, lift up your gates; raise up the doors of the world, that the King of glory may come in!" That is, "Ye princes, open your kingdoms to the *Lord Christ,* and cause his gospel to be preached therein, that God may be truly known, and that the people may obtain eternal life." Matthew 10:33: "Whoever denies me before men, I also will deny before my Father who is in heaven." Matthew 17:5: "This is my beloved Son, with whom I am well pleased; listen to him."

These and similar passages clearly show that the worldly authority himself is obliged to accept the holy gospel, to believe, confess, and direct others to true divine service. Therefore, he is to prohibit external idolatry and false doctrine and to punish stubbornness. It is really deplorable that we have any doubts about whether worldly authorities are to seek God's glory or their own general happiness! This office before all else should serve God, and should regulate and direct everything to the glory of God.

Therefore, although few kings and princes think of God, nevertheless God has always given some large or small regencies for the advancement of the gospel. Because God has established this order, he will not allow it to fall completely into eternal damnation. He will call some persons who will acknowledge him and advance the gospel.

The Holy Spirit, speaking of the true Church in Isaiah 49:23, has commanded all kings, princes, and regencies to advance the gospel. "Kings shall be your foster fathers, and their queens your nursing mothers." That is, the kings and sovereigns shall provide nourishment for preachers and shall not exercise fury against the members of *Christ.*

However, from the beginning such regencies which assist the true Church have been few. Nevertheless God has called and established some whose example and recompense are diligently to be considered—David, Jehosophat, Hezekiah, Josiah, and Judas Maccabeus were laudable princes of Israel. So also in the heathen kingdoms were Nebuchadnezzar and his son Evil-merodach, and later Darius of the Medes, Cyrus, Longimanus,[9]

---

9. Longimanus, more commonly known as Artaxerxes I (465-425 B.C.), is mentioned frequently in Ezra and Nehemiah.

Constantine, Theodosius,[10] Charlemagne, Ludwig the Pious, and Ludwig the Landgrave in Thuringia.[11] Nevertheless, one time has had purer doctrine than another. Note that Nebuchadnezzar and Darius of the Medes had commandments publicly proclaimed, prohibiting blasphemy and persecution of the people who call on the God of Israel.

Such testimonies clearly show that in our time the worldly princes and dominions who have abolished idolatry and false doctrine and established the pure doctrine of the gospel and true worship of God have *acted rightly. All* regencies *are obliged* to do this, according to the passage which I have indicated: *Aperite portas, principes, vestras* [Ye princes, lift up your gates]!

It follows also that the regencies are obliged to prohibit all wrong doctrine, such as the errors of the Anabaptists, and to punish the obstinate, for the regents themselves, as members of the Church, are obliged to have knowledge of the Christian doctrine, and to pass judgment on false doctrine. To do this they should draw near to the other God-fearing, reasonable, skilled Christians, to judge concerning the doctrine, for Christ says, "Where two or three are gathered together in my name, I will be with them." This statement is spoken of the God-fearing who come together for the maintenance and seeking of divine truth, not of those who under the title and name of the Church seek their own tyranny, welfare, pomp, sensual pleasure, and suppression of the truth, as the Pope and his appendages, the councils, assert.

It follows further that the God-fearing sovereigns are obliged for the good of the Church to supply necessary offices, pastors, schools, churches, courts, and hospitals; and it is not right to allow these goods to be squandered by idolatrous, idle, immoral monks and canons. It is not right for the worldly sovereigns to take possession of these properties unless they decree fitting assistance for the pastors, schools, and courts. Sovereigns should note carefully the sermon of *Christ* in Matthew 25:42, "I was hungry and you gave me no food, I was thirsty and you gave me no drink. . . ."

On the other hand, the Son of God has promised rich reward for all who assist in the maintenance and advancement of the doctrine. Matthew

10. Theodosius I, the Great, Roman Emperor (379-395), made Christianity the official religion of the Empire.

11. Ludwig the Pious, Landgrave of Thuringia (1172-1190), distinguished himself at Acre in the Third Crusade. Ludwig IV, also Landgrave of Thuringia (1217-1227), became a celebrated figure in medieval literature. He married St. Elizabeth, the daughter of the King of Hungary, and died during the crusade of Frederick II.

10:42: "And whoever gives to one of these little ones even a cup of cold water because he is a disciple, truly, I say to you, he shall not lose his reward." David and Jehosophat are good examples. The Lord says, "Whoever honors me, him will I also with honor and splendor adorn" [cf. Jn. 5]. That is enough at this time about the first question.

The second question is this: Do the subjects also have property, or do all goods belong to sovereign authority? May the rulers take as many goods as they wish from their subjects?

John the Baptist has answered this question in Luke 3:14, "Rob no one by violence or by false accusation, and be content with your wages."

The sovereign authority has his decreed tribute and tax, which should faithfully be contributed. His goods and the subjects' should be separated. The subjects have property according to divine commandment and the natural laws of the land. The divine commandment says, "You shall not steal!" These words sanction property obtained through inheritance, honorable work, purchases, and other proper means.

To summarize concerning property, that which the subjects have is part of the divine order in worldly government and political society, just as judgment or punishment is. Therefore, the princes should not destroy this order; they should know that they also come under the commandment, "You shall not steal!" They shall not illegally [unverschuldet] take goods from their subjects or burden them too severely.

A frightful example of this is depicted in 1 Kings 21, the story of Naboth, from whom King Ahab wished to buy a vineyard; and, since Naboth wanted to keep his inheritance and did not wish to sell, Jezebel had him put to death. Then Ahab took possession of the vineyard. God punished this tyranny first through Elijah, so that we might know that God is angered over such robbery, and then through the plague which followed on account of the sin. Later God had the robber Ahab and the murderess Jezebel slain.

Bear this example in mind, for such deeds and punishments often occur, even though the world thinks that God sleeps and neither knows nor pays any attention to such things. Because there are some God-fearing rulers, this doctrine is emphasized so that they may remember that the goods of the subjects are not to be appropriated by the master unless the common necessity of the country requires this.

But some will quote the passage from 1 Samuel 8:11, "These will be the ways of the king who will reign over you; he will take your sons, your best fields. . . ." These words do not empower the sovereign power to do anything more than to requisition things for the common protection of the land. For example, if the country is invaded and rescue is needed because of the Turks or other foes who begin unjust wars, then we are obliged to sacrifice not only our goods but our very lives. The First Letter of John clearly states that Christ gave his life for us, and we, accordingly, are obliged to risk our lives to protect our brothers who with us call upon the same eternal God and Father of our Savior *Jesus Christ,* and confess the *Savior Christ.*

The fifth rule: Having said what authority is and indicated in general what the office should be, and that subjects should be submissive, we should now note whether submission and obedience pertain to the entire man or to each man according to his ability. The soul should manifest honor to the authority, and the body should do reasonable work, such as soldiering. Property should also serve with a tax and similar levies.

And here we should be reminded of respect or honor and should know that it consists not only of an external sign, such as bowing to indicate that our head is subject to the sovereign power, but also of true honor which comes from the heart, and of which there are three degrees.

The highest honor is to know and truly to believe that the order of governments is God's work and gift through which he bestows innumerable good things, such as peace, the laws necessary for the protection of wives and children, safeguards for buying and selling . . . and so forth. This order of government is also the shelter of the Church. . . . Knowledge of this and faith should prompt us to love and to be obedient to governmental authorities, not only to the men who rule but to God who created this order.

The second degree of honor is to thank God for his benefits and to beseech him to preserve and protect the government and the rulers against the disturbances of the devil. That the overlords need help from God is obvious, for human ability alone is not sufficient for rule. When the devil sways the human heart, as in the case of Caligula and Nero, human misery follows.

These two degrees of honor are not limited to the subjects; overlords and rulers are also to show such honor, for they should understand that there is a difference between the established order and their person. The person, or the servant in such an order, is himself to acknowledge and love God's work, and be subject to the order. He is not to cause disorder, and is to seek help from God through invocation.

Unfortunately, few sovereigns honor their order; many disgrace it with evil deeds, immorality, and tyranny, and they think that they will not be punished because they are lords, that they have a right to do as they wish. But God has sufficiently warned them against this in his word; before their very eyes he places examples of how he punishes the vices of sovereigns. It is written in Isaiah 10:1 f., "Woe to those who decree in-- iquitous decrees, and the writers who keep writing oppression to turn aside the needy from justice: God's wrath will not be turned away from this." Likewise, 1 Corinthians 6:9 f., "Do not be deceived; fornicators, adulterers, idolaters, thieves, and robbers will not inherit the kingdom of God." Whoever fears God, be he lord or subject, should learn that government is a divine gift, and as such he should honor and love this order.

The third degree of respect, or honor, is to be patient with reasonable rulers, even though mistakes and defects occur. The devil and human weakness combine to hinder both great and small rulers, so that many things are neglected or done erroneously. And human wisdom should not think that it always accomplishes everything, for good government is *God's own work.*

As Solomon says, *"Ut oculus videat, et auris audiat, Deus facit utrumque."* "That which the eye sees and that which the ear hears are God's work" [*cf.* Prov. 20:12]: that is, when a ruler sees and finds good counsel, and follows it, and does not hinder it — in this God is active. For example, that Augustus was a wise ruler and that such a weak man could maintain his authority and obedience was the work of God. Augustus often did what was wrong; he did not hear all things, or he could not give up fighting. So one time was smoother than another, and for this reason we who are subjects should have patience and not rebel against reasonable rulers, as Absalom did against his father, even though some things do not happen justly, because we are obliged to bear our father's and mother's defects.

This is illustrated in the story of the sons of Noah. Ham was cursed because he mocked his father, but the other two, Shem and Japheth, who covered their father, were blessed [*cf.* Gen. 9:20–27].

We are often commanded to forgive others their defects, to bear with the weak, and this is particularly necessary in government, so that revolt and war will not be instigated without great cause, as has happened in the past. *St. Peter* speaks precisely about this when he says, "One is to be obedient to the lords, even though they do not always act kindly" [*cf.* 1 Pet. 2:13–14, 20].

And *St. Paul* says, "Love is the bond that holds people together" [*cf.*

Eph. 5:28–33; 1 Thess. 4:9–10], which is not possible except through the virtue called *Epiikia*, that is, the lenity and patience to bear another's customs and defects, especially if they are near us in our rule, as Cyrus bore with the distrustful Cyaxares, and Fabius, with his companion Minutius, even though the patience is bitter, as those with understanding will discover.[12]

Here I am speaking of reasonable rulers, not tyrants. We should forgive the reasonable ruler, that is, one who devotes himself to doing what is right and who generally does so, even though now and then he may fall or be neglectful, as were David, Jehosophat, and Josiah. There never has been a ruler who has not sooner or later erred or made a false step; with such we should have patience. On the other hand, there are tyrants like Nero who devote themselves to doing wrong and practicing unusual wantonness with immorality and murder; respect and forgiveness do not pertain to these bloodhounds and blood-stainers. Other rulers should restrain them in orderly ways, just as we do mad dogs.

At this point some necessary distinctions should be noted. We should look for the principal goal of each kingdom. For example, some kingdoms were directed above all to maintain God's glory, word, and knowledge; God used the kingdom of Judah for this purpose, and manifested great wonders in it. Some, although they forget God, were not established to persecute God's word, but to maintain peace. Some monarchies have so served, and have enacted honorable laws and maintained good courts, as the history of Rome has shown.

Such kingdoms are to be honored and remembered in prayer; we should pray not only for the kingdom of David but also for the kingdom of Augustus. Jeremiah warned his people to pray for Babylon, for such kingdoms are God's work and gifts, and through them he bestows benefits on men.

On the other hand, there are kingdoms which are established to persecute the divine word, to abolish the name of our *Savior Christ.* Moham-

---

12. Melanchthon is probably referring to Cyaxares II, king of the Medes 585–549 B.C. He was the son and successor of Astyages and the grandson of Cyaxares I. According to Xenophon he was also the nephew and son-in-law of Cyrus. Cyrus had to deal with him as a distrustful relative and political rival and finally found it necessary to dethrone him and unite Media with Persia. Minutius is probably a reference to Marcus Minucius Rufus of the early third century B.C. He was appointed *magister equitum* to Fabius Cunctator by the Comitia. Fabius was pursuing a policy of exhaustion against Hannibal when Minutius, against Fabius' orders, successfully attacked Hannibal at Gerunium. For this valor the people made him co-dictator with Fabius, an action that undermined the office.

med's kingdom was begun for this purpose, particularly for blasphemy, immorality, and murder, not like other nations, to keep peace and justice. For the Mohammedan law, on which the Saracen and Turkish kingdom is founded, commands not that peace be maintained, but that the peaceful be assailed and murdered. They are not particularly hostile to persons, but to the divine Scriptures given in the prophets and apostles and the name of our Savior Jesus Christ. These two things they are sworn to abolish. For this reason, the Mohammedan kingdom is a cruel, ruthless tyranny, founded on blasphemy and murder. It has other stains, for it does not maintain true marriage and it permits frightful immorality. Because this kingdom is just the opposite of the monarchies which were just mentioned, God warned us about it in the prophets Daniel and Ezekiel, so that we might know that God has repudiated it, that it will not completely devour the Church, and that it will be punished. This warning is given so that we may not despair nor depart from the gospel, for the Turkish power and dominion are great and the human heart is greatly moved by fortune and misfortune. Daniel clearly says that after the fourth kingdom after the Fall (the Roman monarchy), the mightiest kingdom of all will come (the Mohammedan), which will speak blasphemy, war triumphantly against the saints, and nevertheless finally be punished.

Seeing that God himself condemns the Mohammedan kingdom and calls it blasphemy and murder, we should not think otherwise of it. Blasphemy and murder are disorders caused by the devil, and we should earnestly beseech God to allay this fury by making an end of it. Note that God's word instructs us through the prophet Daniel not to respect this kingdom which is founded on blasphemy, not to pray for it as we do for others, but on the contrary to pray against the entire Mohammedan kingdom.[13]

This instruction in our time we should carefully note, for verily, the Turkish kingdom is not to be considered a trifling punishment or a simple change of rule, as monarchies have often changed, from the Chaldean to the Persian, from the Persian to the Greek, and from the Greek to the Roman. Although these changes brought great wars and devastation, nevertheless in each monarchy there were some laudable rulers who succored the land. But the Turks hold an entirely different custom. As the name "Turk" means "destroyer," so is he; Gog and Magog mean

---

13. Melanchthon is making a general reference to the rejection of worldly kingdoms in the book of Daniel [cf. 3:13-18; 5:17-30; 7:17-18, 26-28; 10-12].

those who dwell in tents rather than in fixed places of abode, and so dwells the Turk. When he seizes a city, as he did the whole of Asia, he deports the occupants to other lands, and introduces his foreign barbarity. Disorganization and devastation prevail; husbands, wives, mothers, fathers, and children are separated.

Although all this is frightful to see and hear, the words of Daniel are even more frightful, for they indicate a prolonged rage. Nevertheless, they also mention the end, "but previously there will occur great harm." Afterward, says Daniel, shortly before the resurrection, the great prince, the *Son of God*, will come to fight for God's people.

We should draw together and diligently consider all these passages, for the betterment of our lives, for the strengthening of faith, and for exhortation to prayer that God will preserve and protect us against the destruction of our countries and churches by the barbarity of the Turks.

Every reasonable person will note that this article embraces many things that are too lengthy to be treated here, but to most problems these general rules should be applied. . . . And this rule should be remembered: The kingdom of Christ brings eternal benefits [*Güter*], God's grace and activity in man's heart; his kingdom does not alter the reasonable, proper laws of external government, the courts, buying and selling: it allows us to use such orders as we do day and night.

God-fearing people should know that God wants *true faith and love* to enlighten and radiate from this order. For this reason God has bound mankind together with various supports [*Gegenhilfe*], and he wants us to maintain equality in these works in accordance with reasonable, proper laws. He forbids fraud, usury, and other improprieties.

These are the rules which in general we should know. With these rules these matters are not difficult for the God-fearing to determine if they want to be bound in obedience to the eternal God and if they seek equality for their neighbors, an end to which God has bound us.

Bibliography

BALDWIN, T. W., *William Shakspere's Small Latine and Lesse Greeke* (Urbana, Ill., 1944).

BARTON, PETER F., *Melanchthons Werke, Band IV, Frühe exegetische Schriften* (Gütersloh, 1963).

BAUER, CLEMENS, "Melanchthons Naturrechtslehre," in *Archiv für Reformationsgeschichte*, XLII (1951), 64–100.

———, "Melanchthons Wirtschaftsethik," in *Archiv für Reformationsgeschichte*, XLIX (1958), 115–60.

BENZ, ERNST, *Wittenberg und Byzanz* (Marburg, 1949).

BORNKAMM, HEINRICH, *Philip Melanchthon. Zur 450. Wiederkehr seines Geburtstages* (Lüneberg, 1947).

BREEN, QUIRINIUS, "The Terms 'loci communes' and 'loci' in Melanchthon," in *Church History*, XVI (1947), 197–209.

CAEMMERER, R. R., "The Melanchthonian Blight," in *Concordia Theological Monthly*, XVIII (1947).

COHRS, D. FERDINAND, *Philipp Melanchthon, Deutschlands Lehrer* (Halle, 1897).

COX, LEONARD, *The arte or Crafte of Rhetoryke*, F. I. Carpenter, ed. (Chicago, 1899).

EELLS, H., *Martin Bucer* (New Haven, 1931).

ELLIGER, WALTER, *Philipp Melanchthon, Forschungsbeiträge zur vierhundertsten Wiederkehr seines Todestages* (Göttingen, 1961).

ELLINGER, GEORG, *Philipp Melanchthon: Ein Lebensbild* (Berlin, 1902).

ENGELLAND, HANS, "Der Ansatz der Theologie Melanchthons," in *Philip Melanchthon, Forschungsbeiträge zur vierhundertsten Wiederkehr seines Todestages*, Walter Elliger, ed. (Göttingen, 1961).

———, *Melanchthons Werke, II, Loci communes von 1521, Loci praecipui theologici von 1559, und Definitiones* (Gütersloh, 1952).

———, "Melanchthons Bedeutung für Schule und Universität," in *Luther, Mitteilungen der Luthergesellschaft*, 1960.

———, *Melanchthon: Glauben und Handeln* (München, 1931).

FISCHER, ERNST FRIEDRICH, *Melanchthons Lehre von der Bekehrung* (Tübingen, 1905).

FRAENKEL, PETER, *Testimonia Patrum* (Geneve, 1961).

GALLE, F., *Versuch einer Charakteristik Melanchthons als Theologen und eine Entwicklung seines Lehrbegriffs* (Halle, 1840).

HARNACK, ADOLF, *Philip Melanchthon* (Berlin, 1897).

HARTFELDER, K., *Philipp Melanchthon als Praeceptor Germaniae* (Berlin, 1889).

HEIM, KARL, *Das Gewissheitsproblem in der systematischen Theologie bis zu Schleiermacher* (Leipzig, 1911).

HEPPE, H., *Die Bekenntnisschriften der altprotestantischen Kirche Deutschlands* (Cassel, 1855).
————, *Geschichte des deutschen Protestantismus in den Jahren 1555 bis 1581* (Marburg, 1852), I.

HERRLINGER, A., *Die Theologie Melanchthons in ihrer geschichtlichen Entwicklung* (Gotha, 1879).

HILDEBRANDT, FRANZ, *Melanchthon: alien or ally?* (Cambridge, 1946).

HILL, CHARLES L., *The Loci Communes of Philip Melanchthon* (Boston, 1944).
————, FLACK, ELMER E., and SATRE, LOWELL, *Melanchthon: Selected Writings* (Minneapolis, 1962).

HIRSCH, E., *Die Theologie des Andreas Osiander und ihre geschichtlichen Voraussetzungen* (Göttingen, 1919).

HOLL, KARL, *The Cultural Significance of the Reformation*, tr. by Karl and Barbara Hertz and J. H. Lichtblau (New York, 1959).
————, *Die rechtfertigungslehre im Licht der Geschichte des Protestantismus* (Tübingen, 1923).

HÜBNER, FRIEDRICH, *Natürliche Theologie und theokratische Schwärmerei bei Melanchthon* (Gütersloh, 1936).

JACOBS, H. E., ed., *The Book of Concord* (Philadelphia, 1882–93), 2 vols.

JOACHIMSEN, P., *Loci communes. Eine Untersuchung zur Geistesgeschichte des Humanismus und der Reformation*. Jahrbuch der Luthergesellschaft, 8, 1926.

KANTZENBACH, F. W., *Das Ringen um die Einheit der Kirche im Zeitalter der Reformation* (Stuttgart, 1957).

KAWERAU, G., *Johann Agricola von Eisleben* (Berlin, 1881).

KIDD, B. J., *Documents Illustrative of the Continental Reformation* (New York, 1911).

KOETHE, FRIEDRICH A., *Philipp Melanchthons Werke* (Leipzig, 1829), I–VI.

KOLDE, TH., *Die Loci communes Philipp Melanchthonis* (Leipzig and Erlangen, 1925).

KÖSTLIN, J., and KAWERAU, G., *Martin Luther* (Leipzig, 1903).

LENTZ, HAROLD H., *Reformation Crossroads* (Minneapolis, 1948).

McNeill, John T., *Unitive Protestantism* (Richmond, Va., 1964).

Maier, H., *Melanchthon als Philosoph* (Tübingen, 1909).

Manschreck, Clyde L., *Melanchthon: The Quiet Reformer* (New York, 1958).
———, *Prayers of the Reformers* (Philadelphia, 1958).
———, "Reason and Conversion in the Thought of Melanchthon," in *Reformation Studies*, Franklin H. Littell, ed. (Richmond, 1962).
———, "The Role of Melanchthon in the Adiaphora Controversy," in *Archiv für Reformationsgeschichte*, XLIX (1958), 165-82.

Maurer, W., "Lex spiritualis bei Melanchthon," in *Gedenkschrift für W. Elert*, F. Hübner, W. Maurer, and E. Kinder, eds. (Berlin, 1955).
———, "Zur Komposition der Loci Melanchthons von 1521," in *Luther-Jahrbuch*, XXV (1958), 146 ff.

Melanchthon, Philip, *Corpus Reformatorum, Philippi Melanchthonis opera, quae supersunt omnia*, C. G. Bretschneider and H. E. Bindsell, eds. (Halis Saxonium, 1834-60), I-XXVIII.
———, *Heubt artikel Christlicher Lere, Loci Theologici* (Wittenberg, 1555, 1558).
———, *Supplementa Melanchthonia, Dogmatische Schriften Philipp Melanchthons*, O. Clemen, ed. (Leipzig, 1910).
———, *Supplementa Melanchthoniana, Schriften zur praktischen Theologie*, D. F. Cohrs, ed. (Leipzig, 1915).

Muelhaupt, Erwin, *Reformatoren als Erzieher: Luther, Melanchthon, Calvin* (Neukirchen Kreis Moers, 1956).

Neuser, Wilhelm H., *Der Ansatz der Theologie Philipp Melanchthons* (Neukirchen Kreis Moers, 1957).

Nürnberger, Richard, *Melanchthons Werke, Band III, Humanistische Schriften* (Gütersloh, 1961).

Outler, Albert, ed., *John Wesley* (New York, 1964).

Pelikan, Jaroslav, *From Luther to Kierkegaard* (St. Louis, 1950).

Petersen, P., *Geschichte der aristotelischen Philosophie im protestantischen Deutschland* (Leipzig, 1921).

Plitt, G. L., *Die Loci Communes Philipp Melanchthons in ihrer Urgestalt* (Erlangen, 1864).

Reu, M., *Augsburg Confession* (Chicago, 1930).

Richard, James W., *Confessional History of the Lutheran Church* (Philadelphia, 1909).
———, *Philip Melanchthon, the Protestant Preceptor of Germany* (New York, 1898).

Rouse, Ruth, and Neill, Stephen C., *A History of the Ecumenical Movement* (London, 1954).

Schäfer, R., "Christologie und Sittlichkeit in Melanchthons frühen Loci," in *Beiträge zur historischen Theologie*, 29 (Tübingen, 1960).

SCHMIDT, C., *Philipp Melanchthon, Leben und ausgewählte Schriften* (Elberfeld, 1861).

SCHWARZENAU, PAUL, *Der Wandel im theologischen Ansatz bei Melanchthon von 1525–1535* (Gütersloh, 1956).

SEEBERG, R., *Lehrbuch der Dogmengeschichte* (Erlangen and Leipzig, 1920), IV, Pt. 2.

SELL, KARL, *Philipp Melanchthon und die deutsche Reformation bis 1531* (Halle, 1897).

SICK, H., *Melanchthon als Ausleger des Alten Testaments* (Tübingen, 1959).

SMYTH, C. H., *Cranmer and the Reformation under Edward VI* (Cambridge University, 1926).

SPAETH, ADOLPH, "Melanchthon in American Lutheran Theology," in *The Lutheran Church Review*, XVI (1897), 104 ff.

SPERL, A., *Melanchthon zwischen Humanismus und Reformation* (München, 1959).

SPITZ, L. W., "History as a Weapon in Controversy," in *Concordia Theological Monthly*, XVIII (1947), 747 ff.

STROBEL, GEORG T., *Versuch einer Litterär Geschichte von Philipp Melanchthons Loci Theologicis als dem ersten Evangelischen Lehrbuche* (Altdorf and Nürnberg, 1776).

STUPPERICH, ROBERT, *Melanchthons Werke, Band VI, Bekenntnisse und kleine Lehrschriften* (Gütersloh, 1955).
———, "Kirche und Synode bei Melanchthon," in *Gedenkschrift für W. Elert*, F. Hübner, W. Maurer, and E. Kinder, eds. (Berlin, 1955).
———, "Melanchthon und die Täufer," in *Kerygma und Dogma* (Göttingen, 1957), III, 150–70.

THOMPSON, BARD, "The Palatinate Church Order of 1563," in *Church History*, XXIII (December, 1954), 339–54.

TROELTSCH, E., *Vernunft und Offenbarung bei Johann Gerhard und Melanchthon* (Göttingen, 1891).

VAJTA, VILMOS, ed., *Luther and Melanchthon* (Philadelphia, 1961).

WALTER, JOHANNES V., *Luther und Melanchthon während des Augsburger Reichstages* (Gütersloh, 1931).

Index

Wittenberg, ix, xxv f.
Wittenberg Concord, xvi
Wolff, Christian, xli
Works
  good, 87–89, 114, 116 f., 118–21, 136,
    138–40, 175–86, 229, 252 f., 314 ff.
  meritorious, 75, 79, 130–35, 258, 306–16
  of perfection, 130 f.
Worship, 95–97, 136, 305. *See also* Faith;
  Forgiveness.
Wycliffe, John, 261

X

Xenophon, xxxi, 5, 6, 143

Z

Zechariah, 109, 114, 267
Ziba, 120
Zinzendorf, Count Ludwig von, xxii–
  xxiii
Zwingli, Ulrich, xv